I0754715

THE

COMPLETE POETICAL WORKS

OF

SAMUEL ROGERS;

WITH

A Biographical Sketch, and Notes.

EDITED BY

EPES SARGENT.

BOSTON:
PHILLIPS, SAMPSON AND COMPANY.
MDCCCLIV.

PREFACE.

It is now more than a third of a century since Lord Byron alluded to the author of "Human Life" as the Nestor of the living poets. Since that time most of his then celebrated brethren have passed away; but the venerable bard still lives, to enjoy the society he adorns, and the fame which brightens with his years. He has taken leave of Byron, and Campbell, and Moore, and all his poetical rivals and contemporaries; but he has kept alive the sentiments and sympathies of his nature, and is still cheered by the company of younger poets, who regard him with the genial warmth of old friendship.

It was the consolation of Campbell, in his declining years, that he had never written a line against religion or virtue. We may say, with equal truth, of Rogers, that he leaves no verse which, "dying," he could "wish to blot." Exquisite taste and judgment pervade everything from his pen. But, while this purity of style and sentiment renders him a favorite poet for the study of the young, his great and peculiar merits, we think, are better felt and appreciated, in later years, by those who have become wearied with the intense straining for effect, and the passionate eccentricities, of some of our more recent schools of verse, and recur with fresh pleasure to pages that are marked everywhere with simplicity, refinement, and tranquil beauty.

It has been our object to furnish an edition of the Complete Poetical Works of Samuel Rogers, in a form so handsome that everybody might be pleased to possess it, and so cheap that anybody might be able to buy. We have thrown together, in a prefatory memoir, such materials for the personal and literary life of the author as were within our reach; and, among them, we are sure that the admirable critiques of Mackintosh and Jeffrey will be considered as imparting additional value to the volume.

CONTENTS.

MEMOIR OF SAMUEL ROGERS.

Samuel Rogers was born at Newington Green, a village now forming part of London, about the year 1763, and is now (1854) upwards of ninety-one years of age. His birth-place was in a locality distinguished by many associations of interest. "In this neighborhood," says William Howitt, in his entertaining work on the Homes and Haunts of the Most Eminent British Poets, "the Tudor princes used to live a good deal. Canonbury, between this green and Islington, was a favorite hunting-seat of Elizabeth, and no doubt the woods and wastes extended all round this neighborhood. There is Kingsland, now all built on, there is Henry VIII.'s walk, and Queen Elizabeth's walk, all in the vicinity; and this old, quiet green seems to retain a feeling and an aspect of those times. It is built round with houses, evidently of a considerable age. There are trees and quietness about it still. In the centre of the south side is an old house standing back, which is said to have been inhabited by Henry VIII. At the end next to Stoke Newington stands an old Presbyterian chapel, at which the celebrated Dr. Price preached, and of which, afterward, the husband of Mrs. Barbauld was the minister. Near this chapel De Foe was educated, and the house still remains. In this green lived, too, Mary Wolstoncroft, being engaged with another lady in keeping school. Samuel Rogers was born in the stuccoed house at the south-west corner, which is much older than it seems. Adjoining it is a large, old garden. Here his father, and his mother's father, lived before him. By the mother's side he was descended from the celebrated Philip Henry, the father of Matthew

Henry, and was therefore of an old non-conformist family. Mr. Rogers' grandfather was a gentleman, pursuing no profession, but his father engaged in banking." In the banking-house the elder Rogers amassed considerable wealth, which with his business descended to his son.

But little is known of the early life of the poet. His education was liberal, and from an early age he was familiar with the best society of the metropolis. In the year 1786 he published his first volume, with the title of "An Ode to Superstition, and other Poems," in which a critic of the time, writing in the *Monthly Review*, thought he perceived the "hand of a master."

Six years afterwards he published The Pleasures of Memory, a poem that attained an immediate popularity, both in England and in this country. This poem was elaborated with the most consummate care and art. He submitted it very freely to the censure of his friends before publication, one of whom, Mr. Richard Sharpe, since member of Parliament, has said that during the preparation of the first and second editions he had read it with the poet several hundred times, at home and on the continent, and in every temper of mind that varied company and varied scenery could produce. "To the spirit of original observation," says Mr. Allan Cunningham of this poem, in his History of British Literature, "to the fine pictures of men and manners, and to the remarks on the social and domestic condition of the country, which mark the disciples of the newer school of verse, are added the terseness, smoothness and harmony, of the old. The poem abounds with capital and brilliant hits; with passages which remain on the memory, and may be said to please rather than enchant one, — to take silent possession of the heart, rather than fill it with immediate rapture. Hazlitt, with some of that perverseness which even talent is not without, said the chief fault of Rogers was want of genius and taste. Perhaps in the whole list of living men of genius no one can be named whose taste in poetry is so just and delicate. This is apparent in every page of his compositions; nay, he is even fastidious in his taste, and rejects much, in the pictures of manners and feelings which he paints, which other authors, whose taste is unquestioned, would have used without scruple. His diction is pure, and his language has all the necessary strength, without being swelling or redundant: his words are always in keeping with the sentiment. He has, in truth, great strength; he says much in small compass, and may sometimes be charged with a too great anxiety to be brief and terse. It was the error of the school in which his taste was formed to be over anxious about the harmony and polish of the verse; and he may be accused of erring with his teachers. Concerning the composition of The Pleasures of Memory, it is related that he corrected, transposed and changed, till he exhausted his own patience; and then, turning to his friends, he demanded their opinions, listening to every remark, and weighing every observation. This plan of correction is liable to serious objections. The poet is almost sure of losing in dash and vigor more than what he gains by correctness; and, as a whole, the work is apt to be injured, while individual parts are bettered. Poetry is best hit off at one heat of the fancy; the more it is hammered and wrought on, the colder it becomes. The sale of The Pleasures of Memory continued to be large, though The Pleasures of Hope came into the market."

This production gave its author a high position among the men of letters who flourished in London during the early part of the present century. Cumberland, the dramatic author, in the supplement to his Memoirs, published nearly half a century ago, advised Moore, who was then known as the translator of Anacreon and the author of Little's Poems, to "subject his composition to the review of his correct and judicious friend, Mr. Rogers, (and when so done) he may surrender himself without fear to the criticism of the world at large." "I can visit," said the veteran reminiscent, "the justly-admired author of The Pleasures of Memory, and find myself with a friend who together with the brightest genius possesses elegance of manners and excellence of heart. He tells me he remembers the day of our first meeting at Mr. Dilly's; I also remember it, and, though his modest, unassuming nature held back and shrunk from all appearances of ostentation and display of talents, yet even then I take credit for discovering a promise of good things to come, and suspected him of holding secret commerce with the Muse, before the proof appeared in shape of one of the most beautiful and harmonious poems in our language. I do not say that he has not ornamented the age he lives in, though he were to stop where he is; but I hope he will not so totally deliver himself over to the arts, as to neglect the Muses; and I now publicly call upon Samuel Rogers to answer to his name, and stand forth in the title-page of some future work, that shall be in substance greater, in dignity of subject more sublime, and in purity of versification not less charming, than his poem above mentioned."

In November, 1805, Moore wrote to his mother, "I am just going to dine *third* to Rogers and Cumberland: a good poetical step-ladder we make; the former is past forty, and the latter past seventy." It was in the pages of the *Anthologia Hibernica*, for the months of January and February, 1793, that Moore first read, as a schoolboy, *Rogers' Pleasures of Memory*, little dreaming that he should one day become the intimate friend of the author; and such an impression did it then make upon him, as he tells us in his *Memoirs*, that the particular type in which it is there printed, and the very color of the paper, were through life associated with every line of it in his memory.

Rogers was an early friend of Lord Byron. The noble poet had excepted him from the somewhat indiscriminate abuse of the *English Bards and Scotch Reviewers*, and had complimented him in lines which will well bear transcription:

"To the famed throng now paid the tribute due,
Neglected genius! let me turn to you.
Come forth, O Campbell!* give thy talents scope;
Who dares aspire if thou must cease to hope?
And thou, melodious Rogers! rise at last—
Recall the pleasing memory of the past.
Arise! let blest remembrance still inspire,
And strike to wonted tones thy hallowed lyre;
Restore Apollo to his vacant throne,
Assert thy country's honor and thine own."

This eulogy Moore thinks the disinterested and deliberate result of the young poet's judgment, as at that time he had never seen Rogers

* It would be superfluous to recall to the mind of the reader the authors of "The Pleasures of Memory" and "The Pleasures of Hope," the most beautiful didactic poems in our language, if we except Pope's "Essay on Man;" but so many poetasters have started up, that even the names of Campbell and Rogers are become strange.—*Byron's Note.*

(with whom he afterwards became intimate) ; and the opinion he then expressed remained the same through life.

It was in the year 1798 that Rogers published "An Epistle to a Friend, with other Poems," and he did not appear again as an author till the year 1812, when he ventured before the world with a fragmentary poem entitled The Voyage of Columbus. This poem was received by the critics with various favor. In a letter written from Bombay, before its appearance, Sir James Mackintosh had begged to be particularly remembered to Rogers, and added, "I hope Columbus will soon undertake a new voyage to the East, and that he will animate the dulness of the one Indies more quickly than he conquered the barbarism of the other." When the poem appeared, the great whig jurist and statesman, no less eminent as a man of letters and a critic, pronounced his judgment of its merits in the *Edinburgh Review* for October, 1813 ; and we feel that we cannot better occupy the pages we have reserved for a literary memoir of the poet than by giving this article entire :

"POEMS BY SAMUEL ROGERS : *Including Fragments of a Poem called The Voyage of Columbus.* London, 1812.

"It seems very doubtful whether the progress and the vicissitudes of the elegant arts can be referred to the operation of general laws, with the same plausibility as the exertions of the more robust faculties of the human mind, in the severer forms of science and of useful art. The action of fancy and of taste seems to be affected by causes too various and minute to be enumerated with sufficent completeness for the purposes of philosophical theory. To explain them, may appear to be as hopeless an attempt as to account for one summer being more warm and genial than another. The difficulty would be insurmountable, even in framing the most general outline of a theory, if the various forms assumed by imagination, in the fine arts, did not depend on some of the most conspicuous as well as powerful agents in the moral world. But these arise from revolutions of popular sentiments, and are connected with the opinions of the age, and with the manners of the refined class, as certainly, though not in so great a degree, as with the passions of the multitude. The comedy of a polished monarchy never can be of the same character with that of a bold and tumultuous democracy. Changes of religion and of government, civil or foreign wars, conquests which derive splendor from distance or extent or difficulty, long tranquillity, — all these, and indeed every conceivable modification of the state of a community, show themselves in the tone of its poetry, and leave long and deep traces on every part of its literature. Geometry is the same, not only at London and Paris, but in the extremes of Athens and Samarcand; but the state of the general feeling in England, at this moment, requires a different poetry from that which delighted our ancestors in the time of Luther or Alfred.

"During the greater part of the eighteenth century, the connection of the character of English poetry with the state of the country was very easily traced. The period which extended from the English to the French Revolution was the golden age of authentic history. Governments were secure, nations tranquil, improvements rapid, manners mild beyond the example of any former age. The English nation, which possessed the greatest of all human blessings, a wisely constructed popular government, necessarily enjoyed the largest share of every other benefit. The tranquillity of that fortunate period was not disturbed by any of those calamitous, or even extraordinary events, which excite the imagination and inflame the passions. No age was more exempt from the prevalence of any species of popular enthusiasm. Poetry, in this state of things, partook of that calm, argumentative, moral, and directly useful character, into which it naturally subsides when there are no events to call up the higher passions, — when every talent is allured into the immediate service of a prosperous and improving society, — and when wit, taste, diffused literature, and fastidious criticism, combine to deter the young writer from the more arduous enterprises of poetical genius. In such an age, every art becomes rational. Reason is the power which presides in a calm. But reason guides, rather than impels; and, though it must regulate every exertion of genius, it never can rouse it to vigorous action.

"The school of Dryden and Pope, which prevailed till a very late period of the last century, is neither the most poetical nor the most national part of our literary annals. These great poets sometimes, indeed, ventured into the regions of pure poetry; but their general character is, that 'not in fancy's maze they wandered long;' and that they rather approached the elegant correctness of our continental neighbors, than supported the daring flight, which, in the former age, had borne English poetry to a sublimer elevation than that of any other modern people of the West.

"Towards the middle of the century, great, though quiet changes, began to manifest themselves in the republic of letters in every European nation which retained any portion of mental activity. About that time, the exclusive authority of our great rhyming poets began to be weakened, while new tastes and fashions began to show themselves in the political world. A school of poetry must have prevailed long enough to be probably on the verge of downfall, before its practice is embodied in a correspondent system of criticism.

"Johnson was the critic of our second poetical school. As far as his prejudices of a political or religious kind did not disqualify him for all criticism, he was admirably fitted by nature to be the critic of this species of poetry. Without more imagination, sensibility or delicacy, than it required, — not always with perhaps quite enough for its higher parts, — he possessed sagacity, shrewdness, experience, knowledge of mankind, a taste for rational and orderly compositions, and a disposition to accept, instead of poetry, that lofty and vigorous declamation in harmonious verse, of which he himself was capable, and to which his great master sometimes descended. His spontaneous admiration scarcely soared above Dryden. 'Merit of a loftier class he rather saw than felt.' Shakspeare has transcendent excellence of every sort, and for every critic, except those who are repelled by the faults which usually attend sublime virtues, — character and manners, morality and prudence, as well as imagery and passion. Johnson did, indeed, perform a vigorous act of reluctant justice towards Milton; but it was a proof, to use his own words, that

'At length our mighty bard's victorious lays
Fill the loud voice of universal praise;
And baffled Spite, with hopeless anguish dumb,
Yields to renown the centuries to come.'

The deformities of the Life of Gray ought not to be ascribed to jealousy, — for Johnson's mind, though coarse, was not mean, — but to the prejudices of his university, his political faction, and his poetical sect; and this last bigotry is the more remarkable, because it is exerted against the most skilful and tasteful of innovators, who, in reviving more poetical subjects and a more splendid diction, has employed more care and finish than those who aimed only at correctness.

"The interval which elapsed between the death of Goldsmith and the rise of Cowper is perhaps more barren than any other twelve years in the history of our poetry since the accession of Elizabeth. It seemed as if the fertile soil was at length exhausted. But it had in fact only ceased to exhibit its accustomed produce. The established poetry had worn out either its own resources, or the constancy of its readers. Former attempts to introduce novelty had been either too weak or too early. Neither the beautiful fancy of Collins, nor the learned and ingenious industry of Warton, nor even the union of sublime genius with consummate art in Gray, had produced a general change in poetical composition. But the fulness of time was approaching; and a revolution has been accomplished, of which the commencement nearly coincides — not, as we conceive, accidentally — with that of the political revolution which has changed the character, as well as the condition, of Europe. It has been a thousand times observed, that nations become weary even of excellence, and seek a new way of writing, though it should be a worse. But, besides the operation of satiety, — the general cause of literary revolutions, — several particular circumstances seem to have affected the late changes of our poetical taste; of which, two are more conspicuous than the rest.

"In the natural progress of society, the songs which are the effusion of the feelings of a rude tribe are gradually polished into a form of poetry still retaining the marks of the national opinions, sentiments and manners, from which it originally sprung. The plants are improved by cultivation; but they are still the native produce of the soil. The only perfect example which we know, of this sort, is Greece. Knowledge and useful art, and perhaps in a great measure religion, the Greeks received from the East; but, as they studied no foreign language, it was impossible that any foreign literature should influence the progress of theirs. Not even the name of a Persian, Assyrian, Phenician, or Egyptian poet is alluded to by any Greek writer. The Greek poetry was, therefore, wholly national. The

Pelasgic ballads were insensibly formed into Epic, and Tragic, and Lyric poems; but the heroes, the opinions, and the customs, continued as exclusively Grecian as they had been when the Hellenic minstrels knew little beyond the Adriatic and the Ægean. The literature of Rome was a copy from that of Greece. When the classical studies revived amid the chivalrous manners and feudal institutions of Gothic Europe, the imitation of ancient poets struggled against the power of modern sentiments, with various event. in different times and countries, but everywhere in such a manner as to give somewhat of an artificial and exotic character to poetry. Jupiter and the Muses appeared in the poems of Christian nations. The feelings and principles of democracies were copied by the gentlemen of Teutonic monarchies or aristocracies. The sentiments of the poet in his verse were not those which actuated him in his conduct. The forms and rules of composition were borrowed from antiquity, instead of spontaneously arising from the manner of thinking of modern communities. In Italy, when letters first revived, the chivalrous principle was too near the period of its full vigor to be oppressed by his foreign learning. Ancient ornaments were borrowed; but the romantic form was prevalent; and where the forms were classical, the spirit continued to be romantic. The structure of Tasso's poem was that of the Grecian epic; but his heroes were Christian knights. French poetry, having been somewhat unaccountably late in its rise, and slow in its progress, reached its most brilliant period when all Europe had considerably lost its ancient characteristic principles, and was fully imbued with classical ideas. Hence it acquired faultless elegance; hence also it became less natural, — more timid and more imitative, — more like a feeble translation of Roman poetry. The first age of English poetry, in the reign of Elizabeth, displayed a combination, fantastic enough, of chivalrous fancy and feeling with classical pedantry; but, upon the whole, its native genius was unsubdued. The poems of that age, with all their faults, and partly perhaps from their faults, are the most national part of our poetry, as they undoubtedly contain its highest beauties. From the accession of James, to the Civil War, the glory of Shakspeare turned the whole national genius to the drama; and, after the restoration, a new and classical school arose, under whom our old and peculiar literature was abandoned, and

2*

almost forgotten. But all imported tastes in literature must be in some measure superficial. The poetry which once grew in the bosoms of a people is always capable of being revived by a skilful hand. When the brilliant and poignant lines of Pope began to pall on the public ear, it was natural that we should revert to the cultivation of our indigenous poetry.

"Nor was this the sole, or perhaps the chief agent which was working a poetical change. As the condition and character of the former age had produced an argumentative, didactic, sententious, prudential and satirical poetry, so the approaches to a new order (or rather at first disorder) in political society were attended by correspondent movements in the poetical world. Bolder speculations began to prevail. A combination of the science and art of the tranquil period with the hardy enterprises of that which succeeded gave rise to scientific poems, in which a bold attempt was made, by the mere force of diction, to give a political interest and elevation to the coldest parts of knowledge, and to those arts which have been hitherto considered as the meanest. Having been forced above their natural place by the wonder at first elicited, they have not yet recovered from the subsequent depression. Nor will a similar attempt be successful, without a more temperate use of power over style, till the diffusion of physical knowledge renders it familiar to the popular imagination, and till the prodigies worked by the mechanical arts shall have bestowed on them a character of grandeur.

"As the agitation of men's minds approached the period of an explosion, its effects on literature become more visible. The desire of strong emotion succeeded to the solicitude to avoid disgust. Fictions, both dramatic and narrative, were formed according to the school of Rousseau and Goethe. The mixture of comic and tragic pictures once more displayed itself, as in the ancient and national drama. The sublime and energetic feelings of devotion began to be more frequently associated with poetry. The tendency of political speculation concurred in directing the mind of the poet to the intense and undisguised passions of the uneducated, which fastidious politeness had excluded from the subjects of poetical imitation. The history of nations unlike ourselves, the fantastic mythology and ferocious superstition of distant times and countries, or the legends of our own antique faith, and the romances of our fabulous and heroic ages, became themes of poetry. Traces of a higher order of feeling appeared in the contemplations in which the poet indulged, and in the events and scenes which he delighted to describe. The fire with which a chivalrous tale was told made the reader inattentive to negligences in the story or the style. Poetry became more devout, more contemplative, more mystical, more visionary, — more alien from the taste of those whose poetry is only a polished prosaic verse, more full of antique superstition, and more prone to daring innovation. — painting both coarser realities and purer imaginations than she had before hazarded, — sometimes buried in the profound quiet required by the dreams of fancy, sometimes turbulent and martial, — seeking 'fierce wars and faithful loves' in those times long past, when the frequency of the most dreadful dangers produced heroic energy and the ardor of faithful affection.

"Even the direction given to the traveller by the accidents of war has not been without its influence. Greece, the mother of freedom and of poetry in the West, which had long employed only the antiquary, the artist and the philologist, was at length destined, after an interval of many silent and inglorious ages, to awaken the genius of a poet. Full of enthusiasm for those perfect forms of heroism and liberty which his imagination had placed in the recesses of antiquity, he gave vent to his impatience of the imperfections of living men and real institutions in an original strain of sublime satire, which clothes moral anger in imagery of an almost horrible grandeur ; and which, though it cannot coincide with the estimate of reason, yet could only flow from that worship of perfection which is the soul of all true poetry.

"The tendency of poetry to become national was in more than one case remarkable. While the Scottish middle age inspired the most popular poet, perhaps, of the eighteenth century, the national genius of Ireland at length found a poetical representative, whose exquisite ear, and flexible fancy, wantoned in all the varieties of poetical luxury, from the levities to the fondness of love, from polished pleasantry to ardent passion, and from the social joys of private life to a tender and mournful patriotism, taught by the melancholy fortunes of an illustrious country, — with a range adapted to every nerve in the composition of a people susceptible of all feelings which have the color of generosity, and more exempt, probably, than any other from degrading and unpoetical vices.

"The failure of innumerable adventurers is inevitable, in literary, as well as in political, revolutions. The inventor seldom perfects his invention. The uncouthness of the novelty, the clumsiness with which it is managed by an unpractised hand, and the dogmatical contempt of criticism natural to the pride and enthusiasm of the innovator, combine to expose him to ridicule, and generally terminate in his being admired (though warmly) by a few of his contemporaries, remembered only occasionally in after times, and supplanted in general estimation by more cautious and skilful imitators. With the very reverse of unfriendly feelings, we observe that erroneous theories respecting poetical diction, — exclusive and proscriptive notions in criticism, which, in adding new provinces to poetry, would deprive her of ancient dominions and lawful instruments of rule, — and a neglect of that extreme regard to general sympathy, and even accidental prejudice, which is necessary to guard poetical novelties against their natural enemy, the satirist, — have powerfully counteracted an attempt, equally moral and philosophical, made by a writer of undisputed poetical genius, to enlarge the territories of art, by unfolding the poetical interest which lies latent in the common acts of the humblest men, and in the most ordinary modes of feeling, as well as in the most familiar scenes of nature.

"The various opinions which may naturally be formed of the merit of individual writers form no necessary part of our consideration. We consider the present as one of the most flourishing periods of English poetry; but those who condemn all contemporary poets need not on that account dissent from our speculations. It is sufficient to have proved the reality, and in part perhaps to have explained the origin, of a literary revolution. At no time does the success of writers bear so uncertain a proportion to their genius, as when the rules of judging and the habits of feeling are unsettled.

"It is not uninteresting, even as a matter of speculation, to observe the fortune of a poem which, like The Pleasures of Memory, appeared at the commencement of this literary revolution, without paying court to the revolutionary tastes, or seeking distinction by resistance to them. It borrowed no aid either from prejudice or innovation. It neither copied the fashion of the age which was passing away, nor offered any homage to the rising novelties. It resembles, only in measure, the poems of the eighteenth century, which were written in heroic rhyme. Neither the brilliant sententiousness of Pope, nor the frequent languor and negligence perhaps inseparable from the exquisite nature of Goldsmith, could be traced in a poem from which taste and labor equally banished mannerism and inequality. It was patronized by no sect or faction. It was neither imposed on the public by any literary cabal, nor forced into notice by the noisy anger of conspicuous enemies. Yet, destitute as it was of every foreign help, it acquired a popularity originally very great; and which has not only continued amidst extraordinary fluctuation of general taste, but has increased amid a succession of formidable competitors. No production, so popular, was probably ever so little censured by criticism; and thus is combined the applause of contemporaries with the suffrage of the representatives of posterity.

"It is needless to make extracts from a poem which is familiar to every reader. In selection, indeed, no two readers would probably agree; but the description of the Gypsies, of the Boy quitting his Father's house, and of the Savoyard recalling the mountainous scenery of his country, and the descriptive commencement of the tale in Cumberland, have remained most deeply impressed on our minds. We should be disposed to quote the following verses, as not surpassed, in pure and chaste elegance, by any English lines:

'When Joy's bright sun has shed his evening ray,
And Hope's delusive meteors cease to play;
When clouds on clouds the smiling prospect close,
Still through the gloom thy star serenely glows
Like yon fair orb she gilds the brow of Night
With the mild magic of reflected light.'

"The conclusion of the fine passage on the Veterans at Greenwich and Chelsea has a pensive dignity which beautifully corresponds with the scene:

'Long have ye known Reflection's genial ray
Gild the calm close of Valor's various day.'

"And we cannot resist the pleasure of quoting the moral, tender, and elegant lines which close the poem :

'Lighter than air, Hope's summer-visions fly,
If but a fleeting cloud obscure the sky ;
If but a beam of sober Reason play,
Lo ! Fancy's fairy frost-work melts away !
But can the wiles of Art, the grasp of Power,
Snatch the rich relics of a well-spent hour ?
These, when the trembling spirit wings her flight,
Pour round her path a stream of living light ;
And gild those pure and perfect realms of rest,
Where Virtue triumphs, and her sons are blest !'

"The descriptive passages require, indeed, a closer inspection, and a more exercised eye, than those of some celebrated contemporaries who sacrifice elegance to effect, and whose figures stand out, in bold relief, from the general roughness of their more unfinished compositions ; and in the moral parts there is often discoverable a Virgilian art, which suggests, rather than displays, the various and contrasted scenes of human life, and adds to the power of language by a certain air of reflection and modesty, in the preference of measured terms to those of more apparent energy.

"In the View from the House, the scene is neither delightful from very superior beauty, nor striking by singularity, nor powerful from reminding us of terrible passions or memorable deeds. It consists of the more ordinary of the beautiful features of nature, neither exaggerated nor represented with curious minuteness, but exhibited with picturesque elegance, in connection with those tranquil emotions which they call up in the calm order of a virtuous mind, in every condition of society and of life. The verses on the Torso are in a more severe style. The Fragment of a divine artist, which awakened the genius of Michael Angelo, seems to disdain ornament. It would be difficult to name two small poems, by the same writer, in which he has attained such high degrees of kinds of excellence so dissimilar, as are seen in the Sick Chamber and the Butterfly. The first has a truth of detail, which, considered merely as painting, is admirable ; but assumes a higher character, when it is felt to be that minute remembrance with which affection recollects every circumstance that could have affected a beloved sufferer. Though the morality which concludes the second be in itself very beautiful, it may be doubted whether the verses would not have left a more unmixed delight, if the address had remained as a mere sport of fancy, without the seriousness of an object, or an application. The verses written in Westminster Abbey are surrounded by dangerous recollections; they aspire to commemorate Fox, and to copy some of the grandest thoughts in the most sublime work of Bossuet. Nothing can satisfy the expectation awakened by such names; yet we are assured that there are some of them which would be envied by the best writers of this age. The scenery of Loch Long is among the grandest in Scotland; and the description of it shows the power of feeling and painting. In this island the taste for nature has grown with the progress of refinement. It is most alive in those who are most brilliantly distinguished in social and active life. It elevates the mind above the meanness which it might contract in the rivalship for praise; and preserves those habits of reflection and sensibility, which receive so many rude shocks in the coarse contests of the world. Not many summer hours can be passed in the most mountainous solitudes of Scotland, without meeting some who are worthy to be remembered with the sublime objects of nature which they had travelled so far to admire.

"The most conspicuous of the novelties of this volume is the poem, or poems, entitled 'Fragments of the Voyage of Columbus.' The subject of this poem is, politically or philosophically considered, among the most important in the annals of mankind. The introduction of Christianity (humanly viewed), the irruption of the northern barbarians, the contest between the Christian and Mussulman nations in Syria, the two inventions of gunpowder and printing, the emancipation of the human understanding by the Reformation, the discovery of America, and of a maritime passage to Asia, in the last ten years of the fifteenth century, are the events which have produced the greatest and most durable effects since the establishment of civilization, and the consequent commencement of authentic history. But the poetical capabilities of an event bear no proportion to historical importance. None of the consequences that do not strike the senses or the fancy can interest the poet. The greatest of the transactions above enumerated is obviously incapable of entering into poetry. The Crusades were not without permanent effects on the state of men; but their poetical interest does not arise from these effects, and it immeasurably surpasses them.

"Whether the voyage of Columbus be destined to be forever incapable of becoming the subject of an epic poem, is a question which we have scarcely the means of answering. The success of great writers has often so little corresponded with the promise of their subject, that we might be almost tempted to think the choice of a subject indifferent. The story of Hamlet, or of Paradise Lost, would beforehand have been pronounced to be unmanageable. Perhaps the genius of Shakspeare and of Milton has rather compensated for the incorrigible defects of ungrateful subjects, than conquered them. The course of ages may produce the poetical genius, the historical materials and the national feelings, for an American epic poem. There is yet but one state in America, and that state is hardly become a nation. At some future period, when every part of the continent has been the scene of memorable events, when the discovery and conquest have receded into that legendary dimness which allows fancy to mould them at her pleasure, the early history of America may afford scope for the genius of a thousand national poets; and while some may soften the cruelty which darkens the daring energy of Cortez and Pizarro, — while others may, in perhaps new forms of poetry, ennoble the pacific conquests of Penn, — and while the genius, the exploits, and the fate of Raleigh, may render his establishments probably the most alluring of American subjects, every inhabitant of the New World will turn his eyes with filial reverence towards Columbus, and regard with equal enthusiasm the voyage which laid the foundation of so many states, and peopled a continent with civilized men. Most epic subjects, but especially such a subject as Columbus, require either the fire of an actor in the scene, or the religious reverence of a very distant posterity. Homer, as well as Erçilla and Camoens, show what may be done by an epic poet who himself feels the passions of his heroes. It must not be denied that Virgil has borrowed a color of refinement from the court of Augustus, in painting the age of Priam and of Dido. Evander is a solitary and exquisite model of primitive manners divested of grossness, without losing their simplicity. But to an European poet, in this age of the world, the Voyage of Columbus is too naked, and too exactly defined by history. It has no variety, — scarcely any succession of events. It consists of one scene, during which two or three simple passions continue in a state of the highest excitement. It is a voyage with intense anxiety in every bosom, controlled by magnanimous fortitude in the leader, and producing among his followers a fear, — sometimes submissive, sometimes mutinous, always ignoble. It admits of no variety of character, no unexpected revolutions. And even the issue, though of unspeakable importance, and admirably adapted to some kinds of poetry, is not an event of such outward dignity and splendor as ought naturally to close the active and brilliant course of an epic poem.

"It is natural that the Fragments should give a specimen of the marvellous, as well as of the other constituents of epic fiction. We may observe that it is neither the intention nor the tendency of poetical machinery to supersede secondary causes, to fetter the will, and to make human creatures appear as the mere instruments of destiny. It is introduced to satisfy that insatiable demand for a nature more exalted than that which we know by experience, which creates all poetry, and which is most active in its highest species, and in its most perfect productions. It is not to account for thoughts and feelings that superhuman agents are brought down upon earth; it is rather for the contrary purpose, of lifting them into a mysterious dignity beyond the cognizance of reason. There is a material difference between the acts which superior beings perform and the sentiments which they inspire. It is true, that when a god fights against men, there can be no uncertainty or anxiety, and consequently no interest about the event, — unless, indeed, in the rude theology of Homer, where Minerva may animate the Greeks, while Mars excites the Trojans; but it is quite otherwise with these divine persons inspiring passion, or represented as agents in the great phenomena of nature. Venus and Mars inspire love or valor; they give a noble origin and a dignified character to these sentiments; but the sentiments themselves act according to the laws of our nature; and their celestial source has no tendency to impair their power over human sympathy. No event, which has not too much modern vulgarity to be susceptible of alliance with poetry, can be incapable of being ennobled by that eminently poetical art which ascribes it either to the Supreme Will, or to the agency of beings who are greater than

3

human. The wisdom of Columbus is neither less venerable nor less his own because it is supposed to flow more directly than that of other wise men from the inspiration of heaven. The mutiny of his seamen is not less interesting or formidable because the poet traces it to the suggestion of those malignant spirits in whom the imagination, independent of all theological doctrines, is naturally prone to personify and embody the causes of evil.

"Unless, indeed, the marvellous be a part of the popular creed at the period of the action, the reader of a subsequent age will refuse to sympathize with it. His poetical faith is founded in sympathy with that of the poetical personages. Still more objectionable is a marvellous influence neither believed in by the reader nor by the hero; — like a great part of the machinery of the Henriade and the Lusiad, which, indeed, is not only absolutely ineffective, but rather disennobles heroic fiction, by association with light and frivolous ideas. Allegorical persons (if the expression may be allowed) are only in the way to become agents. The abstraction has received a faint outline of form; but it has not yet acquired those individual marks and characteristic peculiarities which render it a really existing being. On the other hand, the more sublime parts of our own religion, and more especially those which are common to all religion, are too awful and too philosophical for poetical effect. If we except Paradise Lost, where all is supernatural, and where the ancestors of the human race are not strictly human beings, it must be owned that no successful attempt has been made to ally a human action with the sublimer principles of the Christian theology. Some opinions, which may, perhaps, without irreverence, be said to be rather appendages to the Christian system than essential parts of it, are in that sort of intermediate state which fits them for the purposes of poetry; — sufficiently exalted to ennoble the human actions with which they are blended, but not so exactly defined, nor so deeply revered, as to be inconsistent with the liberty of imagination. The guardian angels, in the project of Dryden, had the inconvenience of having never taken any deep root in popular belief; the agency of evil spirits was firmly believed in the age of Columbus. With the truth of facts poetry can have no concern; but the truth of manners is necessary to its persons. If the minute investigations of the Notes to this poem had related to historical details, they would have been insignificant; but they are intended to justify the human and the supernatural parts of it, by an appeal to the manners and to the opinions of the age.

"Perhaps there is no volume in our language of which it can be so truly said as of the present that it is equally exempt from the frailties of negligence and the vices of affectation. Exquisite polish of style is, indeed, more admired by the artist than by the people. The gentle and elegant pleasure which it imparts can only be felt by a calm reason, an exercised taste, and a mind free from turbulent passions. But these beauties of execution can exist only in combination with much of the primary beauties of thought and feeling; and poets of the first rank depend on them for no small part of the perpetuity of their fame. In poetry, though not in eloquence, it is less to rouse the passions of a moment than to satisfy the taste of all ages.

"In estimating the poetical rank of Mr. Rogers, it must not be forgotten that popularity never can arise from elegance alone. The vices of a poem may render it popular; and virtues of a faint character may be sufficient to preserve a languishing and cold reputation. But, to be both popular poets and classical writers is the rare lot of those few who are released from all solicitude about their literary fame. It often happens to successful writers that the lustre of their first productions throws a temporary cloud over some of those which follow. Of all literary misfortunes, this is the most easily endured, and the most speedily repaired. It is generally no more than a momentary illusion produced by disappointed admiration, which expected more from the talents of the admired writer than any talents could perform. Mr. Rogers has long passed that period of probation during which it may be excusable to feel some painful solicitude about the reception of every new work. Whatever may be the rank assigned hereafter to his writings, when compared with each other, the writer has most certainly taken his place among the classical poets of his country."

This was, no doubt, a very acceptable offset to a critique on the same poem which had found its way into the *Quarterly Review* for the month of March, in the same year. It was written by Mr. Ward, afterwards Lord Dudley, and was alluded to many years afterwards by the *Quarterly*, as a "masterpiece of damning by faint praise." The review nettled the poet not a little, as we learn from a letter of Byron's, written in September :

"Rogers has returned to town, but not yet recovered of the *Quarterly*. What fellows these reviewers are! 'These boys do fear us all!' They made you fight, and me (the milkiest of men) a satirist, and will end by making Rogers madder than Ajax. I have been reading Memory again, the other day, and Hope together, and retain all my preference of the former. His elegance is really wonderful; there is no such thing as a vulgar line in the book. * * Rogers wants me to go with him on a crusade to the Lakes, and to besiege you on our way. This last is a great temptation, but I fear it will not be in my power, unless you would go on with one of us somewhere — no matter where.

"P. S. No letter — *n'importe*. Rogers thinks the *Quarterly* will be at *me* this time ; if so, it shall be a war of extermination — *no quarter*. From the youngest devil down to the oldest woman of that review, all shall perish by one fatal lampoon. The ties of nature shall be torn asunder, for I will not even spare my bookseller ; nay, if one were to include readers also, all the better."

We do not know if this review prompted a celebrated epigram upon its author by the offended poet, or if the epigram prompted the review. From an allusion to it in Medwin's Conversations with Lord Byron, we should imagine that the poet revenged himself by the satire ; but from an allusion in the *Quarterly Review* we infer that Rogers was the first offender. "Rogers is the only man," said his lordship to Captain Medwin, "who can write epigrams, and sharp bone-cutters, too, in two lines." For instance, that on an M.P. who had reviewed his book, and said he wrote very well for a banker :

> "Ward has no heart, they say, but I deny it ;
> He has a heart, and gets his speeches by it."

The *Quarterly* says that Ward would sometimes quote this distich, admit the point, and return usually a Roland for an Oliver. But even Mr. Ward did not fail to recognize the position which the poet had already secured by The Pleasures of Memory. "The first poem in this collection," he says, "does not fall within the province of our criticism. It has been published many years, and has acquired that sort of popularity which is, perhaps, more decisive than any other *single* test of merit. It has been generally admired, and, what is not always a certain consequence of being admired, it has been generally read. The circulation of it has not been confined to the highly-educated and critical part of the public, but it has received the applause which to works of the imagination is quite as flattering, — of that far more numerous class, who, without attempting to judge by accurate and philosophical rules, read poetry only for the pleasure it affords them, and praise because they are delighted. It is to be found in all libraries, and in most parlor windows." In another part of the review, the critic says, "Endowed with an ear naturally correct, and attuned by practice to the measures of his favorite masters, nice to the very verge of fastidiousness, accurate almost to minuteness, habitually attentive to the finer turns of expression and the more delicate shades of thought, Mr. Rogers was always harmonious, always graceful, and often pathetic. But his beauties are all beauties of execution and detail, arising from the charm of skilful versification, the 'curiosa felicitas' of expression, culled with infinite care and selection, and applied with no vulgar judgment, and with the refined tenderness of a polished and feeling mind."

We must now cite a few sentences in a different vein, to show how far the *Quarterly* was right in its estimate of this critique, and to what extent it might well have annoyed the poet. "We have always been desirous," says the reviewer, after alluding to the poet's early productions, "to see something more from the hand of an author whose first appearance was so auspicious. But year after year rolled on, and we began to fear that indolence, the occupations of a busy life, or the dread of detracting from a reputation already so high, would forever prevent our wishes from being gratified. We were, therefore, both *pleased and surprised* when, upon accidentally taking up the last edition of Mr. Rogers' poem, we found that it was *enriched, not only with several very elegant wooden cuts*, but with an entirely new performance in eleven cantos, called 'Fragments of a Poem on the Voyage of Columbus.'"

After a minute analysis of the poem, the critic thus sums up its merits and faults: "Still, however, and with all its defects both of subject and of execution, the poem is by no means undeserving attention. Mr. Rogers has not been able to depart from his former manner, that which use had made natural to him, so much as he, perhaps, intended. He is often himself, in spite of himself. Habit, good taste and an exquisite ear, are constantly bringing him back to the right path, even when he had set out with a resolution to wander from it. Hence, though the poem will not bear to be looked at as a whole, and though there runs through it an affectation of beauties which it is not in the author's power to produce, yet it contains passages of such merit as would amply repay the trouble of reading a much larger and more faulty work. It will be the more pleasing part of our task to select a few of them, with an assurance to our readers that they are not the only ones, and with a strong recommendation to read the whole, — a recommendation with which they will very easily comply, as the poem does not exceed seven or eight hundred lines."

In this connection the following contemporaneous memoranda of Lord Byron's, touching the poet and his critic, will be read with interest:

"*Nov.* 22, 1813. — Rogers is silent; and, it is said, severe. When he does talk, he talks well; and, on all subjects of taste, his delicacy of expression is pure as his poetry. If you enter his house, his drawing-room, his library, you of yourself say, this is not the dwelling of a common mind. There is not a gem, a coin, a book thrown aside on his chimney-piece, his sofa, his table, that does not bespeak an almost fastidious elegance in the possessor. But this very delicacy must be the misery of his existence. O, the jarrings his disposition must have encountered through life!

"*Nov.* 23. — Ward. I like Ward. By Mahomet! I begin to think I like everybody, — a disposition not to be encouraged; a sort of social gluttony that swallows everything set before it. But I like Ward. He is *piquant;* and, in my opinion, will stand *very* high in the house, and everywhere else, if he applies *regularly*. By the by, I dine with him to-morrow, which may have some influence on my opinion. It is as well not to trust one's gratitude *after* dinner. I have heard many a host libelled by his guests, with his Burgundy yet reeking on their rascally lips."

In 1814 the poem of Jacqueline appeared, in the same volume with the Lara of Lord Byron.

"Rogers and I," wrote his lordship to Moore, in July, 1814, "have almost coalesced into a joint invasion of the public. Whether it will take place or not, I do not yet know; and I am afraid Jacqueline (which is very beautiful) will be in bad company. But in this case the lady will not be the sufferer." To the author he had written a few days previously: "You could not have made me a more acceptable present than Jacqueline; she is all grace, and softness, and poetry; there is so much of the last that we do not feel the want of story, which is simple, yet *enough*. I wonder that you do not oftener unbend to more of the same kind. I have some sympathy with the *softer* affections, though very little in *my* way; and no one can depict them so truly and successfully as yourself. I have half a mind to pay you in kind, or rather *un*-kind, for I have just 'supped full of horror' in two cantos of darkness and dismay." In August he wrote to Moore, "Rogers I have not seen, but Larry and Jacky came out a few days ago. Of their effect I know nothing." He adds in the same letter, "Murray talks of divorcing Larry and Jacky,—a bad sign for the authors, who, I suppose, will be divorced too, and throw the blame upon one another. Seriously, I don't care a cigar about it, and I don't see why Sam should."

"I believe I told you of Larry and Jacky," he again wrote to Moore. "A friend of mine was reading—at least a friend of his was reading—said Larry and Jacky, in a Brighton coach. A passenger took up the book, and queried as to the author. The proprietor said 'there were *two*,' to which the answer of the unknown was 'Ay, ay, a joint concern, I suppose; *summat* like Sternhold and Hopkins.' Is not this excellent? I would not have missed the 'vile comparison' to have 'scaped being one of the 'arcades ambo, et cantare pares.'"

Byron seems to have lived on terms of the most cordial intimacy with Rogers, who is one of the few persons of whom he always spoke with kindness and respect. The full-length portrait of his lordship, by Sanders, was presented to him. "You are one of the few persons," Byron wrote to him in March, 1816, "with whom I have lived in what is called intimacy." "It is a considerable time," Byron wrote in the year following, "since I wrote to you last, and I hardly know why I should trouble you now, except that I think you will not be sorry to hear from me now and then. You and I were never correspondents, but always something better, which is very good friends."

His diaries and letters frequently refer to their social meetings. "On Tuesday last," he writes under date of March 6, 1814. "I dined with Rogers,—Madame de Staël, Mackintosh, Sheridan, Erskine and Payne Knight, Lady Donegal and Miss R., there. Sheridan told a very good story of himself and Madame de Recamier's handkerchief; Erskine a few stories of himself only. * * The party went off very well, and the fish was very much to my gusto. But we got up too soon after the women; and Mrs. Corinne always lingers so long after dinner, that we wish her in —— the drawing-room." The next week he makes another entry. "On Tuesday dined with Rogers, Mackintosh, Sheridan, Sharpe,—much talk and good, all except my own little prattlement. Much of old times, Horne Tooke, the Trials, evidence of Sheridan, and anecdotes of those times, when *I*, alas! was an infant."

Of the nature of the relations between his lordship, Rogers, and their common friend Moore, the last mentioned gives us a vivid impression in his account of an evening in St. James'-street. We quote from Moore's Life of Byron:

"Among the many gay hours we passed together this spring (1813), I remember particularly the wild flow of his spirits one evening, when we had accompanied Mr. Rogers home from some early assembly, and when Lord Byron, who, according to his frequent custom, had not dined for the last two days, found his hunger no longer governable, and called aloud for 'something to eat.' Our repast, of his own choosing, was simple bread and cheese; and seldom have I partaken of so joyous a supper. It happened that our host had just received a presentation copy of a volume of poems, written professedly in imitation of the old English writers, and containing, like many of these models, a good deal that was striking and beautiful, mixed up with much that was trifling, fantastic and absurd. In our mood at the moment, it was only with these latter qualities that either Lord Byron or I felt disposed to indulge ourselves; and, in turning over the pages, we found, it must be owned, abundant matter for mirth. In vain did Mr. Rogers, in justice to the author, endeavor to direct our attention to some of the beauties of the work. It suited better our purpose (as is too often the case with more deliberate critics), to pounce only on such passages as ministered to the laughing humor that possessed us. In this sort of hunt through the volume, we at length lighted on the discovery that our host, in addition to his sincere approbation of some of its contents, had also the motive of gratitude for standing by its author, as one of the poems was a warm, and, I need not add, well-deserved panegyric on himself. We were, however, too far gone in nonsense, for even this eulogy, in which we both heartily agreed, to stop us. The opening line of the poem was, as well as I can recollect, 'When Rogers o'er this labor bent.' And Lord Byron undertook to read it aloud; but he found it impossible to get beyond the first two words. Our laughter had now increased to such a pitch that nothing could restrain it. Two or three times he began; but no sooner had the words 'When Rogers' passed his lips, than our fit burst forth afresh, till even Mr. Rogers himself, with all his feeling of our injustice, found it impossible not to join us; and we were, at last, all three in such a state of inextinguishable laughter, that, had the author himself been of the party, I question much whether he could have resisted the infection."

Byron always entertained and expressed an elevated opinion of Rogers as a man of taste and genius. In one of his letters to Moore he says, "I wrote to Rogers the other day, with a message to you. I hope that he flourishes. He is the Tithonus of poetry, — immortal already. You and I must wait for it." Again he says, "Will you remember me to Rogers? — whom I presume to be flourishing, and whom I regard as our poetical papa. You are his lawful son, and I his illegitimate." So in his journal, under date of November 24, 1813, Byron writes:

"I have not answered W. Scott's last letter, but I will. I regret to hear from others that he has lately been unfortunate in pecuniary involvements. He is, undoubtedly, the Monarch of Parnassus, and the most *English* of bards. I should place Rogers next in the living list (I value him more as the last of the *best* school); Moore and Campbell, both third; Southey and Wordsworth and Coleridge; the rest, ὁι πολλοι — thus:

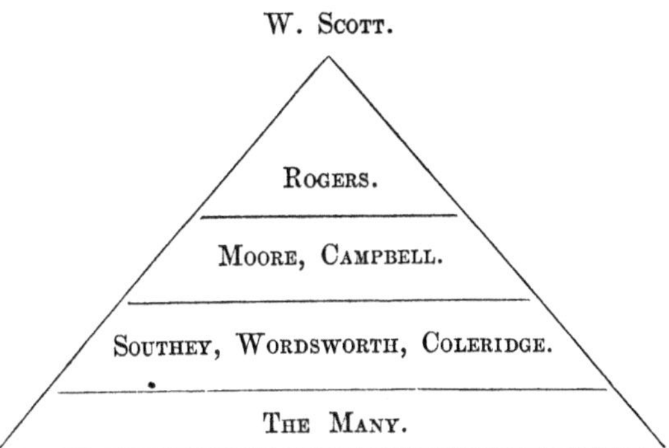

Rogers seems to have cultivated the kindest personal relations with most of his distinguished poetical contemporaries. He was on the most friendly terms with Campbell, who speaks with cordial warmth of the generosity and kindliness of his nature, and his constant search for opportunities of manifesting his benevolence of disposition. With Crabbe, also, he was intimate. This "sternest painter" of nature was introduced to the family of Landsdowne by Bowles, the friend of his latter days; and here he became the acquaintance and friend of Rogers, who invited him to pay a summer visit to London. "He accepted this invitation, and, taking lodgings near his new friend's residence, in St. James' Place, was cordially welcomed by the circle distinguished in politics, fashion, science, art and literature, of which Mr. R. was himself the brightest ornament." The following memoranda from Crabbe's diary show how largely he was indebted to the attentions of Rogers for the enjoyment of his London visit:

"*June* 24, 1817. — Mr. Rogers, his brother and family. Mr. and Mrs. Moore, very agreeable and pleasant people. Foscolo, the Italian gentleman. Dante, &c. Play, Kemble in Coriolanus.

"20*th*. — Mr. Rogers, and the usual company, at breakfast. Lady Holland comes and takes me to Holland House. * * Meet Mr. Campbell. Mr. Moore with us. Mr. Rogers joins us in the course of the day.

"27*th*. — Breakfast with Mr. Brougham and Lady Holland. Lord

Holland to speak at Kemble's retiring, at the meeting at Freemason's Tavern, to-morrow. Difficulty of procuring me an admission ticket, as all are distributed. Trial made by somebody, I knew not who,—failed. This represented to Lady Holland, who makes no reply. Morning, interview with Mr. Brougham. Mr. Campbell's letter. He invites us to Sydenham. I refer it to Mr. Rogers and Mr. Moore. Return to town. The pòrter delivers to me a paper containing the admission ticket, procured by Lady Holland's means; whether request or command, I know not. Call on Mr. Rogers. We go to the Freemason's Tavern. The room filled. We find a place about half-way down the common seats, but not where the managers dine, above the steps. By us, Mr. Smith, one of the authors of the Rejected Addresses. Known, but no introduction. Mr. Perry, editor of the *Morning Chronicle*, and Mr. Campbell, find us, and we are invited into the committee room. Kemble, Perry, Lord Erskine, Mr. Moore, Lord Holland, Lord Ossory, whom I saw at Holland House. Dinner announced. Music. Lord Erskine sits between me and a young man whom I find to be a son of Boswell. Lord Holland's speech after dinner. The ode recited. Campbell's speech. Kemble's — Talma's. We leave the company, and go to Vauxhall to meet Miss Rogers and her party. Stay late.

"28*th*.—Go to St. James' Place. Lord Byron's new works, Manfred and Tasso's Lament. * *

"29*th*.—Breakfast at the coffee-house in Pall Mall, and go to Mr. Rogers and family. Agree to dine, and then join their party after dinner.

"30*th*.—First hour at Mr. Murray's. A much younger and more lively man than I had imagined. A handsome drawing-room, where he receives his friends, usually from two to five o'clock. Pictures by Phillips of Lord Byron, Mr. Scott, Mr. Southey, Mr. Campbell, Rogers (yet unfinished), Moore, by Lawrence (his last picture). Mr. Murray wishes me to sit. Advise with Mr. Rogers. He recommends.

"*July* 1*st*.—I foresee a long train of engagements. Dine with Mr. Rogers. Company: Kemble, Lord Erskine, Lord Ossory, Sir George Beaumont, Mr. Campbell and Mr. Moore. Miss R. retires early, and is not seen any more at home. Meet her at the gallery in Pall Mall, with Mr. Westall.

"*2d.* — Duke of Rutland. List of pictures burned at Belvoir Castle. Dine at Sydenham with Mr. and Mrs. Campbell, Mr. Moore and Mr. Rogers. Poet's Club.

"*4th.*—Morning view, and walk with Mr. Heber and Mr. Stanhope. Afterwards, Mr. Rogers, Lady S., Lady H. A good picture, if I dare draw it accurately; to place in lower life would lose the peculiarities which depend upon their station; yet, in any station. Return with Mr. Rogers. Dine at Landsdowne House. Sir James Mackintosh, Mr. Grenville, elder brother to Lord Grenville. * *

"*6th.* — Call at Mr. Rogers', and go to Lady Spencer. Go with Mr. Rogers to dine at Highbury with his brother and family. Miss Rogers the same at Highbury as in town. * * Mr. Rogers says I must dine with him to-morrow, and that I consented when I was at Sydenham; and now certainly they expect me at Hampstead, though I have made no promise.

"*7th.* —Dinner at Mr. Rogers', with Mr. Moore and Mr. Campbell, Lord Strangford and Mr. Spencer.

"*14th.* — Go to Mr. Rogers', and take a farewell visit to Highbury. Miss Rogers. Promise to go when ——. Return early. Dine there, and purpose to see Mr. Moore and Mr. Rogers in the morning when they set out for Calais.

"*15th.* — Was too late this morning. Messrs. Rogers and Moore were gone. Go to church at St. James'. The sermon good; but the preacher thought proper to apologize for a severity which he had not used. Write some lines in the solitude of Somerset House, not fifty yards from the Thames on one side, and the Strand on the other; but as quiet as the sands of Arabia. I am not quite in good humor with this day; but, happily, I cannot say why."

The dinner at Sydenham, alluded to under the date of July 2d, made a lasting impression on more than one of the party; and Moore has immortalized it in one of his most graceful and exquisite poems, the Verses to the Poet Crabbe's Inkstand. We transcribe the stanzas in which the poet describes the subject of this sketch:

"How freshly doth my mind recall,
'Mong the few days I 've known with thee,
One that most buoyantly of all
Floats in the wake of memory!

"When he, the poet, doubly graced
In life, as in his perfect strain,
With that pure, mellowing power of Taste,
Without which Fancy shines in vain;

"Who in his page will leave behind,
Pregnant with genius though it be,
But half the treasures of a mind,
Where Sense o'er all holds mastery:

"Friend of long years! of friendship tried
Through many a bright and dark event;
In doubts, my judge; in taste, my guide;
In all, my stay and ornament!

"He, too, was of our feast that day,
And all were guests of one whose hand
Hath shed a new and deathless ray
Around the lyre of this great land;

"In whose sea-odes — as in those shells
Where Ocean's voice of majesty
Seems still to sound — immortal dwells
Old Albion's Spirit of the Sea."

In 1819 Rogers appeared again before the world of letters, with the poem entitled Human Life, which found a friendly critic in the accomplished editor of the *Edinburgh Review*. From his beautiful article we copy the following extracts:

"These are very sweet verses. They do not, indeed, stir the spirit like the strong lines of Byron, nor make our hearts dance within us, like the inspiring strains of Scott; but they come over us with a bewitching softness that, in certain moods, is still more delightful, and soothe the troubled spirits with a refreshing sense of truth, purity, and elegance. They are pensive rather than passionate; and more full of wisdom and tenderness than of high flights of fancy, or overwhelming bursts of emotion; while they are moulded into grace at least as much by the effect of the moral beauties they disclose, as by the taste and judgment with which they are constructed.

"The theme is HUMAN LIFE! — not only 'the subject of all verse,' but the great centre and source of all interest in the works of human beings, to which both verse and prose invariably bring us back, when they succeed in riveting our attention, or rousing our emotions, and which turns everything into poetry to which its sensibilities can be ascribed, or by which its vicissitudes can be suggested! Yet it is not by any means to that which, in ordinary language, is termed the poetry or the romance of human life, that the present work is directed. The life which it endeavors to set before us is not life diversified with strange adventures, embodied in extraordinary characters, or agitated with turbulent passions; not the life of warlike paladins, or desperate lovers, or sublime ruffians, or piping shepherds, or sentimental savages, or bloody bigots, or preaching pedlers, or conquerors, poets, or any other species of madmen; but the ordinary, practical, and amiable life of social, intelligent and affectionate men in the upper ranks of society, — such, in short, as multitudes may be seen living every day in this country; for the picture is entirely English, and though not perhaps in the choice of every one, yet open to the judgment, and familiar to the sympathies, of all. It contains, of course, no story, and no individual characters. It is properly and peculiarly contemplative, and consists in a series of reflections on our mysterious nature and condition upon earth, and on the marvellous though unnoticed changes which the ordinary course of our existence is continually bringing about in our being. Its marking peculiarity in this respect is, that it is free from the least alloy of acrimony or harsh judgment, and deals not at all, indeed, in any species of satirical or sarcastic remark. The poet looks here on man, and teaches us to look on him, not merely with love, but with reverence; and, mingling a sort of considerate pity for the shortness of his busy little career, and the disappointments and weaknesses by which it is beset, with a genuine admiration of the great capacities he unfolds, and the high destiny to which he seems to be reserved, works out a very beautiful and engaging picture, both of the affections by which life is endeared, the trials to which it is exposed, and the pure and peaceful enjoyments with which it may often be filled.

"This, after all, we believe, is the tone of true wisdom and true virtue; and that to which all good natures draw nearer, as they approach the close of life, and come to act less, and to know and to meditate more, on the varying and crowded scene of human existence. When the inordinate hopes of early youth, which provoke their own disappointment, have been sobered down by longer experience and more extended views; when the keen contentions, and eager rivalries, which employed our riper age, have expired or been abandoned; when we have seen, year after year, the objects of our fiercest hostility, and of our fondest affections, lie down together in the hallowed peace of the grave; when ordinary pleasures and amusements begin to be insipid, and the gay derision which seasoned them to appear flat and importunate; when we reflect how often we have mourned and been comforted; what opposite opinions we have successively maintained and abandoned; to what inconsistent habits we have gradually been formed, and how frequently the objects of our pride have proved the sources of our shame,— we are naturally led to recur to the careless days of our childhood, and, from that distant starting place, to retrace the whole of our career, and that of our contemporaries, with feelings of far greater humility and indulgence than those by which it had been actually accompanied; — to think all vain but affection and honor, the simplest and cheapest pleasures the truest and most precious, and generosity of sentiment the only mental superiority which ought either to be wished for or admired.

"We are aware that we have said 'something too much of this;' and that our readers would probably have been more edified, as well as more delighted, by Mr. Rogers' text, than with our preachment upon it. But we were anxious to convey to them our sense of the spirit in which this poem is written; — and conceive, indeed, that what we have now said falls more strictly within the line of our critical duty than our general remarks can always be said to do; because the true character and poetical effect of the work seems, in this instance, to depend much more on its moral expression than on any of its merely literary qualities.

"The author, perhaps, may not think it any compliment to be thus told that his verses are likely to be greater favorites with the old than with the young; — and yet it is no small compliment, we think, to say that they are likely to be more favorites with his readers every year they live. And it is, at all events, true, whether it be a compliment or not, that as readers of all ages, if they are any way worth pleasing, have little glimpses and occasional visitations of those truths which longer experience only renders more familiar, so no works ever sink so deep into amiable minds, or recur so often to their remembrance, as those which embody simple, and solemn, and reconciling truths, in emphatic and elegant language, and anticipate, as it were, and bring out with effect, those salutary lessons which it seems to be the great end of our life to inculcate. The pictures of violent passion and terrible emotion, the breathing characters, the splendid imagery and bewitching fancy, of Shakspeare himself, are less frequently recalled, than those great moral aphorisms in which he has so often

> Told us the fashion of our own estate,
> The secrets of our bosoms ;

and, in spite of all that may be said, by grave persons, of the frivolousness of poetry, and of its admirers, we are persuaded that the most memorable and the most generally admired of all its productions are those which are chiefly recommended by their deep practised wisdom, and their coincidence with those salutary imitations with which nature herself seems to furnish us from the passing scenes of our existence.

" The literary character of the work is akin to its moral character; and the diction is as soft, elegant and simple, as the sentiments are generous and true. The whole piece, indeed, is throughout in admirable keeping ; and its beauties, though of a delicate, rather than an obtrusive character, set off each other, to an attentive observer, by the skill with which they are harmonized, and the sweetness with which they slide into each other. The outline, perhaps, is often rather timidly drawn, and there is an occasional want of force and brilliancy in the coloring ; which we are rather inclined to ascribe to the refined and somewhat fastidious taste of the artist, than to any defect of skill or of power. We have none of the broad and blazing tints of Scott, nor the startling contrasts of Byron, nor the anxious and endlessly repeated touch of Southey, but something which comes much nearer to the soft and tender manner of Campbell ; with still more reserve and caution, perhaps, and more frequent sacrifices of strong and popular effect to an abhorrence of glaring beauties, and a disdain of vulgar resources."

Soon after this appearance as a poet, we find him acting in a character which he seems almost as much to have affected, — that of a peace-maker. Among the men of letters whom Dr. Parr visited in

London, we are told by one of his biographers that he "always mentioned with marked distinction Samuel Rogers, whom he admired as a poet, and greatly esteemed as a friend." A clause in his will is in the following words: "I give a ring in token of high regard to Samuel Rogers, author of the justly celebrated poem, The Pleasures of Memory." Rogers had been the medium of reconciling the doctor to Sir James Mackintosh, with whom he had differed, and whom he first met, after a long coldness, at the hospitable board of the poet. The biographer of Mackintosh, after alluding to this difference, says, "It may be interesting to mention that the occasion on which the intimacy was renewed was offered by an acceptance of the following invitation from one whose 'Memory' is prodigal in such 'Pleasures.'

'He best can paint them who can feel them most.'"

"DEAR MACKINTOSH: Dr. Parr dines with me on Thursday, the 3d of August, and he wishes to meet some of his old friends under my roof, as it may be for the last time. He has named Wishaw, and Sharp, and Lord Holland; and he says, 'I want to shake hands with Jemmy Mackintosh before I die.'

"May I ask you to be of the party? That you can forgive, I know full well. That you will forgive in this instance — much as you have to forgive — I hope fervently.

"Some of the pleasantest moments of my life have been spent in the humble office I am now venturing to take upon myself, and I am sure you will not take it amiss, if, on this occasion, I wish to add to the number.

"Yours, very truly, "SAMUEL ROGERS.

"*July 23d*, 1820."

Moore mentions in his diary, that in 1824 he passed an evening in looking over Rogers' Common Place Book with him, where he found highly curious records of his conversations with eminent men, particularly Fox, Grattan and the Duke of Wellington. A diary of Rogers, with his opportunities, and his admirable faculty of compression in his prose style, could hardly fail to be the most entertaining literary history that ever appeared. He has been more familiar with a large number of distinguished persons, for a longer period, than any other man of letters whom we now remember. There is hardly a person distinguished in English history for the last sixty or seventy years, whose name is not in some way connected with that of the venerable poet, — if not otherwise, at least as the partaker of his liberal and elegant hospitality. His social sphere has always been a very large one. It included whigs and tories, wits and statesmen, poets and philanthropists ; not only the habitués of society, but men who were but seldom seen in worldly circles. Sir Samuel Romilly enters in his diary, a few months before his lamented death, — "To-day I dined with Rogers (the poet). A very pleasant dinner with Crabbe (whom I had never before seen), Frere and Jekyll." An extract from the diary of Wilberforce shows that he did not think so well of this dining with poets :

"*Feb.* 19, 1814. — Dined Duke of Gloucester's, to meet Madame de Staël, at her desire. Madame, her son and daughter, duke, two aides-de-camp, Vansittart, Lord Erskine, poet Rogers, and others. Madame de Staël quite like her book, though less hopeful. Complimenting me highly on abolition, and all Europe, &c. But I must not spend time in writing this. She asked me, and I could not well refuse, to dine with her on Friday, to meet Lord Harrowby and Mackintosh, and poet Rogers on Tuesday sennight.

"23*d.* — Breakfast, Mr. Barnett about the poor. Letters. Wrote to Madame de Staël and poet Rogers, to excuse myself from dining with them. It does not seem the line in which I can now glorify God. Dinner quiet, and letters afterwards."

In his diary, under date of the 5th November, 1821, Moore makes the following entry : "By the by, I received the other day a manuscript from the Longmans, requesting me (as they often do) to look over it, and give my opinion whether it would be worth publishing anonymously. Upon opening it, found, to my surprise, that it was 'Rogers' Italy,' which he has sent home thus privately to be published." This work was published in the following year, and is the last and best of its author's productions. Its merits have been set forth with exquisite taste and skill, by a writer in the *New Monthly Magazine :*

"Turn we to the last and greatest of our author's poems, 'Italy.'

"The great character of this poem (Italy) as it is in The Pleasures of Memory, is simplicity ; but here simplicity assumes a nobler shape. Although to a certain degree there is an alteration in the tone of the last from that of the first published poem, an alteration seemingly more marked from the difference between blank verse and rhyme; and although there is something of the new Persian odors, breathing from the myrtle wreaths of a muse, whom 'displicant nexæ philyrâ coronæ,' yet, unlike what we felt inclined to blame in 'Jacqueline' and the 'Human Life,' we see nothing that reminds us of *individual* traits in another; nothing that reminds us of Byron, though he strung his harp to the same theme; nothing that recalls *any* contemporaneous writer, unless it be occasionally Wordsworth, in Wordsworth's purer, if not loftier vein: we see no harsh, constrained abruptness, emulating vigor; no childish *mirauderies*, that would gladly pass themselves off for simplicity. Along the shores and palaces of old glides one calm and serene tide of verse, wooing to its waters every legend and every stream that can hallow and immortalize.

"This poem differs widely from the poems of the day, in that it is wholly void of all that is meretricious. Though nature itself could not be less naked of ornament, yet nature itself could not be more free from all ornament that is tinsel or inappropriate. A contemplative and wise man, skilled in all the arts, and nursing all the beautiful traditions of the past, having seen enough of the world to moralize justly, having so far advanced in the circle of life as to have supplied emotion with meditation, telling you, in sweet and serene strains, all that he sees, hears and feels, in journeying through a country which nature and history combine to consecrate, — this is the character of Rogers' Italy; and the reader will see at once how wholly it differs in complexion from the solemn Harold, or the impassioned Corinne. This poem is perfect as a whole; it is as a whole that it must be judged; its tone, its depth, its *hoard* of thought and description, make its main excellence, and these are the merits that no short extracts can adequately convey.

"Of all things, perhaps the hardest in the world for a poet to effect is to gossip poetically. We are those who think it is in this that Wordsworth rarely succeeds, and Cowper as rarely fails. This graceful and difficult art Rogers has made his own to a degree almost unequalled in the language.

* * * * * * *

"With the author of The Pleasures of Memory — a banker, a wit, a man of high social reputation — we find it is from the stony heart of the great world that the living waters of a pure and transparent poetry have been stricken. Few men of letters have been more personally known in their day, or more generally courted. A vein of agreeable conversation, sometimes amene, and more often caustic; a polished manner, a sense quickly alive to all that passes around; and, above all, perhaps, a taste in the arts, a knowledge of painting and of sculpture, — very rare in this country, — have contributed to make the author of Italy scarce less distinguished in society than in letters."

Moore's diary is full of allusions to his social intercourse with Rogers and his friends. One day the fashionable poet was invited to dine in St. James' Place, to meet Barnes, the editor of the *Times*, in company with Lords Landsdowne and Holland, Luttrell and Tierney; and Moore, on Rogers' advising that he was well worth cultivating, broke off an engagement for the next Sunday with Miss White, and refused Lord Landsdowne, to accept an invitation from Barnes. Another day he would breakfast at Rogers' with Sydney Smith, Sharpe, Luttrell and Lord John; or amuse himself with reading the notes from Sheridan, or passages from the unpublished works of his friend.

On 10th April, 1823, he writes, "Dined at Rogers'. A distinguished party: S. Smith, Ward, Luttrell, Payne Knight, Lord Aberdeen, Abercrombie, Lord Clifden, &c. Smith particularly amusing. Have rather held out against him hitherto; but this day he conquered me; and I am now his victim, in the laughing way, for life. * * What Rogers says of Smith, very true, that whenever the conversation is getting dull he throws in some touch which makes it rebound, and rise again as light as ever. Ward's artificial efforts, which to me are always painful, made still more so by their contrast to Smith's natural and overflowing exuberance. Luttrell, too, considerably extinguished to-day; but there is this difference between Luttrell and Smith, — that after the former you remember what good things he said, and after the latter you merely remember how much you laughed. June 10th. — Breakfasted at Rogers', to meet Luttrell, Lady Davy, Miss Rogers and William Bankes. * * Rogers showed us 'Gray's Poems' in his original hand-writing, with a letter to the printer; also the original MS. of one of Sterne's sermons." Again, he dined with Rogers at the Athenæum, the first time the latter ever dined at a club. He dined with him at Roberts', in Paris, tête-à-tête, at a splendid dinner "at fifteen francs a head, exclusive of wine. Poets did not feed so in the olden time." But the dinners in the poet's own modest but elegant mansion will be remembered as models of refined and intellectual hospitality, as long as the names live of the great men who have delighted to gather round his table.

We have alluded to Rogers' talent for epigram ; a talent which he has very discreetly employed. His conversation seems to have been dry and sarcastic, though he is not to be held responsible for most of the bon-mots and repartees that have been attributed to him. It was at one time the habit of some of the London newspapers to manufacture these things, and ascribe them to Rogers. Of this manufacture, no doubt, is a *mot* that has found its way into a book so respectable as Mr. E. H. Barker's Literary Anecdotes. "Rogers, speaking to Wilberforce of the naked Achilles in the park, said it was strange that one who had made so many *breaches* in Troy should not have a single pair for himself." Moore records some of his observation, which are pithy and pertinent. On one occasion, speaking of the sort of conscription of persons of all kinds that was put in force for the dinner of the Hollands, Rogers said, "There are two parties before whom everybody must appear — them and the police." Again, speaking of their friend Miss White, Rogers said, "How wonderfully she does hold out ! They may say what they will, but Miss White and *Miss*-olonghi arê the most remarkable things going." In talking of the game-laws at a party at Holland House, Rogers said, "If a partridge, on arriving in this country, were to ask what are the game-laws, and somebody would tell him they are laws *for the protection* of game, 'What an excellent country to live in,' the partridge would say, 'where there are so many laws for our protection!'" On somebody remarking that Payne Knight had got very deaf — "'T is from want of practice," said Rogers ; Knight being a notoriously bad listener Rogers thus described Lord Holland's feeling for the arts : "Painting gives him no pleasure, and music absolute pain."

From the reports of his conversation, we are inclined to believe that it is entitled to a good deal of the praise which the *Quarterly Review* bestows upon the *Notes* to his poems. In referring to the venerable poet, the reviewer says, "This most elegant and correct of writers, with a taste matured by the constant study of the classics of our tongue, has amused his leisure hours by trying into how small a compass wit, wisdom and elegance, may be packed. The notes to the last edition of his poems are not merely treasure-houses of anecdote and illustration, but admirable studies in composition for those who will be at the pains of ascertaining the precise language in which the same thoughts or incidents have been expressed in verse or related by others." Of an essay on assassination, written for insertion among the poems on Italy, Mackintosh wrote him that "Hume could not improve the thoughts, nor Addison the language." And Moore says, in his diary, that he feels it would do one good to study such writing, if not as a model, yet as a chastener and simplifier of style, it being the very reverse of ambition or ornament.

It is well said, by a writer in the *Quarterly Review*, that there are few precepts of taste which are not practised in Mr. Rogers' establishment, as well as recommended in his works. In illustration of the remark, he alludes to a novel and ingenious mode of lighting a dining-room, which might be well imitated wherever there are fine pictures. Lamps above or candles on the table there are none, but all the light is reflected by Titians, Reynolds', &c., from lamps projecting out of the frame of the pictures, and screened from the company. His house in St. James' Place is small, but overflowing with the choicest specimens of the fine arts, pictures, antique bronzes, sculptures and literary curiosities of uncounted value. The following detailed description of the works of art which adorn this hospitable mansion is from the pen of Professor Waagen, of Berlin:

"By the kindness of Mr. Solly, who continues to embrace every opportunity of doing me service, I have been introduced to Mr. Rogers the poet, a very distinguished and amiable man. He is one of the few happy mortals to whom it has been granted to be able to gratify, in a worthy manner, the most lively sensibility to everything noble and beautiful. He has accordingly found means, in the course of his long life, to impress this sentiment on everything about him. In his house you are everywhere surrounded and excited with the higher productions of art. In truth, one knows not whether more to admire the diversity or the purity of his taste. Pictures of the most different schools, ancient and modern sculptures, Greek vases, alternately attract the eye; and are so arranged, with a judicious regard to their size, in proportion to the place assigned them, that every room is richly and picturesquely ornamented, without having the appearance of a magazine from being overfilled, as we frequently find. Among all these objects, none is insignificant; several cabinets and portfolios contain, beside the choicest collections of antique ornaments in gold that I have hitherto seen, valuable miniatures of the middle ages, fine drawings by the old masters, and the most agreeable prints of the greatest of the old engravers, Marcantonio, Durer, etc., in the finest impressions. The enjoyment of all these treasures was heightened to the owner by the confidential intercourse with the most eminent, now deceased, English artists, Flaxman and Stothard; both have left him a memorial of their friendship. In two little marble statues of Cupid and Psyche, and a mantel-piece, with a bas-relief representing a muse with a lyre and Mnemosyne by Flaxman, there is the same noble and graceful feeling which has so greatly attracted me, from my childhood, in his celebrated compositions after Homer and Æschylus. The hair and draperies are treated with great, almost too picturesque softness. Among all the English painters, none, perhaps, has so much power of invention as Stothard. His versatile talent has successfully made essays in the domains of history, or fancy and poetry, of humor, and, lastly, even in domestic scenes, in the style of Watteau. To this may be added much feeling for graceful movements, and cheerful, bright coloring. In his pictures, which adorn a chimney-piece, principal characters from Shakspeare's plays are represented with great spirit and humor; among them, Falstaff makes a very distinguished and comical figure. There is also a merry company, in the style of Watteau; the least attractive is an allegorical representation of Peace returning to the earth, for the brilliant coloring, approaching to Rubens, cannot make up for the poorness of the heads and the weakness of the drawing.

"As there are among the pictures some of the best works of Sir Joshua Reynolds, fine specimens of the works of three of the most eminent British artists of an earlier date are here united.

"Beside portraits, properly so called, Sir Joshua Reynolds was the happiest in the representation of children, where he was able, in the main, to remain faithful to nature, and in general an indifferent but naïve action or occupation alone was necessary. In such pictures, he admirably succeeded in representing the youthful bloom and artless manners of the fine English children. This it is which makes his celebrated strawberry-girl, which is in this collection, so attractive. With her hands simply folded, a basket under her arm, she stands in a white frock, and looks full at the spectator, with her fine, large eyes. The admirable impasto, the bright, golden tone, clear as Rembrandt, and the dark landscape back-ground, have a striking effect. Sir Joshua himself looked upon this as one of his best pictures. A sleeping girl is also uncommonly charming, the coloring very glowing; many cracks in the painting, both in the back-ground and the drapery, show the uncertainty of the artist in the mechanical processes of the art. Another girl with a bird does not give me so much pleasure. The rather affected laugh is, in this instance, not stolen from nature, but from the not happy invention of the painter; in the glowing color there is something specky and false. Puck, the merry elf in Shakspeare's Midsummer Night's Dream, called by the English Robin Goodfellow, represented as a child, with an arch look, sitting on a mushroom, and full of wantonness, stretching out arms and legs, is another much admired work of Sir Joshua. But, though this picture is painted with much warmth and clearness, the conception does not at all please me. I find it too childish, and not fantastic enough. In the back-ground, Titania is seen with the ass-headed weaver. Psyche with the lamp, looking at Cupid, figures as large as life, is of the most brilliant effect, and, in the tender, greenish half-tints, also of great delicacy. In the regard for beautiful leading lines, there is an affinity to the rather exaggerated grace of Parmeggiano. In such pictures by Sir Joshua, the incorrect drawing always injures the effect. I was much interested at meeting with a landscape by this master. It is in the style of Rembrandt, and of very strong effect.

"Of older English painters, there are here two pretty pictures by Gainsborough, one by Wilson; of the more recent, I found only one by the rare and spirited Bonington, of a Turk fallen asleep over his pipe, admirably executed in a deep, harmonious chiaro-oscuro. Mr. Rogers' taste and knowledge of the art are too general for him not to feel the profound intellectual value of works of art in which the management of the materials was in some degree restricted. He has, therefore, not disdained to place in his collection the half-figures of St. Paul and St. John, and fragments of a fresco painting from the Carmelite Church at Florence, by Giotto; Salome dancing before

Herod, and the beheading of St. John, by Fiesole ; a coronation of the Virgin, by Lorenzo de Condi, the fellow-scholar and friend of Leonardo da Vinci, whose productions and personal character were so estimable. Next to these pictures is a Christ on the Mount of Olives, by Raphael, at the time when he had not abandoned the manner of Perugio. This little picture was once a part of the predella to the altar-piece which Raphael painted in the year 1505, for the nuns of St. Anthony, at Perugio. It came with the Orleans gallery to England, and was last in the possession of Lord Eldin, in Edinburgh. Unhappily it has been much injured by cleaning and repairing, but in many parts, particularly in the arms of the angel, there are defects in the drawing, such as we do not find in Raphael even at this period. So that, most probably, the composition alone should be ascribed to him, and the execution to one of the assistants, who painted the two saints belonging to the same predella now in Dulwich College.

"From the Orleans gallery, Mr. Rogers has Raphael's Madonna, well known by Flipart's engraving, with the eyes rather cast down, on whom the child standing by her fondly leans. The expression of joyousness in the child is very pleasing. The gray color of the under-dress of the Virgin, with red sleeves, forms an agreeable harmony with the blue mantle. To judge by the character and drawing, the composition may be of the early period of Raphael's residence at Rome. In other respects, this picture admits of no judgment, because many parts have become quite flat by cleaning, and others are painted over. The landscape is in a blue-greenish tone, differing from Raphael's manner.

"Of the Roman school I will mention only one more. Christ bearing his cross, by Andrea Sacchi, a moderate-sized picture from the Orleans gallery, is one of the capital pictures of this master, in composition, depth of coloring, and harmony.

"The crown, however, of the whole collection, is Christ appearing to Mary Magdalene, by Titian. It was formerly in the possession of the family of Muselli at Verona, and afterward adorned the Orleans gallery. In the clear, bright, golden tone of the flesh, the careful execution, the refined feeling, in the impassioned desire of the kneeling Magdalene to touch the Lord, and the calm, dignified refusal of the Saviour, we recognize the earlier time of this master. The beautiful landscape, with the reflection of the glowing horizon upon the blue sea, which is of great importance here, in proportion to the figures, proves how early Titian obtained extraordinary mastery in this point, and confirms that he was the first who carried this branch to a higher degree of perfection. This poetic picture is, on the whole, in very good preservation ; the crimson drapery of the Magdalene is of unusual depth and fulness. The lower part of the legs of Christ have, however, suffered a little. The figures are about a third the size of life.

"The finished sketch for the celebrated picture, known by the name of La Gloria di Tiziano, which he afterward, by the command of Philip II., King of Spain, painted for the church of the convent where the Emperor Charles V. died, is also very remarkable. It is a rich, but not very pleasing composition. The idea of having the coffin of the emperor carried up to heaven, where God the Father and Son are enthroned, is certainly not a happy one. The painting is throughout excellent, and of a rich, deep tone in the flesh. Unfortunately, it is not wanting in re-touches. The large picture is now in the Escurial.

"As the genuine pictures of Giorgione are so very rare, I will briefly mention a young knight, — small, full-length, noble and powerful in face and figure ; the head is masterly, treated in his glowing tone ; the armor with great force and clearness in the chiaro-oscuro.

"The original sketch of Tintoretto, for his celebrated picture of St. Mark coming to the assistance of a martyr, is as spirited as it is full and deep in the tone.

"The rich man and Lazarus, by Giacomo Bassano, is, in execution and glow of coloring, approaching to Rembrandt, one of the best pictures of the master.

"There are some fine cabinet pictures of the school of Carracci : a Virgin and Child, worshipped by six saints, by Lodovico Carracci, is one of his most pleasing pictures in imitation of Corregio. Among four pictures by Domenichino, two landscapes, with the punishment of Marsyas, and Tobit with the fish, are very attractive, from the poetry of the composition and the delicacy of the finish. Another likewise very fine one of Bird-catching, from the Borghese Palace, has unfortunately turned quite dark. A Christ, by Guido, is broadly and spiritedly touched in his finest silver tone.

"There is an exquisite little gem by Claude Lorraine. In a soft evening light, a lonely shepherd, with his peaceful flocks, is playing the pipe. Of the master's earlier time , admirable in the impasto, careful and delicate, decided and soft, all in a warm, golden tone. In the Liber Veritatis, marked No. 11. Few pictures inspire like this a feeling for the delicious stillness of a summer's evening.

"A landscape by Nicolas Poussin, rather large, of a very poetic composition and careful execution, inspires, on the other hand, in the brownish silver tone, the sensation of the freshness of morning. There is quite a reviving coolness in the dark water and under the trees of the fore-ground.

"Two smaller historical pictures by Poussin, of his earlier time, class among his careful and good works.

"Of the Flemish school there are a few, but very good, specimens.

"There is a highly interesting picture by Rubens. During his residence in Mantua, he was so pleased with the triumph of Julius Cæsar, by Mantegna, that he made a fine copy of one of the nine pictures. His love for the fantastic and pompous led him to choose that with the elephants carrying the candelabra ; but his ardent imagination, ever directed to the dramatic, could not be content with this. Instead of a harmless sheep, which in Mantegna is walking by the side of the foremost elephant, Rubens made a lion and a lioness, which growl angrily at the elephant. The latter, on his part, is not idle, but, looking furiously round, is on the point of striking the lion a blow with his trunk. The severe pattern which he had before him in Mantegna has moderated Rubens in his usually very full forms, so that they are more noble and slender than they generally are. The coloring, as in all his earlier pictures, is more subdued than in the later, and yet powerful. Rubens himself seems to have set much value on this study ; for it was among the effects at his death. During the revolution, Mr. Champernowne brought it from the Balbi Palace, at Genoa. It is three feet high, and five feet five inches wide.

"The study for the celebrated picture, the Terrors of War, in the Pitti Palace, at Florence, and respecting which we have a letter in

Rubens' own hand, is likewise well worth notice. Rubens painted this picture for the Grand Duke of Tuscany. Venus endeavors, in vain, to keep Mars, the insatiable warrior, as Homer calls him, from war; he hurries away to prepare indescribable destruction. This picture, one foot eight inches high, and two feet six and a half inches wide, which I have seen in the exhibition of the British Institution, is, by the warmth and power of the coloring, and the spirited and careful execution, one of the most eminent of Rubens' small pictures of this period.

"Lastly, there is a Moonlight by him. The clear reflection of the moon in the water, its effect in the low distance, the contrast of the dark mass of trees in the fore-ground, are a proof of the deep feeling for striking incidents in nature which was peculiar to Rubens. As in another picture the flakes of snow were represented, he has here marked the stars.

"I have now become acquainted with Rembrandt in a new department; he has painted in brown and white a rather obscure allegory on the deliverance of the United Provinces from the union of such great powers as Spain and Austria. It is a rich composition, with many horsemen. One of the most prominent figures is a lion chained at the foot of a rock, on which the the tree of liberty is growing. Over the rock are the words, '*Solo Deo gloria.*' The whole is executed with consummate skill, and the principal effect striking.

"His own portrait, at an advanced age, with very dark ground and shadows, and, for him, a cool tone of the lights, is to be classed, among the great number of them, with that in the Bridgewater Gallery; only it is treated in his broadest manner, which borders on looseness.

"A landscape, with a few trees upon a hill, in the fore-ground, with a horseman and a pedestrian in the back-ground, a plain with a bright horizon, is clearer in the shadows than other landscapes by Rembrandt, and, therefore, with the most powerful effect, the more harmonious.

"Among the drawings, I must at least mention some of the finest.

"Raphael.—The celebrated Entombment, drawn with the utmost spirit with the pen. From the Crozat collection. Mr. Rogers gave one hundred and twenty pounds for it.

"ANDREA DEL SARTO.—Some studies in black chalks, for his fresco paintings in the Chapel del Scalzo. That for the young man who carries the baggage in the visitation of the Virgin is remarkably animated.

"LUCAS VAN LEYDEN.—A pen drawing, executed in the most perfect and masterly manner, for his celebrated and excessively rare engraving of the portrait of the Emperor Maximilian I. This wonderful drawing has hitherto been erroneously ascribed to Albert Durer.

"ALBERT DURER.—A child weeping. In chalk, on colored paper, brightened with white; almost unpleasantly true to reality.

"Among the admirable engravings, I mention only a single female figure, very delicately treated, which is so entirely pervaded with the spirit of Francisco Francia, that I do not hesitate to ascribe it to him. Francia, originally a goldsmith, is well known to have been peculiarly skilled in executing larger compositions in niello. How easily, therefore, might it have occurred to him, instead of working as hitherto in silver, to work with his graver in copper, especially as in his time the engraving on copper had been brought into more general use in Italy, by A. Mantegna and others; and Francia had such energy and diversity of talents that, in his mature age, he successfully made himself master of the art of painting, which was so much more remote from his own original profession. Beside this, the fine delicate lines in which the engraving is executed indicate an artist who had been previously accustomed to work for niello-plates, in which this manner is usually practised. The circumstance, too, that Marcantonio was educated in the workshop of Francia, is favorable to the presumption that he himself had practised engraving.

"Among the old miniatures, that which is framed and glazed and hung up, representing, in a landscape, a knight in golden armor, kneeling down, to whom God the Father, surrounded by cherubim and seraphim, appears in the air, while the damned are tormented by devils in the abyss, is by far the most important. As has been already observed by Passavant, it belongs to a series of forty miniatures, in the possession of Mr. George Brentano, at Frankfort-on-Maine, which were executed for Maître Etienne Chevalier, treasurer of France under King Charles VII., and may probably have adorned his prayer-book. They are by the greatest French miniature-painter of the fifteenth century, Johan Fouquet de Tours, painter to King Louis XI. In regard to the admirable, spirited invention, which betrays a great master, as well as the finished execution, they rank uncommonly high.

"An antique bust of a youth, in Carrara marble, which, in form and expression, resembles the eldest son of Laocoon, is in a very noble style, uncommonly animated, and of admirable workmanship. In particular, the antique piece of the neck and the treatment of the hair are very delicate. The nose and ears are new ; a small part of the chin, too, and the upper lip, are completed in a masterly manner in wax.

"A candelabrum in bronze, about ten inches high, is of the most beautiful kind. The lower part is formed by a sitting female figure holding a wreath. This fine and graceful design belongs to the period when art was in its perfection. This exquisite relic, which was purchased for Mr. Rogers in Italy, by the able connoisseur, Mr. Millingen, is, unfortunately, much damaged in the epidermis.

"Among the elegant articles of antique ornament in gold, the earrings and clasps, by which so many descriptions of the ancient poets are called to mind, there are likewise whole figures beat out in thin gold leaves. The principal article is a golden circlet, about two and a half inches in diameter, the workmanship of which is as rich and skilful as could be made in our times.

"Of the many Greek vases in terra cotta, there are five, some of them large, in the antique taste, with black figures on a yellow ground, which are of considerable importance. A flat dish, on the outer side of which five young men are rubbing themselves with the strigil, and five washing themselves, yellow on a black ground, is to be classed with vases of the first rank, for the gracefulness of the invention, and the beauty and elegance of the execution. In this collection, it is excelled only by a vase, rounded below, so that it must be placed in a peculiar stand. The combat of Achilles with Penthesilia is represented upon it, likewise, in red figures. This composition, consisting of thirteen figures, is by far the most distinguished, not only of all representations of the subject, but, in general, of all representations of combats which I have hitherto seen on vases, in the beauty and variety of the attitudes, in masterly drawing, as well as in the spirit and delicacy of the execution. It is in the happy medium between the severe and the quite free style, so that in the faces there are some traces of the antique manner."

The estimation in which the venerable poet is held, as a judge of art, may be inferred by the following extract from a letter addressed to him by Sir David Wilkie, under date of Constantinople, 30th December, 1840:

"Without any claim for this invasion upon your valuable time, other than being in this distant capital in presence of so many objects which your knowledge of life and materials for art would so enable you to appreciate and put upon record, you will yet, perhaps, excuse the few ideas I try to put together, wishing only that I had your eyes to see, with your taste and judgment to select what were best to note down, and what most worthy to remember."

After condoling with him on the loss of Lord Holland, whom he had last met in company with Moore and Rogers, Wilkie proceeds:

"Could I see you in quiet, as in Brighton and in St. James' Place, and in a suitable frame of mind for lighter subjects, what a deal the journey we have made would suggest for discussion! Mr. William Woodburn, who is with me, frequently speaks of you; and your name was often mentioned, as we passed in review at the Hague, Amsterdam, at Munich and at Vienna, the richest stores of European art; among which we saw in those places two great masters, almost in their greatest triumphs — Rubens and Rembrandt; and we scarcely know any one who could better judge of their splendors than yourself."

It should not be forgotten that Rogers was one of the few who stood by Sheridan in his last days; supplying his pecuniary needs to a great extent, and manifesting a timely sympathy towards him. It was discovered, after Sheridan's death, that sums of money which had been supposed to come from other high quarters to minister to his by no means slender wants were in reality contributed by Rogers.

From an article entitled Gore House, published in the *New Monthly Magazine*, in 1849, we transcribe a passage of gossip, that may pass for what it is worth:

"The number of guests was not yet complete. They arrived in the following order:

"Slowly, with the foot of age, his head bent forward and his hands extended, came Mr. S—— R——, endowed alike with the gifts of Plutus and Apollo, and enjoying, perhaps, a higher reputation for the possession of each than he deserved. If the couplet ascribed to Lady B—— be really hers, her ladyship seems to have thought his most celebrated poem somewhat over-praised; it ran thus:

'Of R——s's Italy, Luttrell relates
That it would have been dished were it not for the plates.'

In this opinion I do not, however, coincide, believing some of his Ausonian fragments — above all, those descriptive of Venice — to be the finest he ever wrote, and worthy, of themselves alone, to place him high amongst poets. Of the peculiarities of which I had heard so much, but one was strikingly exemplified — his fondness for female admiration. Other men have been anxious to engross the attention of a beautiful woman, before it fell to the lot of Mr. R—— to attempt it; but very few, I imagine, have tried to turn it in the same direction. Like a young Frenchman whom I formerly knew in Paris, his motto has been, — not 'comme je l'aime!' but 'comme elle m'adore!' Goldsmith is said to have been jealous if a pretty woman attracted more notice than himself; and it was no uncommon thing for R. to sulk for a whole evening, if the prettiest woman in the company failed to make much of him."

We have the curtain agreeably lifted from the social converse of Rogers, in the following little passage from Mr. Bryant's account of his visit to the veteran bard: "There are not," says Mr. B., "many more beautiful lines in the English language, — there are certainly none so beautiful in the writings of the author, — as those of Mrs. Barbauld, which the poet Rogers is fond of repeating to his friends, in his fine, deliberate manner, with just enough of tremulousness in that grave voice of his to give his recitation the effect of deep feeling:

Life! we 've been long together,
Through pleasant and through cloudy weather.
'T is hard to part when friends are dear;
Perhaps 't will cost a sigh, a tear;
Then steal away, give little warning,
Choose thine own time;
Say not good-night, but, in some happier clime,
Bid me good-morning.'

It makes the thought of death cheerful to represent it thus, as Life looking in upon you with a glad greeting, amidst fresh airs and glorious light. The lines, we infer, were written by Mrs. Barbauld in her late old age, and I do not wonder that the aged poet, who some years since entered upon the fifth score of his years, should find them haunting his memory."

Long may it be before the decease of the venerable poet may open to the world the rich stores for his biography, which must, no doubt, exist in his correspondence and commonplace books! Till that time comes, we must be content with the memoranda which are scattered here and there through the literary history of the century, imperfect and unsatisfactory, but furnishing an index to what remains behind.

But now we cannot bring this sketch to a more acceptable conclusion than by copying the latest notice we have seen of a spot that will long remain classic ground, from the pen of an American traveller. Mr. Tuckerman has been speaking of St. James' Park, and its various associations, which could not long withdraw the literary enthusiast from the bit of green-sward before the window of Rogers, which every spring morning, before the poet's health sent him into suburban exile, was covered with sparrows, expectant of their food from his kindly hand. "The view of the park," he adds, "from this drawing-room bow-window instantly disenchants the sight of all town associations. The room where this vista nature in her genuine English aspect opens, is the same so memorable for the breakfasts for many years enjoyed by the hospitable bard and his fortunate guests. An air of sadness pervaded the apartment, in the absence of him whose taste and urbanity were yet apparent in every object around. The wintry sun threw a gleam, mellow as the light of the fond reminiscence he so gracefully sung, upon the Turkey carpet and veined mahogany. It fell, as if in pensive greeting, on the famous Titian, lit up the cool tints of Watteau, and made the bust found in the sea near Pozzoli wear a creamy hue. When the old housekeeper left the room, and I glanced from the priceless canvas or classic urn to the twinkling turf, all warmed by the casual sunshine, the sensation of comfort, never so completely realized as in a genuine London breakfast-room, was touched to finer issues by the atmosphere of beauty and the memory of genius. The groups of poets, artists and wits, whose commune had filled this room with the electric glow of intellectual life, with gems of art, glimpses of nature, and the charm of intelligent hospitality, to evoke all that was most gifted and cordial, reässembled once more. I could not but appreciate the suggestive character of every ornament. There was a Murillo, to inspire the Spanish traveller with half-forgotten anecdotes ; a fine Reynolds, to whisper of the literary dinners where Garrick and Burke discussed the theatre and the senate ; Milton's agreement for the sale of ' Paradise Lost,' emphatic symbol of the uncertainty of fame ; a sketch of Stonehenge by Turner, provocative of endless discussion to artist and antiquary ; bronzes, medals and choice volumes, whose very names would inspire an affluent talker, in this most charming imaginable nook for a morning colloquy and a social breakfast. I noticed, in a glass vase over the fireplace, numerous sprigs of orange-blossoms in every grade of decay, some crumbling to dust, and others but partially faded. These, it appeared, were all plucked from bridal wreaths, the gift of their fair wearers, on the wedding-day, to the good old poet-friend ; and he, in his bachelor fantasy, thus preserved the withered trophies. They spoke at once of sentiment and of solitude."

POEMS.

O! COULD my mind, unfolded in my page,
Enlighten climes, and mould a future age;
There as it glowed, with noblest frenzy fraught
Dispense the treasures of exalted thought;
To virtue wake the pulses of the heart,
And bid the tear of emulation start!
O! could it still, through each succeeding year,
My life, my manners, and my name endear;
And, when the poet sleeps in silent dust,
Still hold communion with the wise and just! —
Yet should this Verse, my leisure's best resource,
When through the world it steals its secret course,
Revive but once a generous wish suppressed,
Chase but a sigh or charm a care to rest;
In one good deed a fleeting hour employ,
Or flush one faded cheek with honest joy;
Blest were my lines, though limited their sphere,
Though short their date, as his who traced them here.

1793.

THE

PLEASURES OF MEMORY.

IN TWO PARTS.

1792.

. . . . Hoc est
Vivere bis, vitâ posse priore frui. MART.

PART I.

Dolce sentier, ...
Colle, che mi piacesti, . .
Ov' ancor per usanza Amor mi mena;
Ben riconosco in voi l' usate forme,
Non, lasso, in me. PETRARCH.

ANALYSIS OF THE FIRST PART.

The Poem begins with the description of an obscure village, and of the pleasing melancholy which it excites on being revisited after a long absence. This mixed sensation is an effect of the Memory. From an effect we naturally ascend to the cause ; and the subject proposed is then unfolded, with an investigation of the nature and leading principles of this faculty.

It is evident that our ideas flow in continual succession, and introduce each other with a certain degree of regularity. They are sometimes excited by sensible objects, and sometimes by an internal operation of the mind. Of the former species is most probably the memory of brutes ; and its many sources of pleasure to them, as well as to us, are considered in the first part. The latter is the most perfect degree of memory, and forms the subject of the second.

When ideas have any relation whatever, they are attractive of each other in the mind ; and the perception of any object naturally leads to the idea of another, which was connected with it either in time or place, or which can be compared or contrasted with it. Hence arises our attachment to inanimate objects; hence, also, in some degree, the love of our country, and the emotion with which we contemplate the celebrated scenes of antiquity. Hence a picture directs our thoughts to the original ; and, as cold and darkness suggest forcibly the ideas of heat and light, he who feels the infirmities of age dwells most on whatever reminds him of the vigor and vivacity of his youth.

The associating principle, as here employed, is no less conducive to virtue than to happiness ; and, as such, it frequently discovers itself in the most tumultuous scenes of life. It addresses our finer feelings, and gives exercise to every mild and generous propensity.

Not confined to man, it extends through all animated nature ; and its effects are peculiarly striking in the domestic tribes.

PLEASURES OF MEMORY.

PART I.

Twilight's soft dews steal o'er the village-green,
With magic tints to harmonize the scene.
Stilled is the hum that through the hamlet broke,
When round the ruins of their ancient oak
The peasants flocked to hear the minstrel play,
And games and carols closed the busy day.
Her wheel at rest, the matron thrills no more
With treasured tales, and legendary lore.
All, all are fled; nor mirth nor music flows
To chase the dreams of innocent repose.
All, all are fled; yet still I linger here!
What secret charms this silent spot endear?
 Mark yon old Mansion frowning through the trees,
Whose hollow turret woos the whistling breeze.
That casement, arched with ivy's brownest shade,
First to these eyes the light of heaven conveyed.
The mouldering gateway strews the grass-grown court,
Once the calm scene of many a simple sport;
When all things pleased, for life itself was new,
And the heart promised what the fancy drew.

See, through the fractured pediment revealed,
Where moss inlays the rudely-sculptured shield,
The martin's old, hereditary nest.
Long may the ruin spare its hallowed guest!
As jars the hinge, what sullen echoes call!
O, haste,— unfold the hospitable hall!
That hall, where once, in antiquated state,
The chair of justice held the grave debate.
Now stained with dews, with cobwebs darkly hung,
Oft has its roof with peals of rapture rung;
When round yon ample board, in due degree,
We sweetened every meal with social glee.
The heart's light laugh pursued the circling jest;
And all was sunshine in each little breast.
'T was here we chased the slipper by the sound;
And turned the blindfold hero round and round.
'T was here, at eve, we formed our fairy ring;
And Fancy fluttered on her wildest wing.
Giants and Genii chained each wondering ear;
And orphan-sorrows drew the ready tear.
Oft with the babes we wandered in the wood,
Or viewed the forest feats of Robin Hood:
Oft, fancy-led, at midnight's fearful hour,
With startling step we scaled the lonely tower;
O'er infant innocence to hang and weep,
Murdered by ruffian hands, when smiling in its sleep.
Ye Household Deities! whose guardian eye[1]
Marked each pure thought, ere registered on high;
Still, still ye walk the consecrated ground,
And breathe the soul of Inspiration round.
As o'er the dusky furniture I bend,
Each chair awakes the feelings of a friend.

The storied arras, source of fond delight,
With old achievement charms the wildered sight;
And still, with Heraldry's rich hues imprest,
On the dim window glows the pictured crest.
The screen unfolds its many-colored chart.
The clock still points its moral to the heart.
That faithful monitor 't was heaven to hear,
When soft it spoke a promised pleasure near;
And has its sober hand, its simple chime,
Forgot to trace the feathered feet of Time?
That massive beam, with curious carvings wrought,
Whence the caged linnet soothed my pensive thought;
Those muskets, cased with venerable rust;
Those once-loved forms, still breathing through their dust,
Still, from the frame in mould gigantic cast,
Starting to life all whisper of the Past!

As through the garden's desert paths I rove,
What fond illusions swarm in every grove!
How oft, when purple evening tinged the west,[2]
We watched the emmet to her grainy nest;
Welcomed the wild-bee home on weary wing,
Laden with sweets, the choicest of the spring!
How oft inscribed, with Friendship's votive rhyme,
The bark now silvered by the touch of Time;
Soared in the swing, half pleased and half afraid,
Through sister elms that waved their summer-shade;
Or strewed with crumbs yon root-inwoven seat,
To lure the redbreast from his lone retreat!

Childhood's loved group revisits every scene;
The tangled wood-walk and the tufted green!
Indulgent MEMORY wakes, and, lo! they live!
Clothed with far softer hues than Light can give.

Thou first, best friend that Heaven assigns below
To soothe and sweeten all the cares we know;
Whose glad suggestions still each vain alarm,
When nature fades and life forgets to charm;
Thee would the Muse invoke! — to thee belong
The sage's precept and the poet's song.
What softened views thy magic glass reveals,
When o'er the landscape Time's meek twilight steals!
As when in ocean sinks the orb of day,
Long on the wave reflected lustres play;
Thy tempered gleams of happiness resigned
Glance on the darkened mirror of the mind.
  The School's lone porch, with reverend mosses gray,
Just tells the pensive pilgrim where it lay.
Mute is the bell that rung at peep of dawn,
Quickening my truant-feet across the lawn;
Unheard the shout that rent the noontide air,
When the slow dial gave a pause to care.
Up springs, at every step, to claim a tear,[3]
Some little friendship formed and cherished here;
And not the lightest leaf, but trembling teems
With golden visions and romantic dreams!
  Down by yon hazel copse, at evening, blazed
The Gypsy's fagot — there we stood and gazed;
Gazed on her sunburnt face with silent awe,
Her tattered mantle, and her hood of straw;
Her moving lips, her caldron brimming o'er;
The drowsy brood that on her back she bore,
Imps, in the barn with mousing owlet bred,
From rifled roost at nightly revel fed;
Whose dark eyes flashed through locks of blackest shade,
When in the breeze the distant watch-dog bayed: —

And heroes fled the Sibyl's muttered call,
Whose elfin prowess scaled the orchard-wall.
As o'er my palm the silver piece she drew,
And traced the line of life with searching view,
How throbbed my fluttering pulse with hopes and fears,
To learn the color of my future years!
  Ah, then, what honest triumph flushed my breast;
This truth once known — To bless is to be blest!
We led the bending beggar on his way
(Bare were his feet, his tresses silver-gray),
Soothed the keen pangs his aged spirit felt,
And on his tale with mute attention dwelt.
As in his scrip we dropt our little store,
And sighed to think that little was no more,
He breathed his prayer, "Long may such goodness live!"
'T was all he gave, 't was all he had to give.
Angels, when Mercy's mandate winged their flight,
Had stopt to dwell with pleasure on the sight.
  But hark! through those old firs, with sullen swell,
The church-clock strikes! ye tender scenes, farewell!
It calls me hence, beneath their shade, to trace
The few fond lines that Time may soon efface.
  On yon gray stone, that fronts the chancel-door,
Worn smooth by busy feet now seen no more,
Each eve we shot the marble through the ring,
When the heart danced, and life was in its spring;
Alas! unconscious of the kindred earth,
That faintly echoed to the voice of mirth.
  The glow-worm loves her emerald-light to shed
Where now the sexton rests his hoary head.
Oft, as he turned the greensward with his spade,
He lectured every youth that round him played;

And, calmly pointing where our fathers lay,
Roused us to rival each, the hero of his day.
 Hush, ye fond flutterings, hush! while here alone
I search the records of each mouldering stone.
Guides of my life! Instructors of my youth!
Who first unveiled the hallowed form of Truth!
Whose every word enlightened and endeared;
In age beloved, in poverty revered;
In Friendship's silent register ye live,
Nor ask the vain memorial Art can give.
 But when the sons of peace, of pleasure sleep,
When only Sorrow wakes, and wakes to weep,
What spells entrance my visionary mind
With sighs so sweet, with transports so refined?
 Ethereal Power! who at the noon of night
Recall'st the far-fled spirit of delight;
From whom that musing, melancholy mood
Which charms the wise, and elevates the good;
Blest MEMORY, hail! O grant the grateful Muse,
Her pencil dipt in Nature's living hues,
To pass the clouds that round thy empire roll,
And trace its airy precincts in the soul.
 Lulled in the countless chambers of the brain,
Our thoughts are linked by many a hidden chain.
Awake but one, and, lo! what myriads rise![4]
Each stamps its image as the other flies.
Each, as the various avenues of sense
Delight or sorrow to the soul dispense,
Brightens or fades; yet all, with magic art,
Control the latent fibres of the heart.
As studious PROSPERO'S mysterious spell
Drew every subject-spirit to his cell;

Each, at thy call, advances or retires,
As judgment dictates or the scene inspires.
Each thrills the seat of sense, that sacred source
Whence the fine nerves direct their mazy course,
And through the frame invisibly convey
The subtle, quick vibrations as they play;
Man's little universe at once o'ercast,
At once illumined when the cloud is past.
  Survey the globe, each ruder realm explore;
From Reason's faintest ray to NEWTON soar.
What different spheres to human bliss assigned!
What slow gradations in the scale of mind!
Yet, mark in each these mystic wonders wrought;
O, mark the sleepless energies of thought!
  The adventurous boy, that asks his little share,
And hies from home with many a gossip's prayer,
Turns on the neighboring hill, once more to see
The dear abode of peace and privacy;
And, as he turns, the thatch among the trees,
The smoke's blue wreaths ascending with the breeze,
The village-common spotted white with sheep,
The church-yard yews round which his fathers sleep;[5]
All rouse Reflection's sadly-pleasing train,
And oft he looks and weeps, and looks again.
  So, when the mild TUPIA dared explore
Arts yet untaught, and worlds unknown before,
And, with the sons of Science, wooed the gale
That, rising, swelled their strange expanse of sail;
So, when he breathed his firm yet fond adieu,[6]
Borne from his leafy hut, his carved canoe,
And all his soul best loved — such tears he shed,
While each soft scene of summer-beauty fled.

Long o'er the wave a wistful look he cast,
Long watched the streaming signal from the mast;
Till twilight's dewy tints deceived his eye,
And fairy-forests fringed the evening sky.
So Scotia's Queen, as slowly dawned the day,[7]
Rose on her couch and gazed her soul away.
Her eyes had blessed the beacon's glimmering height,
That faintly tipt the feathery surge with light;
But now the morn with orient hues portrayed
Each castled cliff and brown monastic shade:
All touched the talisman's resistless spring,
And, lo! what busy tribes were instant on the wing!
Thus kindred objects kindred thoughts inspire,[8]
As summer-clouds flash forth electric fire.
And hence this spot gives back the joys of youth,
Warm as the life, and with the mirror's truth.
Hence home-felt pleasure prompts the Patriot's sigh;[9]
This makes him wish to live, and dare to die.
For this young FOSCARI, whose hapless fate[10]
Venice should blush to hear the Muse relate,
When exile wore his blooming years away,
To Sorrow's long soliloquies a prey,
When reason, justice, vainly urged his cause,
For this he roused her sanguinary laws;
Glad to return, though Hope could grant no more,
And chains and torture hailed him to the shore.
And hence the charm historic scenes impart;[11]
Hence Tiber awes, and Avon melts the heart.
Aërial forms in Tempe's classic vale
Glance through the gloom and whisper in the gale;
In wild Vaucluse with love and LAURA dwell,
And watch and weep in ELOISA'S cell.[12]

'T was ever thus. Young AMMON, when he sought[13]
Where Ilium stood and where PELIDES fought,
Sate at the helm himself. No meaner hand
Steered through the waves; and, when he struck the land,
Such in his soul the ardor to explore,
PELIDES-like, he leaped the first ashore.
'T was ever thus. As now at VIRGIL'S tomb[14]
We bless the shade and bid the verdure bloom;
So TULLY paused, amid the wrecks of time,[15]
On the rude stone to trace the truth sublime;
When at his feet, in honored dust disclosed,
The immortal Sage of Syracuse reposed.
And as he long in sweet delusion hung,
Where once a PLATO taught, a PINDAR sung;
Who now but meets him musing, when he roves
His ruined Tusculan's romantic groves?
In Rome's great forum, who but hears him roll
His moral thunders o'er the subject soul?
And hence that calm delight the portrait gives:
We gaze on every feature till it lives!
Still the fond lover sees the absent maid;
And the lost friend still lingers in his shade!
Say why the pensive widow loves to weep,[16]
When on her knee she rocks her babe to sleep:
Tremblingly still, she lifts his veil to trace
The father's features in his infant face.
The hoary grandsire smiles the hour away,
Won by the raptures of a game at play;
He bends to meet each artless burst of joy,
Forgets his age, and acts again the boy.
What though the iron school of War erase
Each milder virtue and each softer grace;

What though the fiend's torpedo-touch arrest
Each gentler, finer impulse of the breast;
Still shall this active principle preside,
And wake the tear to Pity's self denied.
 The intrepid Swiss, who guards a foreign shore,
Cóndemned to climb his mountain-cliffs no more,
If chance he hears the song so sweet, so wild,[17]
His heart would spring to hear it when a child,
Melts at the long-lost scenes that round him rise,
And sinks a martyr to repentant sighs.
 Ask not if courts or camps dissolve the charm:
Say why VESPASIAN loved his Sabine farm;[18]
Why great NAVARRE, when France and Freedom bled,[19]
Sought the lone limits of a forest-shed.
When DIOCLETIAN'S self-corrected mind[20]
The imperial fasces of a world resigned,
Say why we trace the labors of his spade
In calm Salona's philosophic shade.
Say, when contentious CHARLES renounced a throne[21]
To muse with monks and meditate alone,[22]
What from his soul the parting tribute drew?
What claimed the sorrows of a last adieu?
The still retreats that soothed his tranquil breast
Ere grandeur dazzled, and its cares oppressed.
 Undamped by time, the generous Instinct glows
Far as Angola's sands, as Zembla's snows;
Glows in the tiger's den, the serpent's nest,
On every form of varied life imprest.
The social tribes its choicest influence hail:—
And when the drum beats briskly in the gale,
The war-worn courser charges at the sound,
And with young vigor wheels the pasture round.

Oft has the aged tenant of the vale
Leaned on his staff to lengthen out the tale;
Oft have his lips the grateful tribute breathed,
From sire to son with pious zeal bequeathed.
When o'er the blasted heath the day declined,
And on the scathed oak warred the winter-wind;
When not a distant taper's twinkling ray
Gleamed o'er the furze to light him on his way;
When not a sheep-bell soothed his listening ear,
And the big rain-drops told the tempest near;
Then did his horse the homeward track descry,[23]
The track that shunned his sad, inquiring eye;
And win each wavering purpose to relent,
With warmth so mild, so gently violent,
That his charmed hand the careless rein resigned,
And doubts and terrors vanished from his mind.
Recall the traveller, whose altered form
Has borne the buffet of the mountain-storm;
And who will first his fond impatience meet?
His faithful dog 's already at his feet!
Yes, though the porter spurn him from the door,
Though all, that knew him, know his face no more,
His faithful dog shall tell his joy to each,
With that mute eloquence which passes speech.—
And see, the master but returns to die!
Yet who shall bid the watchful servant fly?
The blasts of heaven, the drenching dews of earth,
The wanton insults of unfeeling mirth,
These, when to guard Misfortune's sacred grave,
Will firm Fidelity exult to brave.
Led by what chart, transports the timid dove
The wreaths of conquest, or the vows of love?

Say, through the clouds what compass points her flight?
Monarchs have gazed, and nations blessed the sight.
Pile rocks on rocks, bid woods and mountains rise,
Eclipse her native shades, her native skies:—
'T is vain! through Ether's pathless wilds she goes,
And lights at last where all her cares repose.
  Sweet bird! thy truth shall Harlem's walls attest,[24]
And unborn ages consecrate thy nest.
When, with the silent energy of grief,
With looks that asked, yet dared not hope relief,
Want with her babes round generous Valor clung,
To wring the slow surrender from his tongue,
'T was thine to animate her closing eye;
Alas! 't was thine perchance the first to die,
Crushed by her meagre hand when welcomed from the sky.
  Hark! the bee winds her small but mellow horn,[25]
Blithe to salute the sunny smile of morn.
O'er thymy downs she bends her busy course,
And many a stream allures her to its source.
'T is noon, 't is night. That eye so finely wrought,
Beyond the search of sense, the soar of thought,
Now vainly asks the scenes she left behind;
Its orb so full, its vision so confined!
Who guides the patient pilgrim to her cell?
Who bids her soul with conscious triumph swell?
With conscious truth retrace the mazy clue
Of summer-scents, that charmed her as she flew?
Hail, MEMORY, hail! thy universal reign
Guards the least link of Being's glorious chain.

THE

PLEASURES OF MEMORY.

PART II.

Delle cose custode e dispensiera.

TASSO.

ANALYSIS OF THE SECOND PART.

THE Memory has hitherto acted only in subservience to the senses, and so far man is not eminently distinguished from other animals ; but, with respect to man, she has a higher province, and is often busily employed when excited by no external cause whatever. She preserves, for his use, the treasures of art and science, history and philosophy. She colors all the prospects of life ; for we can only anticipate the future by concluding what is possible from what is past. On her agency depends every effusion of the Fancy, who with the boldest effort can only compound or transpose, augment or diminish, the materials which she has collected, and still retains.

When the first emotions of despair have subsided, and sorrow has softened into melancholy, she amuses with a retrospect of innocent pleasures, and inspires that noble confidence which results from the consciousness of having acted well. When sleep has suspended the organs of sense from their office, she not only supplies the mind with images, but assists in their combination. And, even in madness itself, when the soul is resigned over to the tyranny of a distempered imagination, she revives past perceptions, and awakens that train of thought which was formerly most familiar.

Nor are we pleased only with a review of the brighter passages of life. Events the most distressing in their immediate consequences are often cherished in remembrance with a degree of enthusiasm.

But the world and its occupations give a mechanical impulse to the passions, which is not very favorable to the indulgence of this feeling. It is in a calm and well-regulated mind that the memory is most perfect ; and solitude is her best sphere of action. With this sentiment is introduced a Tale illustrative of her influence in solitude, sickness, and sorrow. And the subject having now been considered, so far as it relates to man and the animal world, the Poem concludes with a conjecture that superior beings are blest with a nobler exercise of this faculty.

PART II.

SWEET MEMORY, wafted by thy gentle gale,
Oft up the stream of Time I turn my sail,
To view the fairy-haunts of long-lost hours,
Blest with far greener shades, far fresher flowers.
Ages and climes remote to thee impart
What charms in Genius and refines in Art;
Thee, in whose hands the keys of Science dwell,
The pensive portress of her holy cell;
Whose constant vigils chase the chilling damp
Oblivion steals upon her vestal-lamp.
They in their glorious course the guides of Youth,[1]
Whose language breathed the eloquence of Truth;
Whose life, beyond preceptive wisdom, taught
The great in conduct, and the pure in thought;
These still exist, by thee to Fame consigned,[2]
Still speak and act, the models of mankind.
From thee gay Hope her airy coloring draws:
And Fancy's flights are subject to thy laws.
From thee that bosom-spring of rapture flows,
Which only Virtue, tranquil Virtue, knows.
When Joy's bright sun has shed his evening-ray,
And Hope's delusive meteors cease to play;
When clouds on clouds the smiling prospect close,
Still through the gloom thy star serenely glows:
Like yon fair orb, she gilds the brow of night
With the mild magic of reflected light.

The beauteous maid who bids the world adieu,
Oft of that world will snatch a fond review:
Oft at the shrine neglect her beads, to trace
Some social scene, some dear, familiar face:
And ere, with iron tongue, the vesper-bell
Bursts through the cypress-walk, the convent-cell,
Oft will her warm and wayward heart revive,
To love and joy still tremblingly alive;
The whispered vow, the chaste caress prolong,
Weave the light dance and swell the choral song;
With rapt ear drink the enchanting serenade,
And, as it melts along the moonlight-glade,
To each soft note return as soft a sigh,
And bless the youth that bids her slumbers fly.
But not till Time has calmed the ruffled breast,
Are these fond dreams of happiness confest.
Not till the rushing winds forget to rave,
Is Heaven's sweet smile reflected on the wave.
From Guinea's coast pursue the lessening sail,
And catch the sounds that sadden every gale.
Tell, if thou canst, the sum of sorrows there;
Mark the fixed gaze, the wild and frenzied glare,
The racks of thought, and freezings of despair!
But pause not then — beyond the western wave,
Go, see the captive bartered as a slave!
Crushed till his high, heroic spirit bleeds,
And from his nerveless frame indignantly recedes.
Yet here, even here, with pleasures long resigned,
Lo! MEMORY bursts the twilight of the mind.
Her dear delusions soothe his sinking soul,
When the rude scourge assumes its base control;

And o'er Futurity's blank page diffuse
The full reflection of her vivid hues.
'T is but to die — and then, to weep no more,
Then will he wake on Congo's distant shore;
Beneath his plantain's ancient shade renew
The simple transports that with freedom flew;
Catch the cool breeze that musky Evening blows,
And quaff the palm's rich nectar as it glows;
The oral tale of elder time rehearse,
And chant the rude, traditionary verse
With those, the loved companions of his youth,
When life was luxury, and friendship truth.

Ah, why should Virtue fear the frowns of Fate?[3]
Hers what no wealth can buy, no power create!
A little world of clear and cloudless day,
Nor wrecked by storms, nor mouldered by decay;
A world, with MEMORY'S ceaseless sunshine blest,
The home of Happiness, an honest breast.

But most we mark the wonders of her reign,
When Sleep has locked the senses in her chain.
When sober Judgment has his throne resigned,
She smiles away the chaos of the mind;
And, as warm Fancy's bright Elysium glows,
From her each image springs, each color flows.
She is the sacred guest, the immortal friend,
Oft seen o'er sleeping Innocence to bend,
In that dead hour of night to Silence given,
Whispering seraphic visions of her heaven.

When the blithe son of Savoy, journeying round
With humble wares and pipe of merry sound,
From his green vale and sheltered cabin hies,
And scales the Alps to visit foreign skies;

Though far below the forkéd lightnings play,
And at his feet the thunder dies away,
Oft, in the saddle rudely rocked to sleep,
While his mule browses on the dizzy steep,
With MEMORY'S aid, he sits at home, and sees
His children sport beneath their native trees,
And bends to hear their cherub-voices call,
O'er the loud fury of the torrent's fall.
  But can her smile with gloomy Madness dwell?
Say, can she chase the horrors of his cell?
Each fiery flight on Frenzy's wing restrain,
And mould the coinage of the fevered brain?
  Pass but that grate, which scarce a gleam supplies,
There in the dust the wreck of Genius lies!
He, whose arresting hand divinely wrought
Each bold conception in the sphere of thought;
And round, in colors of the rainbow, threw
Forms ever fair, creations ever new!
But, as he fondly snatched the wreath of Fame,
The spectre Poverty unnerved his frame.
Cold was her grasp, a withering scowl she wore;
And Hope's soft energies were felt no more.
Yet still how sweet the soothings of his art! [4]
From the rude wall what bright ideas start!
Even now he claims the amaranthine wreath,
With scenes that glow, with images that breathe!
And whence these scenes, these images, declare.
Whence but from Her who triumphs o'er despair?
  Awake, arise! with grateful fervor fraught,
Go, spring the mine of elevating thought.
He, who, through Nature's various walk, surveys
The good and fair her faultless line portrays;

Whose mind, profaned by no unhallowed guest,
Culls from the crowd the purest and the best;
May range, at will, bright Fancy's golden clime,
Or, musing, mount where Science sits sublime,
Or wake the Spirit of departed Time.
Who acts thus wisely, mark the moral Muse,
A blooming Eden in his life reviews!
So rich the culture, though so small the space,
Its scanty limits he forgets to trace.
But the fond fool, when evening shades the sky,
Turns but to start, and gazes but to sigh![5]
The weary waste, that lengthened as he ran,
Fades to a blank, and dwindles to a span!
Ah! who can tell the triumphs of the mind,
By truth illumined and by taste refined?
When age has quenched the eye and closed the ear,
Still nerved for action in her native sphere,
Oft will she rise — with searching glance pursue
Some long-loved image vanished from her view;
Dart through the deep recesses of the Past,
O'er dusky forms in chains of slumber cast;
With giant-grasp fling back the folds of night,
And snatch the faithless fugitive to light.
So through the grove the impatient mother flies,
Each sunless glade, each secret pathway, tries;
Till the thin leaves the truant boy disclose,
Long on the wood-moss stretched in sweet repose.
Nor yet to pleasing objects are confined
The silent feasts of the reflecting mind.
Danger and death a dread delight inspire;
And the bald veteran glows with wonted fire,

When, richly bronzed by many a summer-sun,
He counts his scars, and tells what deeds were done.
Go, with Old Thames, view Chelsea's glorious pile,
And ask the shattered hero, whence his smile?
Go, view the splendid domes of Greenwich — Go,
And own what raptures from Reflection flow.
Hail, noblest structures imaged in the wave!
A nation's grateful tribute to the brave.
Hail, blest retreats from war and shipwreck, hail!
That oft arrest the wondering stranger's sail.
Long have ye heard the narratives of age,
The battle's havoc and the tempest's rage;
Long have ye known Reflection's genial ray
Gild the calm close of Valor's various day.
Time's sombrous touches soon correct the piece,
Mellow each tint, and bid each discord cease:
A softer tone of light pervades the whole,
And steals a pensive languor o'er the soul.
Hast thou through Eden's wild-wood vales pursued [6]
Each mountain-scene, majestically rude;
To note the sweet simplicity of life,
Far from the din of Folly's idle strife;
Nor there a while, with lifted eye, revered
That modest stone which pious PEMBROKE reared;
Which still records, beyond the pencil's power,
The silent sorrows of a parting hour;
Still to the musing pilgrim points the place
Her sainted spirit most delights to trace?
Thus, with the manly glow of honest pride,
O'er his dead son the gallant ORMOND sighed.[7]
Thus, through the gloom of SHENSTONE'S fairy grove,
MARIA'S urn still breathes the voice of love.

As the stern grandeur of a Gothic tower
Awes us less deeply in its morning-hour,
Than when the shades of Time serenely fall
On every broken arch and ivied wall;
The tender images we love to trace
Steal from each year a melancholy grace!
And as the sparks of social love expand,
As the heart opens in a foreign land;
And with a brother's warmth, a brother's smile,
The stranger greets each native of his isle;
So scenes of life, when present and confest,
Stamp but their bolder features on the breast;
Yet not an image, when remotely viewed,
However trivial, and however rude,
But wins the heart, and wakes the social sigh,
With every claim of close affinity!

But these pure joys the world can never know;
In gentler climes their silver currents flow.
Oft at the silent, shadowy close of day,
When the hushed grove has sung its parting lay;
When pensive Twilight, in her dusky car,
Comes slowly on to meet the evening-star;
Above, below, aërial murmurs swell,
From hanging wood, brown heath, and bushy dell!
A thousand nameless rills, that shun the light,
Stealing soft music on the ear of night.
So oft the finer movements of the soul,
That shun the sphere of Pleasure's gay control,
In the still shades of calm Seclusion rise,
And breathe their sweet, seraphic harmonies!

Once, and domestic annals tell the time
(Preserved in Cumbria's rude, romantic clime),

When Nature smiled, and o'er the landscape threw
Her richest fragrance, and her brightest hue,
A blithe and blooming Forester explored
Those loftier scenes SALVATOR'S soul adored;
The rocky pass half-hung with shaggy wood,
And the cleft oak flung boldly o'er the flood;
Nor shunned the track, unknown to human tread,
That downward to the night of caverns led;
Some ancient cataract's deserted bed.
High on exulting wing the heath-cock rose,
And blew his shrill blast o'er perennial snows;
Ere the rapt youth, recoiling from the roar,
Gazed on the tumbling tide of dread Lodore;
And through the rifted clifts, that scaled the sky,
Derwent's clear mirror charmed his dazzled eye.
Each osier isle, inverted on the wave,
Through morn's gray mist its melting colors gave;
And, o'er the cygnet's haunt, the mantling grove
Its emerald arch with wild luxuriance wove.
Light as the breeze that brushed the orient dew,
From rock to rock the young Adventurer flew;
And day's last sunshine slept along the shore,
When, lo! a path the smile of welcome wore.
Imbowering shrubs with verdure veiled the sky,
And on the musk-rose shed a deeper die;
Save when a bright and momentary gleam
Glanced from the white foam of some sheltered stream.
O'er the still lake the bell of evening tolled,
And on the moor the shepherd penned his fold;
And on the green hill's side the meteor played;
When, hark! a voice sung sweetly through the shade.

It ceased — yet still in FLORIO'S fancy sung,
Still on each note his captive spirit hung;
Till o'er the mead a cool, sequestered grot
From its rich roof a starry lustre shot.
A crystal water crossed the pebbled floor,
And on the front these simple lines it bore.

Hence away, nor dare intrude!
In this secret, shadowy cell
Musing MEMORY loves to dwell,
With her sister Solitude.
Far from the busy world she flies,
To taste that peace the world denies.
Entranced she sits; from youth to age,
Reviewing Life's eventful page;
And noting, ere they fade away,
The little lines of yesterday.

FLORIO had gained a rude and rocky seat,
When, lo! the Genius of this still retreat!
Fair was her form — but who can hope to trace
The pensive softness of her angel-face?
Can VIRGIL'S verse, can RAPHAEL'S touch, impart
Those finer features of the feeling heart,
Those tenderer tints that shun the careless eye,
And in the world's contagious climate die?

She left the cave, nor marked the stranger there;
Her pastoral beauty and her artless air
Had breathed a soft enchantment o'er his soul!
In every nerve he felt her blest control!
What pure and white-winged agents of the sky,
Who rule the springs of sacred sympathy,
Inform congenial spirits when they meet?
Sweet is their office, as their natures sweet!

Florio, with fearful joy, pursued the maid,
Till through a vista's moonlight-checkered shade,
Where the bat circled, and the rooks reposed
(Their wars suspended, and their councils closed),
An antique mansion burst in solemn state,
A rich vine clustering round the Gothic gate.
Nor paused he there. The master of the scene
Saw his light step imprint the dewy green;
And, slow-advancing, hailed him as his guest,
Won by the honest warmth his looks expressed.
He wore the rustic manners of a Squire;
Age had not quenched one spark of manly fire;
But giant Gout had bound him in her chain,
And his heart panted for the chase in vain.
Yet here Remembrance, sweetly-soothing Power!
Winged with delight Confinement's lingering hour.
The fox's brush still emulous to wear,
He scoured the county in his elbow-chair;
And, with view-halloo, roused the dreaming hound,
That rung, by starts, his deep-toned music round.
Long by the paddock's humble pale confined,
His aged hunters coursed the viewless wind:
And each, with glowing energy portrayed,
The far-famed triumphs of the field displayed;
Usurped the canvas of the crowded hall,
And chased a line of heroes from the wall.
There slept the horn each jocund echo knew,
And many a smile and many a story drew!
High o'er the hearth his forest-trophies hung,
And their fantastic branches wildly flung.
How would he dwell on the vast antlers there!
These dashed the wave, those fanned the mountain-air.

All, as they frowned, unwritten records bore
Of gallant feats and festivals of yore.
  But why the tale prolong? —His only child,
His darling JULIA, on the stranger smiled.
Her little arts a fretful sire to please,
Her gentle gayety and native ease,
Had won his soul; and rapturous Fancy shed
Her golden lights and tints of rosy red.
But, ah! few days had passed, ere the bright vision fled!
  When Evening tinged the lake's ethereal blue,
And her deep shades irregularly threw;
Their shifting sail dropt gently from the cove,
Down by St. Herbert's consecrated grove;[8]
Whence erst the chanted hymn, the tapered rite,
Amused the fisher's solitary night;
And still the mitred window, richly wreathed,
A sacred calm through the brown foliage breathed.
  The wild deer, starting through the silent glade,
With fearful gaze their various course surveyed.
High hung in air the hoary goat reclined,
His streaming beard the sport of every wind;
And, while the coot her jet-wing loved to lave,
Rocked on the bosom of the sleepless wave,
The eagle rushed from Skiddaw's purple crest,
A cloud still brooding o'er her giant-nest.
  And now the moon had dimmed with dewy ray
The few fine flushes of departing day.
O'er the wide water's deep serene she hung,
And her broad lights on every mountain flung;
When, lo! a sudden blast the vessel blew,[9]
And to the surge consigned the little crew.

All, all escaped — but ere the lover bore
His faint and faded JULIA to the shore,
Her sense had fled! — Exhausted by the storm,
A fatal trance hung o'er her pallid form;
Her closing eye a trembling lustre fired;
'T was life's last spark — it fluttered and expired!
  The father strewed his white hairs in the wind,
Called on his child — nor lingered long behind:
And FLORIO lived to see the willow wave,
With many an evening-whisper, o'er their grave.
Yes, FLORIO lived — and, still of each possessed,
The father cherished, and the maid caressed!
  Forever would the fond Enthusiast rove,
With JULIA'S spirit, through the shadowy grove;
Gaze with delight on every scene she planned,
Kiss every floweret planted by her hand.
Ah! still he traced her steps along the glade,
When hazy hues and glimmering lights betrayed
Half-viewless forms; still listened as the breeze
Heaved its deep sobs among the aged trees;
And at each pause her melting accents caught,
In sweet delirium of romantic thought!
Dear was the grot that shunned the blaze of day;
She gave its spars to shoot a trembling ray.
The spring, that bubbled from its inmost cell,
Murmured of JULIA'S virtues as it fell;
And o'er the dripping moss, the fretted stone,
In FLORIO'S ear breathed language not its own.
Her charm around the enchantress MEMORY threw,
A charm that soothes the mind, and sweetens too!
  But is her magic only felt below?
Say, through what brighter realms she bids it flow;

To what pure beings, in a nobler sphere,[10]
She yields delight but faintly imaged here:
All that till now their rapt researches knew,
Not called in slow succession to review;
But, as a landscape meets the eye of day,
At once presented to their glad survey!
Each scene of bliss revealed, since chaos fled,
And dawning light its dazzling glories spread;
Each chain of wonders that sublimely glowed,
Since first Creation's choral anthem flowed;
Each ready flight, at Mercy's call divine,
To distant worlds that undiscovered shine;
Full on her tablet flings its living rays,
And all, combined, with blest effulgence blaze.
There thy bright train, immortal Friendship, soar;
No more to part, to mingle tears no more!
And, as the softening hand of Time endears
The joys and sorrows of our infant-years,
So there the soul, released from human strife,
Smiles at the little cares and ills of life;
Its lights and shades, its sunshine and its showers;
As at a dream that charmed her vacant hours!
Oft may the spirits of the dead descend
To watch the silent slumbers of a friend;
To hover round his evening walk unseen,
And hold sweet converse on the dusky green;
To hail the spot where first their friendship grew,
And heaven and nature opened to their view!
Oft when he trims his cheerful hearth, and sees
A smiling circle emulous to please;
There may these gentle guests delight to dwell,
And bless the scene they loved in life so well!

O thou! with whom my heart was wont to share
From Reason's dawn each pleasure and each care;
With whom, alas! I fondly hoped to know
The humble walks of happiness below;
If thy blest nature now unites above
An angel's pity with a brother's love,
Still o'er my life preserve thy mild control,
Correct my views, and elevate my soul;
Grant me thy peace and purity of mind,
Devout yet cheerful, active yet resigned;
Grant me, like thee, whose heart knew no disguise,
Whose blameless wishes never aimed to rise,
To meet the changes Time and Chance present
With modest dignity and calm content.
When thy last breath, ere Nature sunk to rest,
Thy meek submission to thy God expressed;
When thy last look, ere thought and feeling fled,
A mingled gleam of hope and triumph shed;
What to thy soul its glad assurance gave,
Its hope in death, its triumph o'er the grave?
The sweet Remembrance of unblemished youth,
The still inspiring voice of Innocence and Truth!

Hail, MEMORY, hail! in thy exhaustless mine
From age to age unnumbered treasures shine!
Thought and her shadowy brood thy call obey,
And Place and Time are subject to thy sway!
Thy pleasures most we feel when most alone;
The only pleasures we can call our own.
Lighter than air, Hope's summer-visions die,
If but a fleeting cloud obscure the sky;
If but a beam of sober Reason play,
Lo! Fancy's fairy frost-work melts away!

But can the wiles of Art, the grasp of Power,
Snatch the rich relics of a well-spent hour?
These, when the trembling spirit wings her flight,
Pour round her path a stream of living light;
And gild those pure and perfect realms of rest,
Where Virtue triumphs, and her sons are blest!

NOTES.

PART I.

(1) These were imagined to be the departed souls of virtuous men, who, as a reward of their good deeds in the present life, were appointed after death to the pleasing office of superintending the concerns of their immediate descendants. — *Melmoth.*

(2) Virgil, in one of his Eclogues, describes a romantic attachment as conceived in such circumstances; and the description is so true to nature, that we must surely be indebted for it to some early recollection. — "You were little when I first saw you. You were with your mother gathering fruit in our orchard, and I was your guide. I was just entering my thirteenth year, and just able to reach the boughs from the ground."

So also Zappi, an Italian poet of the last century. — "When I used to measure myself with my goat and my goat was the tallest, even then I loved Clori."

(3) I came to the place of my birth, and cried, "The friends of my youth, where are they?" And an echo answered, "Where are they?" — *From an Arabic MS.*

(4) When a traveller, who was surveying the ruins of Rome, expressed a desire to possess some relic of its ancient grandeur, Poussin, who attended him, stooped down, and gathering up a handful of earth shining with small grains of porphyry, "Take this home," said he, "for your cabinet; and say, boldly, *Questa è Roma Antica.*"

(5) Every man, like Gulliver in Lilliput, is fastened to some spot of earth, by the thousand small threads which habit and association are continually stealing over him. Of these, perhaps, one of the strongest is here alluded to.

When the Canadian Indians were once solicited to emigrate, "What!" they replied, "shall we say to the bones of our fathers, Arise, and go with us into a foreign land?"

(6) He wept; but the effort that he made to conceal his tears concurred with them to do him honor: he went to the mast-head, &c. — *See Cook's First Voyage*, book i. chap. 16.

Another very affecting instance of local attachment is related of his fellow-countryman Potaveri, who came to Europe with M. de Bougainville. — *See Les Jardins*, chant. ii.

(7) Elle se leve sur son lict et se met à contempler la France encore, et tant qu'elle peut. — *Brantôme.*

(8) To an accidental association may be ascribed some of the noblest efforts of human genius. The historian of the Decline and Fall of the Roman Empire first conceived his design among the ruins of the Capitol; * and to the tones of a Welsh harp are we indebted for the Bard of Gray.

* "It was on the 15th of October, 1764, as I sat musing there, while the bare-footed friars were singing verses in the Temple of Jupiter, that the idea first started to my mind." — *Memoirs of my Life.*

(9) Who can enough admire the affectionate attachment of Plutarch, who thus concludes his enumeration of the advantages of a great city to men of letters: "As to myself, I live in a little town; and I choose to live there, lest it should become still less." — *Vit. Demosth.*

(10) He was suspected of murder, and at Venice suspicion was good evidence. Neither the interest of the Doge, his father, nor the intrepidity of conscious innocence, which he exhibited in the dungeon and on the rack, could procure his acquittal. He was banished to the Island of Candia for life.

But here his resolution failed him. At such a distance from home he could not live; and, as it was a criminal offence to solicit the intercession of any foreign prince, in a fit of despair he addressed a letter to the Duke of Milan, and intrusted it to a wretch whose perfidy, he knew, would occasion his being remanded a prisoner to Venice.

(11) Whatever withdraws us from the power of our senses — whatever makes the past, the distant or the future, predominate over the present — advances us in the dignity of thinking beings. Far from me and from my friends be such frigid philosophy as may conduct us indifferent and unmoved over any ground which has been dignified by wisdom, bravery or virtue! That man is little to be envied whose patriotism would not gain force upon the plain of *Marathon*, or whose piety would not grow warmer among the ruins of *Iona*. — *Johnson.*

(12) The Paraclete, founded by Abelard, in Champagne.

(13) Alexander, when he crossed the Hellespont, was in the twenty-second year of his age; and with what feelings must the Scholar of Aristotle have approached the ground described by Homer in that poem which had been his delight from his childhood, and which records the achievements of him from whom he claimed his descent!

It was his fancy, if we may believe tradition, to take the tiller from Menœtius, and be himself the steersman during the passage. It was his fancy also to be the first to land, and to land full-armed. — *Arrian*, i. 11.

(14) Vows and pilgrimages are not peculiar to the religious enthusiast. Silius Italicus performed annual ceremonies on the mountain of Posilipo; and it was there that Boccaccio, *quasi da un divino estro inspirato*, resolved to dedicate his life to the Muses.

(15) When Cicero was quæstor in Sicily, he discovered the tomb of Archimedes by its mathematical inscription. — *Tusc. Quæst.* v. 23.

(16) The influence of the associating principle is finely exemplified in the faithful Penelope, when she sheds tears over the bow of Ulysses. — *Od.* xxi. 55.

(17) The celebrated Ranz des Vaches; cet air si chéri des Suisses qu'il fut défendu sous peine de mort de la jouer dans leurs troupes, parce qu'il faisoit fondre en larmes, déserter ou mourir ceux qui l'entendoient, tant il excitoit en eux l'ardent désir de revoir leur pays. — *Rousseau.*

The maladie de pays is as old as the human heart. Juvenal's little cup-bearer

Suspirat longo non visam tempore matrem,
Et casulam, et notos tristis desiderat hœdos.

And the Argive in the heat of battle

Dulces moriens reminiscitur Argos.

Nor is it extinguished by any injuries, however cruel they may be. Ludlow, write as he would over his door at Vevey,* was still anxious to return home; and how striking is the

* Omne solum forti patria est, quia Patris.

testimony of Camillus, as it is recorded by Livy! "Equidem fatebor vobis," says he in his speech to the Roman people, "etsi minus injuriæ vestræ quam meæ calamitatis meminisse juvat; quum abessem, quotiescunque patria in mentem veniret, hæc omnia occurrebant, colles, campique, et Tiberis, et assueta oculis regio, et hoc cœlum, sub quo natus educatusque essem. Quæ vos, Quirites, nunc moveant potius caritate sua, ut maneatis in sede vestra, quam postea quum reliqueritis ea, macerent desiderio." — V. 54.

(18) This emperor constantly passed the summer in a small villa near Reate, where he was born, and to which he would never add any embellishment; *ne quid scilicet oculorum consuetudini deperiret. — Suet. in Vit. Vesp.* cap. ii.

A similar instance occurs in the life of the venerable Pertinax, as related by J. Capitolinus. Posteaquam in Liguriam venit, multis agris coemptis, tabernam paternam, *manente formâ priore*, infinitis ædificiis circundedit. — *Hist. August.* 54.

And it is said of Cardinal Richelieu, that, when he built his magnificent palace on the site of the old family chateau at Richelieu, he sacrificed its symmetry to preserve the room in which he was born. — *Mém. de Mlle. de Montpensier*, i. 27.

An attachment of this nature is generally the characteristic of a benevolent mind; and a long acquaintance with the world cannot always extinguish it.

"To a friend," says John, Duke of Buckingham, "I will expose my weakness: I am oftener missing a pretty gallery in the old house I pulled down, than pleased with a saloon which I built in its stead, though a thousand times better in all respects." — *See his Letter to the D. of Sh.*

This is the language of the heart, and will remind the reader of that good-humored remark in one of Pope's letters: "I should hardly care to have an old post pulled up, that I remembered ever since I was a child."

The author of Telemachus has illustrated this subject, with equal fancy and feeling, in the story of Alibée, Persan.

(19) That amiable and accomplished monarch, Henry the Fourth of France, made an excursion from his camp, during the long siege of Laon, to dine at a house in the forest of Folambray; where he had often been regaled, when a boy, with fruit, milk and new cheese; and in revisiting which he promised himself great pleasure. — *Mém. de Sully.*

(20) Diocletian retired into his native province, and there amused himself with building, planting and gardening. His answer to Maximian is deservedly celebrated. "If," said he, "I could show him the cabbages which I have planted with my own hands at Salona, he would no longer solicit me to return to a throne."

(21) When the Emperor Charles the Fifth had executed his memorable resolution, and had set out for the monastery of Justé, he stopped a few days at Ghent to indulge that tender and pleasant melancholy, which arises in the mind of every man in the decline of life, on visiting the place of his birth, and the objects familiar to him in his early youth.

(22) Monjes solitarios del glorioso padre San Geronimo, says Sandova.

In a corner of the Convent-garden there is this inscription: En esta santa casa de S. Geronimo de Justé se retiró à acabar su vida Cárlos V. Emperador, &c. — *Ponz.*

(23) The memory of the horse forms the ground-work of a pleasing little romance, entitled, "Lai du Palefroi vair." — *See Fabliaux du* XII. *Siecle.*

Ariosto likewise introduces it in a passage full of truth and nature. When Bayardo meets Angelica in the forest,

. . . . Va mansueto a la Donzella,
. . . .
Ch'in Albracca il servìa già di sua mano.

Orlando Furioso, i. 75.

(24) During the siege of Harlem, when that city was reduced to the last extremity, and on the point of opening its gates to a base and barbarous enemy, a design was formed to relieve it; and the intelligence was conveyed to the citizens by a letter which was tied under the wing of a pigeon. — *Thuanus*, lv. 5.

The same messenger was employed at the siege of Mutina, as we are informed by the elder Pliny. — *Hist. Nat.* x. 37.

(25) This little animal, from the extreme convexity of her eye, cannot see many inches before her.

PART II.

(1) True glory, says one of the ancients, is to be acquired by doing what deserves to be written, and writing what deserves to be read; and by making the world the happier and the better for our having lived in it.

(2) There is a future existence even in this world,— an existence in the hearts and minds of those who shall live after us.*

It is a state of rewards and punishments; and, like that revealed to us in the gospel, has the happiest influence on our lives. The latter excites us to gain the favor of God, the former to gain the love and esteem of wise and good men; and both lead to the same end; for, in framing our conceptions of the Deity, we only ascribe to him exalted degrees of wisdom and goodness.

(3) The highest reward of virtue is virtue herself, as the severest punishment of vice is vice herself.

(4) The astronomer chalking his figures on the wall in Hogarth's view of Bedlam is an admirable exemplification of this idea. — *See the Rake's Progress*, plate 8.

(5) The following stanzas † are said to have been written on a blank leaf of this poem. They present so affecting a reverse of the picture, that I cannot resist the opportunity of introducing them here.

" Pleasures of Memory! O! supremely blest,
And justly proud beyond a poet's praise;
If the pure confines of thy tranquil breast
Contain, indeed, the subject of thy lays!
By me how envied! — for to me,
The herald still of misery,
Memory makes her influence known
By sighs, and tears, and grief alone:
I greet her as the fiend, to whom belong
The vulture's ravening beak, the raven's funeral song.

" She tells of time misspent, of comfort lost,
Of fair occasions gone forever by;
Of hopes too fondly nursed, too rudely crossed,
Of many a cause to wish, yet fear to die;

* De tous les biens humains c'est le seul que la mort ne nous peut ravir. — *Bossuet.*
† By Henry F. R. Soame, of Trinity College, Cambridge.

For what, except the instinctive fear
Lest she survive, detains me here,
When 'all the life of life' is fled ?
What, but the deep inherent dread
Lest she beyond the grave resume her reign,
And realize the hell that priests and beldames feign ?"

(6) On the road side between Penrith and Appleby there stands a small pillar with this inscription :

"This pillar was erected in the year 1656, by Ann, Countess Dowager of Pembroke, &c., for a memorial of her last parting, in this place, with her good and pious mother, Margaret, Countess Dowager of Cumberland, on the 2d of April, 1616 ; in memory whereof she hath left an annuity of 4*l.* to be distributed to the poor of the parish of Brougham, every second day of April forever, upon the stone table placed hard by. Laus Deo ! "

The Eden is the principal river of Cumberland, and rises in the wildest part of Westmoreland.

(7) "I would not exchange my dead son," said he, "for any living son in Christendom." —*Hume.*

The same sentiment is inscribed on an urn at the Leasowes. "Heu, quanto minus est cum reliquis versari, quam tui meminisse ! "

(8) A small island covered with trees, among which were formerly the ruins of a religious house.

(9) In a mountain-lake the agitations are often violent and momentary. The winds blow in gusts and eddies ; and the water no sooner swells than it subsides. — *See Bourn's Hist. of Westmoreland.*

(10) The several degrees of angels may probably have larger views, and some of them be endowed with capacities able to retain together, and constantly set before them, as in one picture, all their past knowledge at once. — *Locke.*

AN EPISTLE TO A FRIEND.

1798.

Villula, . . . et pauper agelle,
Me tibi, et hos unà mecum, quos semper amavi,
Commendo.

PREFACE.

Every reader turns with pleasure to those passages of Horace, and Pope, and Boileau, which describe how they lived and where they dwelt; and which, being interspersed among their satirical writings, derive a secret and irresistible grace from the contrast, and are admirable examples of what in painting is termed repose.

We have admittance to Horace at all hours. We enjoy the company and conversation at his table; and his suppers, like Plato's, "non solum in præsentia, sed etiam postero die jucundæ sunt." But, when we look round as we sit there, we find ourselves in a Sabine farm, and not in a Roman villa. His windows have every charm of prospect; but his furniture might have descended from Cincinnatus; and gems, and pictures, and old marbles, are mentioned by him more than once with a seeming indifference.

His English imitator thought and felt, perhaps, more correctly on the subject; and embellished his garden and grotto with great industry and success. But to these alone he solicits our notice. On the ornaments of his house he is silent; and he appears to have reserved all the minuter touches of his pencil for the library, the chapel, and the banqueting-room of Timon. "Le savoir de notre siècle," says Rousseau, "tend beaucoup plus à détruire qu'à édifier. On censure d'un ton de maître; pour proposer, il en faut prendre un autre."

It is the design of this Epistle to illustrate the virtue of True Taste; and to show how little she requires to secure, not only the comforts, but even the elegances of life. True Taste is an excellent economist. She confines her choice to few objects, and delights in producing great effects by small means: while False Taste is forever sighing after the new and the rare; and reminds us, in her works, of the Scholar of Apelles, who, not being able to paint his Helen beautiful, determined to make her fine.

EPISTLE TO A FRIEND.

An Invitation — The Approach to a Villa described — Its Situation — Its few Apartments — Furnished with Casts from the Antique, &c. — The Dining-room — The Library — A Cold Bath — A Winter Walk — A Summer Walk — The Invitation renewed — Conclusion.

WHEN, with a REAUMUR'S skill, thy curious mind
Has classed the insect-tribes of human kind,
Each with its busy hum, or gilded wing,
Its subtle web-work, or its venomed sting;
Let me, to claim a few unvalued hours,
Point out the green lane rough with fern and flowers;
The sheltered gate that opens to my field,
And the white front through mingling elms revealed.
In vain, alas! a village friend invites
To simple comforts and domestic rites,
When the gay months of Carnival resume
Their annual round of glitter and perfume;
When London hails thee to its splendid mart,
Its hives of sweets and cabinets of art;
And, lo! majestic as thy manly song,
Flows the full tide of human life along.
Still must my partial pencil love to dwell
On the home-prospects of my hermit-cell;
The mossy pales that skirt the orchard-green,
Here hid by shrub-wood, there by glimpses seen;

9*

And the brown pathway, that, with careless flow,
Sinks, and is lost among the trees below.
Still must it trace (the flattering tints forgive)
Each fleeting charm that bids the landscape live.
Oft o'er the mead, at pleasing distance, pass,[1]
Browsing the hedge by fits, the panniered ass;
The idling shepherd-boy, with rude delight,
Whistling his dog to mark the pebble's flight;
And in her kerchief blue the cottage-maid,
With brimming pitcher from the shadowy glade.
Far to the south a mountain-vale retires,
Rich in its groves, and glens, and village spires;
Its upland lawns, and cliffs with foliage hung,
Its wizard-stream, nor nameless nor unsung:
And through the various year, the various day,[2]
What scenes of glory burst, and melt away!
  When April-verdure springs in Grosvenor-square,
And the furred Beauty comes to winter there,
She bids old Nature mar the plan no more;
Yet still the seasons circle as before.
Ah! still as soon the young Aurora plays,
Though moons and flambeaux trail their broadest blaze;
As soon the sky-lark pours his matin-song,
Though Evening lingers at the Masque so long.
  There let her strike with momentary ray,
As tapers shine their little lives away;
There let her practise from herself to steal,
And look the happiness she does not feel;
The ready smile and bidden blush employ
At Faro-routs that dazzle to destroy;
Fan with affected ease the essenced air,
And lisp of fashions with unmeaning stare.

Be thine to meditate an humbler flight,
When morning fills the fields with rosy light;
Be thine to blend, nor thine a vulgar aim,
Repose with dignity, with Quiet fame.
  Here no state-chambers in long line unfold,
Bright with broad mirrors, rough with fretted gold;
Yet modest ornament, with use combined,
Attracts the eye to exercise the mind.
Small change of scene, small space, his home requires,[3]
Who leads a life of satisfied desires.
  What though no marble breathes, no canvas glows,
From every point a ray of genius flows![4]
Be mine to bless the more mechanic skill,
That stamps, renews, and multiplies at will;
And cheaply circulates, through distant climes,
The fairest relics of the purest times.
Here from the mould to conscious being start
Those finer forms, the miracles of art;
Here chosen gems, imprest on sulphur, shine,
That slept for ages in a second mine;
And here the faithful graver dares to trace
A MICHAEL'S grandeur, and a RAPHAEL'S grace!
Thy gallery, Florence, gilds my humble walls;
And my low roof the Vatican recalls!
  Soon as the morning-dream my pillow flies,
To waking sense what brighter visions rise!
O mark! again the coursers of the Sun,
At GUIDO'S call, their round of glory run![5]
Again the rosy hours resume their flight,
Obscured and lost in floods of golden light!
  But could thine erring friend so long forget
(Sweet source of pensive joy and fond regret)

That here its warmest hues the pencil flings,
Lo! here the lost restores, the absent brings;
And still the few best loved and most revered [6]
Rise round the board their social smile endeared? [7]
Selected shelves shall claim thy studious hours;
There shall thy ranging mind be fed on flowers! [8]
There, while the shaded lamp's mild lustre streams,
Read ancient books, or dream inspiring dreams; [9]
And, when a sage's bust arrests thee there, [10]
Pause, and his features with his thoughts compare.
— Ah! most that Art my grateful rapture calls,
Which breathes a soul into the silent walls; [11]
Which gathers round the wise of every tongue, [12]
All on whose words departed nations hung;
Still prompt to charm with many a converse sweet;
Guides in the world, companions in retreat!
Though my thatched bath no rich Mosaic knows,
A limpid spring with unfelt current flows.
Emblem of Life! which, still as we survey,
Seems motionless, yet ever glides away!
The shadowy walls record, with Attic art,
The strength and beauty which its waves impart.
Here THETIS, bending, with a mother's fears
Dips her dear boy, whose pride restrains his tears.
There VENUS, rising, shrinks with sweet surprise,
As her fair self reflected seems to rise! [13]
Far from the joyless glare, the maddening strife,
And all the dull impertinence of life,
These eyelids open to the rising ray, [14]
And close, when Nature bids, at close of day.
Here, at the dawn, the kindling landscape glows;
There noon-day levees call from faint repose.

Here the flushed wave flings back the parting light;
There glimmering lamps anticipate the night.
When from his classic dreams the student steals,[15]
Amid the buzz of crowds, the whirl of wheels,
To muse unnoticed — while around him press
The meteor-forms of equipage and dress;
Alone, in wonder lost, he seems to stand
A very stranger in his native land!
And (though perchance of current coin possest,
And modern phrase by living lips exprest)
Like those blest Youths, forgive the fabling page,[16]
Whose blameless lives deceived a twilight age,
Spent in sweet slumbers; till the miner's spade
Unclosed the cavern, and the morning played.
Ah! what their strange surprise, their wild delight!
New arts of life, new manners, meet their sight!
In a new world they wake, as from the dead;
Yet doubt the trance dissolved, the vision fled!

O, come, and, rich in intellectual wealth,
Blend thought with exercise, with knowledge health;[17]
Long, in this sheltered scene of lettered talk,
With sober step repeat the pensive walk;
Nor scorn, when graver triflings fail to please,
The cheap amusements of a mind at ease;
Here every care in sweet oblivion cast,
And many an idle hour — not idly passed.

No tuneful echoes, ambushed at my gate,
Catch the blest accents of the wise and great.[18]
Vain of its various page, no Album breathes
The sigh that Friendship or the Muse bequeaths.
Yet some good Genii o'er my hearth preside,
Oft the far friend, with secret spell, to guide;

And there I trace, when the gray evening lowers,
A silent chronicle of happier hours!
When Christmas revels in a world of snow,
And bids her berries blush, her carols flow;
His spangling shower when Frost the wizard flings;
Or, borne in ether blue, on viewless wings,
O'er the white pane his silvery foliage weaves,
And gems with icicles the sheltering eaves;
— Thy muffled friend his nectarine-wall pursues,
What time the sun the yellow crocus woos,
Screened from the arrowy North; and duly hies
To meet the morning-rumor as it flies;
To range the murmuring market-place, and view
The motley groups that faithful TENIERS drew.[19]
When Spring bursts forth in blossoms through the vale,
And her wild music triumphs on the gale,
Oft with my book I muse from stile to stile;[20]
Oft in my porch the listless noon beguile,
Framing loose numbers, till declining day
Through the green trellis shoots a crimson ray;
Till the west wind leads on the twilight hours,
And shakes the fragrant bells of closing flowers.
Nor boast, O Choisy! seat of soft delight,
The secret charm of thy voluptuous night.
Vain is the blaze of wealth, the pomp of power!
Lo! here, attendant on the shadowy hour,
Thy closet-supper, served by hands unseen,
Sheds, like an evening-star, its ray serene,[21]
To hail our coming. Not a step profane
Dares, with rude sound, the cheerful rite restrain;
And, while the frugal banquet glows revealed,
Pure and unbought[22] — the natives of my field;

While blushing fruits through scattered leaves invite,
Still clad in bloom, and veiled in azure light;—
With wine, as rich in years as HORACE sings,
With water, clear as his own fountain flings,
The shifting side-board plays its humbler part,
Beyond the triumphs of a Loriot's art.[23]
  Thus, in this calm recess, so richly fraught
With mental light, and luxury of thought,
My life steals on; (O, could it blend with thine!)
Careless my course, yet not without design.
So through the vales of Loire the bee-hives glide,[24]
The light raft dropping with the silent tide;
So, till the laughing scenes are lost in night,
The busy people wing their various flight,
Culling unnumbered sweets from nameless flowers,
That scent the vineyard in its purple hours.
  Rise, ere the watch-relieving clarions play,
Caught through St. James's groves at blush of day;[25]
Ere its full voice the choral anthem flings
Through trophied tombs of heroes and of kings.
Haste to the tranquil shade of learned ease,[26]
Though skilled alike to dazzle and to please;
Though each gay scene be searched with anxious eye,
Nor thy shut door be passed without a sigh.
  If, when this roof shall know thy friend no more,
Some, formed like thee, should once, like thee, explore;
Invoke the lares of his loved retreat,
And his lone walks imprint with pilgrim-feet;
Then be it said (as, vain of better days,
Some gray domestic prompts the partial praise),
"Unknown he lived, unenvied, not unblest;
Reason his guide, and Happiness his guest.

In the clear mirror of his moral page
We trace the manners of a purer age.
His soul, with thirst of genuine glory fraught,
Scorned the false lustre of licentious thought.
— One fair asylum from the world he knew,
One chosen seat, that charms with various view!
Who boasts of more (believe the serious strain)
Sighs for a home, and sighs, alas! in vain.
Through each he roves, the tenant of a day,
And, with the swallow, wings the year away!"[27]

NOTES.

(1) Cosmo of Medicis took most pleasure in his Apennine villa, because all that he commanded from its windows was exclusively his own. How unlike the wise Athenian, who, when he had a farm to sell, directed the crier to proclaim, as its best recommendation, that it had a good neighborhood! — *Plut. in Vit. Themist.*

(2) Well situated is the house, "longos quæ prospicit agros." Distant views contain the greatest variety, both in themselves and in their accidental variations.

(3) Many a great man, in passing through the apartments of his palace, has made the melancholy reflection of the venerable Cosmo: "Questa è troppo gran casa à si poca famiglia." — *Mach. Ist Fior.* lib. vii.

"Parva, sed apta mihi," was Ariosto's inscription over his door in Ferrara; and who can wish to say more? "I confess," says Cowley, "I love littleness almost in all things. A little convenient estate, a little cheerful house, a little company, and a very little feast." — *Essay* vi.

When Socrates was asked why he had built for himself so small a house, "Small as it is," he replied, "I wish I could fill it with friends." — *Phædrus*, iii. 9.

These indeed are all that a wise man can desire to assemble; "for a crowd is not company, and faces are but a gallery of pictures, and talk but a tinkling cymbal, where there is no love."

(4) By these means, when all nature wears a lowering countenance, I withdraw myself into the visionary worlds of art; where I meet with shining landscapes, gilded triumphs, beautiful faces, and all those other objects that fill the mind with gay ideas. — *Addison.*

It is remarkable that Antony, in his adversity, passed some time in a small but splendid retreat, which he called his Timonium, and from which might originate the idea of the Parisian boudoir, that favorite apartment, *où l'on se retire pour être seul, mais où l'on ne boude point.* — *Strabo*, l. xvii. *Plut. in Vit. Anton.*

(5) Alluding to his celebrated fresco in the Rospigliosi Palace, at Rome.

(6) The dining-room is dedicated to Conviviality; or, as Cicero somewhere expresses it, "Communitati vitæ atque victûs." There we wish most for the society of our friends; and, perhaps, in their absence, most require their portraits.

The moral advantages of this furniture may be illustrated by the story of an Athenian courtesan, who, in the midst of a riotous banquet with her lovers, accidentally cast her eye on the portrait of a philosopher, that hung opposite to her seat; the happy character of wisdom and virtue struck her with so lively an image of her own unworthiness, that she instantly left the room, and, retiring home, became ever afterwards an example of temperance, as she had been before of debauchery.

10

(7) "A long table and a square table," says Bacon, "seem things of form, but are things of substance; for at a long table a few at the upper end, in effect, sway all the business." Perhaps Arthur was right when he instituted the order of the round table. In the town-house of Aix-la-Chapelle is still to be seen the round table which may almost literally be said to have given peace to Europe in 1748. Nor is it only at a congress of plenipotentiaries that place gives precedence.

(8) apis Matinæ
More modoque
Grata carpentis thyma . . . — *Hor.*

(9) Before I begin to write, says Bossuet, I always read a little of Homer; for I love to light my lamp at the sun.

The reader will here remember that passage of Horace, *Nunc veterum libris, nunc somno, &c.*, which was inscribed by Lord Chesterfield on the frieze of his library.

(10) Siquidem non solum ex auro argentove, aut certe ex ære in bibliothecis dicantur illi, quorum immortales animæ in iisdem locis ibi loquuntur: quinimo etiam quæ non sunt, finguntur, pariuntque desideria non traditi vultus, sicut in Homero evenit. Quo majus (ut equidem arbitror) nullum est felicitatis specimen, quam semper omnes scire cupere, qualis fuerit aliquis. — *Plin. Nat. Hist.*

Cicero, in the dialogue entitled Brutus, represents Brutus and Atticus as sitting down with him in his garden at Rome by the statue of Plato; and with what delight does he speak of a little seat under Aristotle in the library of Atticus! "Literis sustentor et recreor; maloque in illa tua sedecula, quam habes sub imagine Aristotelis, sedere, quàm in istorum sella curuli!" — *Ep. ad Att.* iv. 10.

Nor should we forget that Dryden drew inspiration from the "majestic face" of Shakspeare; and that a portrait of Newton was the only ornament of the closet of Buffon. — *Ep. to Kneller. Voyage à Montbart.*

In the chamber of a man of genius we

Write all down:
Such and such pictures; — there the window;
. . . . the arras, figures,
Why, such and such.

(11) Postea verò quàm Tyrannio mihi libros disposuit, mens addita videtur meis ædibus. — *Cic.*

(12) Quis tantis non gaudeat et glorietur hospitibus, exclaims Petrarch. — Spectare, etsi nihil aliud, certè juvat. — Homerus apud me mutus, imò verò ego apud illum surdus sum. Gaudeo tamen vel aspectû solo, et sæpe illum amplexus ac suspirans dico: O magne vir, &c. — *Epist. Var.* lib. 20.

(13) After this line, in a former edition,

But hence away! yon rocky cave beware!
A sullen captive broods in silence there!
There, though the dog-star flame, condemned to dwell
In the dark centre of its inmost cell,
Wild Winter ministers his dread control
To cool and crystallize the nectared bowl.
His faded form an awful grace retains;
Stern, though subdued, majestic, though in chains!

(14) Your bed-chamber, and also your library, says Vitruvius, should have an eastern aspect; usus enim matutinum postulat lumen. Not so the picture-gallery: which

requires a north light, uti colores in ope, propter constantiam luminis, immutata permaneant qualitate. This disposition accords with his plan of a Grecian house.

(15) Ingenium, sibi quod vacuas desumsit Athenas,
Et studiis annos septem dedit, insenuitque
Libris et curis, statuâ taciturnius exit
Plerumque . . . . — *Hor.*

(16) See the Legend of the Seven Sleepers. — *Gibbon*, c. 33.

(17) Milton "was up and stirring, ere the sound of any bell awaked men to labor or to devotion;" and it is related of two students in a suburb of Paris, who were opposite neighbors, and were called the morning-star and the evening-star, — the former appearing just as the latter withdrew, — that the morning star continued to shine on, when the evening star was gone out forever.

(18) Mr. Pope delights in enumerating his illustrious guests. Nor is this an exclusive privilege of the poet. The Medici Palace at Florence exhibits a long and imposing catalogue. "Semper hi parietes columnæque eruditis vocibus resonuerunt."

(19) Fallacem circum, vespertinumque pererro
Sæpe forum. — *Hor.*

(20) Tantôt, un livre en main, errant dans les préries . . — *Boileau.*

(21) At a Roman supper statues were sometimes employed to hold the lamps.

—aurea sunt juvenum simulacra per ædes.
Lampadas igniferas manibus retinentia dextris.
Lucr. ii. 24.

A fashion as old as Homer! — *Odyss.* vii. 100.

On the proper degree and distribution of light we may consult a great master of effect. Il lume grande, ed alto, e non troppo potente, sarà quello, che renderà le particole de' corpi molto grate. — *Tratt. della Pittura di Lionardo da Vinci*, c. xli.

Hence every artist requires a broad and high light. Michael Angelo used to work with a candle fixed in his hat. — *Condivi. Vita di Michelagnolo.* Hence also, in a banquet-scene, the most picturesque of all poets has thrown his light from the ceiling. — *Æn.* i. 726.

And hence the "starry lamps" of Milton, that

. . . . from the arched roof
Pendent by subtle magic, ...
. . . . . yielded light
As from a sky.

(22) Dapes inemtas, — *Hor.*

(23) At the petits soupés of Choisy were first introduced those admirable pieces of mechanism, afterwards carried to perfection by Loriot, the Confidente and the Servante; a table and a side-board, which descended, and rose again covered with viands and wines. And thus the most luxurious court in Europe, after all its boasted refinements, was glad to return at last, by this singular contrivance, to the quiet and privacy of humble life. — *Vie privée de Louis XV.* ii. 43.

Between this and the next line were these lines, since omitted:

Hail, sweet Society! in crowds unknown,
Though the vain world would claim thee for its own.

Still where thy small and cheerful converse flows,
Be mine to enter, ere the circle close.
When in retreat Fox lays his thunder by,
And wit and taste their mingled charms supply;
When SIDDONS, born to melt and freeze the heart,
Performs at home her more endearing part;
When he, who best interprets to mankind
The wingéd messengers from mind to mind,
Leans on his spade, and, playful as profound,
His genius sheds its evening sunshine round,
Be mine to listen; pleased yet not elate,
Ever too modest or too proud to rate
Myself by my companions.

These were written in 1796.

(24) An allusion to the floating bee-house, which is seen in some parts of France and Piedmont.

(25) After this line, in the MS.

Groves that Belinda's star illumines still,
And ancient courts and faded splendors fill.

See the Rape of the Lock, Canto V.

(26) Innocuas amo delicias doctamqué quietem.

(27) It was the boast of Lucullus that he changed his climate with the birds of passage.
How often must he have felt the truth here inculcated, that the master of many houses has no home!

THE

VOYAGE OF COLUMBUS.

1812.

Chi se' tu, che vieni — ?
Da me stesso non vegno.
DANTE.

I have seen the day
That I have worn a visor, and could tell
A tale — SHAKSP.

PREFACE.

THE following Poem (or, to speak more properly, what remains of it *) has here and there a lyrical turn of thought and expression. It is sudden in its transitions, and full of historical allusions; leaving much to be imagined by the reader.

The subject is a voyage the most memorable in the annals of mankind. Columbus was a person of extraordinary virtue and piety, acting, as he conceived, under the sense of a divine impulse; and his achievement the discovery of a New World, the inhabitants of which were shut out from the light of revelation, and given up, as they believed, to the dominion of malignant spirits.

Many of the incidents will now be thought extravagant; yet they were once perhaps received with something more than indulgence. It was an age of miracles; and who can say that among the venerable legends in the library of the Escurial, or the more authentic records which fill the great chamber in the *Archivo* of Seville, and which relate entirely to the deep tragedy of America, there are no volumes that mention the marvellous things here described? Indeed, the story, as already told throughout Europe, admits of no heightening. Such was the religious enthusiasm of the early writers, that the author had only to transfuse it into his verse; and he appears to have done little more, though some of the circumstances, which he alludes to as well known, have long ceased to be so. By using the language of that day, he has called up Columbus "in his habit as he lived;" and the authorities, such as exist, are carefully given by the translator.

* The original in the Castilian language, according to the Inscription that follows, was found among other MSS. in an old religious house near Palos, situated on an island formed by the river Tinto, and dedicated to our Lady of La Rábida. The writer describes himself as having sailed with Columbus; but his style and manner are evidently of an after-time.

INSCRIBED ON THE ORIGINAL MANUSCRIPT.

UNCLASP me, Stranger; and unfold,
With trembling care, my leaves of gold,
Rich in Gothic portraiture —
If yet, alas! a leaf endure.

In RABIDA'S monastic fane
I cannot ask, and ask in vain.
The language of CASTILE I speak;
Mid many an Arab, many a Greek,
Old in the days of CHARLEMAIN;
When minstrel-music wandered round,
And Science, waking, blessed the sound.

No earthly thought has here a place,
The cowl let down on every face;
Yet here, in consecrated dust,
Here would I sleep, if sleep I must.
From GENOA when COLUMBUS came
(At once her glory and her shame),
'T was here he caught the holy flame.
'T was here the generous vow he made;
His banners on the altar laid.

Here, tempest-worn and desolate,
A Pilot, journeying through the wild,

* We have an interesting account of his first appearance in Spain, that country which was so soon to be the theatre of his glory. According to

Stopt to solicit at the gate
A pittance for his child.
'T was here, unknowing and unknown,
He stood upon the threshold-stone.
But hope was his — a faith sublime,
That triumphs over place and time;
And here, his mighty labor done,
And his course of glory run,
A while as more than man he stood,
So large the debt of gratitude!

One hallowed morn, methought, I felt
As if a soul within me dwelt!
But who arose and gave to me
The sacred trust I keep for thee,
And in his cell at even-tide
Knelt before the cross and died —
Inquire not now. His name no more
Glimmers on the chancel-floor,
Near the lights that ever shine
Before St. Mary's blessed shrine.

To me one little hour devote,
And lay thy staff and scrip beside thee;

the testimony of Garcia Fernandez, the physician of Palos, a sea-faring man, accompanied by a very young boy, stopped one day at the gate of the Convent of La Rábida, and asked of the porter a little bread and water for his child. While they were receiving this humble refreshment, the prior, Juan Perez, happening to pass by, was struck with the look and manner of the stranger, and, entering into conversation with him, soon learnt the particulars of his story. The stranger was Columbus; the boy was his son Diego; and, but for this accidental interview, America might have remained long undiscovered: for it was to the zeal of Juan Perez that he was finally indebted for the accomplishment of his great purpose. — See Irving's History of Columbus.

Read in the temper that he wrote,
And may his gentle spirit guide thee!
My leaves forsake me, one by one;
The book-worm through and through has gone.
O, haste — unclasp me, and unfold;
The tale within was never told!

PREFACE TO THE SECOND EDITION.

THERE is a spirit in the old Spanish chroniclers of the sixteenth century that may be compared to the freshness of water at the fountain-head. Their simplicity, their sensibility to the strange and the wonderful, their very weaknesses, give an infinite value, by giving a life and a character to everything they touch; and their religion, which bursts out everywhere, addresses itself to the imagination in the highest degree. If they err, their errors are not their own. They think and feel after the fashion of the time; and their narratives are so many moving pictures of the actions, manners and thoughts, of their contemporaries.

What they had to communicate might well make them eloquent; but, inasmuch as relates to Columbus, the inspiration went no further. No national poem appeared on the subject; no Camoëns did honor to his genius and his virtues. Yet the materials that have descended to us are surely not unpoetical; and a desire to avail myself of them, to convey in some instances as far as I could, in others as far as I dared, their warmth of coloring and wildness of imagery, led me to conceive the idea of a poem written not long after his death, when the great consequences of the discovery were beginning to unfold themselves, but while the minds of men were still clinging to the superstitions of their fathers.

The event here described may be thought too recent for the machinery; but I found them together.* A belief in the agency of evil spirits prevailed over both hemispheres; and even yet seems almost necessary to enable us to clear up the darkness,

And justify the ways of God to men.

* Perhaps even a contemporary subject should not be rejected as such, however wild and extravagant it may be, if the manners be foreign and the place distant, — major è longinquo reverentia. L'éloignement des pays, says Racine, répare en quelque sorte la trop grande proximité des temps; car le peuple ne met guere de différence entre ce qui est, si j'ose ainsi parler, à mille ans de lui, et ce qui en est à mille lieues.

THE ARGUMENT.

Columbus, having wandered from kingdom to kingdom, at length obtains three ships, and sets sail on the Atlantic. The compass alters from its ancient direction; the wind becomes constant and unremitting; night and day he advances, till he is suddenly stopped in his course by a mass of vegetation, extending as far as the eye can reach, and assuming the appearance of a country overwhelmed by the sea. Alarm and despondence on board. He resigns himself to the care of Heaven, and proceeds on his voyage.

Meanwhile the deities of America assemble in council; and one of the Zemi, the gods of the islanders, announces his approach. "In vain," says he, "have we guarded the Atlantic for ages. A mortal has baffled our power; nor will our votaries arm against him. Yours are a sterner race. Hence; and, while we have recourse to stratagem, do you array the nations round your altars, and prepare for an exterminating war." They disperse while he is yet speaking; and, in the shape of a condor, he directs his flight to the fleet. His journey described. He arrives there. A panic. A mutiny. Columbus restores order; continues on his voyage; and lands in a New World. Ceremonies of the first interview. Rites of hospitality. The ghost of Cazziva.

Two months pass away, and an angel, appearing in a dream to Columbus, thus addresses him: "Return to Europe; though your adversaries, such is the will of Heaven, shall let loose the hurricane against you. A little while shall they triumph; insinuating themselves into the hearts of your followers, and making the world, which you came to bless, a scene of blood and slaughter. Yet is there cause for rejoicing. Your work is done. The cross of Christ is planted here; and, in due time, all things shall be made perfect!"

THE VOYAGE OF COLUMBUS.

CANTO I.

Night — Columbus on the Atlantic — the Variation of the Compass, &c.

SAY who, when age on age had rolled away,
And still, as sunk the golden orb of day,
The seaman watched him, while he lingered here,
With many a wish to follow, many a fear,
And gazed and gazed and wondered where he went,
So bright his path, so glorious his descent,
Who first adventured? — In his birth obscure,
Yet born to build a Fame that should endure,[1]
Who the great secret of the Deep possessed,
And, issuing through the portals of the west,
Fearless, resolved, with every sail unfurled,
Planted his standard on the unknown world?
Him, by the Paynim bard described of yore,
And ere his coming sung on either shore,
Him could not I exalt — by Heaven designed
To lift the veil that covered half mankind!
Yet, ere I die, I would fulfil my vow;
Praise cannot wound his generous spirit now.

*　　*　　*　　*　　*　　*

*　　*　　*　　*　　*　　*

'T was night. The Moon, o'er the wide wave, disclosed
Her awful face; and Nature's self reposed;
When, slowly rising in the azure sky,
Three white sails shone — but to no mortal eye,
Entering a boundless sea. In slumber cast,
The very ship-boy, on the dizzy mast,
Half breathed his orisons! Alone unchanged,
Calmly, beneath, the great Commander[2] ranged,
Thoughtful, not sad; and, as the planet grew,
His noble form, wrapt in his mantle blue,
Athwart the deck a deepening shadow threw.
"Thee hath it pleased—Thy will be done!" he said,[3]
Then sought his cabin; and, their garments spread,
Around him lay the sleeping as the dead,
When, by his lamp to that mysterious guide,[4]
On whose still counsels all his hopes relied,
That oracle to man in mercy given,
Whose voice is truth, whose wisdom is from heaven,
Who over sands and seas directs the stray,
And, as with God's own finger, points the way,
He turned; but what strange thoughts perplexed his soul,
When, lo! no more attracted to the pole,
The Compass, faithless as the circling vane,
Fluttered and fixed, fluttered and fixed again!
At length, as by some unseen hand imprest,
It sought with trembling energy — the West![5]
"Ah no!" he cried, and calmed his anxious brow.
"Ill, nor the signs of ill, 't is thine to show;
Thine but to lead me where I wished to go!"
COLUMBUS erred not.[6] In that awful hour,
Sent forth to save, and girt with god-like power,

And glorious as the regent of the sun,[7]
An angel came! He spoke, and it was done!
He spoke, and, at his call, a mighty wind,[8]
Not like the fitful blast, with fury blind,
But deep, majestic, in its destined course,
Sprung with unerring, unrelenting force,
From the bright East. Tides duly ebbed and flowed;
Stars rose and set; and new horizons glowed;
Yet still it blew! As with primeval sway
Still did its ample spirit, night and day,
Move on the waters! — All, resigned to Fate,
Folded their arms and sate;[9] and seemed to wait
Some sudden change; and sought, in chill suspense,
New spheres of being, and new modes of sense;
As men departing, though not doomed to die,
And midway on their passage to eternity.

CANTO II.

The Voyage continued.

* * * * *

"WHAT vast foundations in the abyss are there,[1]
As of a former world? Is it not where
ATLANTIC kings their barbarous pomp displayed;[2]
Sunk into darkness with the realms they swayed,
When towers and temples, through the closing wave,
A glimmering ray of ancient splendor gave —
And we shall rest with them? — Or are we thrown"
(Each gazed on each, and all exclaimed as one)
"Where things familiar cease and strange begin,
All progress barred to those without, within?

— Soon is the doubt resolved. Arise, behold —
We stop to stir no more . . .[3] nor will the tale be told."
  The pilot smote his breast; the watchman cried
"Land!" and his voice in faltering accents died.[4]
At once the fury of the prow was quelled;
And (whence or why from many an age withheld)[5]
Shrieks, not of men, were mingling in the blast;
And armèd shapes of god-like stature passed!
Slowly along the evening-sky they went,
As on the edge of some vast battlement;
Helmet and shield, and spear and gonfalon,
Streaming a baleful light that was not of the sun!
  Long from the stern the great adventurer gazed
With awe, not fear; then high his hands he raised.
"Thou All-supreme . . . in goodness as in power,
Who, from his birth to this eventful hour,
Hast led thy servant over land and sea,[6]
Confessing Thee in all, and all in Thee,
O still"— He spoke, and, lo! the charm accurst
Fled whence it came, and the broad barrier burst!
A vain illusion! (such us mocks the eyes
Of fearful men, when mountains round them rise
From less than nothing) nothing now beheld,
But scattered sedge — repelling, and repelled!
  And once again that valiant company
Right onward came, ploughing the unknown sea.
Already borne beyond the range of thought,
With light divine, with truth immortal fraught,
From world to world their steady course they keep,[7]
Swift as the winds along the waters sweep,
Mid the mute nations of the purple deep.

— And now the sound of harpy-wings they hear;
Now less and less, as vanishing in fear!
And see, the heavens bow down, the waters rise,
And, rising, shoot in columns to the skies,[8]
That stand — and still, when they proceed, retire,
As in the desert burned the sacred fire;
Moving in silent majesty, till Night
Descends, and shuts the vision from their sight.

CANTO III.

An Assembly of Evil Spirits.

THOUGH changed my cloth of gold for amice gray[1] —
In my spring-time, when every month was May,
With hawk and hound I coursed away the hour,
Or sung my roundelay in lady's bower.
And though my world be now a narrow cell
(Renounced forever all I loved so well),
Though now my head be bald, my feet be bare,
And scarce my knees sustain my book of prayer,
O, I was there, one of that gallant crew,
And saw — and wondered whence his power he drew,
Yet little thought, though by his side I stood,
Of his great foes in earth and air and flood,
Then uninstructed.— But my sand is run,
And the night coming . . . and my task not done! . .
'T was in the deep, immeasurable cave
Of ANDES,[2] echoing to the Southern wave,
Mid pillars of basalt, the work of fire,
That, giant-like, to upper day aspire,

'T was there that now, as wont in heaven to shine,
Forms of angelic mould and grace divine
Assembled. All, exiled the realms of rest,
In vain the sadness of their souls suppressed;
Yet of their glory many a scattered ray
Shot through the gathering shadows of decay.
Each moved a god; and all, as gods, possessed
One half the globe; from pole to pole confessed![3]

* * * * * *
* * * * * *

O, could I now — but how in mortal verse —
Their numbers, their heroic deeds, rehearse!
These in dim shrines and barbarous symbols reign,
Where PLATA and MARAGNON meet the main.[4]
Those the wild hunter worships as he roves,
In the green shade of CHILI'S fragrant groves;
Or warrior-tribes with rites of blood implore,
Whose night-fires gleam along the sullen shore
Of HURON or ONTARIO, inland seas,[5]
What time the song of death is in the breeze!

* * * * * *

'T was now in dismal pomp and order due,
While the vast concave flashed with lightnings blue,
On shining pavements of metallic ore,
That many an age the fusing sulphur bore,
They held high council. All was silence round,
When, with a voice most sweet, yet most profound,
A sovereign Spirit burst the gates of night,
And from his wings of gold shook drops of liquid light!
MERION, commissioned with his host to sweep
From age to age the melancholy deep!

Chief of the ZEMI, whom the Isles obeyed,
By Ocean severed from a world of shade.[6]

I.

"Prepare, again prepare,"
Thus o'er the soul the thrilling accents came,
"Thrones to resign for lakes of living flame,
And triumph for despair.
He, on whose call afflicting thunders wait,
Has willed it; and his will is fate!
In vain the legions, emulous to save,
Hung in the tempest o'er the troubled main;[7]
Turned each presumptuous prow that broke the wave,
And dashed it on its shores again.
All is fulfilled! Behold, in close array,
What mighty banners stream in the bright track of day!

* * * * *
* * * * *

II.

"No voice as erst shall in the desert rise;[8]
Nor ancient, dread solemnities
With scorn of death the trembling tribes inspire.
Wreaths for the Conqueror's brow the victims bind!
Yet, though we fled yon firmament of fire,
Still shall we fly, all hope of rule resigned?"

* * * * *
* * * * *

He spoke; and all was silence, all was night![9]
Each had already winged his formidable flight.

CANTO IV.

The Voyage continued.

* * * * * * *

"Ah, why look back, though all is left behind?
No sounds of life are stirring in the wind.—
And you, ye birds, winging your passage home,
How blest ye are! — We know not where we roam.
We go," they cried, "go to return no more;
Nor ours, alas! the transport to explore
A human footstep on a desert shore!"

* * * * * * *

— Still, as beyond this mortal life impelled
By some mysterious energy, he held
His everlasting course. Still self-possessed,
High on the deck he stood, disdaining rest
(His amber-chain the only badge he bore,
His mantle blue such as his fathers wore);
Fathomed, with searching hand, the dark profound,
And scattered hope and glad assurance round;
Though, like some strange portentous dream, the Past
Still hovered, and the cloudless sky o'ercast.
At day-break might the Caravels[1] be seen,
Chasing their shadows o'er the deep serene;
Their burnished prows lashed by the sparkling tide,
Their green-cross standards waving far and wide.
And now once more to better thoughts inclined,
The seaman, mounting, clamored in the wind,
The soldier told his tales of love and war;[2]
The courtier sung — sung to his gay guitar.

Round, at Primero, sate a whiskered band;
So Fortune smiled, careless of sea or land![3]
LEON, MONTALVAN (serving side by side;
Two with one soul — and, as they lived, they died),
VASCO the brave, thrice found among the slain,
Thrice, and how soon, up and in arms again,
As soon to wish he had been sought in vain,
Chained down in FEZ, beneath the bitter thong,
To the hard bench and heavy oar so long!
ALBERT of FLORENCE, who, at twilight-time,
In my rapt ear poured DANTE'S tragic rhyme,
Screened by the sail as near the mast we lay,
Our nights illumined by the ocean-spray;
And MANFRED, who espoused with jewelled ring
Young ISABEL, then left her sorrowing:
LERMA "the generous," AVILA "the proud;"[4]
VELASQUEZ, GARCIA, through the echoing crowd
Traced by their mirth — from EBRO'S classic shore,
From golden TAJO, to return no more!

CANTO V.

The Voyage continued.

* * * * *

YET who but he undaunted could explore[1]
A world of waves, a sea without a shore,
Trackless and vast and wild as that revealed
When round the Ark the birds of tempest wheeled;
When all was still in the destroying hour —
No sign of man! no vestige of his power!

One at the stern before the hour-glass stood,
As 't were to count the sands; one o'er the flood
Gazed for St. Elmo;[2] while another cried
"Once more good-morrow!" and sate down and sighed.
Day, when it came, came only with its light.
Though long invoked, 't was sadder than the night!
Look where he would, forever as he turned,
He met the eye of one that inly mourned.
Then sunk his generous spirit, and he wept.
The friend, the father rose; the hero slept.
PALOS, thy port, with many a pang resigned,
Filled with its busy scenes his lonely mind;
The solemn march, the vows in concert given,[3]
The bended knees and lifted hands to heaven,
The incensed rites, and choral harmonies,
The Guardian's blessings mingling with his sighs;
While his dear boys — ah! on his neck they hung,[4]
And long at parting to his garments clung.
Oft in the silent night-watch doubt and fear
Broke in uncertain murmurs on his ear.
Oft the stern Catalan, at noon of day,
Muttered dark threats, and lingered to obey;
Though that brave youth — he, whom his courser bore
Right through the midst, when, fetlock-deep in gore,
The great GONSALVO[5] battled with the Moor
(What time the ALHAMBRA shook — soon to unfold
Its sacred courts, and fountains yet untold,
Its holy texts and arabesques of gold),—
Though ROLDAN, sleep and death to him alike,[6]
Grasped his good sword and half unsheathed to strike.
"O, born to wander with your flocks," he cried,
"And bask and dream along the mountain-side;

To urge your mules, tinkling from hill to hill;
Or at the vintage feast to drink your fill,
And strike your castanets, with gypsy-maid
Dancing Fandangos in the chestnut shade —
Come on," he cried, and threw his glove in scorn,
"Not this your wonted pledge, the brimming horn.
Valiant in peace! Adventurous at home!
O, had ye vowed with pilgrim-staff to roam;
Or with banditti sought the sheltering wood,
Where mouldering crosses mark the scene of blood!—"
He said, he drew; then, at his Master's frown,
Sullenly sheathed, plunging the weapon down.

* * * * * * *

* * * * * * *

CANTO VI.

The Flight of an Angel of Darkness.

War and the Great in War let others sing,[1]
Havoc and spoil, and tears and triumphing;
The morning-march that flashes to the sun,
The feast of vultures when the day is done;
And the strange tale of many slain for one!
I sing a Man, amid his sufferings here,
Who watched and served in humbleness and fear;
Gentle to others, to himself severe.

Still unsubdued by Danger's varying form,
Still, as unconscious of the coming storm,
He looked elate; and, with his wonted smile,
On the great Ordinance leaning, would beguile

The hour with talk. His beard, his mien sublime,
Shadowed by Age — by Age before the time,[2]
From many a sorrow borne in many a clime,
Moved every heart. And now in opener skies
Stars yet unnamed of purer radiance rise!
Stars, milder suns, that love a shade to cast,
And on the bright wave fling the trembling mast!
Another firmament! the orbs that roll,
Singly or clustering, round the Southern pole!
Not yet the four that glorify the Night —
Ah! how forget when to my ravished sight
The Cross shone forth in everlasting light![3]

* * * * * * *
* * * * * * *

'T was the mid hour, when He, whose accents dread
Still wandered through the regions of the dead
(MERION, commissioned with his host to sweep
From age to age the melancholy deep),
To elude the seraph-guard that watched for man,
And mar, as erst, the Eternal's perfect plan,
Rose like the condor, and, at towering height,
In pomp of plumage sailed, deepening the shades of night.
Roc of the West! to him all empire given![4]
Who bears Axalhua's dragon folds to heaven;[5]
His flight a whirlwind, and, when heard afar,
Like thunder, or the distant din of war!

Mountains and seas fled backward as he passed
O'er the great globe, by not a cloud o'ercast
From the ANTARCTIC, from the Land of Fire[6]
To where ALASKA'S wintry wilds retire;[7]
From mines of gold,[8] and giant-sons of earth,
To grots of ice, and tribes of pigmy birth

Who freeze alive, nor, dead, in dust repose,
High-hung in forests to the casing snows.[9]
  Now mid angelic multitudes he flies,
That hourly come with blessings from the skies;
Wings the blue element, and, borne sublime,
Eyes the set sun, gilding each distant clime;
Then, like a meteor shooting to the main,
Melts into pure intelligence again.

* * * * * * *
* * * * * * *

CANTO VII.

A Mutiny excited.

What though Despondence reigned, and wild Affright—
Stretched in the midst, and, through that dismal night,[1]
By his white plume revealed and buskins white,[2]
Slept Roldan. When he closed his gay career,
Hope fled forever, and with Hope fled Fear.
Blest with each gift indulgent Fortune sends,
Birth and its rights, wealth and its train of friends,
Star-like he shone! Now beggared and alone,
Danger he wooed, and claimed her for his own.
O'er him a Vampire his dark wings displayed.[3]
'T was Merion's self, covering with dreadful shade.[4]
He came, and, couched on Roldan's ample breast,
Each secret pore of breathing life possessed,
Fanning the sleep that seemed his final rest;
Then, inly gliding like a subtle flame,[5]
Thrice, with a cry that thrilled the mortal frame,

Called on the Spirit within. Disdaining flight,
Calmly she rose, collecting all her might.[6]
Dire was the dark encounter! Long unquelled,
Her sacred seat, sovereign and pure, she held.
At length the great foe binds her for his prize,
And awful, as in death, the body lies!
Not long to slumber! In an evil hour
Informed and lifted by the unknown power,
It starts, it speaks! "We live, we breathe no more!
The fatal wind blows on the dreary shore!
On yonder cliffs beckoning their fellow-prey,
The spectres stalk, and murmur at delay![7]
—Yet if thou canst (not for myself I plead!
Mine but to follow where 't is thine to lead),
O, turn and save! To thee, with streaming eyes,
To thee each widow kneels, each orphan cries!
Who now, condemned the lingering hours to tell,
Think and but think of those they loved so well!"
All melt in tears! but what can tears avail?
These climb the mast, and shift the swelling sail.
These snatch the helm; and round me now I hear
Smiting of hands, outcries of grief and fear[8]
(That in the aisles at midnight haunt me still,
Turning my lonely thoughts from good to ill).
"Were there no graves—none in our land," they cry,
"That thou hast brought us on the deep to die?"
Silent with sorrow, long within his cloak
His face he muffled—then the HERO spoke.
"Generous and brave! when God himself is here,
Why shake at shadows in your mid career?
He can suspend the laws himself designed,
He walks the waters, and the wingéd wind;

Himself your guide! and yours the high behest,
To lift your voice, and bid a world be blest!
And can you shrink? to you, to you consigned [9]
The glorious privilege to serve mankind!
O, had I perished, when my failing frame [10]
Clung to the shattered oar mid wrecks of flame!
— Was it for this I lingered life away,
The scorn of Folly, and of Fraud the prey;[11]
Bowed down my mind, the gift His bounty gave,
At courts a suitor, and to slaves a slave?
— Yet in His name whom only we should fear
('T is all, all I shall ask, or you shall hear)
Grant but three days." — He spoke not uninspired;[12]
And each in silence to his watch retired.
At length among us came an unknown Voice!
"Go, if ye will; and, if ye can, rejoice.
Go, with unbidden guests the banquet share.
In his own shape shall Death receive you there."[13]

CANTO VIII.

Land discovered.

Twice in the zenith blazed the orb of light;
No shade, all sun, insufferably bright!
Then the long line found rest — in coral groves
Silent and dark, where the sea-lion roves: —
And all on deck, kindling to life again,
Sent forth their anxious spirits o'er the main.
"O whence, as wafted from Elysium, whence
These perfumes, strangers to the raptured sense?

These boughs of gold, and fruits of heavenly hue,
Tinging with vermeil light the billows blue?
And (thrice, thrice blessed is the eye that spied,
The hand that snatched it sparkling in the tide)
Whose cunning carved this vegetable bowl,[1]
Symbol of social rites and intercourse of soul?"
Such to their grateful ear the gush of springs,
Who course the ostrich, as away she wings;
Sons of the desert! who delight to dwell
'Mid kneeling camels round the sacred well;
Who, ere the terrors of his pomp be passed,
Fall to the demon in the reddening blast.[2]
The sails were furled; with many a melting close,
Solemn and slow the evening-anthem rose,
Rose to the Virgin.[3] 'T was the hour of day
When setting suns o'er summer-seas display
A path of glory, opening in the west
To golden climes, and islands of the blest;
And human voices, on the silent air,
Went o'er the waves in songs of gladness there!
Chosen of Men![4] 'T was thine, at noon of night,
First from the prow to hail the glimmering light;[5]
(Emblem of Truth divine, whose secret ray
Enters the soul, and makes the darkness day!)
"PEDRO! RODRIGO![6] there, methought, it shone!
There — in the west! and now, alas! 't is gone! —
'T was all a dream! we gaze and gaze in vain!
— But mark and speak not, there it comes again!
It moves! what form unseen, what being there
With torch-like lustre fires the murky air?
His instincts, passions, say, how like our own?
O! when will day reveal a world unknown?"

CANTO IX.

The New World.

LONG on the deep the mists of morning lay,
Then rose, revealing, as they rolled away,
Half-circling hills, whose everlasting woods
Sweep with their sable skirts the shadowy floods:
And say, when all, to holy transport given,
Embraced and wept as at the gates of Heaven,
When one and all of us, repentant, ran,
And, on our faces, blessed the wondrous man;
Say, was I then deceived, or from the skies
Burst on my ear seraphic harmonies?
"Glory to God!" unnumbered voices sung,
"Glory to God!" the vales and mountains rung,
Voices that hailed Creation's primal morn,
And to the shepherds sung a Saviour born.
  Slowly, bare-headed, through the surf we bore
The sacred cross,[1] and, kneeling, kissed the shore.
But what a scene was there?[2] Nymphs of romance,[3]
Youths graceful as the Faun, with eager glance,
Spring from the glades, and down the alleys peep,
Then headlong rush, bounding from steep to steep,
And clap their hands, exclaiming as they run,
"Come and behold the Children of the Sun!"[4]
When hark, a signal-shot! The voice, it came
Over the sea in darkness and in flame!
They saw, they heard; and up the highest hill,
As in a picture, all at once were still!
Creatures so fair, in garments strangely wrought,
From citadels, with Heaven's own thunder fraught,

Checked their light footsteps — statue-like they stood,
As worshipped forms, the Genii of the Wood!
At length the spell dissolves! The warrior's lance
Rings on the tortoise with wild dissonance!
And see, the regal plumes, the couch of state![5]
Still, where it moves, the wise in council wait!
See now borne forth the monstrous mask of gold,
And ebon chair of many a serpent-fold;
These now exchanged for gifts that thrice surpass
The wondrous ring, and lamp, and horse of brass.[6]
What long-drawn tube transports the gazer home,[7]
Kindling with stars at noon the ethereal dome?
'T is here: and here circles of solid light
Charm with another self the cheated sight;
As man to man another self disclose,
That now with terror starts, with triumph glows!

CANTO X.

Cora — Luxuriant Vegetation — The Humming-bird — The Fountain of Youth.

* * * * * *

THEN CORA came, the youngest of her race,
And in her hands she hid her lovely face;
Yet oft by stealth a timid glance she cast,
And now with playful step the mirror passed,
Each bright reflection brighter than the last!
And oft behind it flew, and oft before;
The more she searched, pleased and perplexed the more!
And looked and laughed, and blushed with quick surprise;
Her lips all mirth, all ecstasy her eyes!

But soon the telescope attracts her view;
And, lo! her lover in his light canoe
Rocking, at noontide, on the silent sea,
Before her lies! It cannot, cannot be.
Late as he left the shore, she lingered there,
Till, less and less, he melted into air! —
Sigh after sigh steals from her gentle frame,
And say — that murmur — was it not his name?
She turns, and thinks; and, lost in wild amaze,
Gazes again, and could forever gaze!
Nor can thy flute, ALONSO, now excite
As in VALENCIA, when, with fond delight,
FRANCISCA, waking, to the lattice flew,
So soon to love and to be wretched too!
Hers through a convent-grate to send her last adieu.
— Yet who now comes uncalled; and round and round,
And near and nearer flutters to the sound;
Then stirs not, breathes not — on enchanted ground?
Who now lets fall the flowers she culled to wear
When he, who promised, should at eve be there;
And faintly smiles, and hangs her head aside
The tear that glistens on her cheek to hide?
Ah, who but CORA? — till, inspired, possessed,
At once she springs, and clasps it to her breast!
Soon from the bay the mingling crowd ascends,
Kindred first met! by sacred instinct Friends!
Through citron-groves, and fields of yellow maize,[1]
Through plantain-walks where not a sunbeam plays.
Here blue savannas fade into the sky,
There forests frown in midnight majesty;
Ceiba,[2] and Indian fig, and plane sublime,
Nature's first-born, and reverenced by Time!

There sits the bird that speaks ! [3] there, quivering, rise
Wings that reflect the glow of evening-skies !
Half bird, half fly,[4] the fairy king of flowers [5]
Reigns there, and revels through the fragrant hours ; [6]
Gem full of life, and joy and song divine,
Soon in the virgin's graceful ear to shine.[7]
'T was he that sung, if ancient Fame speaks truth,
" Come ! follow, follow to the Fount of Youth !
I quaff the ambrosial mists that round it rise,
Dissolved and lost in dreams of Paradise ! "
For there called forth, to bless a happier hour,
It met the sun in many a rainbow-shower !
Murmuring delight, its living waters rolled
'Mid branching palms and amaranths of gold ! [8]

CANTO XI.

Evening — A Banquet — The Ghost of Cazziva.

THE tamarind closed her leaves ; the marmoset
Dreamed on his bough, and played the mimic yet.
Fresh from the lake the breeze of twilight blew,
And vast and deep the mountain-shadows grew ;
When many a fire-fly, shooting through the glade,
Spangled the locks of many a lovely maid,
Who now danced forth to strew our path with flowers,
And hymn our welcome to celestial bowers.[1]
There odorous lamps adorned the festal rite,
And guavas blushed as in the vales of light.[2]
There silent sate many an unbidden guest,[3]
Whose steadfast looks a secret dread impressed ;

Not there forgot the sacred fruit that fed
At nightly feasts the spirits of the dead,
Mingling in scenes that mirth to mortals give,
But by their sadness known from those that live.
  There met, as erst, within the wonted grove,
Unmarried girls and youths that died for love!
Sons now beheld their ancient sires again;
And sires, alas! their sons in battle-slain! [4]
  But whence that sigh? 'T was from a heart that broke!
And whence that voice? As from the grave it spoke!
And who, as unresolved the feast to share,
Sits half-withdrawn in faded splendor there?
'T is he of yore, the warrior and the sage,
Whose lips have moved in prayer from age to age;
Whose eyes, that wandered as in search before,
Now on COLUMBUS fixed — to search no more!
CAZZIVA,[5] gifted in his day to know
The gathering signs of a long night of woe;
Gifted by those who give but to enslave;
No rest in death! no refuge in the grave!
— With sudden spring as at the shout of war,
He flies! and, turning in his flight, from far
Glares through the gloom like some portentous star!
Unseen, unheard! Hence, minister of ill! [6]
Hence, 't is not yet the hour! though come it will!
They that foretold — too soon shall they fulfil; [7]
When forth they rush as with the torrent's sweep,
And deeds are done that make the angels weep!
  Hark, o'er the busy mead the shell proclaims [9]
Triumphs, and masques, and high heroic games.
And now the old sit round; and now the young
Climb the green boughs, the murmuring doves among.

Who claims the prize, when wingéd feet contend;
When twanging bows the flaming arrows send?[10]
Who stands self-centred in the field of fame,
And, grappling, flings to earth a giant's frame?
Whilst all, with anxious hearts and eager eyes,
Bend as he bends, and, as he rises, rise!
And CORA's self, in pride of beauty here,
Trembles with grief and joy, and hope and fear!
(She who, the fairest, ever flew the first,
With cup of balm to quench his burning thirst;
Knelt at his head, her fan-leaf in her hand,
And hummed the air that pleased him, while she fanned)
How blest his lot! — though, by the Muse unsung,
His name shall perish, when his knell is rung.
That night, transported, with a sigh I said
"'T is all a dream!" — Now, like a dream, 't is fled;
And many and many a year has passed away,
And I alone remain to watch and pray!
Yet oft in darkness, on my bed of straw,
Oft I awake and think on what I saw!
The groves, the birds, the youths, the nymphs recall,
And CORA, loveliest, sweetest of them all!

CANTO XII.

A Vision.

STILL would I speak of him, before I went,
Who among us a life of sorrow spent,[1]
And, dying, left a world his monument;

Still, if the time allowed! My hour draws near;
But he will prompt me when I faint with fear.
— Alas, he hears me not! He cannot hear!
  Twice the moon filled her silver urn with light.
Then from the throne an angel winged his flight;
He, who unfixed the compass, and assigned
O'er the wild waves a pathway to the wind;
Who, while approached by none but spirits pure,
Wrought, in his progress through the dread obscure,
Signs like the ethereal bow — that shall endure! [2]
  As he descended through the upper air,
Day broke on day [3] as God himself were there!
Before the great discoverer, laid to rest,
He stood, and thus his secret soul addressed.[4]
  "The wind recalls thee; its still voice obey.
Millions await thy coming; hence, away.
To thee blest tidings of great joy consigned,
Another nature, and a new mankind!
The vain to dream, the wise to doubt, shall cease;
Young men be glad, and old depart in peace! [5]
Hence! though assembling in the fields of air,
Now, in a night of clouds, thy foes prepare
To rock the globe with elemental wars,
And dash the floods of ocean to the stars; [6]
To bid the meek repine, the valiant weep,
And thee restore thy secret to the deep! [7]
  "Not then to leave thee! to their vengeance cast,
Thy heart their aliment, their dire repast! [8]

* * * * * *

To other eyes shall Mexico unfold
Her feathered tapestries, and roofs of gold,

To other eyes, from distant cliff descried,[9]
Shall the PACIFIC roll his ample tide;
There destined soon rich argosies to ride.
Chains thy reward! beyond the ATLANTIC wave
Hung in thy chamber, buried in thy grave![10]
Thy reverend form[11] to time and grief a prey,
A spectre wandering in the light of day![12]
"What though thy gray hairs to the dust descend,
Their scent shall track thee, track thee to the end;
Thy sons reproached with their great father's fame,[13]
And on his world inscribed another's name!
That world a prison-house, full of sights of woe,
Where groans burst forth, and tears in torrents flow!
These gardens of the sun, sacred to song,
By dogs of carnage,[14] howling loud and long,
Swept — till the voyager, in the desert air,[15]
Starts back to hear his altered accents there![16]
"Not thine the olive, but the sword to bring;
Not peace, but war! Yet from these shores shall spring
Peace without end;[17] from these, with blood defiled,
Spread the pure spirit of thy Master mild!
Here, in His train, shall arts and arms attend,[18]
Arts to adorn, and arms but to defend.
Assembling here, all nations shall be blest;[19]
The sad be comforted; the weary rest;
Untouched shall drop the fetters from the slave;[20]
And He shall rule the world he died to save!
"Hence, and rejoice. The glorious work is done.
A spark is thrown that shall eclipse the sun!
And, though bad men shall long thy course pursue
As erst the ravening brood o'er chaos flew,[21]

He, whom I serve, shall vindicate his reign;
The spoiler spoiled of all;[22] the slayer slain;[23]
The tyrant's self, oppressing and opprest,
Mid gems and gold unenvied and unblest:[24]
While to the starry sphere thy name shall rise,
(Not there unsung thy generous enterprise!)
Thine in all hearts to dwell — by Fame enshrined,
With those, the few, that live but for mankind;
Thine evermore, transcendant happiness!
World beyond world to visit and to bless."

On the two last leaves, and written in another hand, are some stanzas in the romance or ballad measure of the Spaniards. The subject is an adventure soon related.

Thy lonely watch-tower, Larenille,
Had lost the western sun;
And loud and long from hill to hill
Echoed the evening-gun,
When Hernan, rising on his oar,
Shot like an arrow from the shore.
— "Those lights are on St. Mary's Isle;
They glimmer from the sacred pile."[1]
The waves were rough; the hour was late.
But soon across the Tinto borne,
Thrice he blew the signal-horn,
He blew and would not wait.
Home by his dangerous path he went;
Leaving, in rich habiliment,
Two strangers at the convent-gate.

They ascended by steps hewn out in the rock; and, having asked for admittance, were lodged there.

Brothers in arms the guests appeared;
The youngest with a princely grace!
Short and sable was his beard,
Thoughtful and wan his face.
His velvet cap a medal bore,
And ermine fringed his broidered vest;
And, ever sparkling on his breast,
An image of St. John he wore.[2]

The eldest had a rougher aspect, and there was craft in his eye He stood a little behind, in a long black mantle, his hand resting on the hilt of his sword; and his white hat and white shoes glittered in the moonshine.[3]

"Not here unwelcome, though unknown.
Enter and rest!" the friar said.
The moon, that through the portal shone,
Shone on his reverend head.
Through many a court and gallery dim
Slowly he led, the burial-hymn
Swelling from the distant choir.
But now the holy men retire;
The arched cloisters issuing through,
In long, long order, two and two.

* * * * * *

When other sounds had died away,
And the waves were heard alone,
They entered, though unused to pray,
Where God was worshipped, night and day,
And the dead knelt round in stone;
They entered, and from aisle to aisle
Wandered with folded arms a while,
Where on his altar-tomb reclined[4]
The crosiered abbot; and the knight,
In harness for the Christian fight,
His hands in supplication joined; —
Then said, as in a solemn mood,
"Now stand we where COLUMBUS stood!"

* * * * * *

"PEREZ,[5] thou good old man," they cried,
"And art thou in thy place of rest? —
Though in the western world his grave,[6]
That other world, the gift he gave,[7]

Would ye were sleeping side by side!
Of all his friends he loved thee best."

* * * * * *
* * * * * *

The supper in the chamber done,
Much of a southern sea they spake,
And of that glorious city[8] won
Near the setting of the sun,
Throned in a silver lake;
Of seven kings in chains of gold,[9]
And deeds of death by tongue untold,
Deeds such as breathed in secret there
Had shaken the confession-chair!

The eldest swore by our Lady,[10] the youngest by his conscience;[11] while the Franciscan, sitting by in his gray habit, turned away and crossed himself again and again. "Here is a little book," said he at last, "the work of him in his shroud below. It tells of things you have mentioned; and, were Cortes and Pizarro here, it might perhaps make them reflect for a moment." The youngest smiled as he took it into his hand. He read it aloud to his companion with an unfaltering voice; but, when he laid it down, a silence ensued; nor was he seen to smile again that night.[12] "The curse is heavy," said he at parting, "but Cortes may live to disappoint it." — "Ay, and Pizarro too!"

*** A circumstance, recorded by Herrera, renders this visit not improbable. "In May, 1528, Cortes arrived unexpectedly at Palos; and, soon after he had landed, he and Pizarro met and rejoiced; and it was remarkable that they should meet, as they were two of the most renowned men in the world." B. Diaz makes no mention of the interview; but, relating an occurrence that took place at this time in Palos, says "that Cortes was now absent at Neustra Senora de la Rábida." The convent is within half a league of the town.

NOTES.

CANTO I.

(1) In him was fulfilled the ancient prophecy,

> . . . . . venient annis
> Secula seris, quibus Oceanus
> Vincula rerum laxet, &c.
>
> *Seneca in Medea*, v. 374.

Which Tasso has imitated in his Gierusalemme Liberata.

> Tempo verrà, che fian d'Ercole i segni
> Favola, vile, &c. c. xv. 30.

The poem opens on Friday the 14th of September, 1492.

(2) In the original, *El Almirante.* "In Spanish America," says M. de Humboldt, "when *El Almirante* is pronounced without the addition of a name, that of Columbus is understood; as, from the lips of a Mexican, *El Marchese* signifies Cortes;" and as, among the Florentines, *Il Segretario* has always signified Machiavel.

(3) "It has pleased our Lord to grant me faith and assurance for this enterprise. He has opened my understanding, and made me most willing to go." — *See his Life by his Son, Ferd. Columbus, entitled, Hist. del Almirante Don Christoval. Colon.* c. 4 & 37.

His will begins thus: "In the name of the most holy Trinity, who inspired me with the idea, and who afterwards made it clear to me, that by traversing the ocean westwardly," &c.

(4) The compass might well be an object of superstition. A belief is said to prevail, even at this day, that it will refuse to traverse when there is a dead body on board.

(5) *Herrera*, dec. I. lib. i. c. 9.

(6) When these regions were to be illuminated, says Acosta, cùm divino concilio decretum esset, prospectum etiam divinitus est, ut tam longi itineris dux certus hominibus præberetur. — *De Natura Novi Orbis.*

A romantic circumstance is related of some early navigator in the Histoire Gén. des Voyages, I. i. 2. "On trouva dans l'île de Cuervo une statue équestre, couverte d'un manteau, mais la tête nue, qui tenoit de la main gauche la bride du cheval, et qui montroit l'occident de la main droite. Il y avoit sur le bas d'un roc quelques lettres gravees, qui ne furent point entendues; mais il parut clairement que le signe de la main regardoit l'Amérique."

(7) Rev. 19: 17.

(8) The more Christian opinion is, that God, with eyes of compassion, as it were, looking down from heaven, called forth those *winds of mercy*, whereby this new world received the hope of salvation. — *Preambles to the Decades of the Ocean.*

(9) To return was deemed impossible, as it blew always from home. — *Hist. del Almirante*, c. 19. *Nos pavidi — at pater Anchises — lætus.*

CANTO II.

(1) Tasso employs preternatural agents on a similar occasion,

Trappassa, et ecco in quel silvestre loco
Sorge improvisa la città del foco. — xiii. 33.

Gli incanti d'Ismeno, che ingannano con delusioni, altro non significano, che la falsità delle ragioni, et delle persuasioni, la qual si genera nella moltitudine, et varietà de' pareri, et de' discorsi humani.

(2) See Plato's Timæus; where mention is made of mighty kingdoms, which, in a day and a night, had disappeared in the Atlantic, rendering its waters unnavigable.

Si quæras Helicen et Burin, Achaïdas urbes,
Invenies sub aquis.

At the destruction of Callao, in 1747, no more than one of all the inhabitants escaped; and he by a providence the most extraordinary. This man was on the fort that overlooked the harbor, going to strike the flag, when he perceived the sea to retire to a considerable distance; and then, swelling mountain-high, it returned with great violence. The people ran from their houses in terror and confusion; he heard a cry of *Miserere* rise from all parts of the city; and immediately all was silent; the sea had entirely overwhelmed it, and buried it forever in its bosom; but the same wave that destroyed it drove a little boat by the place where he stood, into which he threw himself and was saved.

(3) The description of a submarine forest is here omitted by the translator.

League beyond league gigantic foliage spread,
Shadowing old Ocean on his rocky bed;
The lofty summits of resounding woods,
That grasped the depths, and grappled with the floods;
Such as had climbed the mountain's azure height,
When forth he came and reässumed his right.

(4) Historians are not silent on the subject. The sailors, according to Herrera, saw the signs of an inundated country (tierras anegadas); and it was the general expectation that they should end their lives there, as others had done in the frozen sea, "where St. Amaro suffers no ship to stir backward or forward." — *Hist. del Almirante*, c. 19.

(5) The author seems to have anticipated his long slumber in the library of the Fathers.

(6) They may give me what name they please. I am servant of him, &c. — *Hist. del Almirante*, c. 2.

(7) As St. Christopher carried Christ over the deep waters, so Columbus went over safe, himself and his company. — *Hist.* c. 1.

(8) Water-spouts. — *See Edwards' History of the West Indies*, I. 12. Note.

CANTO III.

(1) Many of the first discoverers ended their days in a hermitage or a cloister.

(2) Vast, indeed, must be those dismal regions, if it be true, as conjectured (*Kircher. Mund. Subt.* I. 202), that Ætna, in her eruptions, has discharged twenty times her original bulk. Well might she be called by Euripides (*Troades*, v. 222) the *Mother of Mountains;* yet Ætna herself is but "a mere firework, when compared to the burning summits of the Andes."

(3) Gods, yet confessed later. —*Milton.* Ils ne laissent pas d'en être les esclaves, et de les honorer plus que le grand Esprit, qui de sa nature est bon. —*Lafitau.*

(4) Rivers in South America. Their collision with the tide has the effect of a tempest.

(5) Lakes of North America. Huron is above a thousand miles in circumference. Ontario receives the waters of the Niagara, so famous for its falls, and discharges itself into the Atlantic by the river St. Lawrence.

(6) La plûpart de ces îles ne sont en effet que des pointes de montagnes : et la mer, qui est au-delà, est une vraie mer Méditerranée. —*Buffon.*

(7) The dominion of a bad angel over an unknown sea, *infestandole con torbellinos y tempestades*, and his flight before a Christian hero, are described in glowing language by Ovalle. —*Hist. de Chile.* IV. 8.

(8) Alluding to the oracles of the islanders, so soon to become silent; and particularly to a prophecy, delivered down from their ancestors, and sung with loud lamentations (*Petr. Martyr*, dec. 3, lib. 7) at their solemn festivals (*Herrera*, I. iii. 4), that the country would be laid waste on the arrival of strangers, completely clad, from a region near the rising of the sun. —*Ibid.* II. 5, 2. It is said that Cazziva, a great Cacique, after long fasting and many ablutions, had an interview with one of the Zemi, who announced to him this terrible event (*Hist.* c. 62), as the oracles of Latona, according to Herodotus (II. 152), predicted the overthrow of the eleven kings in Egypt, on the appearance of men of brass, risen out of the sea.

Nor did this prophecy exist among the islanders alone. It influenced the councils of Montezuma, and extended almost universally over the forests of America. —*Cortes. Herrera. Gomara.* "The demons, whom they worshipped," says Acosta, "in this instance told them the truth."

(9) These scattered fragments may be compared to shreds of old arras, or reflections from a river broken and confused by the oar; and now and then perhaps the imagination of the reader may supply more than is lost. Si qua latent, meliora putat. "It is remarkable," says the elder Pliny, "that the Iris of Aristides, the Tyndarides of Nicomachus, and the Venus of Apelles, are held in higher admiration than their finished works." And is it not so in almost everything?

Call up him that left half told
The story of Cambuscan bold.

CANTO IV.

(1) Light vessels, formerly used by the Spaniards and Portuguese.

(2) In the Lusiad, to beguile the heavy hours at sea, Veloso relates to his companions of the second watch the story of the Twelve Knights. — L. vi.

(3) Among those who went with Columbus were many adventurers, and gentlemen of the court. Primero was the game then in fashion. — *See Vega*, p. 2, lib. iii. c. 9.

(4) Many such appellations occur in Bernal Diaz, c. 204.

CANTO V.

(1) Many sighed and wept; and every hour seemed a year, says Herrera. — I. i. 9 and 10.

(2) A luminous appearance, of good omen.

(3) His public procession to the convent of La Rábida on the day before he set sail. It was there that his sons had received their education; and he himself appears to have passed some time there, the venerable guardian, Juan Perez de Marchena, being his zealous and affectionate friend. The ceremonies of his departure and return are represented in many of the fresco-paintings in the palaces of Genoa.

(4) "But I was most afflicted when I thought of my two sons, whom I had left behind me in a strange country . . . . before I had done, or, at least, could be known to have done, anything which might incline your highnesses to remember them. And though I consoled myself with the reflection that our Lord would not suffer so earnest an endeavor for the exaltation of his church to come to nothing, yet I considered that, on account of my unworthiness," &c. — *Hist.* c. 37.

(5) Gonsalvo, or, as he is called in Castilian, Gonzalo Hernandez de Cordova; already known by the name of The Great Captain. Granada surrendered on the second of January, 1492. Columbus set sail on the third of August following.

(6) Probably a soldier of fortune. There were more than one of the name on board.

CANTO VI.

(1) Not but that in the profession of arms there are at all times many noble natures. Let a soldier of the age of Elizabeth speak for those who had commanded under him, those whom he calls "the chief men of action."

"Now that I have tried them, I would choose them for friends, if I had them not; before I had tried them, God and his providence chose them for me. I love them for mine own sake; for I find sweetness in their conversation, strong assistance in their employments with me, and happiness in their friendship. I love them for their virtue's sake, and for their greatness of mind (for little minds, though never so fu'l of virtue, can be but a little virtuous), and for their great understanding; for to undeistand little things, or things not of use, is little better than to understand nothing at all. I love them for their affections; for self-loving men love ease, pleasure and profit; but they that love pains, danger and fame, show that they love public profit more than themselves. I love them for my country's sake; for they are England's best armor of defence, and weapons of offence. If we may have peace, they have purchased it; if we must have war, they must manage it," &c.

(2) Hist. c. 3.

(3) The Cross of the South; "una Croce maravigliosa, e di tanta bellezza," says Andrea Corsali, a Florentine, writing to Giuliano of Medicis in 1515, "che non mi pare ad alcuno segno celeste doverla comparare. E s'io non mi inganno, credo che sia questo il crusero di che Dante parlò nel principio del Purgatorio *con spirito profetico*, dicendo,

I'mi volsi a man destra, e posi mente
All' altro polo, e vidi quattro stelle," &c.

It is still sacred in the eyes of the Spaniards. "Un sentiment religieux les attache à une constellation dont la forme leur rappelle ce signe de la foi planté par leurs ancêtres dans les déserts du nouveau monde."

(4) Le Condor est le même oiseau que le Roc des Orientaux. — *Buffon*. "By the Peruvians," says Vega, "he was anciently worshipped; and there were those who claimed their descent from him." In these degenerate days he still ranks above the eagle.

(5) As the Roc of the east is said to have carried off the elephant. — *See Marco Polo.* Axalhua, or the Emperor, is the name in the Mexican language for the great serpent of America.

(6) Tierra del Fuego.

(7) Northern extremity of the New World. — *See Cook's Last Voyage.*

(8) Mines of Chili; which extend, says Ovalle, to the Strait of Magellan. — I. 4.

(9) A custom not peculiar to the Western Hemisphere. The Tunguses of Siberia hang their dead on trees; "parceque la terre ne se laisse point ouvrir." — *M. Pauw.*

CANTO VII.

(1) "Aquella noche triste." The night on which Cortes made his famous retreat from Mexico through the street of Tlacopan still goes by the name of La Noche Triste. — *Humboldt.*

(2) Pizarro used to dress in this fashion; after Gonsalvo, whom he had served under in Italy.

(3) A species of Bat in South America; which refreshes by the gentle agitation of its wings, while it sucks the blood of the sleeper, turning his sleep into death.

(4) . . . . Now one,
Now other, as their shape served best his end.

Undoubtedly, says Herrera, the Infernal Spirit assumed various shapes in that region of the world.

(5) Many a modern reader will exclaim, in the language of Pococuranté, "Quelle triste extravagance!" Let a great theologian of that day, a monk of the Augustine order, be consulted on the subject. "Corpus ille perimere vel jugulare potest; nec id modò, verùm et animam ita urgere, et in angustum coarctare novit, ut in momento quoque illi excedendum sit." — *Lutherus, De Missa Privata.*

The Roman ritual requires three signs of possession.

(6) —magnum si pectore possit
Excussisse deum.

(7) Euripides in Alcest, v. 255.

(8) Voci alte e fioche, e suon di man con elle. — *Dante.*

(9) The same language had been addressed to Isabella. — *Hist.* c. 15.

(10) His miraculous escape, in early life, during a sea-fight off the coast of Portugal. — *Hist.* c. 5.

(11) Nudo nocchier, promettitor di regni!

By the Genoese and the Spaniards he was regarded as a man resolved on "a wild dedication of himself to unpathed waters, undreamed shores;" and the court of Portugal endeavored to rob him of the glory of his enterprise, by secretly dispatching a vessel in the course which he had pointed out. "Lorsqu'il avait promis un nouvel hémisphère," says Voltaire, "on lui avait soutenu que cet hémisphère ne pouvait exister; et quand il l'eut découvert, on prétendit qu'il avait été connu depuis long-temps."

(12) He used to affirm that he stood in need of God's particular assistance; like Moses, when he led forth the people of Israel, who forbore to lay violent hands upon him, because of the miracles which God wrought by his means. "So," said the Admiral, "did it happen to me on that voyage." — *Hist.* c. 19. — "And so easily," says a commentator, "are the workings of the Evil one overcome by the power of God!"

(13) This denunciation, fulfilled as it appears to be in the eleventh canto, may remind the reader of the Harpy's in Virgil. — *Æn.* III. v. 247.

CANTO VIII.

(1) Ex ligno lucido confectum, et arte mirâ laboratum. — *P. Martyr,* dec. i. 5.

(2) The Simoom.

(3) Salve, regina. — *Herrera,* I. i. 12. It was the usual service, and always sung with great solemnity. "I remember one evening," says Oviedo, "when the ship was in full sail, and all the men were on their knees, singing Salve, regina," &c. — *Relacion Sommaria.* The hymn, O Sanctissima, is still to be heard after sunset along the shores of Sicily, and its effect may be better conceived than described.

(4) I believe that he was *chosen* for this great service; and that, because he was to be so truly an apostle, as in effect he proved to be, therefore was his origin obscure; that

therein he might resemble those who were called to make known the name of the Lord from the seas and rivers, and not from courts and palaces. And I believe also, that, as in most of his doings he was guarded by some special providence, his very name was not without some mystery; for in it is expressed the wonder he performed; inasmuch as he conveyed to a new world the grace of the Holy Ghost, &c. — *Hist.* c. 1.

(5) A light in the midst of darkness, signifying the spiritual light that he came to spread there. — *F. Col.* c. 22. *Herrera*, I. i. 12.

(6) Pedro Gutierrez, a page of the king's chamber. Rodrigo Sanchez of Segovia, Comptroller of the Fleet.

CANTO IX.

(1) Signifying to the Infernal Powers (all' infierno todo) the will of the Most High, that they should renounce a world over which they had tyrannized for so many ages. — *Ovalle*, iv. 5.

(2) "This country excels all others, as far as the day surpasses the night in splendor. Nor is there a better people in the world. They love their neighbor as themselves; their conversation is the sweetest imaginable, their faces always smiling; and so gentle, so affectionate are they, that I swear to your Highnesses," &c. — *Hist.* c. 30, 33.

(3) Dryades formosissimas, aut nativas fontium nymphas de quibus fabulatur antiquitas, se vidisse arbitrati sunt. — *P. Martyr*, dec. i. lib. v.

And an eminent painter of the present day, when he first saw the Apollo of the Belvidere, was struck with its resemblance to an American warrior. — *West's Discourses in the Royal Academy*, 1794.

(4) So, in like manner, when Cortes and his companions appeared at the gates of Mexico, the young exclaimed, "They are Gods!" while the old shook their heads, saying, "They are those of whom the prophets spake; and they are come to reign over us!" — *Herrera.*

(5) "The Cacique came to the shore in a sort of palanquin, attended by his ancient men. The gifts which he received from me were afterwards carried before him." — *Hist.* c. 32.

(6) The ring of Gyges, the lamp of Aladdin, and the horse of the Tartar king.

(7) For the effects of the telescope and the mirror on an uncultivated mind, see *Wallis' Voyage round the World*, c. 2 and 6.

CANTO X.

(1) Ætas est illis aurea. Apertis vivunt hortis. — *P. Martyr*, dec. i. 3.

(2) The wild cotton-tree, often mentioned in history. "Cortes," says Bernal Diaz, "took possession of the country in the following manner: Drawing his sword, he gave three cuts with it into a great Ceiba, and said —."

(3) The parrot, as described by Aristotle.—*Hist. Animal.* viii. 12.

(4) Here are birds so small, says Herrera, that, though they are birds, they are taken for bees or butterflies.

(5) The Humming bird. Kakopit (florum regulus) is the name of an Indian bird, referred to this class by Seba.

(6) There also was heard the wild cry of the Flamingo.

> What clarion winds along the yellow sands?
> Far in the deep the giant-fisher stands,
> Folding his wings of flame.

(7) Il sert après sa mort à parer les jeunes Indiennes, qui portent en pendans d'oreilles deux de ces charmans oiseaux.—*Buffon.*

(8) According to an ancient tradition.—See *Oviedo, Vega, Herrera,* &c. Not many years afterwards a Spaniard of distinction wandered everywhere in search of it; and no wonder, as Robertson observes, when Columbus himself could imagine that he had found the seat of Paradise.

CANTO XI.

(1) *P. Martyr,* dec. i.

(2) They believed that the souls of good men were conveyed to a pleasant valley, abounding in guavas and other delicious fruits.—*Herrera,* I. iii. 3. *Hist. del Almirante,* c. 62.

(3) "The dead walk abroad at night, and feast with the living" (*F. Columbus,* c. 62); and "eat of the fruit called Guannàba."—*P. Martyr,* dec. i. 9.

(4) War reverses the order of nature. In time of peace, says Herodotus, the sons bury their fathers; in time of war, the fathers bury their sons! But the gods have willed it so.—I. 87.

(5) An ancient Cacique, in his lifetime and after his death, employed by the Zemi to alarm his people.—*See Hist.* c. 62.

(6) The author is speaking in his inspired character. Hidden things are revealed to him, and placed before his mind as if they were present.

(7) Nor could they (the Powers of Darkness) have more effectually prevented the progress of the faith, than by desolating the New World; by burying nations alive in mines, or consigning them, in all their errors, to the sword.—*Relacion de B. de las Casas.*

(8) Not man alone, but many other animals, became extinct there.

(9) *P. Martyr,* dec. iii. c 7.

(10) *Rocheforte,* c. xx.

CANTO XII.

(1) For a summary of his life and character, see "An Account of the European Settlements." — P. I. c. 8. Of him it might have been said, as it was afterwards said of Bacon, and a nobler tribute there could not be: "In his adversity I ever prayed that God would give him strength, for greatness he could not want. Neither could I condole for him in a word or syllable, as knowing no accident could do harm to virtue, but rather help to make it manifest." — *B. Jonson.*

(2) It is remarkable that these phenomena still remain among the mysteries of nature.

(3) E disubito parve giorno a giorno
Essere aggiunto, come quei, che puote,
Avesse'l Ciel d'un' altro Sole adorno.
Paradiso, I. 61.

(4) Te tua fata docebo. — *Virg.*
Saprai di tua vita il viaggio. — *Dante.*

(5) P. Martyr, *Epist.* 133, 152.

(6) When he entered the Tagus, all the seamen ran from all parts to behold, as it were some wonder, a ship that had escaped so terrible a storm. — *Hist.* c. 40.

(7) I wrote on a parchment that I had discovered what I had promised; and, having put it into a cask, I threw it into the sea. — *Ibid.* c. 37.

(8) See the *Eumenides of Æschylus*, v. 305, &c.

(9) Balboa immediately concluded it to be the ocean for which Columbus had searched in vain; and when, at length, after a toilsome march among the mountains, his guides pointed out to him the summit from which it might be seen, he commanded his men to halt, and *went up alone.* — *Herrera*, I. x. 1.

(10) I always saw them in his room, and he ordered them to be buried with his body. — *Hist.* c. 86.

(11) His person, says Herrera, had an air of grandeur. His hair, from many hardships, had long been gray. In him you saw a man of an unconquerable courage and high thoughts; patient of wrongs, calm in adversity, ever trusting in God; and, had he lived in ancient times, statues and temples would have been erected to him without number, and his name would have been placed among the stars.

(12) See the *Eumenides of Æschylus*, v. 246. *Agamemnon of Æschylus*, v. 82.

(13) "There go the sons of him who discovered those fatal countries," &c. — *Hist.* c. 85.

(14) One of these, on account of his extraordinary sagacity and fierceness, received the full allowance of a soldier. His name was Berezillo.

(15) With my own eyes I saw kingdoms as full of people as hives are full of bees; and now where are they? — *Las Casas.*

(16) No unusual effect of an exuberant vegetation. "The air was so vitiated," says an African traveller, "that our torches burnt dim, and seemed ready to be extinguished; and even the human voice lost its natural tone."

(17) See Washington's Farewell Address to his fellow-citizens.

(18) "There are those alive," said an illustrious orator, "whose memory might touch the two extremities. Lord Bathurst, in 1704, was of an age to comprehend such things; and, if his angel had then drawn up the curtain, and, while he was gazing with admiration, had pointed out to him a speck, and had told him, 'Young man, there is America, which, at this day, serves for little more than to amuse you with stories of savage men and uncouth manners; yet shall, before you taste of death,'" &c. — *Burke in* 1775.

(19) How simple were the manners of the early colonists! The first ripening of any European fruit was distinguished by a family festival. Garcilasso de la Vega relates how his dear father, the valorous Andres, collected together in his chamber seven or eight gentlemen to share with him three asparaguses, the first that ever grew on the table-land of Cusco. When the operation of dressing them was over (and it is minutely described) he distributed the two largest among his friends; begging that the company would not take it ill if he reserved the third for himself, *as it was a thing from Spain.*

North America became instantly an asylum for the oppressed; Huguenots, and Catholics, and sects of every name and country. Such were the first settlers in Carolina and Maryland, Pennsylvania and New England. Nor is South America altogether without a claim to the title. Even now, while I am writing, the ancient house of Braganza is on its passage across the Atlantic,

Cum sociis, natoque, Penatibus, et magnis dis.

(20) Je me transporte quelquefois au delà d'un siècle. J'y vois le bonheur à côté de l'industrie, la douce tolérance remplaçant la farouche inquisition; j'y vois un jour de fête; Péruviens, Mexicains, Américains libres, François s'embrassant comme des frères, et bénissant le règne de la liberté, qui doit amener partout une harmonie universelle. Mais les mines, les esclaves, que deviendront-ils? Les mines se fermeront; les esclaves seront les frères de leurs maitres. — *Brissot.*

There is a prophetic stanza, written a century ago by Bp. Berkeley, which I must quote, though I may suffer by the comparison:

Westward the course of empire takes its way.
The four first acts already past,
A fifth shall close the drama with the day.
Time's noblest offspring is the last.

(21) See *Paradise Lost*, X.

(22) Cortes. A peine put-il obtenir audience de Charles-Quint: un jour il fendit la presse qui entourait le coche de l'empereur, et monta sur l'étrier de la portière. Charles demanda quel était cet homme; "C'est," répondit Cortes, "celui qui vous a donné plus d'états que vos pères ne vous ont laissé de villes." — *Voltaire.*

(17) "Almost all," says Las Casas, "have perished. The innocent blood which they had shed cried aloud for vengeance; the sighs, the tears of so many victims, went up before God."

(24) L'Espagne a fait comme ce roi insensé qui demanda que tout ce qu'il toucheroit se convertit en or, et qui fut obligé de revenir aux dieux pour les prier de finir sa misère. — *Montesquieu.*

(1) The Convent of La Rábida.

(2) See *Bernal Diaz*, c. 203; and also a well-known portrait of Cortes, ascribed to Titian. Cortes was now in the forty-third, Pizarro in the fiftieth year of his age.

(3) *Augustin Zaratè*, lib. iv. c. 9.

(4) An interpolation.

(5) Late Superior of the House.

(6) In the chancel of the cathedral of St. Domingo.
An anachronism. The body of Columbus was not yet removed from Seville.
It is almost unnecessary to point out another in the Ninth Canto. The telescope was not then in use; though described long before, with great accuracy, by Roger Bacon.

(7) The words of the epitaph. "A Castilia y a Leon nuevo Mundo dio Colon."

(8) Mexico.

(9) Afterwards the arms of Cortes and his descendants.

(10) *Fernandez*, lib. ii. c. 63.

(11) *B. Diaz*, c. 203.

(12) "After the death of Guatimotzin," says B. Diaz, "he became gloomy and restless; rising continually from his bed, and wandering about in the dark." "Nothing prospered with him; and it was ascribed to the curses he was loaded with."

JACQUELINE.

1813.

JACQUELINE.

I.

'T WAS Autumn; through Provence had ceased
The vintage, and the vintage-feast.
The sun had set behind the hill,
The moon was up, and all was still,
And from the convent's neighboring tower
The clock had tolled the midnight-hour,
When Jacqueline came forth alone,
Her kerchief o'er her tresses thrown;
A guilty thing and full of fears,
Yet, ah! how lovely in her tears!
She starts, and what has caught her eye?
What — but her shadow gliding by?
She stops, she pants; with lips apart
She listens — to her beating heart!
Then, through the scanty orchard stealing,
The clustering boughs her track concealing,
She flies, nor casts a thought behind,
But gives her terrors to the wind;
Flies from her home, the humble sphere
Of all her joys and sorrows here,
Her father's house of mountain-stone,
And by a mountain-vine o'ergrown.

At such an hour in such a night,
So calm, so clear, so heavenly bright,
Who would have seen, and not confessed
It looked as all within were blest?
What will not woman, when she loves?
Yet lost, alas! who can restore her? —
She lifts the latch, the wicket moves;
And now the world is all before her.
  Up rose St. Pierre, when morning shone;
— And Jacqueline, his child, was gone!
O, what the maddening thought that came?
Dishonor coupled with his name!
By Condé at Rocroy he stood;
By Turenne, when the Rhine ran blood.
Two banners of Castile he gave
Aloft in Notre Dame to wave;
Nor did thy cross, St. Louis, rest
Upon a purer, nobler breast.
He slung his old sword by his side,
And snatched his staff and rushed to save;
Then sunk — and on his threshold cried,
"O, lay me in my grave!
— Constance! Claudine! where were ye then?
But stand not there. Away! away!
Thou, Frederic, by thy father stay.
Though old, and now forgot of men,
Both must not leave him in a day."
Then, and he shook his hoary head,
"Unhappy in thy youth!" he said.
"Call as thou wilt, thou call'st in vain;
No voice sends back thy name again.

To mourn is all thou hast to do;
Thy playmate lost, and teacher too."
And who but she could soothe the boy,
Or turn his tears to tears of joy?
Long had she kissed him as he slept,
Long o'er his pillow hung and wept;
And, as she passed her father's door,
She stood as she would stir no more.
But she is gone, and gone forever!
No, never shall they clasp her — never!
They sit and listen to their fears;
And he, who through the breach had led
Over the dying and the dead,
Shakes if a cricket's cry he hears!
O! she was good as she was fair.
None — none on earth above her!
As pure in thought as angels are,
To know her was to love her.
When little, and her eyes, her voice,
Her every gesture, said "rejoice,"
Her coming was a gladness;
And, as she grew, her modest grace,
Her downcast look, 't was heaven to trace,
When, shading with her hand her face,
She half inclined to sadness.
Her voice, whate'er she said, enchanted;
Like music to the heart it went.
And her dark eyes — how eloquent!
Ask what they would, 't was granted.
Her father loved her as his fame;
— And Bayard's self had done the same!

Soon as the sun the glittering pane
On the red floor in diamonds threw,
His songs she sung and sung again,
Till the last light withdrew.
Every day, and all day long,
He mused or slumbered to a song.
But she is dead to him, to all !
Her lute hangs silent on the wall ;
And on the stairs, and at the door,
Her fairy-step is heard no more !
At every meal an empty chair
Tells him that she is not there ;
She, who would lead him where he went,
Charm with her converse while he leant ;
Or, hovering, every wish prevent ;
At eve light up the chimney-nook,
Lay there his glass within his book ;
And that small chest of curious mould
(Queen Mab's, perchance, in days of old),
Tusk of elephant and gold ;
Which, when a tale is long, dispenses
Its fragrant dust to drowsy senses.
In her who mourned not, when they missed her,
The old a child, the young a sister ?
No more the orphan runs to take
From her loved hand the barley-cake.
No more the matron in the school
Expects her in the hour of rule,
To sit amid the elfin brood,
Praising the busy and the good.
The widow trims her hearth in vain.
She comes not — nor will come again.

Not now, his little lesson done,
With Frederic blowing bubbles in the sun;
Nor spinning by the fountain side
(Some story of the days of old,
Barbe Bleue or Chaperon Rouge half-told
To him who would not be denied);
Not now, to while an hour away,
Gone to the falls in Valombrè,
Where 't is night at noon of day;
Nor wandering up and down the wood,
To all but her a solitude,
Where once a wild deer, wild no more,
Her chaplet on his antlers wore,
And at her bidding stood.

II.

The day was in the golden west;
And, curtained close by leaf and flower,
The doves had cooed themselves to rest
In Jacqueline's deserted bower;
The doves — that still would at her casement peck,
And in her walks had ever fluttered round
With purple feet and shining neck,
True as the echo to the sound.
That casement, underneath the trees,
Half open to the western breeze,
Looked down, enchanting Garonnelle,
Thy wild and mulberry-shaded dell,
Round which the Alps of Piedmont rose,
The blush of sunset on their snows:

While, blithe as lark on summer-morn,
When green and yellow waves the corn,
When harebells blow in every grove,
And thrushes sing "I love! I love!"*
Within (so soon the early rain
Scatters, and 't is fair again;
Though many a drop may yet be seen
To tell us where a cloud has been) —
Within lay Frederick, o'er and o'er,
Building castles on the floor,
And feigning, as they grew in size,
New troubles and new dangers;
With dimpled cheeks and laughing eyes,
As he and fear were strangers.
St. Pierre sat by, nor saw nor smiled.
His eyes were on his loved Montaigne;
But every leaf was turned in vain.
For in that hour remorse he felt,
And his heart told him he had dealt
Unkindly with his child.
A father may a while refuse;
But who can for another choose?
When her young blushes had revealed
The secret from herself concealed,
Why promise what her tears denied,
That she should be De Courcy's bride?
— Wouldst thou, presumptuous as thou art,
O'er Nature play the tyrant's part,
And with the hand compel the heart?
O rather, rather hope to bind
The ocean-wave, the mountain-wind;

* Cantando "Io amo! Io amo!" — TASSO.

Or, fix thy foot upon the ground
To stop the planet rolling round.
  The light was on his face; and there
You might have seen the passions driven —
Resentment, Pity, Hope, Despair —
Like clouds across the face of Heaven.
Now he sighed heavily; and now,
His hand withdrawing from his brow,
He shut the volume with a frown,
To walk his troubled spirit down:
— When (faithful as that dog of yore*
Who wagged his tail and could no more)
Manchon, who long had snuffed the ground,
And sought and sought, but never found,
Leapt up and to the casement flew,
And looked and barked, and vanished through.
"'T is Jacqueline! 'T is Jacqueline!"
Her little brother laughing cried.
"I know her by her kirtle green,
She comes along the mountain-side;
Now turning by the traveller's seat,—
Now resting in the hermit's cave,—
Now kneeling, where the pathways meet,
To the cross on the stranger's grave.
And, by the soldier's cloak, I know
(There, there along the ridge they go)
D'Arcy, so gentle and so brave!
Look up — why will you not?" he cries,
His rosy hands before his eyes;
For on that incense-breathing eve
The sun shone out, as loth to leave.

* Argus.

"See—to the rugged rock she clings!
She calls, she faints, and D'Arcy springs;
D'Arcy, so dear to us, to all;
Who, for you told me on your knee,
When in the fight he saw you fall,
Saved you for Jacqueline and me!"

And true it was! And true the tale!
When did she sue and not prevail?
Five years before—it was the night
That on the village-green they parted,
The lilied banners streaming bright
O'er maids and mothers broken-hearted;
The drum—it drowned the last adieu,
When D'Arcy from the crowd she drew.
"One charge I have, and one alone,
Nor that refuse to take,
My father—if not for his own,
O, for his daughter's sake!"
Inly he vowed—'t was all he could;
And went and sealed it with his blood.
Nor can ye wonder. When a child,
And in her playfulness she smiled,
Up many a ladder-path* he guided
Where meteor-like the chamois glided,
Through many a misty grove.
They loved—but under Friendship's name;
And Reason, Virtue fanned the flame,
Till in their houses Discord came,
And 't was a crime to love.

* Called in the language of the country *Pas-de-l'Echelle.*

Then what was Jacqueline to do?
Her father's angry hours she knew,
And when to soothe, and when persuade;
But now her path De Courcy crossed,
Led by his falcon through the glade—
He turned, beheld, admired the maid;
And all her little arts were lost!
De Courcy, Lord of Argentiere!
Thy poverty, thy pride, St. Pierre,
Thy thirst for vengeance, sought the snare.
The day was named, the guests invited;
The bridegroom, at the gate, alighted;
When up the windings of the dell
A pastoral pipe was heard to swell,
And, lo! an humble Piedmontese,
Whose music might a lady please,
This message through the lattice bore
(She listened, and her trembling frame
Told her at once from whom it came),
"O, let us fly—to part no more!"

III.

THAT morn ('t was in Ste. Julienne's cell,
As at Ste. Julienne's sacred well
Their dream of love began)—
That morn, ere many a star was set,
Their hands had on the altar met
Before the holy man.

— And now, her strength, her courage spent,
And more than half a penitent,
She comes along the path she went.
And now the village gleams at last;
The woods, the golden meadows passed,
Where, when, Toulouse, thy splendor shone,
The Troubadour, from grove to grove,
Chanting some roundelay of love,
Would wander till the day was gone.
"All will be well, my Jacqueline!
O, tremble not — but trust in me.
The good are better made by ill,
As odors crushed are sweeter still;
And, gloomy as thy past has been,
Bright shall thy future be!"
So saying, through the fragrant shade
Gently along he led the maid,
While Manchon round and round her played:
And, as that silent glen they leave,
Where by the spring the pitchers stand,
Where glow-worms light their little lamps at eve,
And fairies revel as in fairy-land
(When Lubin calls, and Blanche steals round,
Her finger on her lip, to see;
And many an acorn-cup is found
Under the greenwood tree),
From every cot above, below,
They gather as they go —
Sabot, and coif, and collerette,
The housewife's prayer, the grandame's blessing!
Girls that adjust their locks of jet,
And look and look and linger yet,
The lovely bride caressing;

Babes that had learnt to lisp her name,
And heroes he had led to fame.
But what felt D'Arcy, when at length
Her father's gate was open flung?
Ah! then he found a giant's strength;
For round him, as for life, she clung!
And when, her fit of weeping o'er,
Onward they moved a little space,
And saw an old man sitting at the door,—
Saw his wan cheek, and sunken eye
That seemed to gaze on vacancy,—
Then, at the sight of that beloved face,
At once to fall upon his neck she flew;
But — not encouraged — back she drew,
And trembling stood in dread suspense,
Her tears her only eloquence!
All, all — the while — an awful distance keeping;
Save D'Arcy, who nor speaks nor stirs;
And one, his little hand in hers,
Who weeps to see his sister weeping.
Then Jacqueline the silence broke.
She clasped her father's knees and spoke,
Her brother kneeling too;
While D'Arcy as before looked on,
Though from his manly cheek was gone
Its natural hue.
"His praises from your lips I heard,
Till my fond heart was won;
And, if in aught his sire has erred,
O, turn not from the son! —
She, whom in joy, in grief, you nursed;
Who climbed and called you father first,

By that dear name conjures —
On her you thought — but to be kind !
When looked she up, but you inclined ?
These things, forever in her mind,
O, are they gone from yours ?
Two kneeling at your feet behold ;
One — one how young ! — nor yet the other old.
O, spurn them not —nor look so cold ! —
If Jacqueline be cast away,
Her bridal be her dying day.
— Well, well might she believe in you !
She listened, and she found it true."
He shook his aged locks of snow ;
And twice he turned, and rose to go.
She hung ; and was St. Pierre to blame,
If tears and smiles together came ?
"O, no — begone ! I 'll hear no more."
But, as he spoke, his voice relented.
"That very look thy mother wore
When she implored, and old Le Roc consented.
True, I have erred and will atone ;
For still I love him as my own.
And now, in my hands, yours with his unite ;
A father's blessing on your heads alight !
. . . Nor let the least be sent away.
All hearts shall sing 'Adieu to sorrow !'
St. Pierre has found his child to-day ;
And old and young shall dance to-morrow."

Had Louis* then before the gate dismounted,
Lost in the chase at set of sun ;

* Louis the Fourteenth.

Like Henry when he heard recounted *
The generous deeds himself had done
(What time the miller's maid Colette
Sung, while he supped, her chansonnette),
Then — when St. Pierre addressed his village-train,
Then had the monarch with a sigh confessed
A joy by him unsought and unpossessed,
— Without it what are all the rest? —
To love, and to be loved again.

* Alluding to a popular story related of Henry the Fourth, of France, similar to ours of "The King and Miller of Mansfield."

HUMAN LIFE.

1819.

THE ARGUMENT.

Introduction. Ringing of Bells in a neighboring Village on the Birth of an Heir. General Reflections on Human Life. The subject proposed. Childhood. Youth. Manhood. Love. Marriage. Domestic Happiness and Affliction. War. Peace. Civil Dissension. Retirement from Active Life. Old Age and its Enjoyments. Conclusion.

HUMAN LIFE.

The lark has sung his carol in the sky;
The bees have hummed their noon-tide harmony.
Still in the vale the village-bells ring round,
Still in Llewellyn-hall the jests resound:
For now the caudle-cup is circling there,
Now, glad at heart, the gossips breathe their prayer,
And, crowding, stop the cradle to admire
The babe, the sleeping image of his sire.
A few short years — and then these sounds shall hail
The day again, and gladness fill the vale;
So soon the child a youth, the youth a man,
Eager to run the race his fathers ran.
Then the huge ox shall yield the broad sirloin;
The ale, now brewed, in floods of amber shine:
And, basking in the chimney's ample blaze,
Mid many a tale told of his boyish days,
The nurse shall cry, of all her ills beguiled,
"'Twas on these knees he sate so oft and smiled."
And soon again shall music swell the breeze;
Soon, issuing forth, shall glitter through the trees
Vestures of nuptial white; and hymns be sung,
And violets scattered round; and old and young,

In every cottage-porch with garlands green,
Stand still to gaze,[1] and, gazing, bless the scene;
While, her dark eyes declining, by his side
Moves in her virgin-veil the gentle bride.
And once, alas! nor in a distant hour,
Another voice shall come from yonder tower;
When in dim chambers long black weeds are seen,
And weepings heard where only joy has been;
When by his children borne, and from his door
Slowly departing to return no more,
He rests in holy earth with them that went before.
And such is Human Life; so, gliding on,
It glimmers like a meteor, and is gone!
Yet is the tale, brief though it be, as strange,
As full, methinks, of wild and wondrous change,
As any that the wandering tribes require,
Stretched in the desert round their evening-fire;
As any sung of old in hall or bower
To minstrel-harps at midnight's witching-hour!
Born in a trance, we wake, observe, inquire;
And the green earth, the azure sky, admire.
Of Elfin-size — forever as we run,
We cast a longer shadow in the sun!
And now a charm, and now a grace is won!
We grow in stature, and in wisdom too!
And, as new scenes, new objects, rise to view,
Think nothing done while aught remains to do.[2]
Yet, all forgot, how oft the eye-lids close,
And from the slack hand drops the gathered rose!
How oft, as dead, on the warm turf we lie,
While many an emmet comes with curious eye;
And on her nest the watchful wren sits by!

Nor do we speak or move, or hear or see;
So like what once we were, and once again shall be!
  And say, how soon, where, blithe as innocent,
The boy at sunrise carolled as he went,
An aged pilgrim on his staff shall lean,
Tracing in vain the footsteps o'er the green;
The man himself how altered, not the scene!
Now journeying home with nothing but the name;
Way-worn and spent, another and the same!
  No eye observes the growth or the decay.
To-day we look as we did yesterday;
And we shall look to-morrow as to-day.
Yet while the loveliest smiles, her locks grow gray!
And in her glass could she but see the face
She'll see so soon among another race,
How would she shrink! — Returning from afar,
After some years of travel, some of war,
Within his gate Ulysses stood unknown
Before a wife, a father, and a son!
  And such is Human Life, the general theme.
Ah! what at best, what but a longer dream?
Though with such wild romantic wanderings fraught,
Such forms in Fancy's richest coloring wrought,
That, like the visions of a love-sick brain,
Who would not sleep and dream them o'er again?
  Our pathway leads but to a precipice;[3]
And all must follow, fearful as it is!
From the first step 't is known; but — No delay!
On, 't is decreed. We tremble and obey.
A thousand ills beset us as we go.
— "Still, could I shun the fatal gulf" — Ah, no,

16

'T is all in vain — the inexorable Law!
Nearer and nearer to the brink we draw.
Verdure springs up; and fruits and flowers invite,
And groves and fountains — all things that delight.
"O, I would stop, and linger if I might!" —
We fly; no resting for the foot we find;[4]
All dark before, all desolate behind!
At length the brink appears — but one step more!
We faint — On, on! — we falter — and 't is o'er!
  Yet here high passions, high desires unfold,
Prompting to noblest deeds; here links of gold
Bind soul to soul; and thoughts divine inspire
A thirst unquenchable, a holy fire
That will not, cannot but with life expire!
  Now, seraph-winged, among the stars we soar;[5]
Now distant ages, like a day, explore,
And judge the act, the actor now no more;
Or, in a thankless hour, condemned to live,[6]
From others claim what these refuse to give,
And dart, like MILTON, an unerring eye
Through the dim curtains of Futurity.[7]
  Wealth, pleasure, ease, all thought of self resigned,
What will not man encounter for mankind?
Behold him now unbar the prison-door,[8]
And, lifting Guilt, Contagion, from the floor,
To peace and health, and light and life restore;
Now in Thermopylæ remain to share
Death — nor look back, nor turn a footstep there,
Leaving his story to the birds of air;
And now like Pylades (in Heaven they write
Names such as his in characters of light)

Long with his friend in generous enmity,[9]
Pleading, insisting in his place to die!
Do what he will, he cannot realize
Half he conceives — the glorious vision flies.
Go where he may, he cannot hope to find
The truth, the beauty pictured in his mind.
But if by chance an object strike the sense,
The faintest shadow of that excellence,
Passions, that slept, are stirring in his frame;
Thoughts undefined, feelings without a name!
And some, not here called forth, may slumber on
Till this vain pageant of a world is gone;
Lying too deep for things that perish here,
Waiting for life — but in a nobler sphere!
Look where he comes! Rejoicing in his birth,
A while he moves as in a heaven on earth!
Sun, moon, and stars — the land, the sea, the sky,
To him shine out as in a galaxy!
But soon 't is past[10] — the light has died away!
With him it came (it was not of the day)
And he himself diffused it, like the stone
That sheds a while a lustre all its own,[11]
Making night beautiful. 'T is past, 't is gone,
And in his darkness as he journeys on,
Nothing revives him but the blessed ray
That now breaks in, nor ever knows decay,
Sent from a better world to light him on his way.
How great the Mystery! Let others sing
The circling Year,— the promise of the Spring,
The Summer's glory, and the rich repose
Of Autumn, and the Winter's silvery snows.

Man through the changing scene let us pursue,
Himself how wondrous in his changes too!
Not Man, the sullen savage in his den;
But Man called forth in fellowship with men;
Schooled and trained up to wisdom from his birth; [12]
God's noblest work — His image upon earth!

The day arrives, the moment wished and feared; [13]
The child is born, by many a pang endeared.
And now the mother's ear has caught his cry;
O, grant the cherub to her asking eye!
He comes . . . she clasps him. To her bosom pressed,
He drinks the balm of life and drops to rest.
Her by her smile how soon the stranger knows;
How soon by his the glad discovery shows!
As to her lips she lifts the lovely boy,
What answering looks of sympathy and joy!
He walks, he speaks. In many a broken word
His wants, his wishes, and his griefs, are heard.
And ever, ever to her lap he flies,
When rosy Sleep comes on with sweet surprise.
Locked in her arms, his arms across her flung
(That name most dear forever on his tongue),
As with soft accents round her neck he clings,
And, cheek to cheek, her lulling song she sings,
How blest to feel the beatings of his heart,
Breathe his sweet breath, and kiss for kiss impart;
Watch o'er his slumbers like the brooding dove,
And, if she can, exhaust a mother's love!
But soon a nobler task demands her care.
Apart she joins his little hands in prayer,
Telling of Him who sees in secret there! —

And now the volume on her knee has caught
His wandering eye — now many a written thought,
Never to die, with many a lisping sweet,
His moving, murmuring lips endeavor to repeat.
  Released, he chases the bright butterfly;
O, he would follow — follow through the sky!
Climbs the gaunt mastiff slumbering in his chain,
And chides and buffets, clinging by the mane;
Then runs, and, kneeling by the fountain-side,
Sends his brave ship in triumph down the tide,
A dangerous voyage; or, if now he can,
If now he wears the habit of a man,
Flings off the coat so much his pride and pleasure,
And, like a miser digging for his treasure,
His tiny spade in his own garden plies,
And in green letters sees his name arise!
Where'er he goes, forever in her sight,
She looks, and looks, and still with new delight!
  Ah! who, when fading of itself away,
Would cloud the sunshine of his little day!
Now is the May of life. Exulting round,
Joy wings his feet, Joy lifts him from the ground!
Pointing to such, well might Cornelia say,
When the rich casket shone in bright array,
"These are MY Jewels!"[14] Well of such as he,
When JESUS spake, well might the language be,
"Suffer these little ones to come to me!"[15]
  Thoughtful by fits, he scans and he reveres
The brow engraven with the thoughts of years;[16]
Close by her side his silent homage given
As to some pure intelligence from Heaven;

His eyes cast downward with ingenuous shame,
His conscious cheeks, conscious of praise or blame,
At once lit up as with a holy flame!
He thirsts for knowledge, speaks but to inquire;
And soon with tears relinquished to the sire,
Soon in his hand to Wisdom's temple led,
Holds secret converse with the mighty dead;
Trembles and thrills and weeps as they inspire,
Burns as they burn, and with congenial fire![17]
Like her most gentle, most unfortunate,[18]
Crowned but to die — who in her chamber sate
Musing with Plato, though the horn was blown,
And every ear and every heart was won,
And all in green array were chasing down the sun!
 Then is the Age of Admiration![19] — Then
Gods walk the earth, or beings more than men;
Who breathe the soul of inspiration round,
Whose very shadows consecrate the ground!
Ah! then comes thronging many a wild desire,
And high imagining and thought of fire!
Then from within a voice exclaims "Aspire!"
Phantoms, that upward point, before him pass,
As in the cave athwart the wizard's glass;
They, that on youth a grace, a lustre shed,
Of every age — the living and the dead!
Thou, all-accomplished SURREY, thou art known;
The flower of knighthood, nipt as soon as blown!
Melting all hearts but Geraldine's alone!
And, with his beaver up, discovering there
One who loved less to conquer than to spare,
Lo! the Black Warrior, he, who, battle-spent,
Bare-headed served the captive in his tent!

Young B——— in the groves of Academe,
Or where Ilyssus winds his whispering stream;
Or where the wild bees swarm with ceaseless hum,
Dreaming old dreams — a joy for years to come;
Or on the rock within the sacred fane; —
Scenes such as MILTON sought, but sought in vain: [20]
And MILTON'S self (at that thrice-honored name
Well may we glow — as men, we share his fame) — [21]
And MILTON'S self, apart with beaming eye,
Planning he knows not what — that shall not die!
O, in thy truth secure, thy virtue bold,
Beware the poison in the cup of gold,
The asp among the flowers! Thy heart beats high,
As bright and brighter breaks the distant sky!
But every step is on enchanted ground.
Danger thou lov'st, and Danger haunts thee round.
Who spurs his horse against the mountain-side;
Then, plunging, slakes his fury in the tide?
Draws, and cries ho! and, where the sunbeams fall,
At his own shadow thrusts along the wall?
Who dances without music; and anon
Sings like the lark — then sighs as woe-begone,
And folds his arms, and, where the willows wave,
Glides in the moonshine by a maiden's grave?
Come hither, boy, and clear thy open brow.
Yon summer-clouds, now like the Alps, and now
A ship, a whale, change not so fast as thou.
He hears me not! — Those sighs were from the heart.
Too, too well taught, he plays the lover's part.
He who at masques, nor feigning nor sincere,
With sweet discourse would win a lady's ear,

Lie at her feet and on her slipper swear
That none were half so faultless, half so fair,
Now through the forest hies, a stricken deer,
A banished man, flying when none are near;
And writes on every tree, and lingers long
Where most the nightingale repeats her song;
Where most the nymph, that haunts the silent grove,
Delights to syllable the names we love.
  Two on his steps attend, in motley clad;
One woful-wan, one merry but as mad;
Called Hope and Fear. Hope shakes his cap and bells,
And flowers spring up among the woodland dells.
To Hope he listens, wandering without measure
Through sun and shade, lost in a trance of pleasure;
And, if to Fear but for a weary mile,
Hope follows fast and wins him with a smile.
  At length he goes — a pilgrim to the shrine,
And for a relic would a world resign!
A glove, a shoe-tie, or a flower let fall —
What though the least, Love consecrates them all!
And now he breathes in many a plaintive verse;
Now wins the dull ear of the wily nurse
At early matins ('t was at matin-time [22]
That first he saw and sickened in his prime),
And soon the Sibyl, in her thirst for gold,
Plays with young hearts that will not be controlled.
  "Absence from thee — as self from self it seems!"
Scaled is the garden-wall; and, lo! her beams
Silvering the east, the moon comes up, revealing
His well-known form along the terrace stealing.
— O, ere in sight he came, 't was his to thrill
A heart that loved him though in secret still.

"Am I awake? or is it . . . can it be
An idle dream? Nightly it visits me!
— That strain," she cries, "as from the water rose;
Now near and nearer through the shade it flows! —
Now sinks departing — sweetest in its close!"
No casement gleams; no Juliet, like the day,
Comes forth and speaks and bids her lover stay.
Still, like aërial music heard from far
As through the doors of Paradise ajar,
Nightly it rises with the evening-star.
— "She loves another! Love was in that sigh!"
On the cold ground he throws himself to die.
Fond youth, beware! Thy heart is most deceiving.
Who wish are fearful; who suspect, believing.
— And soon her looks the rapturous truth avow.
Lovely before, O, say how lovely now![23]
She flies not, frowns not, though he pleads his cause;
Nor yet — nor yet her hand from his withdraws;
But by some secret power surprised, subdued,
(Ah! how resist? And would she if she could?)
Falls on his neck as half unconscious where,
Glad to conceal her tears, her blushes, there.
Then come those full confidings of the past;
All sunshine now, where all was overcast.
Then do they wander till the day is gone,
Lost in each other; and when night steals on,
Covering them round, how sweet her accents are!
O, when she turns and speaks, her voice is far,
Far above singing! — But soon nothing stirs
To break the silence — joy like his, like hers,
Deals not in words; and now the shadows close,
Now in the glimmering, dying light she grows

Less and less earthly! As departs the day,
All that was mortal seems to melt away,
Till, like a gift resumed as soon as given,
She fades at last into a spirit from Heaven!
  Then are they blest indeed; and swift the hours
Till her young sisters wreathe her hair in flowers,
Kindling her beauty — while, unseen, the least
Twitches her robe, then runs behind the rest,
Known by her laugh that will not be suppressed.
Then before All they stand — the holy vow
And ring of gold, no fond illusions now,
Bind her as his. Across the threshold led,
And every tear kissed off as soon as shed,
His house she enters — there to be a light
Shining within, when all without is night;
A guardian-angel o'er his life presiding,
Doubling his pleasures, and his cares dividing;
Winning him back, when mingling in the throng,
From a vain world we love, alas! too long,
To fireside happiness, and hours of ease
Blest with that charm, the certainty to please.
How oft her eyes read his! her gentle mind
To all his wishes, all his thoughts inclined;
Still subject — ever on the watch to borrow
Mirth of his mirth, and sorrow of his sorrow.
The soul of music slumbers in the shell,
Till waked and kindled by the master's spell;
And feeling hearts — touch them but rightly — pour
A thousand melodies unheard before! [24]
  Nor many moons o'er hill and valley rise
Ere to the gate with nymph-like step she flies,

And their first-born holds forth, their darling boy,
With smiles how sweet, how full of love and joy,
To meet him coming; theirs through every year
Pure transports, such as each to each endear!
And laughing eyes and laughing voices fill
Their home with gladness. She, when all are still,
Comes and undraws the curtain as they lie,
In sleep how beautiful! He, when the sky
Gleams, and the wood sends up its harmony,
When, gathering round his bed, they climb to share
His kisses, and with gentle violence there
Break in upon a dream not half so fair,
Up to the hill-top leads their little feet;
Or by the forest-lodge, perchance to meet
The stag-herd on its march, perchance to hear
The otter rustling in the sedgy mere;
Or to the echo near the Abbot's tree,
That gave him back his words of pleasantry —
When the House stood, no merrier man than he!
And, as they wander with a keen delight,
If but a leveret catch their quicker sight
Down a green alley, or a squirrel then
Climb the gnarled oak, and look and climb again,
If but a moth flit by, an acorn fall,
He turns their thoughts to Him who made them all;
These with unequal footsteps following fast,
These clinging by his cloak, unwilling to be last.
  The shepherd on Tornaro's misty brow,
And the swart seaman, sailing far below,
Not undelighted watch the morning ray
Purpling the orient — till it breaks away,
And burns and blazes into glorious day!

But happier still is he who bends to trace
That sun, the soul, just dawning in the face;
The burst, the glow, the animating strife,
The thoughts and passions stirring into life;
The forming utterance, the inquiring glance,
The giant waking from his ten-fold trance,
Till up he starts as conscious whence he came,
And all is light within the trembling frame!
  What then a father's feelings? Joy and fear
In turn prevail, — joy most; and through the year
Tempering the ardent, urging night and day
Him who shrinks back or wanders from the way,
Praising each highly — from a wish to raise
Their merits to the level of his praise,
Onward in their observing sight he moves,
Fearful of wrong, in awe of whom he loves!
Their sacred presence who shall dare profane?
Who, when he slumbers, hope to fix a stain?
He lives a model in his life to show,
That, when he dies and through the world they go,
Some men may pause and say, when some admire,
"They are his sons, and worthy of their sire!"
  But man is born to suffer. On the door
Sickness has set her mark; and now no more
Laughter within we hear, or wood-notes wild
As of a mother singing to her child.
All now in anguish from that room retire,
Where a young cheek glows with consuming fire,
And innocence breathes contagion — all but one,
But she who gave it birth — from her alone
The medicine-cup is taken. Through the night,[26]
And through the day, that with its dreary light

Comes unregarded, she sits silent by,[27]
Watching the changes with her anxious eye;
While they without, listening below, above,
(Who but in sorrow know how much they love?)
From every little noise catch hope and fear,
Exchanging still, still as they turn to hear,
Whispers and sighs, and smiles all tenderness,
That would in vain the starting tear repress.
  Such grief was ours — it seems but yesterday —
When in thy prime, wishing so much to stay,
'T was thine, Maria, thine without a sigh
At midnight in a sister's arms to die!
O, thou wert lovely — lovely was thy frame,
And pure thy spirit as from Heaven it came!
And, when recalled to join the blest above,
Thou diedst a victim to exceeding love,
Nursing the young to health. In happier hours,
When idle Fancy wove luxuriant flowers,
Once in thy mirth thou bad'st me write on thee;
And now I write — what thou shalt never see!
  At length the father, vain his power to save,
Follows his child in silence to the grave
(That child how cherished, whom he would not give,
Sleeping the sleep of death, for all that live);
Takes a last look, when, not unheard, the spade
Scatters the earth as "dust to dust"[28] is said,
Takes a last look and goes; his best relief
Consoling others in that hour of grief,
And with sweet tears and gentle words infusing
The holy calm that leads to heavenly musing.
  But hark, the din of arms! no time for sorrow.
To horse, to horse! A day of blood to-morrow!

One parting pang, and then — and then I fly,
Fly to the field, to triumph — or to die! —
He goes, and night comes as it never came! [29]
With shrieks of horror! — and a vault of flame!
And, lo! when morning mocks the desolate,
Red runs the river by; and at the gate
Breathless a horse without his rider stands!
But hush! . . a shout from the victorious bands!
And, O, the smiles and tears, a sire restored!
One wears his helm, one buckles on his sword;
One hangs the wall with laurel-leaves, and all
Spring to prepare the soldier's festival;
While she best-loved, till then forsaken never,
Clings round his neck as she would cling forever!
Such golden deeds lead on to golden days,
Days of domestic peace — by him who plays
On the great stage how uneventful thought!
Yet with a thousand busy projects fraught,
A thousand incidents that stir the mind
To pleasure, such as leaves no sting behind!
Such as the heart delights in — and records
Within how silently [30] — in more than words!
A holiday — the frugal banquet spread
On the fresh herbage near the fountain-head
With quips and cranks — what time the wood-lark there
Scatters his loose notes on the sultry air,
What time the king-fisher sits perched below,
Where, silver-bright, the water-lilies blow: —
A Wake — the booths whitening the village green,
Where Punch and Scaramouch aloft are seen;
Sign beyond sign in close array unfurled,
Picturing at large the wonders of the world;

And far and wide, over the vicar's pale,
Black hoods and scarlet crossing hill and dale,
All, all abroad, and music in the gale: —
A wedding dance — a dance into the night
On the barn-floor, when maiden-feet are light;
When the young bride receives the promised dower,
And flowers are flung, herself a fairer flower: —
A morning-visit to the poor man's shed,
(Who would be rich while one was wanting bread?)
When all are emulous to bring relief,
And tears are falling fast — but not for grief: —
A walk in Spring — GRATTAN, like those with thee[31]
By the heath-side (who had not envied me?)
When the sweet limes, so full of bees in June,
Led us to meet beneath their boughs at noon;
And thou didst say which of the great and wise,
Could they but hear and at thy bidding rise,
Thou wouldst call up and question.

Graver things
Come in due order. Every morning brings
Its holy office; and the Sabbath-bell,
That over wood and wild and mountain-dell
Wanders so far, chasing all thoughts unholy
With sounds most musical, most melancholy,
Not on his ear is lost. Then he pursues
The pathway leading through the aged yews,
Nor unattended; and, when all are there,[32]
Pours out his spirit in the house of prayer,
That house with many a funeral-garland hung[33]
Of virgin-white — memorials of the young,
The last yet fresh when marriage-chimes were ringing,
And hope and joy in other hearts were springing;

That house, where Age led in by Filial Love,
Their looks composed, their thoughts on things above,
The world forgot, or all its wrongs forgiven —
Who would not say they trod the path to Heaven?
  Nor at the fragrant hour — at early dawn —
Under the elm-tree on his level lawn,
Or in his porch, is he less duly found,
When they that cry for justice gather round,
And in that cry her sacred voice is drowned;
His then to hear, and weigh and arbitrate,
Like ALFRED judging at his palace-gate.
Healed at his touch, the wounds of discord close;
And they return as friends, that came as foes.
  Thus, while the world but claims its proper part,
Oft in the head but never in the heart,
His life steals on; within his quiet dwelling
That home-felt joy all other joys excelling.
Sick of the crowd, when enters he — nor then
Forgets the cold indifference of men?
  Soon through the gadding vine the sun looks in,[34]
And gentle hands the breakfast-rite begin.
Then the bright kettle sings its matin-song,
Then fragrant clouds of Mocha and Souchong
Blend as they rise; and (while without are seen,
Sure of their meal, the small birds on the green;
And in from far a school-boy's letter flies,
Flushing the sister's cheek with glad surprise)
That sheet unfolds (who reads, and reads it not?)
Born with the day and with the day forgot;
Its ample page various as human life,
The pomp, the woe, the bustle, and the strife!
  But nothing lasts. In Autumn at his plough
Met and solicited, behold him now

Leaving that humbler sphere his fathers knew,
The sphere that Wisdom loves, and Virtue too;
They who subsist not on the vain applause
Misjudging man now gives and now withdraws.
'T was morn — the sky-lark o'er the furrow sung
As from his lips the slow consent was wrung;
As from the glebe his fathers tilled of old,
The plough they guided in an age of gold,
Down by the beechwood-side he turned away: —
And now behold him in an evil day
Serving the State again — not as before,
Not foot to foot, the war-whoop at his door, —
But in the Senate; and (though round him fly
The jest, the sneer, the subtle sophistry)
With honest dignity,[35] with manly sense,
And every charm of natural eloquence,
Like HAMPDEN struggling in his country's cause,[36]
The first, the foremost to obey the laws,
The last to brook oppression. On he moves,
Careless of blame while his own heart approves,
Careless of ruin — [37] ("For the general good
'T is not the first time I shall shed my blood.")
On through that gate misnamed,[38] through which before
Went Sidney, Russell, Raleigh, Cranmer, More,
On into twilight within walls of stone,
Then to the place of trial;[39] and alone,[40]
Alone before his judges in array
Stands for his life: there, on that awful day,
Counsel of friends — all human help denied —
All but from her who sits the pen to guide,
Like that sweet saint who sate by RUSSELL's side
Under the judgment-seat.[41]

But guilty men
Triumph not always. To his hearth again,
Again with honor to his hearth restored,
Lo! in the accustomed chair and at the board,
Thrice greeting those who most withdraw their claim [42]
(The lowliest servant calling by his name),
He reads thanksgiving in the eyes of all,
All met as at a holy festival!
— On the day destined for his funeral!
Lo! there the friend,[43] who, entering where he lay,
Breathed in his drowsy ear "Away, away!
Take thou *my* cloak! — Nay, start not, but obey —
Take it and leave me." And the blushing maid,
Who through the streets as through a desert strayed;
And, when her dear, dear father passed along,[44]
Would not be held — but, bursting through the throng,
Halberd and battle-axe — kissed him o'er and o'er;
Then turned and went — then sought him as before,
Believing she should see his face no more!
And, O, how changed at once — no heroine here,
But a weak woman worn with grief and fear,
Her darling mother! 'T was but now she smiled;
And now she weeps upon her weeping child!
— But who sits by, her only wish below
At length fulfilled — and now prepared to go?
His hands on hers — as through the mists of night,
She gazes on him with imperfect sight;
Her glory now, as ever her delight! [45]
To her, methinks, a second youth is given;
The light upon her face a light from Heaven!
An hour like this is worth a thousand passed
In pomp or ease. — 'T is present to the last!

Years glide away untold — 't is still the same!
As fresh, as fair, as on the day it came!
And now once more where most he loved to be,
In his own fields — breathing tranquillity —
We hail him — not less happy, Fox, than thee,
Thee at St. Anne's so soon of care beguiled,
Playful, sincere, and artless as a child!
Thee, who wouldst watch a bird's nest on the spray,
Through the green leaves exploring, day by day.
How oft from grove to grove, from seat to seat,
With thee conversing in thy loved retreat,
I saw the sun go down! — Ah! then 't was thine
Ne'er to forget some volume half divine,
Shakspeare's or Dryden's — through the checkered shade
Borne in thy hand behind thee as we strayed;
And where we sate (and many a halt we made)
To read there with a fervor all thy own,
And in thy grand and melancholy tone,
Some splendid passage not to thee unknown,
Fit theme for long discourse.— Thy bell has tolled!
— But in thy place among us we behold
One who resembles thee.
'T is the sixth hour.
The village-clock strikes from the distant tower.
The ploughman leaves the field; the traveller hears,
And to the inn spurs forward. Nature wears
Her sweetest smile; the day-star in the west
Yet hovering, and the thistle's down at rest.
And such, his labor done, the calm he knows,[46]
Whose footsteps we have followed. Round him glows
An atmosphere that brightens to the last;
The light, that shines, reflected from the past,

— And from the future too! Active in thought
Among old books, old friends; and not unsought
By the wise stranger — in his morning-hours,
When gentle airs stir the fresh-blowing flowers,
He muses, turning up the idle weed;
Or prunes or grafts, or in the yellow mead
Watches his bees at hiving-time;[47] and now,
The ladder resting on the orchard-bough,
Culls the delicious fruit that hangs in air,
The purple plum, green fig, or golden pear,
Mid sparkling eyes, and hands uplifted there.
At night, when all, assembling round the fire,
Closer and closer draw till they retire,
A tale is told of India or Japan,
Of merchants from Golconde or Astracan,
What time wild nature revelled unrestrained,
And Sinbad voyaged and the Caliphs reigned: —
Of knights renowned from holy Palestine,
And minstrels, such as swept the lyre divine,
When Blondel came, and Richard in his cell[48]
Heard, as he lay, the song he knew so well: —
Of some Norwegian, while the icy gale
Rings in her shrouds and beats her iron-sail,
Among the shining Alps of polar seas
Immovable — forever there to freeze![49]
Or some great caravan, from well to well
Winding as darkness on the desert fell,
In their long march, such as the Prophet bids,
To Mecca from the land of Pyramids,
And in an instant lost — a hollow wave
Of burning sand their everlasting grave! —
Now the scene shifts to Cashmere — to a glade
Where, with her loved gazelle, the dark-eyed maid

(Her fragrant chamber for a while resigned,
Her lute, by fits discoursing with the wind)
Wanders well-pleased, what time the nightingale
Sings to the rose, rejoicing hill and dale;
And now to Venice — to a bridge, a square,
Glittering with light, all nations masking there,
With light reflected on the tremulous tide,
Where gondolas in gay confusion glide,
Answering the jest, the song on every side;
To Naples next — and at the crowded gate,
Where Grief and Fear and wild Amazement wait,
Lo! on his back a son brings in his sire,[50]
Vesuvius blazing like a world on fire! —
Then, at a sign that never was forgot,
A strain breaks forth (who hears and loves it not?)
From harp or organ![51] 'T is at parting given,
That in their slumbers they may dream of Heaven;
Young voices mingling, as it floats along,
In Tuscan air or Handel's sacred song!
  And she inspires, whose beauty shines in all;
So soon to weave a daughter's coronal,
And at the nuptial rite smile through her tears; —
So soon to hover round her full of fears,
And with assurance sweet her soul revive
In child-birth —[52] when a mother's love is most alive!
  No, 't is not here that Solitude is known.
Through the wide world he only is alone
Who lives not for another.[53] Come what will,
The generous man has his companion still:
The cricket on his hearth; the buzzing fly,
That skims his roof, or, be his roof the sky,
Still with its note of gladness passes by:

And, in an iron cage condemned to dwell,
The cage that stands within the dungeon-cell,
He feeds his spider — happier at the worst
Than he at large who in himself is curst!
O thou all-eloquent, whose mighty mind[54]
Streams from the depth of ages on mankind,
Streams like the day — who, angel-like, hast shed
Thy full effulgence on the hoary head,
Speaking in Cato's venerable voice,
"Look up, and faint not — faint not, but rejoice!"
From thy Elysium guide him! Age has now
Stamped with his signet that ingenuous brow;
And, 'mid his old hereditary trees,
Trees he has climbed so oft, he sits and sees
His children's children playing round his knees:
Then happiest, youngest, when the quoit is flung,
When side by side the archers' bows are strung;
His to prescribe the place, adjudge the prize,
Envying no more the young their energies
Than they an old man when his words are wise;
His a delight how pure . . . without alloy;
Strong in their strength, rejoicing in their joy!
Now in their turn assisting, they repay
The anxious cares of many and many a day;
And now by those he loves relieved, restored,
His very wants and weaknesses afford
A feeling of enjoyment. In his walks,
Leaning on them, how oft he stops and talks,
While they look up! Their questions, their replies,
Fresh as the welling waters, round him rise,
Gladdening his spirit: and, his theme the past,
How eloquent he is! His thoughts flow fast;

And, while his heart (O! can the heart grow old?
False are the tales that in the world are told!)
Swells in his voice, he knows not where to end;
Like one discoursing of an absent friend.
But there are moments which he calls his own.
Then, never less alone than when alone,
Those whom he loved so long and sees no more,
Loved and still loves—not dead—but gone before,
He gathers round him; and revives at will
Scenes in his life—that breathe enchantment still—
That come not now at dreary intervals—
But where a light as from the Blessed falls,
A light such guests bring ever—pure and holy—
Lapping the soul in sweetest melancholy!
—Ah! then less willing (nor the choice condemn)
To live with others than to think of them!
And now behold him up the hill ascending,
Memory and Hope like evening-stars attending;
Sustained, excited, till his course is run,
By deeds of virtue done or to be done.
When on his couch he sinks at length to rest,
Those by his counsel saved, his power redressed,
Those by the world shunned ever as unblest,
At whom the rich man's dog growls from the gate,
But whom he sought out, sitting desolate,
Come and stand round—the widow with her child,
As when she first forgot her tears and smiled!
They, who watch by him, see not; but he sees,
Sees and exults.—Were ever dreams like these?
They, who watch by him, hear not; but he hears,
And earth recedes, and Heaven itself appears!
'T is past! That hand we grasped, alas! in vain!
Nor shall we look upon his face again!

But to his closing eyes, for all were there,
Nothing was wanting; and, through many a year
We shall remember with a fond delight
The words so precious which we heard to-night;
His parting, though a while our sorrow flows,
Like setting suns or music at the close!
 Then was the drama ended. Not till then,
So full of chance and change the lives of men,
Could we pronounce him happy. Then secure
From pain, from grief, and all that we endure,
He slept in peace — say rather soared to Heaven,
Upborne from earth by Him to whom 't is given
In his right hand to hold the golden key
That opes the portals of Eternity.
— When by a good man's grave I muse alone,
Methinks an angel sits upon the stone,
And, with a voice inspiring joy, not fear,
Says, pointing upward, "Know, he is not here!"
 But let us hence; for now the day is spent,
And stars are kindling in the firmament,[55]
To us how silent! — though like ours perchance
Busy and full of life and circumstance;
Where some the paths of Wealth and Power pursue,
Of Pleasure some, of Happiness a few;
And, as the sun goes round — a sun not ours —
While from her lap another Nature showers
Gifts of her own, some from the crowd retire,
Think on themselves, within, without inquire;
At distance dwell on all that passes there,
All that their world reveals of good and fair;
Trace out the journey through their little day,
And dream, like me, an idle hour away.

NOTES.

(1) See the *Iliad*, l. xviii. v. 496.

(2) "Nil actum credens, dum quid superesset agendum." — *Lucan* II. 657.

(3) See Bossuet, Sermon sur la Résurrection.

(4) "I have considered," says Solomon, "all the works that are under the sun, and behold, all is vanity and vexation of spirit." But who believes it, till Death tells it us? It is Death alone that can make man to know himself. He tells the proud and insolent that they are but abjects, and humbles them at the instant. He takes the account of the rich man, and proves him a beggar, — a naked beggar. He holds a glass before the eyes of the most beautiful, and makes them see therein their deformity; and they acknowledge it

O eloquent, just and mighty Death! whom none could advise, thou hast persuaded; what none have dared, thou hast done; and whom all the world have flattered, thou only hast cast out and despised; thou hast drawn together all the far-stretched greatness, all the pride, cruelty and ambition of man, and covered it all over with these two narrow words, *Hic jacet*. — *Raleigh*.

(5) Among the most precious gifts with which the Almighty has rewarded us for our diligence in the investigation of his works are the Telescope and the Microscope. They came as it were by chance; they came we know not how; and "they have laid open the infinite in both directions." But what may not come in like manner; when from the situation of a pebble may be learnt the state of the earth, many myriads of ages ago, before it was inhabited by man; and when the fall of an apple to the ground has led us to the knowledge of those laws which regulate every world as it revolves in its orbit? — *See Sir John Herschel's excellent Discourse on the Study of Natural Philosophy.*

(6) How much is it to be lamented that the greatest benefactors of mankind, being beyond the age they live in, are so seldom understood before they are gone!

(7) Fancy can hardly forbear to conjecture with what temper Milton surveyed the silent progress of his work, and marked his reputation stealing its way in a kind of subterraneous current through fear and silence. I cannot but conceive him calm and confident, little disappointed, not at all dejected, relying on his own merit with steady consciousness, and waiting, without impatience, the vicissitudes of opinion and the impartiality of a future generation. — *Johnson*.

After this line, in the MS.

O'er place and time we triumph; on we go,
Ranging at will the realms above, below;
Yet, ah! how little of ourselves we know!

And why the heart beats on, or how the brain
Says to the foot, "Now move, now rest again."
From age to age we search, and search in vain.

(8) An allusion to John Howard. "Wherever he came, in whatever country, the prisons and hospitals were thrown open to him as to the general censor. Such is the force of pure and exalted virtue!"

(9) Aristotle's definition of Friendship, "one soul in two bodies," is well exemplified by some ancient author in a dialogue between Ajax and Achilles. "Of all the wounds you ever received in battle," says Ajax, "which was the most painful to you?"—"That which I received from Hector," replies Achilles. — "But Hector never gave you a wound?" — "Yes, and a mortal one; when he slew my friend, Patroclus."

(10) This light, which is so heavenly in its lustre, and which is everywhere and on everything when we look round us on our arrival here; which, while it lasts, never leaves us, rejoicing us by night as well as by day and lighting up our very dreams; yet, when it fades, fades so fast, and, when it goes, goes out forever, — we may address it in the words of the poet, words which we might apply so often in this transitory life:

Too soon your value from your loss we learn!
R. Sharp's Epistles in Verse, ii.

(11) See "Observations on a Diamond that shines in the dark." —*Boyle's Works*, I. 789

(12) Cicero, in his Essay *De Senectute*, has drawn his images from the better walks of life; and Shakspeare, in his Seven Ages, has done so too. But Shakspeare treats his subject satirically; Cicero, as a philosopher. In the venerable portrait of Cato we discover no traces of "the lean and slippered pantaloon."

Every object has a bright and a dark side; and I have endeavored to look at things as Cicero has done. By some, however, I may be thought to have followed too much my own dream of happiness; and in such a dream indeed I have often passed a solitary hour. It was castle-building once; now it is no longer so. But whoever would try to realize it would not perhaps repent of his endeavor.

(13) A Persian poet has left us a beautiful thought on this subject, which the reader, if he has not met with it, will be glad to know, and, if he has, to remember.

Thee on thy mother's knees, a new-born child,
In tears we saw, when all around thee smiled.
So live, that, sinking in thy last long sleep,
Smiles may be thine, when all around thee weep.

(14) The anecdote here alluded to is related by Valerius Maximus, Lib. iv. c. 4.

(15) In our early youth, while yet we live only among those we love, we love without restraint, and our hearts overflow in every look, word and action. But when we enter the world, and are repulsed by strangers, forgotten by friends, we grow more and more timid in our approaches even to those we love best.

How delightful to us, then, are the little caresses of children! All sincerity, all affection, they fly into our arms; and then, and then only, do we feel our first confidence, our first pleasure.

(16) This is a law of nature. Age was anciently synonymous with power; and we may always observe that the old are held in more or less honor as men are more or less virtuous. "Shame," says Homer, "bids the youth beware how he accosts the man of many

years." "Thou shalt rise up before the hoary head, and honor the face of an old man." —*Leviticus.*

Among us, and wherever birth and possessions give rank and authority, the young and the profligate are seen continually above the old and the worthy ; there age can never find its due respect. But among many of the ancient nations it was otherwise ; and they reaped the benefit of it. : Rien ne maintient plus les mœurs, qu'une extrême subordination des jeunes gens envers les vieillards. Les uns et les autres seront contenus, ceuxlà par le respect qu'ils auront pour les vieillards, et ceuxci par le respect qu'ils auront pour eux-mêmes. — *Montesquieu.*

(17) How many generations have passed away, how many empires and how many languages, since Homer sung his verses to the Greeks ! Yet the words which he uttered, and which were only so much fleeting breath, remain almost entire to this day, and will now, in all probability, continue to delight and instruct mankind as long as the world endures.

(18) Before I went into Germany, I came to Brodegate in Leicestershire, to take my leave of that noble Lady Jane Grey, to whom I was exceeding much beholding. Her parents, the duke and duchess, with all the household, gentlemen and gentlewomen, were hunting in the park. I found her in her chamber reading Phædo Platonis in Greek, and that with as much delight as some gentlemen would read a merry tale in Boccace. After salutation, and duty done, with some other talk, I asked her why she would lose such pastime in the park ? Smiling, she answered me, "I wist, all their sport in the park is but a shadow to that pleasure which I find in Plato." — *Roger Ascham.*

(19) Dante in his old age was pointed out to Petrarch when a boy ; and Dryden to Pope.

Who does not wish that Dante and Dryden could have known the value of the homage that was paid them, and foreseen the greatness of their young admirers ?

(20) He had arrived at Naples, and was preparing to visit Sicily and Greece, when, hearing of the troubles in England, he thought it proper to hasten home.

(21) I began thus far to assent . . . to an inward prompting which now grew daily upon me, that by labor and intent study (which I take to be my portion in this life), joined with the strong propensity of nature, I might perhaps leave something so written to aftertimes as they should not willingly let it die. — *Milton.*

Nor can his wish be unfulfilled. Calumniated in his lifetime and writing what few would read, he left it to a voice which none could silence, — a voice which would deliver it to all nations, — in the Old World and the New.

A good book (to quote his own words) is the precious life-blood of a master spirit, and to destroy it is to slay an immortality rather than a life.

(22) Love and devotion are said to be nearly allied. Boccaccio fell in love at Naples in the church of St. Lorenzo ; as Petrarch had done at Avignon in the church of St. Clair.

(23) Is it not true that the young not only appear to be, but really are, most beautiful in the presence of those they love ? It calls forth all their beauty.

(24) Xenophon has left us a delightful instance of conjugal affection.

The King of Armenia not fulfilling his promise, Cyrus entered the country, and having taken him and all his family prisoners, ordered them instantly before him. Armenian, said he, you are free ; for you are now sensible of your error. And what will you give me, if I restore your wife to you ?— All that I am able. —What, if I restore your children ? — All that I am able. — And you, Tigranes, said he, turning to the son, what would *you* do to save your wife from servitude ? Now, Tigranes was but lately married, and had a great love for his wife. Cyrus, he replied, to save her from servitude, I would willingly lay down my life.

Let each have his own again, said Cyrus; and, when he was departed, one spoke of his clemency, and another of his valor, and another of his beauty and the graces of his person. Upon which Tigranes asked his wife if she thought him handsome. Really, said she, I did not look at him.— At whom then did you look?— At him who said he would lay down his life for me. — *Cyropædia*, L. III.

(25) "When such is the ruling, the habitual sentiment of our minds," says Paley, "the world becomes a temple, and life itself one continued act of worship." We breathe aspirations all day long.

(26) Hers the mournful privilege, "adsidere valetudini, fovere deficientem, satiari vultu, complexu." — *Tacitus*.

(27) We may have many friends in life; but we can only have one mother; "a discovery," says Gray, "which I never made till it was too late."

The child is no sooner born than he clings to his mother; nor, while she lives, is her image absent from him in the hour of his distress. Sir John Moore, when he fell from his horse in the battle of Corunna, faltered out with his dying breath some message to his mother; and who can forget the last words of Conradin, when, in his fifteenth year, he was led forth to die at Naples, "O my mother! how great will be your grief, when you hear of it!"

(28) How exquisite are those lines of Petrarch!

Le crespe chiome d'or puro lucente,
E'l lampeggiar d'ell angelico riso,
Che solean far in terrà un paradiso,
Poca polvere son, che nulla sente.

(29) These circumstances, as well as some others that follow, are happily, as far as they regard England, of an ancient date. To us the miseries inflicted by a foreign invader are now known only by description. Many generations have passed away since our country-women saw the smoke of an enemy's camp.

But the same passions are always at work everywhere, and their effects are always nearly the same; though the circumstances that attend them are infinitely various.

(30) Si tout cela consistoit en faits, en actions, en paroles, on pourroit le décrire et le rendre en quelque façon: mais comment dire ce qui n'étoit ni dit, ni fait, ni pensé même, mais goûté, mais senti. Le vrai bonheur ne se décrit pas. — *Rousseau*.

(31) How welcome to an old man is the society of a young one! He, who is here mentioned, would propose a walk wherever we were, unworthy as I was of his notice; and one as great, if not greater, when we were interrupted in his library at St. Anne's, and I withdrew but for a moment to write down what I wished so much to remember, would say when I returned, "Why do you leave me?" words which few would forget, and which come again and again to me when half a century is gone by.

(32) So many pathetic affections are awakened by every exercise of social devotion, that most men, I believe, carry away from public worship a better temper towards the rest of mankind than they brought with them. Having all one interest to secure, one Lord to serve, one judgment to look forward to, we cannot but remember our common relationship, and our natural equality is forced upon our thoughts. The distinctions of civil life are almost always insisted upon too much, and whatever conduces to restore the level improves the character on both sides. If ever the poor man holds up his head, it is at

church ; if ever the rich man looks upon him with respect, it is there; and both will be the better the oftener they meet where the feeling of superiority is mitigated in the one and the spirit of the other is erected and confirmed. — *Paley.*

(33) A custom in some of our country churches.

(34) An English breakfast ; which may well excite in others what in Rousseau continued through life, un goût vif pour les déjeûnés. C'est le temps de la journée où nous sommes le plus tranquilles, où nous causons le plus à notre aise.

The luxuries here mentioned, familiar to us as they now are, were almost unknown before the Revolution.

(35) He who resolves to rise in the world by politics or religion can degrade his mind to any degree, when he sets about it. Overcome the first scruple, and the work is done. "You hesitate," said one who spoke from experience. "Put on the mask, young man ; and in a very little while you will not know it from your own face."

(36) Zeuxis is said to have drawn his Helen from an assemblage of the most beautiful women ; and many a writer of fiction, in forming a life to his mind, has recourse to the brightest moments in the lives of others.

I may be suspected of having done so here, and of having designed, as it were, from living models ; but, by making an allusion now and then to those who have really lived, I thought I should give something of interest to the picture, as well as better illustrate my meaning.

(37) "By the Mass !" said the Duke of Norfolk to Sir Thomas More, "by the Mass ! Master More, it is perilous striving with princes ; the anger of a prince is death."—"And is that all, my lord ? then the difference between you and me is but this — *That I shall die to-day, and you to-morrow.*" — *Roper's Life.*

(38) Traitor's gate, the water-gate in the Tower of London.

(39) This very slight sketch of Civil Dissension is taken from our own annals ; but, for an obvious reason, not from those of our own age.

The persons here immediately alluded to lived more than a hundred years ago, in a reign which Blackstone has justly represented as wicked, sanguinary and turbulent ; but such times have always afforded the most signal instances of heroic courage and ardent affection.

Great reverses, like theirs, lay open the human heart. They occur indeed but seldom ; yet all men are liable to them ; all, when they occur to others, make them more or less their own ; and, were we to describe our condition to an inhabitant of some other planet, could we omit what forms so striking a circumstance in human life ?

(40) A prisoner, prosecuted for high treason, may now make his defence by counsel. In the reign of William the Third the law was altered ; and it was in rising to urge the necessity of an alteration, that Lord Shaftesbury, with such admirable quickness, took advantage of the embarrassment that seized him. "If I," said he, "who rise only to give my opinion of this bill, am so confounded that I cannot say what I intended, what must be the condition of that man, who, without any assistance, is pleading for his life ?"

(41) *Lord Russell.* May I have somebody to write, to assist my memory ?

Mr. Attorney General. Yes, a servant.

Lord Chief Justice. Any of your servants shall assist you in writing anything you please for you.

Lord Russell. My wife is here, my Lord, to do it. — *State Trials*, II.

(42) See the *Alcestis of Euripides*, v. 194.

(43) Such as Russell found in Cavendish ; and such as many have found.

(44) An allusion to the last interview of Sir Thomas More and his daughter Margaret. "Dear Meg," said he, when afterwards with a coal he wrote to bid her farewell, "I never liked your manner towards me better ; for I like when daughterly love and dear charity have no leisure to look to worldly courtesy." — *Roper's Life.*

(45) Epaminondas, after his victory at Leuctra, rejoiced most of all at the pleasure which it would give his father and mother ; and who would not have envied them their feelings ?

Cornelia was called at Rome the mother-in-law of Scipio. "When," said she to her sons, "shall I be called the mother of the Gracchi ? "

(46) At illa quanti sunt, animum tanquam emeritis stipendiis libidinis, ambitionis, contentionis, inimicitiarum, cupiditatum omnium, secum esse, secumque (ut dicitur) vivere ? — *Cic de Senectute.*

(47) Hinc ubi jam emissum caveis ad sidera cœli
Nare per æstatem liquidam suspexeris agmen,
Contemplator. — *Virg.*

(48) Richard the First. For the romantic story here alluded to we are indebted to the French chroniclers. — *See Fauchet.* Recueil de l'Origine de la Langue et Poësie Fr.

(49) She was under all her sails, and looked less like a ship incrusted with ice than ice in the fashion of a ship. — *See the Voyage of Captain Thomas James, in* 1631.

(50) An act of filial piety represented on the coins of Catana, a Greek city, some remains of which are still to be seen at the foot of Mount Ætna.* The story is told of two brothers who, in this manner, saved both their parents. The place from which they escaped was long called the field of the pious ; and public games were annually held there to commemorate the event.

(51) What a pleasing picture of domestic life is given to us by Bishop Berkeley in his letters ! "The more we have of good instruments, the better ; for all my children, not excepting my little daughter, learn to play, and are preparing to fill my house with harmony against all events , that, if we have worse times, we may have better spirits."

(52) See the *Alcestis of Euripides*, v. 328.

(53) How often, says an excellent writer, do we err in our estimate of happiness ! When I hear of a man who has noble parks, splendid palaces, and every luxury in life, I always inquire whom he has to love ; and, if I find he has nobody, or does not love those he has, in the midst of all his grandeur I pronounce him a being in deep adversity.

(54) Cicero. It is remarkable that, among the comforts of old age, he has not mentioned those arising from the society of women and children. Perhaps the husband of Terentia and "the father of Marcus felt something on the subject, of which he was willing to spare himself the recollection."

(55) An old writer breaks off in a very lively manner at a later hour of the night. "But the Hyades run low in the heavens, and to keep our eyes open any longer were to act our Antipodes. The huntsmen are up in America, and they are already past their first sleep in Persia."

* It is introduced also, and very happily, by two great masters ; by Virgil in the Sack of Troy, and by Raphael in the Incendio di Borgo.

Before I conclude I would say something in favor of the old-fashioned triplet, which I have here ventured to use so often. Dryden seems to have delighted in it, and in many of his poems has used it much oftener than I have done, as for instance in the Hind and Panther,* and in Theodore and Honoria, where he introduces it three, four and even five times in succession.

If I have erred anywhere in the structure of my verse from a desire to follow yet earlier end higher examples, I rely on the forgiveness of those *in whose ear the music of our old versification is still sounding*.†

* Pope used to mention this poem as the most correct specimen of Dryden's versification. It was, indeed, written when he had completely formed his manner, and may be supposed to exhibit, negligence excepted, his deliberate and ultimate scheme of metre.—*Johnson.*

† With regard to trisyllables, as their accent is very rarely on the last, they cannot properly be any rhymes at all; yet nevertheless I highly commend those who have judiciously and sparingly introduced them as such.—*Gray.*

MISCELLANEOUS POEMS.

MISCELLANEOUS POEMS.

ODE TO SUPERSTITION.[1]

HENCE to the realms of Night, dire Demon, hence!
  Thy chain of adamant can bind
  That little world, the human mind,
And sink its noblest powers to impotence.
  Wake the lion's loudest roar,
  Clot his shaggy mane with gore,
  With flashing fury bid his eye-balls shine;
  Meek is his savage, sullen soul, to thine!
  Thy touch, thy deadening touch, has steeled the breast,
  Whence, through her April-shower, soft Pity smiled;
  Has closed the heart each godlike virtue blessed,
  To all the silent pleadings of his child.[2]
  At thy command he plants the dagger deep,
At thy command exults, though Nature bids him weep!

When, with a frown that froze the peopled earth,[3]
  Thou dartedst thy huge head from high,
  Night waved her banners o'er the sky,
And, brooding, gave her shapeless shadows birth.

Rocking on the billowy air,
Ha! what withering phantoms glare!
As blows the blast with many a sudden swell,
At each dead pause, what shrill-toned voices yell!
The sheeted spectre, rising from the tomb,
Points to the murderer's stab, and shudders by;
In every grove is felt a heavier gloom,
That veils its genius from the vulgar eye:
The spirit of the water rides the storm,
And, through the mist, reveals the terrors of his form.

I. 3.

O'er solid seas, where Winter reigns,
And holds each mountain-wave in chains,
The fur-clad savage, ere he guides his deer
By glistering star-light through the snow,
Breathes softly in her wondering ear
Each potent spell thou bad'st him know.
By thee inspired, on India's sands,
Full in the sun the Brahmin stands;
And, while the panting tigress hies
To quench her fever in the stream,
His spirit laughs in agonies,
Smit by the scorchings of the noontide beam.
Mark who mounts the sacred pyre,[4]
Blooming in her bridal vest:
She hurls the torch! she fans the fire!
To die is to be blest:
She clasps her lord to part no more,
And, sighing, sinks! but sinks to soar.
O'ershadowing Scotia's desert coast,
The Sisters sail in dusky state,[5]

And, wrapt in clouds, in tempests tost,
Weave the airy web of Fate;
While the lone shepherd, near the shipless main,[6]
Sees o'er her hills advance the long-drawn funeral train.

II. 1.

Thou spak'st, and, lo! a new creation glowed.
Each unhewn mass of living stone
Was clad in horrors not its own,
And at its base the trembling nations bowed.
Giant Error, darkly grand,
Grasped the globe with iron hand.
Circled with seats of bliss, the Lord of Light
Saw prostrate worlds adore his golden height.
The statue, waking with immortal powers,[7]
Springs from its parent earth, and shakes the spheres;
The indignant pyramid sublimely towers,
And braves the efforts of a host of years.
Sweet Music breathes her soul into the wind;
And bright-eyed Painting stamps the image of the mind.

II. 2.

Round the rude ark old Egypt's sorcerers rise!
A timbrelled anthem swells the gale,
And bids the God of Thunders hail;[8]
With lowings loud the captive god replies.
Clouds of incense woo thy smile,
Scaly monarch of the Nile![9]
But, ah! what myriads claim the bended knee![10]
Go, count the busy drops that swell the sea.
Proud land! what eye can trace thy mystic lore,
Locked up in characters as dark as night?[11]

What eye those long, long labyrinths dare explore,[12]
To which the parted soul oft wings her flight;
Again to visit her cold cell of clay,
Charmed with perennial sweets, and smiling at decay?

II. 3.

On yon hoar summit, mildly bright[13]
With purple ether's liquid light,
High o'er the world, the white-robed Magi gaze
On dazzling bursts of heavenly fire;
Start at each blue, portentous blaze,
Each flame that flits with adverse spire.
But say, what sounds my ear invade
From Delphi's venerable shade?
The temple rocks, the laurel waves!
"The god! the god!" the Sibyl cries.[14]
Her figure swells! she foams, she raves!
Her figure swells to more than mortal size!
Streams of rapture roll along,
Silver notes ascend the skies:
Wake, Echo, wake and catch the song,
O, catch it, ere it dies!
The Sibyl speaks, the dream is o'er,
The holy harpings charm no more.
In vain she checks the god's control;
His madding spirit fills her frame,
And moulds the features of her soul,
Breathing a prophetic flame.
The cavern frowns; its hundred mouths unclose!
And, in the thunder's voice, the fate of empire flows!

III. 1.

Mona, thy Druid-rites awake the dead!
Rites thy brown oaks would never dare
Even whisper to the idle air;
Rites that have chained old Ocean on his bed.
Shivered by thy piercing glance,
Pointless falls the hero's lance.
Thy magic bids the imperial eagle fly,[15]
And blasts the laureate wreath of victory.
Hark, the bard's soul inspires the vocal string!
At every pause dread Silence hovers o'er:
While murky Night sails round on raven wing,
Deepening the tempest's howl, the torrent's roar;
Chased by the Morn from Snowdon's awful brow,
Where late she sate and scowled on the black wave below.

III. 2.

Lo! steel-clad War his gorgeous standard rears!
The red-cross squadrons madly rage,[16]
And mow through infancy and age;
Then kiss the sacred dust and melt in tears.
Veiling from the eye of day,
Penance dreams her life away;
In cloistered solitude she sits and sighs,
While from each shrine still, small responses rise.
Hear, with what heartfelt beat the midnight bell
Swings its slow summons through the hollow pile!
The weak, wan votarist leaves her twilight cell,
To walk, with taper dim, the winding aisle;
With choral chantings vainly to aspire
Beyond this nether sphere, on Rapture's wing of fire.

III. 3.

Lord of each pang the nerves can feel,
Hence with the rack and reeking wheel.
Faith lifts the soul above this little ball!
While gleams of glory open round,
And circling choirs of angels call,
Canst thou, with all thy terrors crowned,
Hope to obscure that latent spark,
Destined to shine when suns are dark?
Thy triumphs cease! through every land,
Hark! Truth proclaims, thy triumphs cease!
Her heavenly form, with glowing hand,
Benignly points to piety and peace.
Flushed with youth, her looks impart
Each fine feeling as it flows;
Her voice the echo of a heart
Pure as the mountain snows:
Celestial transports round her play,
And softly, sweetly die away.
She smiles! and where is now the cloud
That blackened o'er thy baleful reign?
Grim darkness furls his leaden shroud,
Shrinking from her glance in vain.
Her touch unlocks the day-spring from above,
And, lo! it visits man with beams of light and love.

THE SAILOR.

1786.

THE Sailor sighs as sinks his native shore,
  As all its lessening turrets bluely fade;
He climbs the mast to feast his eye once more,
  And busy Fancy fondly lends her aid.

Ah! now, each dear, domestic scene he knew,
  Recalled and cherished in a foreign clime,
Charms with the magic of a moonlight view;
  Its colors mellowed, not impaired, by time.

True as the needle, homeward points his heart,
  Through all the horrors of the stormy main;
This, the last wish that would with life depart,
  To meet the smile of her he loves again.

When Morn first faintly draws her silver line,
  Or Eve's gray cloud descends to drink the wave;
When sea and sky in midnight darkness join,
  Still, still he sees the parting look she gave.

Her gentle spirit, lightly hovering o'er,
  Attends his little bark from pole to pole;
And, when the beating billows round him roar,
  Whispers sweet hope to soothe his troubled soul.

Carved is her name in many a spicy grove,
  In many a plantain-forest, waving wide;
Where dusky youths in painted plumage rove,
  And giant palms o'erarch the golden tide.

But, lo! at last he comes with crowded sail!
  Lo! o'er the cliff what eager figures bend!
And hark, what mingled murmurs swell the gale!
  In each he hears the welcome of a friend.

'T is she, 't is she herself! she waves her hand!
  Soon is the anchor cast, the canvas furled;
Soon through the whitening surge he springs to land,
  And clasps the maid he singled from the world.

A WISH.

MINE be a cot beside the hill;
  A bee-hive's hum shall soothe my ear;
A willowy brook, that turns a mill,
  With many a fall shall linger near.

The swallow, oft, beneath my thatch,
  Shall twitter from her clay-built nest;
Oft shall the pilgrim lift the latch,
  And share my meal, a welcome guest.

Around my ivied porch shall spring
  Each fragrant flower that drinks the dew;
And Lucy, at her wheel, shall sing
  In russet gown and apron blue.

The village church, among the trees,
  Where first our marriage vows were given,
With merry peals shall swell the breeze,
  And point with taper spire to heaven.

AN ITALIAN SONG.

Dear is my little native vale,
  The ring-dove builds and murmurs there;
Close by my cot she tells her tale
  To every passing villager.
The squirrel leaps from tree to tree,
And shells his nuts at liberty.

In orange-groves and myrtle-bowers,
  That breathe a gale of fragrance round,
I charm the fairy-footed hours
  With my loved lute's romantic sound;
Or crowns of living laurel weave,
For those that win the race at eve.

The shepherd's horn at break of day,
  The ballet danced in twilight glade,
The canzonet and roundelay
  Sung in the silent green-wood shade;
These simple joys, that never fail,
Shall bind me to my native vale.

THE ALPS AT DAY-BREAK.

The sunbeams streak the azure skies,
  And line with light the mountain's brow:
With hounds and horns the hunters rise,
  And chase the roebuck through the snow.

From rock to rock, with giant-bound,
High on their iron poles they pass;
Mute, lest the air, convulsed by sound,
Rend from above a frozen mass.

The goats wind slow their wonted way,
Up craggy steeps and ridges rude;
Marked by the wild wolf for his prey,
From desert cave or hanging wood.

And while the torrent thunders loud,
And as the echoing cliffs reply,
The huts peep o'er the morning-cloud,
Perched, like an eagle's nest, on high.

ON A TEAR.

O! THAT the chemist's magic art
Could crystallize this sacred treasure!
Long should it glitter near my heart,
A secret source of pensive pleasure.

The little brilliant, ere it fell,
Its lustre caught from CHLOE'S eye;
Then, trembling, left its coral cell —
The spring of Sensibility!

Sweet drop of pure and pearly light!
In thee the rays of Virtue shine;
More calmly clear, more mildly bright,
Than any gem that gilds the mine.

Benign restorer of the soul!
  Who ever fly'st to bring relief,
When first we feel the rude control
  Of Love or Pity, Joy or Grief.

The sage's and the poet's theme,
  In every clime, in every age;
Thou charm'st in Fancy's idle dream,
  In Reason's philosophic page.

That very law[17] which moulds a tear,
  And bids it trickle from its source,
That law preserves the earth a sphere,
  And guides the planets in their course.

WRITTEN IN A SICK CHAMBER.

1793.

THERE, in that bed so closely curtained round,
  Worn to a shade and wan with slow decay,
A father sleeps! O, hushed be every sound!
  Soft may we breathe the midnight hours away!

He stirs—yet still he sleeps. May heavenly dreams
  Long o'er his smooth and settled pillow rise;
Nor fly, till morning through the shutter streams,
  And on the hearth the glimmering rush-light dies!

* * * * * *

TO TWO SISTERS.[18]

1795.

WELL may you sit within, and, fond of grief,
  Look in each other's face, and melt in tears.
Well may you shun all counsel, all relief.
  O, she was great in mind, though young in years!

Changed is that lovely countenance, which shed
  Light when she spoke; and kindled sweet surprise,
As o'er her frame each warm emotion spread,
  Played round her lips, and sparkled in her eyes.

Those lips so pure, that moved but to persuade,
  Still to the last enlivened and endeared.
Those eyes at once her secret soul conveyed,
  And ever beamed delight when you appeared.

Yet has she fled the life of bliss below,
  That youthful Hope in bright perspective drew?
False were the tints! false as the feverish glow
  That o'er her burning cheek Distemper threw!

And now in joy she dwells, in glory moves!
  (Glory and joy reserved for you to share.)
Far, far more blest in blessing those she loves,
  Than they, alas! unconscious of her care.

TO A FRIEND ON HIS MARRIAGE.

On thee, blest youth, a father's hand confers
  The maid thy earliest, fondest wishes knew.
Each soft enchantment of the soul is hers;
  Thine be the joys to firm attachment due.

As on she moves with hesitating grace,
  She wins assurance from his soothing voice;
And, with a look the pencil could not trace,
  Smiles through her blushes, and confirms the choice.

Spare the fine tremors of her feeling frame!
  To thee she turns — forgive a virgin's fears!
To thee she turns with surest, tenderest claim;
  Weakness that charms, reluctance that endears!

At each response the sacred rite requires,
  From her full bosom bursts the unbidden sigh.
A strange mysterious awe the scene inspires;
  And on her lips the trembling accents die.

O'er her fair face what wild emotions play!
  What lights and shades in sweet confusion blend!
Soon shall they fly, glad harbingers of day,
  And settled sunshine on her soul descend!

Ah! soon, thine own confest, ecstatic thought!
  That hand shall strew thy summer-path with flowers;
And those blue eyes, with mildest lustre fraught,
  Gild the calm current of domestic hours!

WRITTEN TO BE SPOKEN BY MRS. SIDDONS.[19]

YES, 't is the pulse of life! my fears were vain;
I wake, I breathe, and am myself again.
Still in this nether world; no seraph yet!
Nor walks my spirit, when the sun is set,
With troubled step to haunt the fatal board,
Where I died last — by poison or the sword;
Blanching each honest cheek with deeds of night,
Done here so oft by dim and doubtful light.
— To drop all metaphor, that little bell
Called back reality, and broke the spell.
No heroine claims your tears with tragic tone;
A very woman — scarce restrains her own!
Can she, with fiction, charm the cheated mind,
When to be grateful is the part assigned?
Ah, no! she scorns the trappings of her art;
No theme but truth, no prompter but the heart!
But, Ladies, say, must I alone unmask?
Is here no other actress, let me ask.
Believe me, those, who best the heart dissect,
Know every woman studies stage-effect.
She moulds her manners to the part she fills,
As Instinct teaches, or as Humor wills;
And, as the grave or gay her talent calls,
Acts in the drama, till the curtain falls.
First, how her little breast with triumph swells,
When the red coral rings its golden bells!
To play in pantomime is then the *rage*,
Along the carpet's many-colored stage;

Or lisp her merry thoughts with loud endeavor,
Now here, now there,— in noise and mischief ever!
  A school-girl next, she curls her hair in papers,
And mimics father's gout, and mother's vapors;
Discards her doll, bribes Betty for romances;
Playful at church, and serious when she dances;
Tramples alike on customs and on toes,
And whispers all she hears to all she knows;
Terror of caps, and wigs, and sober notions!
A romp! that *longest* of perpetual motions!
— Till, tamed and tortured into foreign graces,
She sports her lovely face at public places;
And with blue, laughing eyes, behind her fan,
First acts her part with that great actor, MAN.
  Too soon a flirt, approach her and she flies!
Frowns when pursued, and, when entreated, sighs!
Plays with unhappy men as cats with mice;
Till fading beauty hints the late advice.
Her prudence dictates what her pride disdained,
And now she sues to slaves herself had chained!
  Then comes that good old character, a Wife,
With all the dear, distracting cares of life;
A thousand cards a day at doors to leave,
And, in return, a thousand cards receive;
Rouge high, play deep, to lead the ton aspire,
With nightly blaze set PORTLAND-PLACE on fire;
Snatch half a glimpse at concert, opera, ball,
A meteor, traced by none, though seen by all;
And, when her shattered nerves forbid to roam,
In very spleen — rehearse the girls at home.
  Last the gray Dowager, in ancient flounces,
With snuff and spectacles the age denounces;

Boasts how the sires of this degenerate Isle
Knelt for a look, and duelled for a smile.
The scourge and ridicule of Goth and Vandal,
Her tea she sweetens, as she sips, with scandal;
With modern belles eternal warfare wages,
Like her own birds that clamor from their cages;
And shuffles round to bear her tale to all,
Like some old Ruin, "nodding to its fall!"
  Thus WOMAN makes her entrance and her exit;
Not least an actress when she least suspects it.
Yet Nature oft peeps out and mars the plot,
Each lesson lost, each poor pretence forgot;
Full oft, with energy that scorns control,
At once lights up the features of the soul;
Unlocks each thought chained down by coward Art,
And to full day the latent passions start!
— And she, whose first, best wish is your applause,
Herself exemplifies the truth she draws.
Born on the stage — through every shifting scene,
Obscure or bright, tempestuous or serene,
Still has your smile her trembling spirit fired!
And can she act, with thoughts like these inspired?
No! from her mind all artifice she flings,
All skill, all practice, now unmeaning things!
To you, unchecked, each genuine feeling flows;
For all that life endears — to you she owes.

TO * * * * * * *.

Go — you may call it madness, folly;
  You shall not chase my gloom away.
There 's such a charm in melancholy,
  I would not, if I could, be gay.

O, if you knew the pensive pleasure
  That fills my bosom when I sigh,
You would not rob me of a treasure
  Monarchs are too poor to buy.

A FAREWELL.

Adieu! A long, a long adieu!
  I must be gone while yet I may.
Oft shall I weep to think of you;
  But here I will not, cannot stay.

The sweet expression of that face,
  Forever changing, yet the same,
Ah no! I dare not turn to trace.
  It melts my soul, it fires my frame!

Yet give me, give me, ere I go,
  One little lock of those so blest,
That lend your cheek a warmer glow,
  And on your white neck love to rest.

— Say, when, to kindle soft delight,
  That hand has chanced with mine to meet,
How could its thrilling touch excite
  A sigh so short, and yet so sweet?

O say — but no, it must not be.
Adieu ! A long, a long adieu !
— Yet still, methinks, you frown on me ;
Or never could I fly from you.

FROM A GREEK EPIGRAM.

While on the cliff with calm delight she kneels,
And the blue vales a thousand joys recall,
See, to the last, last verge her infant steals !
O, fly ! — yet stir not, speak not, lest it fall.
Far better taught, she lays her bosom bare,
And the fond boy springs back to nestle there.

FROM EURIPIDES.

There is a streamlet issuing from a rock.
The village-girls, singing wild madrigals,
Dip their white vestments in its waters clear,
And hang them to the sun. There first we met,
There on that day. Her dark and eloquent eyes
'T was heaven to look upon ; and her sweet voice,
As tunable as harp of many strings,
At once spoke joy and sadness to my soul !

Dear is that valley to the murmuring bees ;
And all, who know it, come and come again.
The small birds build there ; and at summer-noon
Oft have I heard a child, gay among flowers,
As in the shining grass she sate concealed,
Sing to herself. . . . . . .

FROM AN ITALIAN SONNET.

Love, under Friendship's vesture white,
Laughs, his little limbs concealing;
And oft in sport, and oft in spite,
Like Pity meets the dazzled sight,
Smiles through his tears revealing.
  But now as Rage the god appears!
He frowns, and tempests shake his frame! —
Frowning, or smiling, or in tears,
'T is Love; and Love is still the same.

CAPTIVITY.

Caged in old woods, whose reverend echoes wake
When the hern screams along the distant lake,
Her little heart oft flutters to be free,
Oft sighs to turn the unrelenting key.
In vain! the nurse that rusted relic wears,
Nor moved by gold — nor to be moved by tears;
And terraced walls their black reflection throw
On the green-mantled moat that sleeps below.

WRITTEN AT MIDNIGHT.

While through the broken pane the tempest sighs,
And my step falters on the faithless floor,
Shades of departed joys around me rise,
With many a face that smiles on me no more;
With many a voice that thrills of transport gave,
Now silent as the grass that tufts their grave!

20*

A CHARACTER.

As through the hedge-row shade the violet steals,
And the sweet air its modest leaf reveals;
Her softer charms, but by their influence known,
Surprise all hearts, and mould them to her own.

TO AN OLD OAK.

TRUNK of a giant now no more!
Once did thy limbs to heaven aspire;
Once, by a track untried before,
Strike as resolving to explore
  Realms of infernal fire.[20]

Round thee, alas! no shadows move!
From thee no sacred murmurs breathe!
Yet within thee, thyself a grove,
Once did the eagle scream above,
  And the wolf howl beneath.

There once the red-cross knight reclined,
His resting-place, a house of prayer;
And, when the death-bell smote the wind
From towers long fled by human kind,
  He knelt and worshipped there!

Then Culture came, and days serene;
And village-sports, and garlands gay.
Full many a pathway crossed the green;
And maids and shepherd-youths were seen
  To celebrate the May.

Father of many a forest deep,
Whence many a navy thunder-fraught!
Erst in thy acorn-cells asleep,
Soon destined o'er the world to sweep,
  Opening new spheres of thought!

Wont in the night of woods to dwell,
The holy Druid saw thee rise;
And, planting there the guardian-spell,
Sung forth, the dreadful pomp to swell
  Of human sacrifice!

Thy singed top and branches bare
Now straggle in the evening-sky;
And the wan moon wheels round to glare
On the long corse that shivers there
  Of him who came to die!

TO THE YOUNGEST DAUGHTER OF LADY * *.

1800.

Ah! why with tell-tale tongue reveal[21]
What most her blushes would conceal?
Why lift that modest veil to trace
The seraph-sweetness of her face?
Some fairer, better sport prefer;
And feel for us, if not for her.
  For this presumption, soon or late,
Know thine shall be a kindred fate.
Another shall in vengeance rise —
Sing Harriet's cheeks, and Harriet's eyes;
And, echoing back her wood-notes wild,
— Trace all the mother in the child!

TO THE GNAT.

When by the greenwood side, at summer eve,
Poetic visions charm my closing eye;
And fairy-scenes, that Fancy loves to weave,
Shift to wild notes of sweetest minstrelsy;
'T is thine to range in busy quest of prey,
Thy feathery antlers quivering with delight,
Brush from my lids the hues of heaven away,
And all is solitude, and all is night!
— Ah! now thy barbéd shaft, relentless fly,
Unsheaths its terrors in the sultry air!
No guardian sylph, in golden panoply,
Lifts the broad shield, and points the glittering sp
Now near and nearer rush thy whirring wings,
Thy dragon-scales still wet with human gore.
Hark, thy shrill horn its fearful larum flings!
— I wake in horror, and dare sleep no more!

TO A VOICE THAT HAD BEEN LOST.[22]

Vane, quid affectas faciem mihi ponere, pictor?
Aeris et linguæ sum filia;
Et, si vis similem pingere, pinge sonum. — Ausonius.

Once more, Enchantress of the soul,
Once more we hail thy soft control.
— Yet whither, whither didst thou fly?
To what bright region of the sky?
Say, in what distant star to dwell?
(Of other worlds thou seem'st to tell)

Or trembling, fluttering here below,
Resolved and unresolved to go,
In secret didst thou still impart
Thy raptures to the pure in heart?
  Perhaps to many a desert shore,
Thee, in his rage, the tempest bore;
Thy broken murmurs swept along,
Mid echoes yet untuned by song;
Arrested in the realms of frost,
Or in the wilds of ether lost.
  Far happier thou! 't was thine to soar,
Careering on the wingéd wind.
Thy triumphs who shall dare explore?
Suns and their systems left behind.
No tract of space, no distant star,
No shock of elements at war,
Did thee detain. Thy wing of fire
Bore thee amid the cherub-choir;
And there a while to thee 't was given
Once more that voice[23] beloved to join,
Which taught thee first a flight divine,
And nursed thy infant years with many a strain from
    Heaven!

TO THE BUTTERFLY.

Child of the sun! pursue thy rapturous flight,
Mingling with her thou lov'st in fields of light;
And, where the flowers of Paradise unfold,
Quaff fragrant nectar from their cups of gold.

There shall thy wings, rich as an evening-sky,
Expand and shut with silent ecstasy!
— Yet wert thou once a worm, a thing that crept
On the bare earth, then wrought a tomb and slept.
And such is man; soon from his cell of clay
To burst a seraph in the blaze of day!

AN EPITAPH ON A ROBIN-REDBREAST.[24]

Tread lightly here, for here, 't is said,
When piping winds are hushed around,
A small note wakes from underground,
Where now his tiny bones are laid.
No more in lone and leafless groves,
With ruffled wing and faded breast,
His friendless, homeless spirit roves;
— Gone to the world where birds are blest!
Where never cat glides o'er the green,
Or school-boy's giant form is seen;
But Love, and Joy, and smiling Spring,
Inspire their little souls to sing!

TO THE FRAGMENT OF A STATUE OF HERCULES.

COMMONLY CALLED THE TORSO.

And dost thou still, thou mass of breathing stone
(Thy giant limbs to night and chaos hurled),
Still sit as on the fragment of a world;
Surviving all, majestic and alone?

What though the Spirits of the North, that swept
Rome from the earth when in her pomp she slept,
Smote thee with fury, and thy headless trunk
Deep in the dust mid tower and temple sunk;
Soon to subdue mankind 't was thine to rise,
Still, still unquelled thy glorious energies!
Aspiring minds, with thee conversing, caught
Bright revelations of the Good they sought;[25]
By thee that long-lost spell in secret given,
To draw down gods, and lift the soul to Heaven![26]

TO . . . .[27]

Ah! little thought she, when, with wild delight,
  By many a torrent's shining track she flew,
When mountain-glens and caverns full of night
  O'er her young mind divine enchantment threw,

That in her veins a secret horror slept,
  That her light footsteps should be heard no more,
That she should die — nor watched, alas! nor wept
  By thee, unconscious of the pangs she bore.

Yet round her couch indulgent Fancy drew
  The kindred forms her closing eye required.
There didst thou stand — there, with the smile she knew;
  She moved her lips to bless thee, and expired.

And now to thee she comes; still, still the same
  As in the hours gone unregarded by!
To thee, how changed, comes as she ever came;
  Health on her cheek, and pleasure in her eye!

Nor less, less oft, as on that day, appears,
  When lingering, as prophetic of the truth,
By the way-side she shed her parting tears —
  Forever lovely in the light of Youth!

THE BOY OF EGREMOND.

"SAY, what remains when Hope is fled?"
She answered, "Endless weeping!"
For in the herdsman's eye she read
Who in his shroud lay sleeping.
  At Embsay rung the matin-bell,
The stag was roused on Barden-fell;
The mingled sounds were swelling, dying,
And down the Wharfe a hern was flying;
When near the cabin in the wood,
In tartan-clad and forest-green,
With hound in leash and hawk in hood,
The Boy of Egremond was seen.[28]
Blithe was his song, a song of yore;
But where the rock is rent in two,
And the river rushes through,
His voice was heard no more!
'T was but a step! the gulf he passed;
But that step — it was his last!
As through the mist he winged his way
(A cloud that hovers night and day),
The hound hung back, and back he drew
The master and his merlin too.

That narrow place of noise and strife
Received their little all of life!
  There now the matin-bell is rung;
The "Miserere!" duly sung;
And holy men in cowl and hood
Are wandering up and down the wood.
But what avail they? Ruthless Lord,
Thou didst not shudder when the sword
Here on the young its fury spent,
The helpless and the innocent.
Sit now and answer, groan for groan.
The child before thee is thy own.
And she who wildly wanders there,
The mother in her long despair,
Shall oft remind thee, waking, sleeping,
Of those who by the Wharfe were weeping;
Of those who would not be consoled
When red with blood the river rolled.

WRITTEN IN THE HIGHLANDS OF SCOTLAND,

September 2, 1812.

Blue was the loch, the clouds were gone,
Ben-Lomond in his glory shone,
When, Luss, I left thee; when the breeze
Bore me from thy silver sands,
Thy kirk-yard wall among the trees,
Where, gray with age, the dial stands;
That dial so well known to me!
—Though many a shadow it had shed,

Beloved sister, since with thee
The legend on the stone was read.
  The fairy-isles fled far away;
That with its woods and uplands green,
Where shepherd-huts are dimly seen,
And songs are heard at close of day;
That too, the deer's wild covert, fled,
And that, the asylum of the dead:
While, as the boat went merrily,
Much of ROB ROY the boatman told;
His arm that fell below his knee,
His cattle-ford and mountain-hold.
  Tarbat,[29] thy shore I climbed at last;
And, thy shady region passed,
Upon another shore I stood,
And looked upon another flood;[30]
Great Ocean's self! ('T is He who fills
That vast and awful depth of hills);
Where many an elf was playing round,
Who treads unshod his classic ground;
And speaks, his native rocks among,
As FINGAL spoke, and OSSIAN sung.
  Night fell; and dark and darker grew
That narrow sea, that narrow sky,
As o'er the glimmering waves we flew;
The sea-bird rustling, wailing by.
And now the grampus, half-descried,
Black and huge above the tide;
The cliffs and promontories there,
Front to front, and broad and bare;
Each beyond each, with giant-feet
Advancing as in haste to meet;

The shattered fortress, whence the Dane
Blew his shrill blast, nor rushed in vain,
Tyrant of the drear domain;
All into midnight-shadow sweep —
When day springs upward from the deep![31]
Kindling the waters in its flight,
The prow wakes splendor; and the oar,
That rose and fell unseen before,
Flashes in a sea of light!
Glad sign, and sure! for now we hail
Thy flowers, Glenfinnart, in the gale;
And bright indeed the path should be,
That leads to Friendship and to thee!
O blest retreat, and sacred too!
Sacred as when the bell of prayer
Tolled duly on the desert air,
And crosses decked thy summits blue.
Oft, like some loved romantic tale,
Oft shall my weary mind recall,
Amid the hum and stir of men,
Thy beechen-grove and waterfall,
Thy ferry with its gliding sail,
And her — the Lady of the Glen!

ON . . . ASLEEP.

Sleep on, and dream of Heaven a while.
Though shut so close thy laughing eyes,
Thy rosy lips still wear a smile,
And move, and breathe delicious sighs! —

Ah! now soft blushes tinge her cheeks,
And mantle o'er her neck of snow.
Ah! now she murmurs, now she speaks,
What most I wish — and fear to know.

She starts, she trembles, and she weeps!
Her fair hands folded on her breast.
— And now, how like a saint she sleeps!
A seraph in the realms of rest!

Sleep on secure! Above control,
Thy thoughts belong to Heaven and thee!
And may the secret of thy soul
Remain within its sanctuary!

AN INSCRIPTION IN THE CRIMEA.

SHEPHERD, or Huntsman, or worn Mariner,
Whate'er thou art, who wouldst allay thy thirst,
Drink and be glad. This cistern of white stone,
Arched, and o'erwrought with many a sacred verse,
This iron-cup chained for the general use,
And these rude seats of earth within the grove,
Were given by FATIMA. Borne hence a bride,
'T was here she turned from her beloved sire,
To see his face no more.[32] O, if thou canst
('T is not far off), visit his tomb with flowers;
And with a drop of this sweet water fill
The two small cells scooped in the marble there,
That birds may come and drink upon his grave,
Making it holy[33] . . . .

AN INSCRIPTION FOR A TEMPLE DEDICATED TO THE GRACES.[34]

APPROACH with reverence. There are those within
Whose dwelling-place is Heaven. Daughters of Jove,
From them flow all the decencies of life;
Without them nothing pleases, Virtue's self
Admired, not loved: and those on whom they smile,
Great though they be, and wise, and beautiful,
Shine forth with double lustre.

REFLECTIONS.

MAN to the last is but a froward child;
So eager for the future, come what may,
And to the present so insensible!
O, if he could in all things as he would,
Years would as days and hours as moments be;
He would, so restless is his spirit here,
Give wings to Time, and wish his life away!

ALAS! to our discomfort and his own,
Oft are the greatest talents to be found
In a fool's keeping. For what else is he,
However worldly wise and worldly strong,
Who can pervert and to the worst abuse
The noblest means to serve the noblest ends;
Who can employ the gift of eloquence,
That sacred gift, to dazzle and delude;
Or, if achievement in the field be his,

Climb but to gain a loss, suffering how much,
And how much more inflicting! Everywhere,
Cost what they will, such cruel freaks are played;
And hence the turmoil in this world of ours,
The turmoil never ending, still beginning,
The wailing and the tears.—When CÆSAR came,
He who could master all men but himself,
Who did so much and could so well record it;
Even he, the most applauded in his part,
Who, when he spoke, all things summed up in him,
Spoke to convince, nor ever, when he fought,
Fought but to conquer — what a life was his,
Slaying so many, to be slain at last,[35]
A life of trouble and incessant toil,
And all to gain what is far better missed!

THE heart, they say, is wiser than the schools;
And well they may. All that is great in thought,
That strikes at once as with electric fire,
And lifts us, as it were, from earth to heaven,
Comes from the heart; and who confesses not
Its voice as sacred, nay, almost divine,
When inly it declares on what we do,
Blaming, approving? Let an erring world
Judge as it will, we care not while we stand
Acquitted there; and oft, when clouds on clouds
Compass us round and not a track appears,
Oft is an upright heart the surest guide,
Surer and better than the subtlest head;
Still with its silent counsels through the dark
Onward and onward leading.

This Child, so lovely and so cherub-like
(No fairer spirit in the heaven of heavens),
Say, must he know remorse? Must Passion come,
Passion in all or any of its shapes,
To cloud and sully what is now so pure?
Yes, come it must. For who, alas! has lived,
Nor in the watches of the night recalled
Words he has wished unsaid and deeds undone?
Yes, come it must. But if, as we may hope,
He learns ere long to discipline his mind,
And onward goes, humbly and cheerfully,
Assisting them that faint, weak though he be,
And in his trying hours trusting in God —
Fair as he is, he shall be fairer still;
For what was Innocence will then be Virtue.

O, if the Selfish knew how much they lost,
What would they not endeavor, not endure,
To imitate, as far as in them lay,
Him who his wisdom and his power employs
In making others happy!

Hence to the Altar and with her thou lov'st,
With her who longs to strew thy way with flowers;
Nor lose the blessed privilege to give
Birth to a race immortal as yourselves.
Which, trained by you, shall make a Heaven on earth,
And tread the path that leads from earth to Heaven.

WRITTEN AT MIDNIGHT.

SEPTEMBER 3, 1848.

IF Day reveals such wonders by her light,
What by her darkness cannot Night reveal ?
For at her bidding, when she mounts her throne
The heavens unfold, and from the depths of space
Sun beyond sun, as when called forth they came,
Each with the worlds that round him rolled rejoicing,
Sun beyond sun in numbers numberless
Shine with a radiance that is all their own !

FROM AN ITALIAN SONNET.

I SAID to Time, " This venerable pile,
Its floor the earth, its roof the firmament,
Whose was it once ? " He answered not, but fled
Fast as before. I turned to Fame, and asked.
" Names such as his, to thee they must be known.
Speak ! " But she answered only with a sigh,
And, musing mournfully, looked on the ground.
Then to Oblivion I addressed myself,
A dismal phantom, sitting at the gate ;
And, with a voice as from the grave, he cried,
" Whose it was once I care not ; now 't is mine."

WRITTEN IN WESTMINSTER ABBEY.[36]

OCTOBER 10, 1806.

WHOE'ER thou art, approach, and, with a sigh,
Mark where the small remains of Greatness lie.[37]
There sleeps the dust of Fox forever gone;
How near the place where late his glory shone!
And, though no more ascends the voice of prayer,
Though the last footsteps cease to linger there,
Still, like an awful dream that comes again,
Alas! at best, as transient and as vain,
Still do I see (while through the vaults of night
The funeral-song once more proclaims the rite)
The moving pomp along the shadowy aisle,
That, like a darkness, filled the solemn pile;
The illustrious line, that in long order led,
Of those, that loved him living, mourned him dead;
Of those the few, that for their country stood
Round him who dared be singularly good;
All, of all ranks, that claimed him for their own;
And nothing wanting — but himself alone! [38]
O, say, of him now rests there but a name;
Wont, as he was, to breathe ethereal flame?
Friend of the absent, guardian of the dead!
Who but would here their sacred sorrows shed?
(Such as he shed on NELSON'S closing grave;
How soon to claim the sympathy he gave!)
In him, resentful of another's wrong,
The dumb were eloquent, the feeble strong.
Truth from his lips a charm celestial drew —
Ah! who so mighty and so gentle too?

What though with war the madding nations rung,
"Peace," when he spoke, was ever on his tongue!
Amid the frowns of power, the tricks of state,
Fearless, resolved, and negligently great!
In vain malignant vapors gathered round;
He walked, erect, on consecrated ground.
The clouds, that rise to quench the orb of day,
Reflect its splendor, and dissolve away!
When in retreat he laid his thunder by,
For lettered ease and calm philosophy,
Blest were his hours within the silent grove,
Where still his godlike spirit deigns to rove;
Blest by the orphan's smile, the widow's prayer,
For many a deed, long done in secret there.
There shone his lamp on Homer's hallowed page.
There, listening, sate the hero and the sage;
And they, by virtue and by blood allied,
Whom most he loved, and in whose arms he died.
Friend of all human-kind! not here alone
(The voice, that speaks, was not to thee unknown)
Wilt thou be missed. — O'er every land and sea
Long, long shall England be revered in thee!
And, when the storm is hushed — in distant years —
Foes on thy grave shall meet, and mingle tears!

WRITTEN AT DROPMORE,

JULY, 1831.

GRENVILLE, to thee my gratitude is due
For many an hour of studious musing here,
For many a day-dream, such as hovered round
Hafiz or Sadi; through the golden East,

Search where we would, no fairer bowers than these,
Thine own creation; where, called forth by thee,
"Flowers worthy of Paradise, with rich inlay,
Broider the ground," and every mountain-pine
Elsewhere unseen (his birth-place in the clouds,
His kindred sweeping with majestic march
From cliff to cliff along the snowy ridge
Of Caucasus, or nearer yet the moon)
Breathes heavenly music. — Yet much more I owe
For what so few, alas! can hope to share,
Thy converse; when, among thy books reclined,
Or in thy garden-chair that wheels its course
Slowly and silently through sun and shade,
Thou speak'st, as ever thou art wont to do,
In the calm temper of philosophy;
— Still to delight, instruct, whate'er the theme.

WRITTEN AT STRATHFIELD SAYE.

These are the groves a grateful people gave
For noblest service; and, from age to age,
May they, to such as come with listening ear,
Relate the story! Sacred is their shade;
Sacred the calm they breathe — O, how unlike
What in the field 't was his so long to know!
Where many a mournful, many an anxious thought,[39]
Troubling, perplexing, on his weary mind
Preyed, ere to arms the morning-trumpet called;
Where, till the work was done and darkness fell,
Blood ran like water, and, go where thou wouldst,
Death in thy pathway met thee, face to face.

For on, regardless of himself, he went;
And, by no change elated or depressed,
Fought, till he won the imperishable wreath,
Leading the conquerors captive; on he went,
Bating nor heart nor hope, whoe'er opposed;
The greatest warriors, in their turn, appearing;
The last that came, the greatest of them all —
One scattering hosts as born but to subdue,
And even in bondage withering hearts with fear.
When such the service, what the recompense?
Yet, and I err not, a renown as fair,
And fairer still, awaited him at home;
Where to the last, day after day, he stood,
The party-zeal, that round him raged, restraining;
— His not to rest, while his the strength to serve.[40]

WRITTEN IN JULY, 1834.

GREY, thou hast served, and well, the sacred cause
That Hampden, Sydney died for. Thou hast stood,
Scorning all thought of self, from first to last,
Among the foremost in that glorious field;
From first to last; and, ardent as thou art,
Held on with equal step as best became
A lofty mind, loftiest when most assailed;
Never, though galled by many a barbed shaft,
By many a bitter taunt from friend and foe,
Swerving or shrinking. Happy in thy youth,
Thy youth the dawn of a long summer-day;
But in thy age still happier; thine to earn
The gratitude of millions yet unborn;

Thine to conduct, through ways how difficult,
A mighty people in their march sublime
From Good to Better. Great thy recompense,
When in their eyes thou read'st what thou hast done;
And may'st thou long enjoy it; may'st thou long
Preserve for them what they still claim as theirs,
That generous fervor and pure eloquence,
Thine from thy birth and Nature's noblest gifts,
To guard what they have gained!

WRITTEN IN 1834.

Well, when her day is over, be it said
That, though a speck on the terrestrial globe,
Found with long search and in a moment lost,
She made herself a name — a name to live
While science, eloquence, and song divine,
And wisdom, in self-government displayed,
And valor, such as only in the Free,
Shall among men be honored.
Every sea
Was covered with her sails; in every port
Her language spoken; and, where'er you went,
Exploring, to the east or to the west,
Even to the rising or the setting day,
Her arts and laws and institutes were there,
Moving with silent and majestic march,
Onward and onward, where no pathway was;
There her adventurous sons, like those of old,
Founding vast empires [41] — empires in their turn

Destined to shine through many a distant age
With sun-like splendor.
                                        Wondrous was her wealth,
The world itself her willing tributary;
Yet, to accomplish what her soul desired,
All was as nothing; and the mightiest kings,
Each in his hour of strife exhausted, fallen,
Drew strength from her, their coffers from her own
Filled to o'erflowing. When her fleets of war
Had swept the main,—had swept it and were gone,
Gone from the eyes and from the minds of men,
Their dreadful errand so entirely done,—
Up rose her armies; on the land they stood,
Fearless, erect; and in an instant smote
Him with his legions.[42]
                                        Yet ere long 't was hers,
Great as her triumphs, to eclipse them all,
To do what none had done, none had conceived,
An act how glorious, making joy in Heaven;
When, such her prodigality, condemned
To toil and toil, alas! how hopelessly,
Herself in bonds, for ages unredeemed—
As with a godlike energy she sprung,
All else forgot, and, burdened as she was,
Ransomed the African.[43]

NOTES.

(1) Written in 1785.

(2) The sacrifice of Iphigenia.

(3) Lucretius, I. 63.

(4) The funeral rite of the Hindoos.

(5) The Fates of the northern mythology. — *See Mallet's Antiquities.*

(6) An allusion to the second sight.

(7) *Æn.* II. 172, &c.

(8) The bull, Apis.

(9) The crocodile.

(10) According to an ancient proverb, it was less difficult in Egypt to find a god than a man.

(11) The Hieroglyphics.

(12) The Catacombs.

(13) "The Persians," says Herodotus, "have no temples, altars or statues. They sacrifice on the tops of the highest mountains." — I. 131.

(14) *Æn.* VI. 46, &c.

(15) See *Tacitus*, I. xiv. c. 29.

(16) This remarkable event happened at the siege and sack of Jerusalem, in the last year of the eleventh century. — *Matth. Paris*, IV. 2.

(17) The law of gravitation.

(18) On the death of a young sister.

(19) After a tragedy, performed for her benefit at the Theatre Royal, in Drury Lane, April 27, 1795.

(20) Radice in Tartara tendit. — *Virg.*

(21) Alluding to some verses which she had written on an elder sister.

(22) In the winter of 1805.

(23) Mrs. Sheridan's.

(24) Inscribed on an urn in the flower-garden at Hafod.

(25) In the gardens of the Vatican, where it was placed by Julius II., it was long the favorite study of those great men to whom we owe the revival of the arts, Michael Angelo, Raphael and the Caracci.

(26) Once in the possession of Praxiteles, if we may believe an ancient epigram on the Guidian Venus. —*Analecta Vet. Poetarum*, III. 200.

(27) On the death of her sister, in 1805.

(28) In the twelfth century William Fitz-Duncan laid waste the valleys of Craven with fire and sword; and was afterwards established there by his uncle, David, King of Scotland.

He was the last of the race; his son, commonly called the Boy of Egremond, dying before him in the manner here related; when a Priory was removed from Embsay to Bolton, that it might be as near as possible to the place where the accident happened. That place is still known by the name of the *Strid;* and the mother's answer, as given in the first stanza, is to this day often repeated in Wharfedale. —*See Whitaker's Hist. of Craven.*

(29) Signifying in the Gaelic language an isthmus.

(30) Loch-Long.

(31) A phenomenon described by many navigators.

(32) There is a beautiful story, delivered down to us from antiquity, which will here, perhaps, occur to the reader.

Icarius, when he gave Penelope in marriage to Ulysses, endeavored to persuade him to dwell in Lacedæmon, and, when all he urged was to no purpose, he entreated his daughter to remain with him. When Ulysses set out with his bride for Ithaca, the old man followed the chariot till, overcome by his importunity, Ulysses consented that it should be left to Penelope to decide whether she would proceed with him or return with her father. It is related, says Pausanias, that she made no reply, but that she covered herself with her veil; and that Icarius, perceiving at once by it that she inclined to Ulysses, suffered her to depart with him.

A statue was afterwards placed by her father as a memorial in that part of the road where she had covered herself with her veil. It was still standing there in the days of Pausanias, and was called the statue of Modesty.

(33) A Turkish superstition.

(34) At Woburn Abbey.

(35) He is said to have slain a million of men in Gaul alone.

(36) After the funeral of the Right Hon. CHARLES JAMES FOX.

(37) Venez voir le peu qui nous reste de tant de grandeur, &c. —*Bossuet. Oraison funèbre de Louis de Bourbon.*

(38) Et rien enfin ne manque dans tous ces honneurs, que celui à qui on les rend. —*Bossuet. Oraison funèbre de Louis de Bourbon.*

(39) How strange, said he to me, are the impressions that sometimes follow a battle! After the battle of Assaye I slept in a farm-house, and so great had been the slaughter that whenever I awoke, which I did continually through the night, it struck me that I had lost all my friends, nor could I bring myself to think otherwise till morning came, and one by one I saw those that were living.

(40) On Friday, the 19th of November, 1830, there was an assembly at Bridgewater House, a house which has long ceased to be, and of which no stone is now resting on another. It was there that I saw a lady whose beauty was the least of her attractions, and she said, "I never see you now." — "When may I come?" — "Come on Sunday at five." — "At five, then, you shall see me." — "Remember five." — And through the evening, wherever I went, a voice followed me, repeating, in a tone of mock solemnity, "Remember five!" It was the voice of one who had overheard us; and little did he think what was to take place at five.

On Sunday, when the time drew near, it struck me as I was leaving Lord Holland's, in Burlington-street, that I had some engagement, so little had I thought of it, and I repaired to the house, No. 4, in Carlton Gardens. There were the Duke of Wellington's horses at the door, and I said, "The duke is here." — "But you are expected, sir." — I went in and found him sitting with the lady of the house, the lady who had made the appointment, nor was it long before he spoke as follows:

"They want me to place myself at the head of a faction, but I tell them that I never will.

"To-morrow I shall give up my office and go down into my county, to restore order there, if I can restore it. When I return, I shall take my place in Parliament, to approve when I can approve; and when I cannot, to say so. I have now served my country forty years, twenty in the field and ten — if not more — in the cabinet; nor, while I live, shall I be found wanting, wherever I may be. But never — no, never — will I place myself at the head of a faction."

Having met Lord Grey, who was to succeed him in his office, again and again under my roof, and knowing our intimacy, he meant that these words should be repeated to him; and so they were, word for word, on that very night.

(41) North America speaks for itself; and so indeed may we say of India, when such a territory is ours in a region so remote; when a company of merchants, from such small beginnings, have established a dominion so absolute, — a dominion over a people for ages civilized and cultivated, while we were yet in the woods.

(42) Alluding to the battle of Waterloo. The illustrious man who commanded there on our side, and who, in his anxiety to do justice to others, never fails to forget himself, said to me many years afterwards, with some agitation, when relating an occurrence of that day, "It was a battle of giants! a battle of giants!"

(43) Parliament had only to register the edict of the people. — *Channing.*

ITALY.

PREFACE.

In this poem the author has endeavored to describe his journey through a beautiful country; and it may not perhaps be uninteresting to those who have learnt to live in past times as well as present, and whose minds are familiar with the events and the people that have rendered Italy so illustrious; for, wherever he came, he could not but remember; nor is he conscious of having slept over any ground that has been "dignified by wisdom, bravery or virtue."

Much of it was originally published as it was written on the spot. He has since, on a second visit, revised it throughout, and added many stories from the old chroniclers, and many notes illustrative of the manners, customs and superstitions, there.

ITALY.

THE LAKE OF GENEVA.

Day glimmered in the east, and the white Moon
Hung like a vapor in the cloudless sky,
Yet visible, when on my way I went,
Glad to be gone; a pilgrim from the North,
Now more and more attracted as I drew
Nearer and nearer. Ere the artisan
Had from his window leant, drowsy, half-clad,
To snuff the morn, or the caged lark poured forth,
From his green sod upspringing as to heaven
(His tuneful bill o'erflowing with a song
Old in the days of Homer, and his wings
With transport quivering), on my way I went,
Thy gates, Geneva, swinging heavily,
Thy gates so slow to open, swift to shut;
As on that Sabbath-eve when he arrived,[1]
Whose name is now thy glory, now by thee,
Such virtue dwells in those small syllables,
Inscribed to consecrate the narrow street,
His birth-place,—when, but one short step too late,
In his despair, as though the die were cast,

He flung him down to weep, and wept till dawn;
Then rose to go, a wanderer through the world.
'T is not a tale that every hour brings with it.[2]
Yet at a city-gate, from time to time,
Much may be learnt; nor, London, least at thine,
Thy hive the busiest, greatest of them all,
Gathering, enlarging still. Let us stand by,
And note who passes. Here comes one, a youth,
Glowing with pride, the pride of conscious power,
A CHATTERTON — in thought admired, caressed,
And crowned like PETRARCH in the Capitol;
Ere long to die, to fall by his own hand,
And fester with the vilest. Here come two,
Less feverish, less exalted — soon to part,
A GARRICK and a JOHNSON; Wealth and Fame
Awaiting one, even at the gate; Neglect
And Want the other. But what multitudes,
Urged by the love of change, and, like myself,
Adventurous, careless of to-morrow's fare,
Press on — though but a rill entering the sea,
Entering and lost! Our task would never end.
Day glimmered and I went, a gentle breeze
Ruffling the LEMAN Lake. Wave after wave,
If such they might be called, dashed as in sport,
Not anger, with the pebbles on the beach
Making wild music, and far westward caught
The sunbeam — where, alone and as entranced,
Counting the hours, the fisher in his skiff
Lay with his circular and dotted line
On the bright waters. When the heart of man
Is light with hope, all things are sure to please;
And soon a passage-boat swept gayly by,

Laden with peasant-girls and fruits and flowers,
And many a chanticleer and partlet caged
For VEVEY's market-place — a motley group
Seen through the silvery haze. But soon 't was gone.
The shifting sail flapped idly to and fro,
Then bore them off. I am not one of those
So dead to all things in this visible world,
So wondrously profound, as to move on
In the sweet light of heaven, like him of old [3]
(His name is justly in the Calendar)
Who through the day pursued this pleasant path
That winds beside the mirror of all beauty,[4]
And, when at eve his fellow-pilgrims sate,
Discoursing of the lake, asked where it was.
They marvelled, as they might; and so must all,
Seeing what now I saw: for now 't was day,
And the bright sun was in the firmament,
A thousand shadows of a thousand hues
Checkering the clear expanse. A while his orb
Hung o'er thy trackless fields of snow, MONT BLANC,
Thy seas of ice and ice-built promontories,
That change their shapes forever as in sport;
Then travelled onward and went down behind
The pine-clad heights of JURA, lighting up
The woodman's casement, and perchance his axe
Borne homeward through the forest in his hand;
And, on the edge of some o'erhanging cliff,
That dungeon-fortress [5] never to be named,[6]
Where, like a lion taken in the toils,
Toussaint breathed out his brave and generous spirit.
Little did he, who sent him there to die,
Think, when he gave the word, that he himself,

Great as he was, the greatest among men,
Should in like manner be so soon conveyed
Athwart the deep,—and to a rock so small
Amid the countless multitude of waves,
That ships have gone and sought it, and returned,
Saying it was not!

MEILLERIE.

THESE gray majestic cliffs that tower to heaven,
These glimmering glades and open chestnut groves,
That echo to the heifer's wandering bell,
Or woodman's axe, or steers-man's song beneath,
As on he urges his fir-laden bark,
Or shout of goatherd boy above them all,
Who loves not? And who blesses not the light,
When through some loop-hole he surveys the lake
Blue as a sapphire-stone, and richly set
With chateaux, villages, and village-spires,
Orchards and vineyards, alps and alpine snows?
Here would I dwell; nor visit, but in thought,
FERNEY far south, silent and empty now
As now thy once luxurious bowers, RIPAILLE;[7]
VEVEY, so long an exiled patriot's[8] home;
Or CHILLON'S dungeon-floors beneath the wave,
Channelled and worn by pacing to and fro;
LAUSANNE, where GIBBON in his sheltered walk
Nightly called up the shade of ancient ROME;[9]
Or COPPET, and that dark untrodden grove[10]
Sacred to Virtue, and a daughter's tears!
Here would I dwell, forgetting and forgot;

And oft methinks (of such strange potency
The spells that Genius scatters where he will)
Oft should I wander forth like one in search,
And say, half-dreaming, "Here St. Preux has stood!"
Then turn and gaze on Clarens.
Yet there is,
Within an eagle's flight and less, a scene
Still nobler if not fairer (once again
Would I behold it ere these eyes are closed,
For I can say, "I also have been there!")
That sacred lake[11] withdrawn among the hills,
Its depth of waters flanked as with a wall
Built by the giant-race before the flood;
Where not a cross or chapel but inspires
Holy delight, lifting our thoughts to God
From godlike men,— men in a barbarous age
That dared assert their birthright, and displayed
Deeds half-divine, returning good for ill;
That in the desert sowed the seeds of life,
Framing a band of small republics there,
Which still exist, the envy of the world!
Who would not land in each, and tread the ground;
Land where Tell leaped ashore; and climb to drink
Of the three hallowed fountains? He that does
Comes back the better; and relates at home
That he was met and greeted by a race
Such as he read of in his boyish days;
Such as Miltiades at Marathon
Led, when he chased the Persians to their ships.
There, while the well-known boat is heaving in,
Piled with rude merchandise, or launching forth,
Thronged with wild cattle for Italian fairs,

There in the sunshine, 'mid their native snows,
Children, let loose from school, contend to use
The cross-bow of their fathers; and o'errun
The rocky field where all, in every age,
Assembling sit, like one great family,
Forming alliances, enacting laws;
Each cliff and head-land and green promontory
Graven to their eyes with records of the past
That prompt to hero-worship, and excite
Even in the least, the lowliest, as he toils,
A reverence nowhere else or felt or feigned;
Their chronicler great Nature; and the volume
Vast as her works — above, below, around!
The fisher on thy beach, THERMOPYLÆ,
Asks of the lettered stranger why he came,
First from his lips to learn the glorious truth!
And who that whets his scythe in RUNNEMEDE,
Though but for them a slave, recalls to mind
The barons in array, with their great charter?
Among the everlasting Alps alone,
There to burn on as in a sanctuary,
Bright and unsullied lives the ethereal flame;
And 'mid those scenes unchanged, unchangeable,
Why should it ever die?

ST. MAURICE.

STILL by the LEMAN Lake, for many a mile,
Among those venerable trees I went,
Where damsels sit and weave their fishing-nets,
Singing some national song by the wayside.

But now the fly was gone, the gnat was come;
Now glimmering lights from cottage-windows broke.
'T was dusk; and, journeying upward by the RHONE,
That there came down, a torrent from the Alps,
I entered where a key unlocks a kingdom;
The road and river, as they wind along,
Filling the mountain pass. There, till a ray
Glanced through my lattice, and the household-stir
Warned me to rise, to rise and to depart,
A stir unusual, and accompanied
With many a tuning of rude instruments,
And many a laugh that argued coming pleasure,
Mine host's fair daughter for the nuptial rite
And nuptial feast attiring — there I slept,
And in my dreams wandered once more, well pleased.
But now a charm was on the rocks and woods
And waters; for, methought, I was with those
I had at morn and even wished for there.

THE GREAT ST. BERNARD.

NIGHT was again descending, when my mule,
That all day long had climbed among the clouds,
Higher and higher still, as by a stair
Let down from heaven itself, transporting me,
Stopped, to the joy of both, at that low door,
That door which ever, as self-opened, moves
To them that knock, and nightly sends abroad
Ministering spirits. Lying on the watch,
Two dogs of grave demeanor welcomed me,

All meekness, gentleness, though large of limb;
And a lay-brother of the hospital,
Who, as we toiled below, had heard by fits
The distant echoes gaining on his ear,
Came and held fast my stirrup in his hand
While I alighted. Long could I have stood,
With a religious awe contemplating
That house, the highest in the ancient world,
And destined to perform from age to age
The noblest service, welcoming as guests
All of all nations and of every faith;
A temple, sacred to Humanity! [12]
It was a pile of simplest masonry,
With narrow window and vast buttresses,
Built to endure the shocks of time and chance;
Yet showing many a rent, as well it might,
Warred on forever by the elements,
And in an evil day, nor long ago,
By violent men — when on the mountain-top
The French and Austrian banners met in conflict.
On the same rock beside it stood the church,
Reft of its cross, not of its sanctity;
The vesper-bell, for 't was the vesper hour,
Duly proclaiming through the wilderness,
"All ye who hear, whatever be your work,
Stop for an instant — move your lips in prayer!"
And, just beneath it, in that dreary dale,—
If dale it might be called, so near to heaven,–
A little lake, where never fish leaped up,
Lay like a spot of ink amid the snow;
A star, the only one in that small sky,
On its dead surface glimmering. 'T was a place

Resembling nothing I had left behind,
As if all worldly ties were now dissolved ; —
And, to incline the mind still more to thought,
To thought and sadness, on the eastern shore
Under a beetling cliff stood half in gloom
A lonely chapel destined for the dead,
For such as, having wandered from their way,
Had perished miserably. Side by side,
Within they lie, a mournful company,
All in their shrouds, no earth to cover them ;
Their features full of life, yet motionless
In the broad day, nor soon to suffer change,
Though the barred windows, barred against the wolf,
Are always open ! — But the North blew cold ;
And, bidden to a spare but cheerful meal,
I sate among the holy brotherhood
At their long board. The fare indeed was such
As is prescribed on days of abstinence,
But might have pleased a nicer taste than mine ;
And through the floor came up, an ancient crone
Serving unseen below ; while from the roof
(The roof, the floor, the walls, of native fir)
A lamp hung flickering, such as loves to fling
Its partial light on apostolic heads,
And sheds a grace on all. Theirs Time as yet
Had changed not. Some were almost in the prime ;
Nor was a brow o'ercast. Seen as they sate,
Ranged round their ample hearth-stone in an hour
Of rest, they were as gay, as free from guile,
As children ; answering, and at once, to all
The gentler impulses, to pleasure, mirth ;
Mingling, at intervals, with rational talk

Music; and gathering news from them that came,
As of some other world. But when the storm
Rose, and the snow rolled on in ocean-waves,
When on his face the experienced traveller fell,
Sheltering his lips and nostrils with his hands,
Then all was changed; and, sallying with their pack
Into that blank of nature, they became
Unearthly beings. "Anselm, higher up,
Just where it drifts, a dog howls loud and long,
And now, as guided by a voice from Heaven,
Digs with his feet. That noble vehemence,
Whose can it be, but his who never erred?[13]
A man lies underneath! Let us to work! —
But who descends MONT VELAN? 'T is La Croix.
Away, away! if not, alas! too late.
Homeward he drags an old man and a boy,
Faltering and falling, and but half awaked,
Asking to sleep again." Such their discourse.
  Oft has a venerable roof received me;
St. BRUNO's once[14] — where, when the winds were hushed,
Nor from the cataract the voice came up,
You might have heard the mole work underground,
So great the stillness there; none seen throughout,
Save when from rock to rock a hermit crossed
By some rude bridge — or one at midnight tolled
To matins, and white habits, issuing forth,
Glided along those aisles interminable,[15]
All, all observant of the sacred law
Of Silence. Nor is that sequestered spot,
Once called "Sweet Waters," now "The Shady Vale,"[16]
To me unknown; that house so rich of old,
So courteous,[17] and, by two that passed that way,[18]

Amply requited with immortal verse,
The poet's payment. — But, among them all,
None can with this compare, the dangerous seat
Of generous, active Virtue. What though Frost
Reign everlastingly, and ice and snow
Thaw not, but gather — there is that within,
Which, where it comes, makes Summer; and, in thought,
Oft am I sitting on the bench beneath
Their garden-plot, where all that vegetates
Is but some scanty lettuce, to observe
Those from the south ascending, every step
As though it were their last,— and instantly
Restored, renewed, advancing as with songs,
Soon as they see, turning a lofty crag,
That plain, that modest structure, promising
Bread to the hungry, to the weary rest.

THE DESCENT.

My mule refreshed — and, let the truth be told,
He was nor dull nor contradictory,[19]
But patient, diligent, and sure of foot,
Shunning the loose stone on the precipice,
Snorting suspicion while with sight, smell, touch,
Trying, detecting, where the surface smiled;
And with deliberate courage sliding down,
Where in his sledge the Laplander had turned
With looks aghast — my mule refreshed, his bells
Jingled once more, the signal to depart,
And we set out in the gray light of dawn,
Descending rapidly — by waterfalls

Fast-frozen, and among huge blocks of ice
That in their long career had stopped mid-way.
At length, unchecked, unbidden, he stood still;
And all his bells were muffled. Then my guide,
Lowering his voice, addressed me: "Through this gap
On and say nothing — lest a word, a breath
Bring down a winter's snow — enough to whelm
The armed files that, night and day, were seen
Winding from cliff to cliff in loose array
To conquer at MARENGO. Though long since,
Well I remember how I met them here,
As the sun set far down, purpling the west;
And how NAPOLEON, he himself, no less,
Wrapt in his cloak,— I could not be deceived,—
Reined in his horse, and asked me, as I passed,
How far 't was to St. Remi. Where the rock
Juts forward, and the road, crumbling away,
Narrows almost to nothing at the base,
'T was there; and down along the brink he led
To victory! — DESAIX,[20] who turned the scale,
Leaving his life-blood in that famous field
(When the clouds break, we may discern the spot
In the blue haze), sleeps, as you saw at dawn,
Just where we entered, in the Hospital-church."
So saying, for a while he held his peace,
Awe-struck beneath that dreadful canopy;
But soon, the danger passed, launched forth again.

JORASSE.

JORASSE was in his three-and-twentieth year;
Graceful and active as a stag just roused;
Gentle withal, and pleasant in his speech,
Yet seldom seen to smile. He had grown up
Among the hunters of the Higher Alps;
Had caught their starts and fits of thoughtfulness,
Their haggard looks, and strange soliloquies,
Arising (so say they that dwell below)
From frequent dealings with the Mountain-Spirits.
But other ways had taught him better things;
And now he numbered, marching by my side,
The great, the learnéd, that with him had crossed
The frozen tract — with him familiarly
Through the rough day and rougher night conversed
In many a chalêt round the Peak of Terror,[21]
Round Tacul, Tour, Well-horn, and Rosenlau,
And her whose throne is inaccessible,[22]
Who sits, withdrawn in virgin majesty,
Nor oft unveils. Anon an Avalanche
Rolled its long thunder; and a sudden crash,
Sharp and metallic, to the startled ear
Told that far-down a continent of ice
Had burst in twain. But he had now begun;
And with what transport he recalled the hour
When, to deserve, to win his blooming bride,
Madelaine of Annecy, to his feet he bound
The iron crampons, and, ascending, trod
The upper realms of frost; then, by a cord
Let half-way down, entered a grot star-bright,
And gathered from above, below, around,[23]

The pointed crystals! — Once, nor long before[24]
(Thus did his tongue run on, fast as his feet,
And with an eloquence that Nature gives
To all her children — breaking off by starts
Into the harsh and rude, oft as the mule
Drew his displeasure), once, nor long before,
Alone at day-break on the Mettenberg
He slipped and fell; and, through a fearful cleft
Gliding insensibly from ledge to ledge,
From deep to deeper and to deeper still,
Went to the Under-world! Long while he lay
Upon his rugged bed — then waked like one
Wishing to sleep again and sleep forever!
For, looking round, he saw, or thought he saw,
Innumerable branches of a cave,
Winding beneath that solid crust of ice;
With here and there a rent that showed the stars!
What then, alas! was left him but to die?
What else in those immeasurable chambers,
Strewn with the bones of miserable men,
Lost like himself? Yet must he wander on,
Till cold and hunger set his spirit free!
And, rising, he began his dreary round;
When hark! the noise as of some mighty flood
Working its way to light! Back he withdrew,
But soon returned, and, fearless from despair,
Dashed down the dismal channel; and all day
If day could be where utter darkness was,
Travelled incessantly; the craggy roof
Just overhead, and the impetuous waves,
Nor broad nor deep, yet with a giant's strength,
Lashing him on. At last as in a pool

The water slept; a pool sullen, profound,
Where, if a billow chanced to heave and swell,
It broke not; and the roof, descending, lay
Flat on the surface. Statue-like he stood,
His journey ended; when a ray divine
Shot through his soul. Breathing a prayer to Her
Whose ears are never shut, the Blessed Virgin,
He plunged and swam — and in an instant rose,
The barrier passed, in sunshine! Through a vale,
Such as in ARCADY, where many a thatch
Gleams through the trees, half seen and half embowered,
Glittering the river ran; and on the bank
The young were dancing ('t was a festival-day)
All in their best attire. There first he saw
His Madelaine. In the crowd she stood to hear,
When all drew round, inquiring; and her face,
Seen behind all and varying, as he spoke,
With hope and fear and generous sympathy,
Subdued him. From that very hour he loved.
  The tale was long, but coming to a close,
When his wild eyes flashed fire; and, all forgot,
He listened and looked up. I looked up too;
And twice there came a hiss that through me thrilled!
'T was heard no more. A chamois on the cliff
Had roused his fellows with that cry of fear,
And all were gone. But now the theme was changed;
And he recounted his hair-breadth escapes,
When with his friend, Hubert of Bionnay
(His ancient carbine from his shoulder slung,
His axe to hew a stair-way in the ice),
He tracked their wanderings. By a cloud surprised,
Where the next step had plunged them into air,

Long had they stood, locked in each other's arms,
Amid the gulfs that yawned to swallow them;
Each guarding each through many a freezing hour.
As on some temple's highest pinnacle,
From treacherous slumber. O, it was a sport
Dearer than life, and but with life relinquished!
"My sire, my grandsire died among these wilds.
As for myself," he cried, and he held forth
His wallet in his hand, "this do I call
My winding-sheet — for I shall have no other!"
And he spoke truth. Within a little month
He lay among these awful solitudes
('T was on a glacier — half-way up to heaven),
Taking his final rest. Long did his wife,
Suckling her babe, her only one, look out
The way he went at parting,— but he came not;
Long fear to close her eyes, from dusk till dawn
Plying her distaff through the silent hours,
Lest he appear before her — lest in sleep,
If sleep steal on, he come as all are wont,
Frozen and ghastly blue or black with gore,
To plead for the last rite.

MARGUERITE DE TOURS.

Now the gray granite, starting through the snow,
Discovered many a variegated moss [25]
That to the pilgrim resting on his staff
Shadows out capes and islands; and ere long
Numberless flowers, such as disdain to live
In lower regions, and delighted drink

The clouds before they fall, flowers of all hues,
With their diminutive leaves covered the ground.
There, turning by a venerable larch,
Shivered in two yet most majestical
With his long level branches, we observed
A human figure sitting on a stone
Far down by the way-side — just where the rock
Is riven asunder, and the Evil One
Has bridged the gulf, a wondrous monument[26]
Built in one night, from which the flood beneath,
Raging along, all foam, is seen, not heard,
And seen as motionless! — Nearer we drew;
And, lo! a woman young and delicate,
Wrapt in a russet cloak from head to foot,
Her eyes cast down, her cheek upon her hand,
In deepest thought. Over her tresses fair,
Young as she was, she wore the matron-cap:
And, as we judged, not many moons would change
Ere she became a mother. Pale she looked,
Yet cheerful; though, methought, once, if not twice,
She wiped away a tear that would be coming;
And in those moments her small hat of straw,
Worn on one side, and glittering with a band
Of silk and gold, but ill concealed a face
Not soon to be forgotten. Rising up
On our approach, she travelled slowly on;
And my companion, long before we met,
Knew, and ran down to greet her. She was born
(Such was her artless tale, told with fresh tears)
In Val d'Aosta; and an Alpine stream,
Leaping from crag to crag in its short course
To join the Dora, turned her father's mill.

There did she blossom, till a Valaisan,
A townsman of MARTIGNY, won her heart,
Much to the old man's grief. Long he refused,
Loth to be left; disconsolate at the thought.
She was his only one, his link to life;
And in despair — year after year gone by —
One summer-morn they stole a match and fled.
The act was sudden; and, when far away,
Her spirit had misgivings. Then, full oft,
She pictured to herself that aged face
Sickly and wan, in sorrow, not in wrath;
And, when at last she heard his hour was near,
Went forth unseen, and, burdened as she was,
Crossed the high Alps on foot to ask forgiveness,
And hold him to her heart before he died.
Her task was done. She had fulfilled her wish,
And now was on her way, rejoicing, weeping.
A frame like hers had suffered; but her love
Was strong within her; and right on she went,
Fearing no ill. May all good angels guard her!
And should I once again, as once I may,
Visit MARTIGNY, I will not forget
Thy hospitable roof, MARGUERITE DE TOURS;
Thy sign the silver swan. Heaven prosper thee!

THE BROTHERS.

IN the same hour the breath of life receiving,
They came together and were beautiful;
But, as they slumbered in their mother's lap,
How mournful was their beauty! She would sit,

And look and weep, and look and weep again;
For Nature had but half her work achieved,
Denying, like a step-dame, to the babes
Her noblest gifts; denying speech to one,
And to the other — reason.

But at length
(Seven years gone by, seven melancholy years)
Another came, as fair and fairer still;
And then, how anxiously the mother watched
Till reason dawned and speech declared itself!
Reason and speech were his; and down she knelt,
Clasping her hands in silent ecstasy.

On the hill-side, where still their cottage stands
('T is near the upper falls in Lauterbrounn;
For there I sheltered now, their frugal hearth
Blazing with mountain-pine when I appeared,
And there, as round they sate, I heard their story),
On the hill-side, among the cataracts,
In happy ignorance the children played;
Alike unconscious, through their cloudless day,
Of what they had and had not; everywhere
Gathering rock-flowers; or, with their utmost might,
Loosening the fragment from the precipice,
And, as it tumbled, listening for the plunge;
Yet, as by instinct, at the customed hour
Returning; the two eldest, step by step,
Lifting along, and with the tenderest care,
Their infant brother.

Once the hour was past;
And, when she sought, she sought and could not find;
And when she found — where was the little one?

Alas! they answered not; yet still she asked,
Still in her grief forgetting.
With a scream,
Such as an eagle sends forth when he soars,
A scream that through the wild scatters dismay,
The idiot-boy looked up into the sky,
And leaped and laughed aloud and leaped again;
As if he wished to follow in its flight
Something just gone, and gone from earth to heaven:
While he, whose every gesture, every look,
Went to the heart, for from the heart it came,[27]
He who nor spoke nor heard — all things to him,
Day after day, as silent as the grave
(To him unknown the melody of birds,
Of waters — and the voice that should have soothed
His infant sorrows, singing him to sleep),
Fled to her mantle as for refuge there,
And, as at once o'ercome with fear and grief,
Covered his head and wept. A dreadful thought
Flashed through her brain. "Has not some bird of prey,
Thirsting to dip his beak in innocent blood —
It must, it must be so!" — And so it was.

There was an eagle that had long acquired
Absolute sway, the lord of a domain
Savage, sublime; nor from the hills alone
Gathering large tribute, but from every vale;
Making the ewe, whene'er he deigned to stoop,
Bleat for the lamb. Great was the recompense
Assured to him who laid the tyrant low;
And near his nest in that eventful hour,
Calmly and patiently, a hunter stood,

A hunter, as it chanced, of old renown,
And, as it chanced, their father.
In the South
A speck appeared, enlarging; and ere long,
As on his journey to the golden sun,
Upward he came, the felon in his flight,
Ascending through the congregated clouds,
That, like a dark and troubled sea, obscured
The world beneath. "But what is in his grasp?
Ha! 't is a child — and may it not be ours?
I dare not, cannot; and yet why forbear,
When, if it lives, a cruel death awaits it? —
May He who winged the shaft when Tell stood forth
And shot the apple from the youngling's head,[28]
Grant me the strength, the courage!" As he spoke,
He aimed, he fired; and at his feet they fell,
The eagle and the child — the child unhurt —
Though, such the grasp, not even in death relinquished.[29]

THE ALPS.

Who first beholds those everlasting clouds,
Seed-time and harvest, morning, noon and night,
Still where they were, steadfast, immovable,—
Those mighty hills, so shadowy, so sublime,
As rather to belong to heaven than earth,—
But instantly receives into his soul
A sense, a feeling that he loses not,
A something that informs him 't is an hour
Whence he may date henceforward and forever?
To me they seemed the barriers of a world,

Saying, Thus far, no further! and as o'er
The level plain I travelled silently,
Nearing them more and more, day after day,
My wandering thoughts my only company,
And they before me still — oft as I looked,
A strange delight was mine, mingled with fear,
A wonder as at things I had not heard of!
And still and still I felt as if I gazed
For the first time! Great was the tumult there,
Deafening the din when in barbaric pomp
The Carthaginian on his march to ROME
Entered their fastnesses. Trampling the snows,
The war-horse reared; and the towered elephant
Upturned his trunk into the murky sky,
Then tumbled headlong, swallowed up and lost,
He and his rider.

Now the scene is changed;
And o'er the Simplon, o'er the Splugen, winds
A path of pleasure. Like a silver zone
Flung about carelessly, it shines afar,
Catching the eye in many a broken link,
In many a turn and traverse as it glides;
And oft above and oft below appears,
Seen o'er the wall by him who journeys up,
As if it were another, through the wild
Leading along he knows not whence or whither.
Yet through its fairy course, go where it will,
The torrent stops it not, the rugged rock
Opens and lets it in; and on it runs,
Winning its easy way from clime to clime
Through glens locked up before. — Not such *my* path!
The very path for them that dare defy

Danger, nor shrink, wear he what shape he will;
That o'er the caldron, when the flood boils up,
Hang as in air, gazing and shuddering on
Till fascination comes and the brain turns![30]
The very path for them, that list, to choose
Where best to plant a monumental cross,
And live in story like EMPEDOCLES;
A track for heroes, such as he who came,
Ere long, to win, to wear the iron crown;
And (if aright I judge from what I felt
Over the DRANCE, just where the Abbot fell,
Rolled downward in an after-dinner's sleep)[31]
The same as HANNIBAL'S. But now 't is passed,
That turbulent chaos; and the promised land
Lies at my feet in all its loveliness!
To him who starts up from a terrible dream,
And, lo! the sun is shining, and the lark
Singing aloud for joy — to him is not
Such sudden ravishment as now I feel
At the first glimpses of fair ITALY.

COMO.

I LOVE to sail along the LARIAN Lake[32]
Under the shore — though not, where'er he dwelt,[33]
To visit PLINY; not, in loose attire,
When from the bath or from the tennis-court,
To catch him musing in his plane-tree walk,
Or angling from his window:[34] and, in truth,
Could I recall the ages past and play
The fool with Time, I should perhaps reserve

My leisure for Catullus on *his* lake,[35]
Though to fare worse, or VIRGIL at his farm
A little further on the way to MANTUA.
But such things cannot be. So I sit still,
And let the boatman shift his little sail,
His sail so forkéd and so swallow-like,
Well-pleased with all that comes. The morning-air
Plays on my cheek how gently, flinging round
A silvery gleam! and now the purple mists
Rise like a curtain; now the sun looks out,
Filling, o'erflowing with his glorious light
This noble amphitheatre of hills;
And now appear as on a phosphor-sea
Numberless barks, from MILAN, from PAVIA;
Some sailing up, some down, and some at rest,
Lading, unlading at that small port-town
Under the promontory — its tall tower
And long flat roofs, just such as GASPAR drew,
Caught by a sunbeam slanting through a cloud;
A quay-like scene, glittering and full of life,
And doubled by reflection.
What delight,
After so long a sojourn in the wild,
To hear once more the peasant at his work!
— But in a clime like this where is he not?
Along the shores, among the hills, 'tis now
The hey-day of the vintage; all abroad,
But most the young and of the gentler sex,
Busy in gathering; all among the vines,
Some on the ladder and some underneath,
Filling their baskets of green wicker-work,
While many a canzonet and frolic laugh

Come through the leaves; the vines in light festoons
From tree to tree, the trees in avenues,
And every avenue a covered walk
Hung with black clusters. 'T is enough to make
The sad man merry, the benevolent one
Melt into tears — so general is the joy!
While up and down the cliffs, over the lake,
Wains oxen-drawn and panniered mules are seen,
Laden with grapes and dropping rosy wine.
Here I received from thee, BASILICO,
One of those courtesies so sweet, so rare!
When, as I rambled through thy vineyard ground
On the hill-side, thy little son was sent,
Charged with a bunch almost as big as he,
To press it on the stranger. May thy vats
O'erflow, and he, thy willing gift-bearer,
Live to become a giver; and, at length,
When thou art full of honor and wouldst rest,
The staff of thine old age!

In a strange land
Such things, however trivial, reach the heart,
And through the heart the head, clearing away
The narrow notions that grow up at home,
And in their place grafting good-will to all.
At least I found it so, nor less at eve,
When, bidden as a lonely traveller
('T was by a little boat that gave me chase
With oar and sail, as homeward-bound I crossed
The bay of TRAMEZZINE), right readily
I turned my prow and followed, landing soon
Where steps of purest marble met the wave;

Where, through the trellises and corridors,
Soft music came as from ARMIDA'S palace,
Breathing enchantment o'er the woods and waters
And through a bright pavilion, bright as day,
Forms such as hers were flitting, lost among
Such as of old in sober pomp swept by,
Such as adorn the triumphs and the feasts
By PAOLO[36] painted; where a fairy-queen,
That night her birth-night, from her throne recei
(Young as she was, no floweret in her crown,
Hyacinth or rose, so fair and fresh as she)
Our willing vows, and by the fountain-side
Led in the dance, disporting as she pleased,
Under a starry sky — while I looked on,
As in a glade of CASHMERE or SHIRAZ,
Reclining, quenching my sherbet in snow,
And reading in the eyes that sparkled round
The thousand love-adventures written there.
Can I forget — no, never, such a scene,
So full of witchery. Night lingered still,
When with a dying breeze I left BELLAGGIO;
But the strain followed me; and still I saw
Thy smile, ANGELICA; and still I heard
Thy voice — once and again bidding adieu.

BERGAMO.

THE song was one that I had heard before,
But where I knew not. It inclined to sadness;
And, turning round from the delicious fare
My landlord's little daughter BARBARA

Had from her apron just rolled out before me,
Figs and rock-melons — at the door I saw
Two boys of lively aspect. Peasant-like
They were, and poorly clad, but not unskilled;
With their small voices and an old guitar
Winning their way to my unguarded heart
In that, the only universal tongue.
But soon they changed the measure, entering on
A pleasant dialogue of sweet and sour,
A war of words, with looks and gestures waged
Between TRAPPANTI and his ancient dame,
MONA LUCILIA. To and fro it went;
While many a titter on the stairs was heard,
And BARBARA'S among them. When it ceased,
Their dark eyes flashed no longer, yet, methought,
In many a glance as from the soul, disclosed
More than enough to serve them. Far or near,
Few looked not for their coming ere they came,
Few, when they went, but looked till they were gone;
And not a matron, sitting at her wheel,
But could repeat their story. Twins they were,
And orphans, as I learnt, cast on the world;
Their parents lost in an old ferry-boat
That, three years since, last Martinmas, went down,
Crossing the rough BENACUS.[37] — May they live
Blameless and happy — rich they cannot be,
Like him who, in the days of minstrelsy,[38]
Came in a beggar's weeds to PETRARCH'S door,
Asking, beseeching for a lay to sing,
And soon in silk (such then the power of song)
Returned to thank him; or like that old man,
Old not in heart, who by the torrent-side

Descending from the TYROL, as night fell,
Knocked at a city-gate near the hill-foot,
The gate that bore so long, sculptured in stone,
An eagle on a ladder, and at once
Found welcome — nightly in the bannered hall
Tuning his harp to tales of chivalry
Before the great MASTINO, and his guests,[39]
The three-and-twenty kings, by adverse fate,
By war or treason or domestic strife,
Reft of their kingdoms, friendless, shelterless,
And living on his bounty.
But who comes,
Brushing the floor with what was once, methinks,
A hat of ceremony? On he glides,
Slip-shod, ungartered; his long suit of black
Dingy, thread-bare, though, patch by patch, renewed
Till it has almost ceased to be the same.
At length arrived, and with a shrug that pleads
"'T is my necessity!" he stops and speaks,
Screwing a smile into his dinnerless face.
"Blame not a poet, signor, for his zeal —
When all are on the wing, who would be last?
The splendor of thy name has gone before thee;
And ITALY from sea to sea exults,
As well indeed she may! But I transgress.[40]
He, who has known the weight of praise himself,
Should spare another." Saying so, he laid
His sonnet, an impromptu, at my feet
(If his, then PETRARCH must have stolen it from him),
And bowed and left me; in his hollow hand
Receiving my small tribute, a zecchine,
Unconsciously, as doctors do their fees.

My omelet, and a flagon of hill-wine,[41]
Pure as the virgin-spring, had happily
Fled from all eyes; or, in a waking dream,
I might have sat as many a great man has,
And many a small, like him of Santillane,
Bartering my bread and salt for empty praise.[42]

ITALY.

AM I in ITALY? Is this the Mincius?
Are those the distant turrets of Verona?
And shall I sup where JULIET at the masque [43]
Saw her loved MONTAGUE, and now sleeps by him?
Such questions hourly do I ask myself; [44]
And not a stone, in a cross-way, inscribed
"To Mantua"—"To Ferrara" [45]—but excites
Surprise, and doubt, and self-congratulation.
O ITALY, how beautiful thou art!
Yet I could weep—for thou art lying, alas!
Low in the dust; and we admire thee now
As we admire the beautiful in death.
Thine was a dangerous gift, when thou wert born,
The gift of Beauty. Would thou hadst it not;
Or wert as once, awing the caitiffs vile
That now beset thee, making thee their slave!
Would they had loved thee less, or feared thee more![46]
——But why despair? Twice hast thou lived already;[47]
Twice shone among the nations of the world,
As the sun shines among the lesser lights
Of heaven; and shalt again. The hour shall come,
When they who think to bind the ethereal spirit,

25

Who, like the eagle cowering o'er his prey,
Watch with quick eye, and strike and strike again
If but a sinew vibrate,[48] shall confess
Their wisdom folly. Even now the flame
Bursts forth where once it burnt so gloriously,
And, dying, left a splendor like the day,
That like the day diffused itself, and still
Blesses the earth — the light of genius, virtue,
Greatness in thought and act, contempt of death,
Godlike example. Echoes that have slept
Since ATHENS, LACEDÆMON, were themselves,
Since men invoked "By those in MARATHON!"
Awake along the ÆGEAN; and the dead,
They of that sacred shore, have heard the call,
And through the ranks, from wing to wing, are seen
Moving as once they were — instead of rage
Breathing deliberate valor.

COLL'ALTO.

"IN this neglected mirror (the broad frame
Of massy silver serves to testify
That many a noble matron of the house
Has sat before it) once, alas! was seen
What led to many sorrows. From that time
The bat came hither for a sleeping place;[49]
And he, who cursed another in his heart,
Said, 'Be thy dwelling, through the day and night,
Shunned like COLL'ALTO.'"—'T was in that old pile,
Which flanks the cliff with its gray battlements
Flung here and there, and, like an eagle's nest,

Hangs in the TREVISAN, that thus the steward,
Shaking his locks, the few that Time had left,
Addressed me, as we entered what was called
"My Lady's Chamber." On the walls, the chairs,
Much yet remained of the rich tapestry;
Much of the adventures of SIR LAUNCELOT
In the green glades of some enchanted wood.
The toilet-table was of silver wrought,
Florentine art, when Florence was renowned;
A gay confusion of the elements,
Dolphins and boys, and shells and fruits and flowers:
And from the ceiling, in his gilded cage,
Hung a small bird of curious workmanship,
That, when his mistress bade him, would unfold
(So says the babbling dame, Tradition, there)
His emerald-wings, and sing and sing again
The song that pleased her. While I stood and looked,
A gleam of day yet lingering in the west,
The steward went on. "She had ('t is now long since)
A gentle serving-maid, the fair CRISTINE,
Fair as a lily, and as spotless too;
None so admired, beloved. They had grown up
As play-fellows; and some there were, that said,
Some that knew much, discoursing of CRISTINE,
'She is not what she seems.' When unrequired,
She would steal forth; her custom, her delight,
To wander through and through an ancient grove
Self-planted half-way down, losing herself
Like one in love with sadness; and her veil
And vesture white, seen ever in that place,
Ever as surely as the hours came round,
Among those reverend trees, gave her below

The name of The White Lady. — But the day
Is gone, and I delay thee.
                                        In that chair
The Countess, as it might be now, was sitting,
Her gentle serving-maid, the fair CRISTINE,
Combing her golden hair; and through this door
The Count, her lord, was hastening, called away
By letters of great urgency to VENICE;
When in the glass she saw, as she believed
('T was an illusion of the Evil One —
Some say he came and crossed it at the time),
A smile, a glance at parting, given and answered,
That turned her blood to gall. That very night
The deed was done. That night, ere yet the moon
Was up on Monte Calvo, and the wolf
Baying as still he does (oft is he heard,
An hour and more, by the old turret-clock),
They led her forth, the unhappy lost CRISTINE,
Helping her down in her distress — to die.
  "No blood was spilt; no instrument of death
Lurked — or stood forth, declaring its bad purpose;
Nor was a hair of her unblemished head
Hurt in that hour. Fresh as a flower just blown,
And warm with life, her youthful pulses playing,
She was walled up within the castle-wall.[50]
The wall itself was hollowed secretly;
Then closed again, and done to line and rule.
Wouldst thou descend? ——'T is in a darksome vault
Under the chapel: and there nightly now,
As in the narrow niche, when smooth and fair,
And as if nothing had been done or thought,
The stone-work rose before her, till the light

Glimmered and went — there, nightly at that hour,
(Thou smil'st, and would it were an idle tale!)
In her white veil and vesture white she stands
Shuddering — her eyes uplifted, and her hands
Joined as in prayer; then, like a blessed soul
Bursting the tomb, springs forward, and away
Flies o'er the woods and mountains. Issuing forth,
The hunter meets her in his hunting-track;[51]
The shepherd on the heath, starting, exclaims
(For still she bears the name she bore of old)
''T is the White Lady!'"

VENICE.

There is a glorious city in the sea.
The sea is in the broad, the narrow streets,
Ebbing and flowing; and the salt sea-weed
Clings to the marble of her palaces.
No track of men, no footsteps to and fro,
Lead to her gates. The path lies o'er the sea,
Invisible; and from the land we went,
As to a floating city — steering in,
And gliding up her streets as in a dream,
So smoothly, silently — by many a dome,
Mosque-like, and many a stately portico,
The statues ranged along an azure sky;
By many a pile in more than Eastern pride,
Of old the residence of merchant-kings;
The fronts of some, though Time had shattered them,
Still glowing with the richest hues of art,[52]
As though the wealth within them had run o'er.

Thither I come, and in a wondrous ark
(That, long before we slipt our cable, rang
As with the voices of all living things),
From PADUA, where the stars are, night by night,
Watched from the top of an old dungeon-tower,
Whence blood ran once, the tower of Ezzelin —[53]
Not as he watched them, when he read his fate
And shuddered. But of him I thought not then,
Him or his horoscope;[54] far, far from me
The forms of Guilt and Fear; though some were there,
Sitting among us round the cabin-board,
Some who, like him, had cried, "Spill blood enough!"
And could shake long at shadows. They had played
Their parts at PADUA, and were floating home,
Careless and full of mirth; to-morrow a day
Not in their calendar.[55]— Who, in a strain
To make the hearer fold his arms and sigh,
Sings, "Caro, Caro"?— 'T is the Prima Donna,
And to her monkey, smiling in his face.
Who, as transported, cries, "Brava! Ancora"?
—'T is a grave personage, an old macaw,
Perched on her shoulder. But who leaps ashore,
And with a shout urges the lagging mules;[56]
Then climbs a tree that overhangs the stream,
And, like an acorn, drops on deck again?
'T is he who speaks not, stirs not, but we laugh;
That child of fun and frolic, Arlecchino.[57]
And mark their poet — with what emphasis
He prompts the young soubrette, conning her part!
Her tongue plays truant, and he raps his box,
And prompts again; forever looking round
As if in search of subjects for his wit,

His satire; and as often whispering
Things, though unheard, not unimaginable.
  Had I thy pencil, CRABBE (when thou hast done,
Late may it be . . it will, like PROSPERO'S staff,
Be buried fifty fathoms in the earth),
I would portray the Italian. — Now I cannot.
Subtle, discerning, eloquent, the slave
Of Love, of Hate, forever in extremes;
Gentle when unprovoked, easily won,
But quick in quarrel — through a thousand shades
His spirit flits, chameleon-like; and mocks
The eye of the observer.
                                        Gliding on,
At length we leave the river for the sea.
At length a voice aloft proclaims "Venezia!"
And, as called forth, she comes.
                                                  A few in fear,
Flying away from him whose boast it was[58]
That the grass grew not where his horse had trod,
Gave birth to VENICE. Like the water-fowl,
They built their nests among the ocean-waves;
And where the sands were shifting, as the wind
Blew from the north or south — where they that came
Had to make sure the ground they stood upon,
Rose, like an exhalation from the deep,
A vast metropolis,[59] with glistering spires,
With theatres, basilicas adorned;
A scene of light and glory, a dominion,
That has endured the longest among men.[60]
  And whence the talisman, whereby she rose,
Towering? 'T was found there in the barren sea.
Want led to Enterprise;[61] and, far or near,

Who met not the Venetian ? — now among
The ÆGEAN Isles, steering from port to port,
Landing and bartering ; now, no stranger there,
In CAIRO, or without the eastern gate,
Ere yet the Cafila[62] came, listening to hear
Its bells approaching from the Red-Sea coast;
Then on the Euxine, and that smaller Sea
Of Azoph, in close converse with the Russ,
And Tartar; on his lowly deck receiving
Pearls from the Persian Gulf, gems from Golconde;
Eyes brighter yet, that shed the light of love,
From Georgia, from Circassia. Wandering round,
When in the rich bazaar he saw, displayed,
Treasures from climes unknown, he asked and learnt,
And, travelling slowly upward, drew ere long
From the well-head, supplying all below ;
Making the imperial city of the East,
Herself, his tributary. — If we turn
To those black forests, where, through many an age,
Night without day, no axe the silence broke,
Or seldom, save where Rhine or Danube rolled ;
Where o'er the narrow glen a castle hangs,
And, like the wolf that hungered at his door,
The baron lived by rapine — there we meet,
In warlike guise, the caravan from VENICE ;
When on its march, now lost and now beheld,
A glittering file (the trumpet heard, the scout
Sent and recalled), but at a city-gate
All gayety, and looked for ere it comes ;
Winning regard with all that can attract,
Cages, whence every wild cry of the desert,
Jugglers, stage-dancers. Well might CHARLEMAIN,

And his brave peers, each with his visor up,
On their long lances lean and gaze a while,
When the Venetian to their eyes disclosed
The wonders of the East! Well might they then
Sigh for new conquests!
Thus did VENICE rise,
Thus flourish, till the unwelcome tidings came,
That in the TAGUS had arrived a fleet
From INDIA, from the region of the sun,
Fragrant with spices — that a way was found,
A channel opened, and the golden stream
Turned to enrich another. Then she felt
Her strength departing, yet a while maintained
Her state, her splendor; till a tempest shook
All things most held in honor among men,
All that the giant with the scythe had spared,
To their foundations, and at once she fell;[63]
She who had stood yet longer than the last
Of the four kingdoms — who, as in an ark,
Had floated down, amid a thousand wrecks,
Uninjured, from the Old World to the New,
From the last glimpse of civilized life — to where
Light shone again, and with the blaze of noon.
Through many an age in the mid-sea she dwelt,
From her retreat calmly contemplating
The changes of the earth, herself unchanged.
Before her passed, as in an awful dream,
The mightiest of the mighty. What are these,
Clothed in their purple? O'er the globe they fling
Their monstrous shadows; and, while yet we speak,
Phantom-like, vanish with a dreadful scream!
What—but the last that styled themselves the Cæsars?

And who in long array (look where they come;
Their gestures menacing so far and wide)
Wear the green turban and the heron's plume?
Who — but the Caliphs? followed fast by shapes
As new and strange — Emperor, and King, and Czar,
And Soldan, each, with a gigantic stride,
Trampling on all the flourishing works of peace
To make his greatness greater, and inscribe
His name in blood — some, men of steel, steel-clad;
Others, nor long, alas! the interval,
In light and gay attire, with brow serene
Wielding Jove's thunder, scattering sulphurous fire
Mingled with darkness; and, among the rest,
Lo! one by one, passing continually,
Those who assume a sway beyond them all;
Men gray with age, each in a triple crown,
And in his tremulous hands grasping the keys
That can alone, as he would signify,
Unlock Heaven's gate.

LUIGI.

HAPPY is he who loves companionship,
And lights on thee, LUIGI. Thee I found,
Playing at MORA[64] on the cabin-roof
With Punchinello. — 'T is a game to strike[65]
Fire from the coldest heart. What then from thine?
And, ere the twentieth throw, I had resolved,
Won by thy looks. Thou wert an honest lad;
Wert generous, grateful, not without ambition.
Had it depended on thy will alone,

Thou wouldst have numbered in thy family
At least six Doges and the first in fame.
But that was not to be. In thee I saw
The last, if not the least, of a long line,
Who in their forest, for three hundred years,
Had lived and labored, cutting, charring wood;
Discovering where they were, to those astray,
By the reëchoing stroke, the crash, the fall,
Or the blue wreath that travelled slowly up
Into the sky. Thy nobler destinies
Led thee away to justle in the crowd;
And there I found thee — trying once again,
What for thyself thou hadst prescribed so oft,
A change of air and diet — once again
Crossing the sea, and springing to the shore
As though thou knewest where to dine and sleep.
First in BOLOGNA didst thou plant thyself,
Serving behind a cardinal's gouty chair,
Listening and oft replying, jest for jest;
Then in FERRARA, everything by turns,
So great thy genius and so Proteus-like!
Now serenading in a lover's train,
And measuring swords with his antagonist;
Now carving, cup-bearing in halls of state;
And now a guide to the lorn traveller,
A very Cicerone — yet, alas!
How unlike him who fulmined in old ROME!
Dealing out largely in exchange for pence
Thy scraps of knowledge — through the grassy street
Leading, explaining — pointing to the bars
Of TASSO's dungeon, and the Latin verse,
Graven in the stone, that yet denotes the door
Of ARIOSTO.

Many a year is gone
Since on the RHINE we parted; yet, methinks,
I can recall thee to the life, LUIGI,
In our long journey ever by my side;
Thy locks jet-black, and clustering round a face
Open as day and full of manly daring.
Thou hadst a hand, a heart for all that came,
Herdsman or pedler, monk or muleteer;
And few there were that met thee not with smiles.
Mishap passed o'er thee like a summer-cloud.[66]
Cares thou hadst none; and they that stood to hear thee
Caught the infection and forgot their own.
Nature conceived thee in her merriest mood,
Her happiest — not a speck was in the sky;
And at thy birth the cricket chirped, LUIGI,
Thine a perpetual voice — at every turn
A larum to the echo. In a clime
Where all were gay, none were so gay as thou;
Thou, like a babe, hushed only by thy slumbers;
Up hill and down hill, morning, noon and night,
Singing or talking; singing to thyself
When none gave ear, but to the listener talking.

ST. MARK'S PLACE.

OVER how many tracts, vast, measureless,
Ages on ages roll, and none appear
Save the wild hunter ranging for his prey;
While on this spot of earth, the work of man,
How much has been transacted! Emperors, Popes,
Warriors, from far and wide, laden with spoil,

Landing, have here performed their several parts,
Then left the stage to others. Not a stone
In the broad pavement, but to him who has
An eye, an ear for the inanimate world,
Tells of past ages.
In that temple-porch
(The brass is gone, the porphyry remains[67])
Did BARBAROSSA fling his mantle off,
And kneeling, on his neck receive the foot
Of the proud Pontiff[68] — thus at last consoled
For flight, disguise, and many an aguish shake
On his stone pillow.
In that temple-porch,
Old as he was, so near his hundredth year,
And blind — his eyes put out — did DANDOLO
Stand forth, displaying on his crown the cross.
There did he stand, erect, invincible,
Though wan his cheeks, and wet with many tears,
For in his prayers he had been weeping much;
And now the pilgrims and the people wept
With admiration, saying in their hearts,
"Surely those aged limbs have need of rest!"[69]
There did he stand, with his old armor on,
Ere, gonfalon in hand, that streamed aloft,
As conscious of its glorious destiny,
So soon to float o'er mosque and minaret,
He sailed away, five hundred gallant ships,
Their lofty sides hung with emblazoned shields,
Following his track to fame. He went to die;
But of his trophies four arrived ere long,
Snatched from destruction — the four steeds divine,
That strike the ground, resounding with their feet,[70]

And from their nostrils snort ethereal flame
Over that very porch; and in the place
Where in an aftertime, beside the Doge,
Sate one yet greater,[71] one whose verse shall live
When the wave rolls o'er VENICE. High he sate,
High over all, close by the ducal chair,
At the right hand of his illustrious host,
Amid the noblest daughters of the realm,
Their beauty shaded from the western ray
By many-colored hangings; while, beneath,
Knights of all nations,[72] some of fair renown
From ENGLAND,[73] from victorious EDWARD'S court,
Their lances in the rest, charged for the prize.
Here, among other pageants, and how oft
It met the eye, borne through the gazing crowd,
As if returning to console the least,
Instruct the greatest, did the Doge go round;
Now in a chair of state, now on his bier.
They were his first appearance, and his last.
The sea, that emblem of uncertainty,
Changed not so fast, for many and many an age,
As this small spot. To-day 't was full of masks;[74]
And, lo! the madness of the Carnival,
The monk, the nun, the holy legate masked!
To-morrow came the scaffold and the wheel;
And he died there by torch-light, bound and gagged,
Whose name and crime they knew not. Underneath
Where the Archangel,[75] as alighted there,
Blesses the city from the topmost tower,
His arms extended — there, in monstrous league,
Two phantom-shapes were sitting, side by side,
Or up, and, as in sport, chasing each other;

Horror and Mirth. Both vanished in one hour!
But ocean only, when again he claims
His ancient rule, shall wash away their footsteps.
  Enter the palace by the marble stairs [76]
Down which the grizzly head of old FALIER
Rolled from the block. Pass onward through the hall,
Where, among those drawn in their ducal robes,
But one is wanting — where, thrown off in heat,
A brief inscription on the Doge's chair
Led to another on the wall as brief; [77]
And thou wilt track them — wilt from rooms of state,
Where kings have feasted, and the festal song
Rung through the fretted roof, cedar and gold,
Step into darkness; and be told, "'T was here,
Trusting, deceived, assembled but to die,
To take a long embrace and part again,
CARRARA [78] and his valiant sons were slain;
He first — then they, whose only crime had been
Struggling to save their father." —— Through that door,
So soon to cry, smiting his brow, "I am lost!"
Was with all courtesy, all honor, shown
The great and noble captain, CARMAGNOLA.[79] —
That deep descent [80] (thou canst not yet discern
Aught as it is) leads to the dripping vaults
Under the flood, where light and warmth were never!
Leads to a covered bridge, the Bridge of Sighs;
And to that fatal closet at the foot,
Lurking for prey.—
                    But let us to the roof,
And, when thou hast surveyed the sea, the land,
Visit the narrow cells that cluster there,
As in a place of tombs. There burning suns,

Day after day, beat unrelentingly;
Turning all things to dust, and scorching up
The brain, till Reason fled, and the wild yell
And wilder laugh burst out on every side,
Answering each other as in mockery!
  Few houses of the size were better filled;
Though many came and left it in an hour.
"Most nights," so said the good old Nicolo
(For three-and-thirty years his uncle kept
The water-gate below, but seldom spoke,
Though much was on his mind), "most nights arrived
The prison-boat, that boat with many oars,
And bore away as to the Lower World,
Disburdening in the Cànal ORFANO,[81]
That drowning-place, where never net was thrown,
Summer or Winter, death the penalty;
And where a secret, once deposited,
Lay till the waters should give up their dead."
  Yet what so gay as VENICE?[82] Every gale
Breathed music! and who flocked not, while she reigned,
To celebrate her Nuptials with the Sea;
To wear the mask, and mingle in the crowd
With Greek, Armenian, Persian — night and day
(There, and there only, did the hour stand still)
Pursuing through her thousand labyrinths
The enchantress Pleasure; realizing dreams
The earliest, happiest — for a tale to catch
Credulous ears, and hold young hearts in chains,
Had only to begin, "There lived in VENICE" ——
  "Who were the six we supped with yesternight?"[83]
"Kings, one and all! Thou couldst not but remark
The style and manner of the six that served them."

"Who answered me just now?[84] Who, when I said,
''T is nine,' turned round and said so solemnly,
'Signor, he died at nine'?"—"'T was the Armenian;
The mask that follows thee, go where thou wilt."
"But who moves there, alone among them all?"[85]
"The Cypriot. Ministers from distant courts
Beset his doors, long ere his rising-hour;
His the great secret! Not the golden house
Of Nero, nor those fabled in the East,
Rich though they were, so wondrous rich as his!
Two dogs, coal-black, in collars of pure gold,
Walk in his footsteps.—Who but his familiars?
They walk, and cast no shadow in the sun!
"And mark him speaking. They, that listen, stand
As if his tongue dropped honey; yet his glance
None can endure! He looks nor young nor old;
And at a tourney, where I sat and saw,
A very child (full threescore years are gone)
Borne on my father's shoulder through the crowd,
He looked not otherwise. Where'er he stops,
Though short the sojourn, on his chamber-wall,
Mid many a treasure gleaned from many a clime,
His portrait hangs—but none must notice it!
For TITIAN glows in every lineament,
(Where is it not inscribed, The work is his?)
And TITIAN died two hundred years ago."
—Such their discourse. Assembling in St. Mark's,
All nations met as on enchanted ground!
What though a strange mysterious power was there,
Moving throughout, subtle, invisible,
And universal as the air they breathed;
A power that never slumbered, nor forgave?

All eye, all ear, nowhere and everywhere,[86]
Entering the closet and the sanctuary,
No place of refuge for the Doge himself;
Most present when least thought of[87]— nothing drop
In secret, when the heart was on the lips,
Nothing in feverish sleep, but instantly
Observed and judged — a power, that if but named
In casual converse, be it where it might,
The speaker lowered at once his eyes, his voice,
And pointed upward as to God in heaven ——
What though that power was there, he who lived thu
Pursuing Pleasure, lived as if it were not.
But let him in the midnight air indulge
A word, a thought against the laws of VENICE,
And in that hour he vanished from the earth !

THE GONDOLA.

BOY, call the Gondola; the sun is set.——
It came, and we embarked; but instantly,
As at the waving of a magic wand,
Though she had stept on board so light of foot,
So light of heart, laughing she knew not why,
Sleep overcame her; on my arm she slept.
From time to time I waked her; but the boat
Rocked her to sleep again. The moon was now
Rising full-orbed, but broken by a cloud.
The wind was hushed, and the sea mirror-like.
A single zephyr, as enamored, played
With her loose tresses, and drew more and more
Her veil across her bosom. Long I lay

Contemplating that face so beautiful,
That rosy mouth, that cheek dimpled with smiles,
That neck but half concealed, whiter than snow.
'T was the sweet slumber of her early age.
I looked and looked, and felt a flush of joy
I would express, but cannot. Oft I wished
Gently — by stealth — to drop asleep myself,
And to incline yet lower that sleep might come;
Oft closed my eyes as in forgetfulness.
'T was all in vain. Love would not let me rest.
But how delightful when at length she waked!
When, her light hair adjusting, and her veil
So rudely scattered, she resumed her place
Beside me; and, as gayly as before,
Sitting unconsciously nearer and nearer,
Poured out her innocent mind!

So, nor long since,
Sung a Venetian; and his lay of love,[88]
Dangerous and sweet, charmed VENICE. For myself
(Less fortunate, if Love be Happiness),
No curtain drawn, no pulse beating alarm,
I went alone beneath the silent moon;
Thy square, ST. MARK, thy churches, palaces,
Glittering and frost-like, and, as day drew on,
Melting away, an emblem of themselves.

Those porches passed, through which the water-breeze
Plays, though no longer on the noble forms[89]
That moved there, sable-vested — and the quay,
Silent, grass-grown[90] — adventurer-like I launched
Into the deep, ere long discovering
Isles such as cluster in the Southern seas,
All verdure. Everywhere, from bush and brake,

The musky odor of the serpents came;
Their slimy track across the woodman's path
Bright in the moonshine; and, as round I went,
Dreaming of GREECE, whither the waves were gliding,
I listened to the venerable pines
Then in close converse, and, if right I guessed,
Delivering many a message to the winds,
In secret, for their kindred on Mount IDA.[91]
Nor when again in VENICE, when again
In that strange place, so stirring and so still,
Where nothing comes to drown the human voice
But music, or the dashing of the tide,
Ceased I to wander. Now a JESSICA
Sung to her lute, her signal as she sate
At her half-open window. Then, methought,
A serenade broke silence, breathing hope
Through walls of stone, and torturing the proud heart
Of some PRIULI. Once, we could not err
(It was before an old Palladian house,
As between night and day we floated by),
A gondolier lay singing; and he sung,
As in the time when VENICE was herself,
Of TANCRED and ERMINIA.[92] On our oars
We rested; and the verse was verse divine!
We could not err — perhaps he was the last —
For none took up the strain, none answered him;
And, when he ceased, he left upon my ear
A something like the dying voice of VENICE!
The moon went down; and nothing now was seen
Save where the lamp of a Madonna shone
Faintly — or heard, but when he spoke, who stood
Over the lantern at the prow and cried,

Turning the corner of some reverend pile,
Some school or hospital of old renown,
Though haply none were coming, none were near,
"Hasten or slacken."[93] But at length Night fled;
And with her fled, scattering, the sons of Pleasure.
Star after star shot by, or, meteor-like,
Crossed me and vanished — lost at once among
Those hundred isles that tower majestically,
That rise abruptly from the water-mark,
Not with rough crag, but marble, and the work
Of noblest architects. I lingered still;
Nor sought my threshold,[94] till the hour was come
And past, when, flitting home in the gray light,
The young BIANCA found her father's door,[95]
That door so often with a trembling hand,
So often — then so lately left ajar,
Shut; and, all terror, all perplexity,
Now by her lover urged, now by her love,
Fled o'er the waters to return no more.

THE BRIDES OF VENICE.[96]

IT was St. Mary's Eve, and all poured forth
For some great festival. The fisher came
From his green islet, bringing o'er the waves
His wife and little one; the husbandman
From the firm land, with many a friar and nun,
And village-maiden, her first flight from home,
Crowding the common ferry. All arrived;
And in his straw the prisoner turned to hear,
So great the stir in VENICE. Old and young

Thronged her three hundred bridges; the grave Tu
Turbaned, long-vested, and the cozening Jew
In yellow hat and threadbare gabardine,
Hurrying along. For, as the custom was,
The noblest sons and daughters of the state,
Whose names are written in the Book of Gold,
Were on that day to solemnize their nuptials.
  At noon a distant murmur, through the crowd
Rising and rolling on, proclaimed them near;
And never from their earliest hour was seen
Such splendor or such beauty.[97] Two and two
(The richest tapestry unrolled before them),
First came the brides; each in her virgin-veil,
Nor unattended by her bridal maids,
The two that, step by step, behind her bore
The small but precious caskets that contained
The dowry and the presents. On she moved
In the sweet seriousness of virgin-youth;
Her eyes cast down, and holding in her hand
A fan, that gently waved, of ostrich-plumes.
Her veil, transparent as the gossamer,[98]
Fell from beneath a starry diadem;
And on her dazzling neck a jewel shone,
Ruby or diamond or dark amethyst;
A jewelled chain, in many a winding wreath,
Wreathing her gold brocade.
                                        Before the church,
That venerable structure now no more[99]
On the sea-brink, another train they met,
No strangers, nor unlooked for ere they came,
Brothers to some, still dearer to the rest;
Each in his hand bearing his cap and plume,

And, as he walked, with modest dignity
Folding his scarlet mantle. At the gate
They join; and slowly up the bannered aisle
Led by the choir, with due solemnity
Range round the altar. In his vestments there
The Patriarch stands; and, while the anthem flows,
Who can look on unmoved — the dream of years
Just now fulfilling! Here a mother weeps,
Rejoicing in her daughter. There a son
Blesses the day that is to make her his;
While she shines forth through all her ornament,
Her beauty heightened by her hopes and fears.
At length the rite is ending. All fall down,
All of all ranks; and, stretching out his hands,
Apostle-like, the holy man proceeds
To give the blessing — not a stir, a breath;
When, hark! a din of voices from without,
And shrieks and groans and outcries as in battle!
And, lo! the door is burst, the curtain rent,
And armed ruffians, robbers from the deep,
Savage, uncouth, led on by BARBERIGO
And his six brothers in their coats of steel,
Are standing on the threshold! Statue-like
A while they gaze on the fallen multitude,
Each with his sabre up, in act to strike;
Then, as at once recovering from the spell,
Rush forward to the altar, and as soon
Are gone again — amid no clash of arms
Bearing away the maidens and the treasures.
Where are they now? — ploughing the distant waves,
Their sails outspread and given to the wind,
They on their decks triumphant. On they speed,

Steering for ISTRIA; their accursed barks
(Well are they known[100] the galliot and the galley)
Freighted, alas! with all that life endears!
The richest argosies were poor to them!
  Now hadst thou seen along that crowded shore
The matrons running wild, their festal dress
A strange and moving contrast to their grief;
And through the city, wander where thou wouldst,
The men half armed and arming — everywhere
As roused from slumber by the stirring trump;
One with a shield, one with a casque and spear;
One with an axe severing in two the chain
Of some old pinnace. Not a raft, a plank,
But on that day was drifting. In an hour
Half VENICE was afloat. But long before,
Frantic with grief and scorning all control,
The youths were gone in a light brigantine,
Lying at anchor near the arsenal;
Each having sworn, and by the holy rood,
To slay or to be slain.
                                        And from the tower
The watchman gives the signal. In the east
A ship is seen, and making for the port;
Her flag St. Mark's. And now she turns the point,
Over the waters like a sea-bird flying!
Ha! 't is the same, 't is theirs! from stern to prow
Green with victorious wreaths, she comes to bring
All that was lost.
                                        Coasting, with narrow search,
FRIULI — like a tiger in his spring,
They had surprised the corsairs where they lay[101]
Sharing the spoil in blind security

And casting lots — had slain them, one and all,
All to the last, and flung them far and wide
Into the sea, their proper element;
Him first, as first in rank, whose name so long
Had hushed the babes of VENICE, and who yet,
Breathing a little, in his look retained
The fierceness of his soul.[102]
Thus were the brides
Lost and recovered; and what now remained
But to give thanks? Twelve breast-plates and twe
crowns,
By the young victors to their patron-saint
Vowed in the field, inestimable gifts
Flaming with gems and gold, were in due time
Laid at his feet;[103] and ever to preserve
The memory of a day so full of change,
From joy to grief, from grief to joy again,
Through many an age, as oft as it came round,
'T was hèld religiously. The Doge resigned
His crimson for pure ermine, visiting
At earliest dawn St. Mary's silver shrine;
And through the city, in a stately barge
Of gold, were borne with songs and symphonies
Twelve ladies young and noble.[104] Clad they were
In bridal white with bridal ornaments,
Each in her glittering veil; and on the deck,
As on a burnished throne, they glided by;
No window or balcóny but adorned
With hangings of rich texture, not a roof
But covered with beholders, and the air
Vocal with joy. Onward they went, their oars
Moving in concert with the harmony,

Through the Rialto[105] to the Ducal Palace,
And at a banquet, served with honor there,
Sat representing, in the eyes of all,
Eyes not unwet, I ween, with grateful tears,
Their lovely ancestors, the Brides of VENICE.

FOSCARI.

LET us lift up the curtain, and observe
What passes in that chamber. Now a sigh,
And now a groan is heard. Then all is still.
Twenty are sitting as in judgment there;[106]
Men who have served their country and grown gray
In governments and distant embassies,
Men eminent alike in war and peace;
Such as in effigy shall long adorn
The walls of VENICE — to show what she was!
Their garb is black, and black the arras is,
And sad the general aspect. Yet their looks
Are calm, are cheerful; nothing there like grief,
Nothing or harsh or cruel. Still that noise,
That low and dismal moaning.
                                        Half withdrawn,
A little to the left, sits one in crimson,
A venerable man, fourscore and five.
Cold drops of sweat stand on his furrowed brow.
His hands are clenched; his eyes half-shut and glazed;
His shrunk and withered limbs rigid as marble.
'T is FOSCARI, the Doge. And there is one,
A young man, lying at his feet, stretched out
In torture. 'T is his son. 'T is GIACOMO,

His only joy (and has he lived for this?)
Accused of murder. Yesternight the proofs,
If proofs they be, were in the Lion's mouth
Dropt by some hand unseen; and he, himself,
Must sit and look on a beloved son
Suffering the Question.

Twice, to die in peace,
To save, while yet he could, a falling house,
And turn the hearts of his fell adversaries,
Those who had now, like hell-hounds in full cry,
Chased down his last of four, twice did he ask
To lay aside the crown, and they refused,
An oath exacting, never more to ask;
And there he sits, a spectacle of woe,
Condemned in bitter mockery to wear
The bauble he had sighed for.

Once again
The screw is turned; and, as it turns, the son
Looks up, and, in a faint and broken tone,
Murmurs "My father!" The old man shrinks back,
And in his mantle muffles up his face.
"Art thou not guilty?" says a voice, that once
Would greet the sufferer long before they met,
"Art thou not guilty?"—"No! Indeed I am not!"
But all is unavailing. In that court
Groans are confessions; patience, fortitude,
The work of magic; and, released, revived,
For condemnation, from his father's lips
He hears the sentence, "Banishment to CANDIA.
Death, if he leaves it." And the bark sets sail;
And he is gone from all he loves in life!
Gone in the dead of night—unseen of any—

Without a word, a look of tenderness,
To be called up, when, in his lonely hours,
He would indulge in weeping. Like a ghost,
Day after day, year after year, he haunts
An ancient rampart that o'erhangs the sea;
Gazing on vacancy, and hourly there
Starting as from some wild and uncouth dream,
To answer to the watch.——Alas! how changed
From him the mirror of the youth of VENICE;
Whom in the slightest thing, or whim or chance,
Did he but wear his doublet so and so,
All followed; at whose nuptials, when he won
That maid at once the noblest, fairest, best,[107]
A daughter of the house that now among
Its ancestors in monumental brass
Numbers eight Doges — to convey her home,
The Bucentaur went forth; and thrice the sun
Shone on the chivalry, that, front to front,
And blaze on blaze reflecting, met and ranged
To tourney in ST. MARK'S.—But, lo! at last,
Messengers come. He is recalled: his heart
Leaps at the tidings. He embarks: the boat
Springs to the oar, and back again he goes—
Into that very chamber! there to lie
In his old resting-place, the bed of steel;
And thence look up (five long, long years of grief
Have not killed either) on his wretched sire,
Still in that seat — as though he had not stirred;
Immovable, and muffled in his cloak.
  But now he comes convicted of a crime
Great by the laws of VENICE. Night and day,
Brooding on what he had been, what he was,

'T was more than he could bear. His longing-fits
Thickened upon him. His desire for home
Became a madness; and, resolved to go,
If but to die, in his despair he writes
A letter to the sovereign-prince of MILAN
(To him whose name, among the greatest now,[108]
Had perished, blotted out at once and razed,
But for the rugged limb of an old oak),
Soliciting his influence with the state,
And drops it to be found.——"Would ye know all?
I have transgressed, offended wilfully;[109]
And am prepared to suffer as I ought.
But let me, let me, if but for an hour
(Ye must consent—for all of you are sons,
Most of you husbands, fathers)—let me first
Indulge the natural feelings of a man,
And, ere I die, if such my sentence be,
Press to my heart ('t is all I ask of you)
My wife, my children—and my aged mother—
Say, is she yet alive?"

He is condemned
To go ere set of sun, go whence he came,
A banished man; and for a year to breathe
The vapor of a dungeon. But his prayer
(What could they less?) is granted.

In a hall
Open and crowded by the common herd,
'T was there a wife and her four sons yet young,
A mother borne along, life ebbing fast,
And an old Doge, mustering his strength in vain,
Assembled now, sad privilege! to meet
One so long lost, one who for them had braved,

For them had sought—death and yet worse than death!
To meet him, and to part with him forever ! —
Time and their wrongs had changed them all — him most!
Yet when the wife, the mother, looked again,
'T was he — 't was he himself — 't was GIACOMO !
And all clung round him, weeping bitterly;
Weeping the more, because they wept in vain.
  Unnerved, and now unsettled in his mind
From long and exquisite pain, he sobs and cries,
Kissing the old man's cheek, "Help me, my father!
Let me, I pray thee, live once more among ye:
Let me go home." —— "My son," returns the Doge,
"Obey. Thy country wills it." [110]
                                        GIACOMO
That night embarked; sent to an early grave
For one whose dying words, "The deed was mine!
He is most innocent! 'T was I who did it!"
Came when he slept in peace. The ship, that sailed
Swift as the winds with his deliverance,
Bore back a lifeless corse. Generous as brave,
Affection, kindness, the sweet offices
Of duty and love were from his tenderest years
To him as needful as his daily bread;
And to become a by-word in the streets,
Bringing a stain on those who gave him life,
And those, alas! now worse than fatherless —
To be proclaimed a ruffian, a night-stabber,
He on whom none before had breathed reproach —
He lived but to disprove it. That hope lost,
Death followed. O! if justice be in heaven,
A day must come of ample retribution!
  Then was thy cup, old man, full to the brim.

But thou wert yet alive; and there was one,
The soul and spring of all that enmity,
Who would not leave thee; fastening on thy flank,
Hungering and thirsting, still unsatisfied;
One of a name illustrious as thine own!
One of the Ten! one of the Invisible Three! [111]
'T was LOREDANO. When the whelps were gone,
He would dislodge the lion from his den;
And, leading on the pack he long had led,
The miserable pack that ever howled
Against fallen greatness, moved that FOSCARI
Be Doge no longer; urging his great age;
Calling the loneliness of grief neglect
Of duty, sullenness against the laws.
—— "I am most willing to retire," said he:
"But I have sworn, and cannot of myself.
Do with me as ye please."—— He was deposed,
He, who had reigned so long and gloriously;
His ducal bonnet taken from his brow,
His robes stript off, his seal and signet-ring
Broken before him. But now nothing moved
The meekness of his soul. All things alike!
Among the six that came with the decree,
FOSCARI saw one he knew not, and inquired
His name. "I am the son of MARCO MEMMO."
"Ah!" he replied, "thy father was my friend."
And now he goes. "It is the hour and past.
I have no business here." —— "But wilt thou not
Avoid the gazing crowd? That way is private."
"No! as I entered, so will I retire."
And, leaning on his staff, he left the house,
His residence for five-and-thirty years,

By the same stairs up which he came in state;
Those where the giants stand, guarding the ascent,
Monstrous, terrific. At the foot he stopt,
And, on his staff still leaning, turned and said,
"By mine own merits did I come. I go,
Driven by the malice of mine enemies."
Then to his boat withdrew, poor as he came,
Amid the sighs of them that dared not speak.
This journey was his last. When the bell rang
At dawn, announcing a new Doge to VENICE,
It found him on his knees before the cross,
Clasping his aged hands in earnest prayer;
And there he died. Ere half its task was done,
It rang his knell.
But whence the deadly hate
That caused all this — the hate of LOREDANO?
It was a legacy his father left,
Who, but for FOSCARI, had reigned in Venice,
And, like the venom in the serpent's bag,
Gathered and grew! Nothing but turned to hate! [112]
In vain did FOSCARI supplicate for peace,
Offering in marriage his fair ISABEL.
He changed not, with a dreadful piety
Studying revenge; listening to those alone
Who talked of vengeance; grasping by the hand
Those in their zeal (and none were wanting there)
Who came to tell him of another wrong,
Done or imagined. When his father died,
They whispered, "'T was by poison!" and the words
Struck him as uttered from his father's grave.
He wrote it on the tomb [113] ('t is there in marble),
And with a brow of care, most merchant-like,

Among the debtors in his leger-book[114]
Entered at full (nor month nor day forgot)
"FRANCESCO FOSCARI — for my father's death."
Leaving a blank — to be filled up hereafter.
When FOSCARI'S noble heart at length gave way,
He took the volume from the shelf again
Calmly, and with his pen filled up the blank,
Inscribing, "He has paid me."
Ye who sit
Brooding from day to day, from day to day
Chewing the bitter cud, and starting up
As though the hour was come to whet your fangs,
And, like the Pisan,[115] gnaw the hairy scalp
Of him who had offended — if ye must,
Sit and brood on; but, O! forbear to teach
The lesson to your children.

MARCOLINI.

IT was midnight; the great clock had struck and was still echoing through every porch and gallery in the quarter of ST. MARK, when a young citizen, wrapped in his cloak, was hastening home under it from an interview with his mistress. His step was light, for his heart was so. Her parents had just consented to their marriage; and the very day was named. "Lovely GIULIETTA!" he cried. "And shall I then call thee mine at last? Who was ever so blest as thy MARCOLINI?" But, as he spoke, he stopped; for something glittered on the pavement before him. It was a scabbard of rich workmanship; and the discovery, what was it but an earnest of good fortune? "Rest thou there!"

he cried, thrusting it gayly into his belt. "If another claims thee not, thou hast changed masters!" And on he went as before, humming the burden of a song which he and his GIULIETTA had been singing together. But how little do we know what the next minute will bring forth! He turned by the Church of ST. GEMINIANO, and in three steps he met the watch. A murder had just been committed. The senator RENALDI had been found dead at his door, the dagger left in his heart; and the unfortunate MARCOLINI was dragged away for examination. The place, the time, everything served to excite, to justify suspicion; and no sooner had he entered the guard-house than a damning witness appeared against him. The bravo in his flight had thrown away his scabbard; and, smeared with blood, with blood not yet dry, it was now in the belt of MARCOLINI. Its patrician ornaments struck every eye; and, when the fatal dagger was produced and compared with it, not a doubt of his guilt remained. Still there is in the innocent an energy and a composure, an energy when they speak and a composure when they are silent, to which none can be altogether insensible; and the judge delayed for some time to pronounce the sentence, though he was a near relation of the dead. At length, however, it came; and MARCOLINI lost his life, GIULIETTA her reason.

Not many years afterwards the truth revealed itself, the real criminal in his last moments confessing the crime: and hence the custom in VENICE, a custom that long prevailed, for a crier to cry out in the court before a sentence was passed, "Ricordatevi del povero MARCOLINI!"[116]

Great, indeed, was the lamentation throughout the city, and the judge, dying, directed that thenceforth and forever a mass should be sung every night in a chapel of the ducal church for his own soul, and the soul of MARCOLINI, and the souls of all who had suffered by an unjust judgment. Some land on the BRENTA was left by him for the purpose: and still is the mass sung in the chapel; still every night, when the great square is illuminating and the casinos are filling fast with the gay and the dissipated, a bell is rung as for a service, and a ray of light seen to issue from a small Gothic window that looks toward the place of execution,— the place where, on a scaffold, MARCOLINI breathed his last.

ARQUÀ.

THREE leagues from PADUA stands and long has stood
(The Paduan student knows it, honors it)
A lonely tomb beside a mountain-church;
And I arrived there as the sun declined
Low in the west. The gentle airs, that breathe
Fragrance at eve, were rising, and the birds
Singing their farewell-song — the very song
They sung the night that tomb received a tenant;
When, as alive, clothed in his canon's stole,
And slowly winding down the narrow path,
He came to rest there. Nobles of the land,
Princes and prelates, mingled in his train,
Anxious by any act, while yet they could,
To catch a ray of glory by reflection;
And from that hour have kindred spirits flocked [117]
From distant countries, from the north, the south,
To see where he is laid.
Twelve years ago,
When I descended the impetuous RHONE,

Its vineyards of such great and old renown,[118]
Its castles, each with some romantic tale,
Vanishing fast — the pilot at the stern,
He who had steered so long, standing aloft,
His eyes on the white breakers, and his hands
On what was now his rudder, now his oar,
A huge misshapen plank — the bark itself
Frail and uncouth, launched to return no more,
Such as a shipwrecked man might hope to build,[119]
Urged by the love of home. —Twelve years ago,
When like an arrow from the cord we flew,
Two long, long days, silence, suspense on board,
It was to offer at thy fount, VAUCLUSE,
Entering the archéd cave, to wander where
PETRARCH had wandered, to explore and sit
Where in his peasant-dress he loved to sit,
Musing, reciting — on some rock moss-grown,
Or the fantastic root of some old beech,
That drinks the living waters as they stream
Over their emerald-bed; and could I now
Neglect the place where, in a graver mood,[120]
When he had done and settled with the world,
When all the illusions of his youth were fled,
Indulged perhaps too much, cherished too long,
He came for the conclusion? Half-way up
He built his house,[121] whence as by stealth he caught,
Among the hills, a glimpse of busy life
That soothed, not stirred. — But knock, and enter in.
This was his chamber. 'T is as when he went;
As if he now were in his orchard-grove.
And this his closet. Here he sat and read.
This was his chair; and in it, unobserved,

Reading, or thinking of his absent friends,
He passed away as in a quiet slumber.
Peace to this region! Peace to each, to all!
They know his value — every coming step,
That draws the gazing children from their play,
Would tell them, if they knew not. — But could aught
Ungentle or ungenerous spring up
Where he is sleeping; where, and in an age
Of savage warfare and blind bigotry,
He cultured all that could refine, exalt;[122]
Leading to better things?

GINEVRA.

If thou shouldst ever come by choice or chance
To Modena,[123] where still religiously
Among her ancient trophies is preserved
Bologna's bucket (in its chain it hangs[124]
Within that reverend tower, the Guirlandine),
Stop at a palace near the Reggio-gate,
Dwelt in of old by one of the Orsini.
Its noble gardens, terrace above terrace,
And rich in fountains, statues, cypresses,
Will long detain thee; through their archéd walks,
Dim at noon-day, discovering many a glimpse
Of knights and dames such as in old romance,
And lovers such as in heroic song,—
Perhaps the two, for groves were their delight,
That in the spring-time, as alone they sate,
Venturing together on a tale of love,
Read only part that day.[125]——A summer-sun

Sets ere one-half is seen; but, ere thou go,
Enter the house — prithee, forget it not —
And look a while upon a picture there.
'T is of a lady in her earliest youth,[126]
The very last of that illustrious race,
Done by ZAMPIERI[127] — but by whom I care not.
He who observes it, ere he passes on,
Gazes his fill, and comes and comes again,
That he may call it up when far away.
She sits, inclining forward as to speak,
Her lips half-open, and her finger up,
As though she said "Beware!" her vest of gold
Broidered with flowers, and clasped from head to foot,
An emerald-stone in every golden clasp;
And on her brow, fairer than alabaster,
A coronet of pearls. But then her face,
So lovely, yet so arch, so full of mirth,
The overflowings of an innocent heart —
It haunts me still, though many a year has fled,
Like some wild melody!
Alone it hangs
Over a mouldering heirloom, its companion,
An oaken-chest, half-eaten by the worm,
But richly carved by ANTONY of Trent
With scripture-stories from the life of Christ;
A chest that came from VENICE, and had held
The ducal robes of some old ancestor.
That by the way — it may be true or false —
But don't forget the picture; and thou wilt not,
When thou hast heard the tale they told me there.
She was an only child; from infancy
The joy, the pride, of an indulgent sire.

Her mother dying of the gift she gave,
That precious gift, what else remained to him?
The young GINEVRA was his all in life,
Still as she grew, forever in his sight;
And in her fifteenth year became a bride,
Marrying an only son, FRANCESCO DORIA,
Her playmate from her birth, and her first love.
  Just as she looks there in her bridal dress,
She was all gentleness, all gayety,
Her pranks the favorite theme of every tongue.
But now the day was come, the day, the hour;
Now, frowning, smiling, for the hundredth time,
The nurse, that ancient lady, preached decorum;
And, in the lustre of her youth, she gave
Her hand, with her heart in it, to FRANCESCO.
  Great was the joy; but at the bridal feast,
When all sate down, the bride was wanting there.
Nor was she to be found! Her father cried,
" 'T is but to make a trial of our love!"
And filled his glass to all; but his hand shook,
And soon from guest to guest the panic spread.
'T was but that instant she had left FRANCESCO,
Laughing and looking back and flying still,
Her ivory-tooth imprinted on his finger
But now, alas! she was not to be found;
Nor from that hour could anything be guessed
But that she was not! — Weary of his life,
FRANCESCO flew to VENICE, and forthwith
Flung it away in battle with the Turk.
ORSINI lived; and long was to be seen
An old man wandering[128] as in quest of something,
Something he could not find — he knew not what.

When he was gone, the house remained a while
Silent and tenantless — then went to strangers.
  Full fifty years were past, and all forgot,
When on an idle day, a day of search
'Mid the old lumber in the gallery,
That mouldering chest was noticed; and 't was said
By one as young, as thoughtless as GINEVRA,
"Why not remove it from its lurking-place?"
'T was done as soon as said; but on the way
It burst, it fell; and, lo! a skeleton,
With here and there a pearl, an emerald-stone,
A golden clasp, clasping a shred of gold.
All else had perished — save a nuptial ring,
And a small seal, her mother's legacy,
Engraven with a name, the name of both,
"GINEVRA."——There, then, had she found a grave!
Within that chest had she concealed herself,
Fluttering with joy, the happiest of the happy;
When a spring-lock, that lay in ambush there,
Fastened her down forever!

BOLOGNA.

'T WAS night; the noise and bustle of the day
Were o'er. The mountebank no longer wrought
Miraculous cures — he and his stage were gone;
And he who, when the crisis of his tale
Came, and all stood breathless with hope and fear,
Sent round his cap; and he who thrummed his wire
And sang, with pleading look and plaintive strain,
Melting the passenger. Thy thousand cries,[19]

So well portrayed, and by a son of thine,
Whose voice had swelled the hubbub in his youth,
Were hushed, BOLOGNA, silence in the streets,
The squares, when, hark! the clattering of fleet hoofs;
And soon a courier, posting as from far,
Housing and holster, boot and belted coat
And doublet, stained with many a various soil,
Stopt and alighted. 'T was where hangs aloft
That ancient sign, the pilgrim, welcoming
All who arrive there, all perhaps save those
Clad like himself, with staff and scallop-shell,
Those on a pilgrimage. And now approached
Wheels, through the lofty porticos resounding,
Arch beyond arch, a shelter or a shade
As the sky changes. To the gate they came;
And, ere the man had half his story done,
Mine host received the master — one long used
To sojourn among strangers, everywhere
(Go where he would, along the wildest track)
Flinging a charm that shall not soon be lost,
And leaving footsteps to be traced by those
Who love the haunts of genius; one who saw,
Observed, nor shunned the busy scenes of life,
But mingled not, and 'mid the din, the stir,
Lived as a separate spirit.
Much had passed
Since last we parted; and those five short years —
Much had they told! His clustering locks were turned
Gray; nor did aught recall the youth that swam
From SESTOS to ABYDOS. Yet his voice,
Still it was sweet; still from his eye the thought
Flashed lightning-like, nor lingered on the way,

Waiting for words. Far, far into the night
We sat, conversing — no unwelcome hour,
The hour we met; and when Aurora rose,
Rising, we climbed the rugged Apennine.
  Well I remember how the golden sun
Filled with its beams the unfathomable gulfs,
As on we travelled, and along the ridge,
'Mid groves of cork and cistus and wild-fig,
His motley household came. — Not last nor least,
BATTISTA, who, upon the moonlight-sea
Of VENICE, had so ably, zealously,
Served, and, at parting, thrown his oar away
To follow through the world; who without stain
Had worn so long that honorable badge,
The gondolier's, in a patrician house
Arguing unlimited trust.[130] — Not last nor least,
Thou, though declining in thy beauty and strength,
Faithful MORETTO, to the latest hour
Guarding his chamber-door, and now along
The silent, sullen strand of MISSOLONGHI
Howling in grief. — He had just left that place
Of old renown, once in the ADRIAN sea,[131]
RAVENNA! where from DANTE'S sacred tomb
He had so oft, as many a verse declares,[132]
Drawn inspiration; where, at twilight-time,
Through the pine-forest wandering with loose rein,
Wandering and lost, he had so oft beheld
(What is not visible to a poet's eye?)
The spectre-knight, the hell-hounds and their prey,
The chase, the slaughter, and the festal mirth
Suddenly blasted.[133] 'T was a theme he loved,
But others claimed their turn; and many a tower,[134]

Shattered, uprooted from its native rock,
Its strength the pride of some heroic age,
Appeared and vanished (many a sturdy steer
Yoked and unyoked) while as in happier days
He poured his spirit forth. The past forgot,
All was enjoyment. Not a cloud obscured
Present or future.
He is now at rest;
And praise and blame fall on his ear alike,
Now dull in death. Yes, BYRON, thou art gone,
Gone like a star that through the firmament
Shot and was lost, in its eccentric course
Dazzling, perplexing. Yet thy heart, methinks,
Was generous, noble — noble in its scorn
Of all things low or little; nothing there
Sordid or servile. If imagined wrongs
Pursued thee, urging thee sometimes to do
Things long regretted, oft, as many know,
None more than I, thy gratitude would build
On slight foundations: and, if in thy life
Not happy, in thy death thou surely wert,
Thy wish accomplished; dying in the land
Where thy young mind had caught ethereal fire —
Dying in GREECE, and in a cause so glorious!
They in thy train — ah! little did they think,
As round we went, that they so soon should sit
Mourning beside thee, while a nation mourned,
Changing her festal for her funeral song;
That they so soon should hear the minute-gun,
As morning gleamed on what remained of thee,
Roll o'er the sea, the mountains, numbering
Thy years of joy and sorrow.

Thou art gone;
And he who would assail thee in thy grave,
O, let him pause! For who among us all,
Tried as thou wert — even from thine earliest years,
When wandering, yet unspoilt, a highland-boy —
Tried as thou wert, and with thy soul of flame;
Pleasure, while yet the down was on thy cheek,
Uplifting, pressing, and to lips like thine,
Her charméd cup — ah! who among us all
Could say he had not erred as much, and more?

FLORENCE.

Of all the fairest cities of the earth,
None is so fair as Florence. 'T is a gem
Of purest ray; and what a light broke forth,[136]
When it emerged from darkness! Search within,
Without; all is enchantment! 'T is the Past
Contending with the Present; and in turn
Each has the mastery.
In this chapel wrought [137]
One of the few, Nature's interpreters,
The few, whom genius gives as lights to shine,
Masaccio; and he slumbers underneath.
Wouldst thou behold his monument? Look round!
And know that where we stand stood oft and long,
Oft till the day was gone, Raphael himself;
Nor he alone, so great the ardor there,
Such, while it reigned, the generous rivalry;
He and how many as at once called forth,
Anxious to learn of those who came before,

To steal a spark from their authentic fire,
Theirs who first broke the universal gloom,
Sons of the Morning.
On that ancient seat,
The seat of stone that runs along the wall,[138]
South of the church, east of the belfry-tower [139]
(Thou canst not miss it), in the sultry time
Would DANTE sit conversing, and with those
Who little thought that in his hand he held
The balance, and assigned at his good pleasure
To each his place in the invisible world,
To some an upper region, some a lower;
Many a transgressor sent to his account,[140]
Long ere in FLORENCE numbered with the dead;
The body still as full of life and stir
At home, abroad; still and as oft inclined
To eat, drink, sleep; still clad as others were,
And at noon-day, where men were wont to meet,
Met as continually; when the soul went,
Relinquished to a demon, and by him
(So says the bard, and who can read and doubt?)
Dwelt in and governed.
Sit thee down a while;[141]
Then, by the gates so marvellously wrought,
That they might serve to be the gates of Heaven,[142]
Enter the Baptistery. That place he loved,
Loved as his own;[143] and in his visits there
Well might he take delight! For when a child,
Playing, as many are wont, with venturous feet
Near and yet nearer to the sacred font,
Slipped and fell in, he flew and rescued him,
Flew with an energy, a violence,

That broke the marble — a mishap ascribed
To evil motives; his, alas! to lead
A life of trouble,[144] and ere long to leave
All things most dear to him, ere long to know
How salt another's bread is, and the toil
Of going up and down another's stairs.[145]
Nor then forget that chamber of the dead,[146]
Where the gigantic shapes of Night and Day,
Turned into stone, rest everlastingly;
Yet still are breathing, and shed round at noon
A two-fold influence — only to be felt —
A light, a darkness, mingling each with each;
Both and yet neither. There, from age to age,
Two ghosts are sitting on their sepulchres.
That is the Duke LORENZO. Mark him well.[147]
He meditates, his head upon his hand.
What from beneath his helm-like bonnet scowls?
Is it a face, or but an eyeless skull?
'T is lost in shade; yet, like the basilisk,
It fascinates, and is intolerable.
His mien is noble, most majestical!
Then most so, when the distant choir is heard
At morn or eve — nor fail thou to attend
On that thrice-hallowed day, when all are there;[148]
When all, propitiating with solemn songs,
Visit the dead. Then wilt thou feel his power!
But let not Sculpture, Painting, Poesy,
Or they, the masters of these mighty spells,
Detain us. Our first homage is to Virtue.
Where, in what dungeon of the citadel
(It must be known — the writing on the wall[149]
Cannot be gone — 't was with the blade cut in,

Ere, on his knees to God, he slew himself),
Did he, the last, the noblest citizen,[150]
Breathe out his soul, lest in the torturing hour
He might accuse the guiltless?
That debt paid,
But with a sigh, a tear for human frailty,
We may return, and once more give a loose
To the delighted spirit — worshipping,
In her small temple of rich workmanship,[151]
VENUS herself, who, when she left the skies,
Came hither.

DON GARZÌA.

AMONG those awful forms, in elder time
Assembled, and through many an after-age
Destined to stand as Genii of the place
Where men most meet in FLORENCE, may be seen
His who first played the tyrant. Clad in mail,
But with his helmet off — in kingly state,
Aloft he sits upon his horse of brass;[152]
And they, that read the legend underneath,
Go and pronounce him happy. Yet, methinks,
There is a chamber that, if walls could speak,
Would turn their admiration into pity.
Half of what passed died with him; but the rest,
All he discovered when the fit was on,
All that, by those who listened, could be gleaned
From broken sentences and starts in sleep,
Is told, and by an honest chronicler.[153]
Two of his sons, GIOVANNI and GARZÌA

(The eldest had not seen his nineteenth summer),
Went to the chase; but only one returned.
GIOVANNI, when the huntsman blew his horn
O'er the last stag that started from the brake,
And in the heather turned to stand at bay,
Appeared not; and at close of day was found
Bathed in his innocent blood. Too well, alas!
The trembling COSMO guessed the deed, the doer;
And, having caused the body to be borne
In secret to that chamber — at an hour
When all slept sound, save she who bore them both,[154]
Who little thought of what was yet to come,
And lived but to be told — he bade GARZÌA
Arise and follow him. Holding in one hand
A winking lamp, and in the other a key
Massive and dungeon-like, thither he led;
And, having entered in and locked the door,
The father fixed his eyes upon the son,
And closely questioned him. No change betrayed
Or guilt or fear. Then COSMO lifted up
The bloody sheet. "Look there! Look there!" he cried.
"Blood calls for blood — and from a father's hand!
— Unless thyself wilt save him that sad office.
What!" he exclaimed, when, shuddering at the sight,
The boy breathed out, "I stood but on my guard!"
"Dar'st thou then blacken one who never wronged thee,
Who would not set his foot upon a worm?
Yes, thou must die, lest others fall by thee,
And thou shouldst be the slayer of us all."
Then from GARZÌA's belt he drew the blade,
That fatal one which spilt his brother's blood;
And, kneeling on the ground, "Great God!" he cried,

"Grant me the strength to do an act of justice.
Thou knowest what it costs me; but, alas!
How can I spare myself, sparing none else?
Grant me the strength, the will — and, O! forgive
The sinful soul of a most wretched son!
'T is a most wretched father who implores it."
Long on GARZÌA'S neck he hung and wept,
Long pressed him to his bosom tenderly;
And then, but while he held him by the arm,
Thrusting him backward, turned away his face,
And stabbed him to the heart.
Well might a youth,[155]
Studious of men, anxious to learn and know,
When in the train of some great embassy
He came, a visitant, to COSMO'S court,
Think on the past; and, as he wandered through
The ample spaces of an ancient house,[156]
Silent, deserted — stop a while to dwell
Upon two portraits there, drawn on the wall[157]
Together, as of two in bonds of love,
Those of the unhappy brothers, and conclude,
From the sad looks of him who could have told,
The terrible truth.[158] — Well might he heave a sigh
For poor humanity, when he beheld
That very COSMO shaking o'er his fire,
Drowsy and deaf and inarticulate,
Wrapt in his night-gown, o'er a sick man's mess,
In the last stage — death-struck and deadly pale;
His wife, another, not his ELEANOR,
At once his nurse and his interpreter.

THE CAMPAGNA OF FLORENCE.

'T IS morning. Let us wander through the fields,
Where CIMABUÈ[159] found a shepherd-boy
Tracing his idle fancies on the ground;
And let us from the top of FIESOLE,
Whence GALILEO'S glass[160] by night observed
The phases of the moon, look round below
On ARNO'S vale, where the dove-colored steer
Is ploughing up and down among the vines,
While many a careless note is sung aloud,
Filling the air with sweetness — and on thee,
Beautiful FLORENCE![161] all within thy walls,
Thy groves and gardens, pinnacles and towers,
Drawn to our feet.
From that small spire, just caught
By the bright ray, that church among the rest
By one of old distinguished as The Bride,[162]
Let us in thought pursue (what can we better?)
Those who assembled there at matin-time;[163]
Who, when vice revelled and along the street
Tables were set, what time the bearer's bell
Rang to demand the dead at every door,
Came out into the meadows; and, a while
Wandering in idleness, but not in folly,
Sate down in the high grass and in the shade
Of many a tree sun-proof — day after day,
When all was still and nothing to be heard
But the cicala's voice among the olives,
Relating in a ring, to banish care,
Their hundred tales.[164]

Round the green hill they went,[165]
Round underneath — first to a splendid house,
Gherardi, as an old tradition runs,
That on the left, just rising from the vale;
A place for luxury — the painted rooms,
The open galleries and middle court,
Not unprepared, fragrant and gay with flowers.
Then westward to another, nobler yet;
That on the right, now known as the Palmieri,
Where Art with Nature vied — a Paradise
With verdurous walls, and many a trellised walk
All rose and jasmine, many a twilight-glade
Crossed by the deer. Then to the Ladies' Vale;
And the clear lake, that as by magic seemed
To lift up to the surface every stone
Of lustre there, and the diminutive fish
Innumerable, dropt with crimson and gold,
Now motionless, now glancing to the sun.
Who has not dwelt on their voluptuous day?
The morning banquet by the fountain-side,[166]
While the small birds rejoiced on every bough;
The dance that followed, and the noontide slumber;
Then the tales told in turn, as round they lay
On carpets, the fresh waters murmuring;
And the short interval of pleasant talk
Till supper-time, when many a siren-voice
Sung down the stars; and, as they left the sky,
The torches, planted in the sparkling grass,
And everywhere among the glowing flowers,
Burnt bright and brighter.—He [167] whose dream it was
(It was no more) sleeps in a neighboring vale;
Sleeps in the church, where, in his ear, I ween,

The friar poured out his wondrous catalogue; [168]
A ray, imprimis, of the star that shone
To the Wise Men; a vial-full of sounds,
The musical chimes of the great bells that hung
In SOLOMON'S Temple; and, though last not least,
A feather from the Angel GABRIEL'S wing,
Dropt in the Virgin's chamber. That dark ridge,
Stretching south-east, conceals it from our sight;
Not so his lowly roof and scanty farm,
His copse and rill, if yet a trace be left,
Who lived in Val di Pesa, suffering long
Want and neglect and (far, far worse) reproach,
With calm, unclouded mind.[169] The glimmering tower
On the gray rock beneath, his landmark once,
Now serves for ours, and points out where he ate
His bread with cheerfulness. Who sees him not
('T is his own sketch — he drew it from himself)[170]
Laden with cages from his shoulder slung,
And sallying forth, while yet the morn is gray,
To catch a thrush on every lime-twig there;
Or in the wood among his wood-cutters;
Or in the tavern by the highway-side
At tric-trac with the miller; or at night,
Doffing his rustic suit, and, duly clad,
Entering his closet, and, among his books,
Among the great of every age and clime,[171]
A numerous court, turning to whom he pleased,
Questioning each why he did this or that,
And learning how to overcome the fear
Of poverty and death?

Nearer we hail
Thy sunny slope, ARCETRI, sung of old

For its green wine;[172] dearer to me, to most,
As dwelt on by that great astronomer,[173]
Seven years a prisoner at the city-gate,
Let in but in his grave-clothes.[174] Sacred be
His villa (justly was it called The Gem!)[175]
Sacred the lawn, where many a cypress threw
Its length of shadow, while he watched the stars!
Sacred the vineyard, where, while yet his sight
Glimmered, at blush of morn he dressed his vines,
Chanting aloud in gayety of heart
Some verse of ARIOSTO![176] — There, unseen,[177]
In manly beauty MILTON stood before him,
Gazing with reverent awe — MILTON, his guest,
Just then come forth, all life and enterprise;
He in his old age and extremity,
Blind, at noon-day exploring with his staff;[178]
His eyes upturned as to the golden sun,
His eyeballs idly rolling. Little then
Did GALILEO think whom he received;
That in his hand he held the hand of one
Who could requite him — who would spread his name
O'er lands and seas[179] — great as himself, nay, greater;
MILTON as little that in him he saw,
As in a glass, what he himself should be,[180]
Destined so soon to fall on evil days
And evil tongues — so soon, alas! to live
In darkness, and with dangers compassed round,
And solitude.

Well pleased, could we pursue
The ARNO, from his birthplace in the clouds,
So near the yellow TIBER'S — springing up[181]
From his four fountains on the Apennine,

That mountain-ridge a sea-mark to the ships
Sailing on either sea. Downward he runs,
Scattering fresh verdure through the desolate wild,
Down by the City of Hermits,[182] and the woods
That only echo to the choral hymn;
Then through these gardens to the TUSCAN sea,
Reflecting castles, convents, villages,
And those great rivals in an elder day,
FLORENCE and PISA[183] — who have given him fame,
Fame everlasting, but who stained so oft
His troubled waters. Oft, alas! were seen,
When flight, pursuit, and hideous rout were there,
Hands, clad in gloves of steel, held up imploring;[184]
The man, the hero, on his foaming steed
Borne underneath, already in the realms
Of darkness. — Nor did night or burning noon
Bring respite. Oft, as that great artist saw,[185]
Whose pencil had a voice, the cry "To arms!"
And the shrill trumpet hurried up the bank
Those who had stolen an hour to breast the tide,
And wash from their unharnessed limbs the blood
And sweat of battle. Sudden was the rush,[186]
Violent the tumult; for, already in sight,
Nearer and nearer yet the danger drew;
Each every sinew straining, every nerve,
Each snatching up, and girding, buckling on
Morion and greave and shirt of twisted mail,
As for his life — no more perchance to taste,
ARNO, the grateful freshness of thy glades,
Thy waters — where, exulting, he had felt
A swimmer's transport, there, alas! to float
And welter. — Nor between the gusts of war,

When flocks were feeding, and the shepherd's pipe
Gladdened the valley,—when, but not unarmed,
The sower came forth, and, following him that ploughed,
Threw in the seed,—did thy indignant waves
Escape pollution. Sullen was the splash,
Heavy and swift the plunge, when they received
The key that just had grated on the ear
Of UGOLINO, ever closing up
That dismal dungeon thenceforth to be named
The Tower of Famine.—Once indeed 't was thine,
When many a winter-flood, thy tributary,
Was through its rocky glen rushing, resounding,
And thou wert in thy might, to save, restore
A charge most precious. To the nearest ford,
Hastening, a horseman from Arezzo came,
Careless, impatient of delay, a babe
Slung in a basket to the knotty staff
That lay athwart his saddle-bow. He spurs,
He enters; and his horse, alarmed, perplexed,
Halts in the midst. Great is the stir, the strife;
And, lo! an atom on that dangerous sea,[187]
The babe is floating! Fast and far he flies;
Now tempest-rocked, now whirling round and round
But not to perish. By thy willing waves
Borne to the shore, among the bulrushes
The ark has rested; and unhurt, secure
As on his mother's breast, he sleeps within,
All peace! or never had the nations heard
That voice so sweet, which still enchants, inspires;
That voice, which sung of love, of liberty.
PETRARCH lay there!—And such the images
That here spring up forever, in the young

Kindling poetic fire! Such they that came
And clustered round our MILTON, when at eve,
Reclined beside thee, ARNO;[188] when at eve,
Led on by thee, he wandered with delight,
Framing Ovidian verse, and through thy groves
Gathering wild myrtle. Such the poet's dreams;
Yet not such only. For, look round and say,
Where is the ground that did not drink warm blood,
The echo that had learnt not to articulate
The cry of murder? — Fatal was the day
To FLORENCE, when ('t was in a narrow street
North of that temple, where the truly great
Sleep, not unhonored, not unvisited;
That temple sacred to the Holy Cross —
There is the house — that house of the DONATI,
Towerless,[189] and left long since, but to the last
Braving assault — all rugged, all embossed
Below, and still distinguished by the rings
Of brass, that held in war and festival-time
Their family-standards) — fatal was the day
To Florence, when, at morn, at the ninth hour,
A noble dame in weeds of widowhood,
Weeds by so many to be worn so soon,
Stood at her door; and, like a sorceress, flung
Her dazzling spell. Subtle she was, and rich,
Rich in a hidden pearl of heavenly light,
Her daughter's beauty; and too well she knew
Its virtue! Patiently she stood and watched;
Nor stood alone — but spoke not. — In her breast
Her purpose lay; and, as a youth passed by,
Clad for the nuptial rite, she smiled and said,
Lifting a corner of the maiden's veil,

"This had I treasured up in secret for thee.
This hast thou lost!" He gazed and was undone!
Forgetting — not forgot — he broke the bond,
And paid the penalty, losing his life
At the bridge-foot;[190] and hence a world of woe![191]
Vengeance for vengeance crying, blood for blood;
No intermission! Law, that slumbers not,
And, like the angel with the flaming sword,
Sits over all, at once chastising, healing,
Himself the avenger, went; and every street
Ran red with mutual slaughter — though sometimes
The young forgot the lesson they had learnt,
And loved when they should hate — like thee, Imelda,
Thee and thy Paolo. When last ye met
In that still hour (the heat, the glare was gone,
Not so the splendor — through the cedar-grove
A radiance streamed like a consuming fire,
As though the glorious orb, in its descent,
Had come and rested there) — when last ye met,
And thy relentless brothers dragged him forth,
It had been well hadst thou slept on, Imelda,[192]
Nor from thy trance of fear awaked, as night
Fell on that fatal spot, to wish thee dead,
To track him by his blood, to search, to find,
Then fling thee down to catch a word, a look,
A sigh, if yet thou couldst (alas! thou couldst not),
And die, unseen, unthought of — from the wound
Sucking the poison.[193]

Yet, when slavery came,
Worse followed.[194] Genius, Valor left the land,
Indignant — all that had from age to age
Adorned, ennobled; and headlong they fell,

Tyrant and slave. For deeds of violence,
Done in broad day and more than half redeemed
By many a great and generous sacrifice
Of self to others, came the unpledged bowl,
The stab of the stiletto. Gliding by
Unnoticed, in slouched hat and muffling cloak,
That just discovered, Caravaggio-like,
A swarthy cheek, black brow, and eye of flame,
The bravo stole, and o'er the shoulder plunged
To the heart's core, or from beneath the ribs
Slanting (a surer path, as some averred)
Struck upward — then slunk off, or, if pursued,
Made for the sanctuary, and there along
The glimmering aisle among the worshippers
Wandered with restless step and jealous look,
Dropping thick blood. — Misnamed to lull alarm,
In every palace was The Laboratory,[105]
Where he within brewed poisons swift and slow,
That scattered terror till all things seemed poisonous,
And brave men trembled if a hand held out
A nosegay or a letter; while the great
Drank only from the Venice-glass, that broke,
That shivered, scattering round it as in scorn,
If aught malignant, aught of thine was there,
Cruel TOPHANA;[106] and pawned provinces
For that miraculous gem, the gem that gave
A sign infallible of coming ill,[107]
That clouded though the vehicle of death
Were an invisible perfume. Happy then
The guest to whom at sleeping-time 't was said,
But in an under voice (a lady's page
Speaks in no louder), "Pass not on. That door

Leads to another which awaits thy coming,
One in the floor — now left, alas! unlocked.[198]
No eye detects it — lying under-foot,
Just as thou enterest, at the threshold-stone;
Ready to fall and plunge thee into night
And long oblivion!" — In that evil hour
Where lurked not danger? Through the fairy-land
No seat of pleasure glittering half-way down,
No hunting-place — but with some damning spot
That will not be washed out! There, at Caïano,[199]
Where, when the hawks were mewed and evening came,
PULCI would set the table in a roar
With his wild lay[200] — there, where the sun descends,
And hill and dale are lost, veiled with his beams,
The fair Venetian[201] died, she and her lord —
Died of a posset drugged by him who sate
And saw them suffer, flinging back the charge;
The murderer on the murdered.— Sobs of grief,
Sounds inarticulate . . suddenly stopt,
And followed by a struggle and a gasp,
A gasp in death, are heard yet in Cerreto,
Along the marble halls and staircases,
Nightly at twelve; and, at the self-same hour,
Shrieks, such as penetrate the inmost soul,
Such as awake the innocent babe to long,
Long wailing, echo through the emptiness
Of that old den far up among the hills,[202]
Frowning on him who comes from Pietra-Mala:
In them, alas! within five days and less,
Two unsuspecting victims, passing fair,
Welcomed with kisses, and slain cruelly,
One with the knife, one with the fatal noose.

But, lo! the sun is setting;[203] earth and sky[204]
One blaze of glory.—What we saw but now,
As though it were not, though it had not been!
He lingers yet; and, lessening to a point,
Shines like the eye of Heaven—then withdraws;
And from the zenith to the utmost skirts
All is celestial red! The hour is come
When they that sail along the distant seas
Languish for home; and they that in the morn
Said to sweet friends "farewell" melt as at parting;
When, just gone forth, the pilgrim, if he hears,
As now we hear it, wandering round the hill,
The bell that seems to mourn the dying day,
Slackens his pace and sighs, and those he loved
Loves more than ever. But who feels it not?
And well may we, for we are far away.

THE PILGRIM.

It was an hour of universal joy.[205]
The lark was up and at the gate of heaven,
Singing, as sure to enter when he came;
The butterfly was basking in my path,
His radiant wings unfolded. From below
The bell of prayer rose slowly, plaintively;
And odors, such as welcome in the day,
Such as salute the early traveller,
And come and go, each sweeter than the last,
Were rising. Hill and valley breathed delight;
And not a living thing but blessed the hour!

In every bush and brake there was a voice
Responsive!
From the THRASYMENE, that now
Slept in the sun, a lake of molten gold,
And from the shore that once, when armies met,[206]
Rocked to and fro unfelt, so terrible
The rage, the slaughter, I had turned away;
The path, that led me, leading through a wood,
A fairy-wilderness of fruits and flowers,
And by a brook that, in the day of strife,[207]
Ran blood, but now runs amber — when a glade,
Far, far within, sunned only at noon-day,
Suddenly opened. Many a bench was there,
Each round its ancient elm; and many a track,
Well known to them that from the highway loved
A while to deviate. In the midst a cross
Of mouldering stone as in a temple stood,
Solemn, severe; coëval with the trees
That round it in majestic order rose;
And on the lowest step a pilgrim knelt
In fervent prayer. He was the first I saw
(Save in the tumult of a midnight-masque,
A revel, where none cares to play his part,
And they, that speak, at once dissolve the charm) —
The first in sober truth, no counterfeit;
And, when his orisons were duly paid,
He rose, and we exchanged, as all are wont,
A traveller's greeting.
Young, and of an age
When youth is most attractive, when a light
Plays round and round, reflected, while it lasts,
From some attendant spirit, that ere long

(His charge relinquished with a sigh, a tear)
Wings his flight upward — with a look he won
My favor; and, the spell of silence broke,
I could not but continue. — "Whence," I asked,
"Whence art thou?" — "From Mont' alto," he replied,
"My native village in the Apennines." —
"And whither journeying?" — "To the holy shrine
Of Saint Antonio in the city of PADUA.
Perhaps, if thou hast ever gone so far,
Thou wilt direct my course." — "Most willingly;
But thou hast much to do, much to endure,
Ere thou hast entered where the silver lamps
Burn ever. Tell me . . . I would not transgress,
Yet ask I must . . . what could have brought thee forth,
Nothing in act or thought to be atoned for?" —
"It was a vow I made in my distress.
We were so blest, none were so blest as we,
Till sickness came. First, as death-struck, I fell;
Then my beloved sister; and ere long,
Worn with continual watchings, night and day,
Our saint-like mother. Worse and worse she grew;
And in my anguish, my despair, I vowed,
That if she lived, if Heaven restored her to us,
I would forthwith, and in a pilgrim's weeds,
Visit that holy shrine. My vow was heard;
And therefore am I come." — "Blest be thy steps;
And may those weeds, so reverenced of old,
Guard thee in danger!" — "They are nothing worth.
But they are worn in humble confidence;
Nor would I for the richest robe resign them,
Wrought, as they were, by those I love so well,
Lauretta and my sister; theirs the task,

But none to them, a pleasure, a delight,
To ply their utmost skill, and send me forth
As best became this service. Their last words,
'Fare thee well, Carlo. We shall count the hours!'
Will not go from me."—"Health and strength be thine
In thy long travel! May no sunbeam strike;
No vapor cling and wither! May'st thou be,
Sleeping or waking, sacred and secure;
And when again thou com'st, thy labor done,
Joy be among ye! In that happy hour
All will pour forth to bid thee welcome, Carlo;
And there is one, or I am much deceived,
One thou hast named, who will not be the last."—
"O, she is true as Truth itself can be!
But, ah! thou know'st her not. Would that thou couldst!
My steps I quicken when I think of her;
For, though they take me further from her door,
I shall return the sooner."

AN INTERVIEW.

PLEASURE that comes unlooked-for is thrice welcome;
And, if it stir the heart, if aught be there
That may hereafter in a thoughtful hour
Wake but a sigh, 't is treasured up among
The things most precious! and the day it came
Is noted as a white day in our lives.
  The sun was wheeling westward, and the cliffs
And nodding woods, that everlastingly
(Such the dominion of thy mighty voice,[208]
Thy voice, VELINO, uttered in the mist)

Hear thee and answer thee, were left at length
For others still as noon; and on we strayed
From wild to wilder, nothing hospitable
Seen up or down, no bush or green or dry,[209]
That ancient symbol at the cottage-door,
Offering refreshment — when LUIGI cried,
"Well, of a thousand tracks we chose the best!"
And, turning round an oak, oracular once,
Now lightning-struck, a cave, a thoroughfare
For all that came, each entrance a broad arch,
Whence many a deer, rustling his velvet coat,
Had issued, many a gypsy and her brood
Peered forth, then housed again — the floor yet gray
With ashes, and the sides, where roughest, hung
Loosely with locks of hair — I looked and saw
What, seen in such an hour by Sancho Panza,
Had given his honest countenance a breadth,
His cheeks a blush of pleasure and surprise,
Unknown before, had chained him to the spot,
And thou, Sir Knight, hadst traversed hill and dale,
Squire-less. —— Below and winding far away,
A narrow glade unfolded, such as Spring
Broiders with flowers, and, when the moon is high,
The hare delights to race in, scattering round
The silvery dews.[210] Cedar and cypress threw
Singly their depth of shadow, checkering
The greensward, and, what grew in frequent tufts,
An underwood of myrtle, that by fits
Sent up a gale of fragrance. Through the midst,
Reflecting, as it ran, purple and gold,
A rainbow's splendor (somewhere in the east
Rain-drops were falling fast), a rivulet

Sported as loth to go; and on the bank
Stood (in the eyes of one, if not of both,
Worth all the rest and more) a sumpter-mule
Well laden, while two menials as in haste
Drew from his ample panniers, ranging round
Viands and fruits on many a shining salver,
And plunging in the cool translucent wave
Flasks of delicious wine. — Anon a horn
Blew, through the champaign bidding to the feast,
Its jocund note to other ears addressed,
Not ours; and, slowly coming by a path,
That, ere it issued from an ilex-grove,
Was seen far inward, though along the glade
Distinguished only by a fresher verdure,
Peasants approached, one leading in a leash
Beagles yet panting, one with various game
In rich confusion slung, before, behind,
Leveret and quail and pheasant. All announced
The chase as over; and ere long appeared,
Their horses full of fire, champing the curb,
For the white foam was dry upon the flank,
Two in close converse, each in each delighting,
Their plumage waving as instinct with life;
A lady young and graceful, and a youth,
Yet younger, bearing on a falconer's glove,
As in the golden, the romantic time,
His falcon hooded. Like some spirit of air,
Or fairy-vision, such as feigned of old,
The lady, while her courser pawed the ground,
Alighted; and her beauty, as she trod
The enamelled bank, bruising nor herb nor flower,
That place illumined. Ah! who should she be,

And with her brother, as when last we met
(When the first lark had sung ere half was said,
And as she stood, bidding adieu, her voice,
So sweet it was, recalled me like a spell) —
Who but Angelica? —— That day we gave
To pleasure, and, unconscious of their flight,
Another and another! hers a home
Dropt from the sky amid the wild and rude,
Loretto-like; where all was as a dream,
A dream spun out of some Arabian tale
Read or related in a jasmine bower,
Some balmy eve. The rising moon we hailed,
Duly, devoutly, from a vestibule
Of many an arch, o'er-wrought and lavishly
With many a labyrinth of sylphs and flowers,
When RAPHAEL and his school from FLORENCE came,
Filling the land with splendor[211] — nor less oft
Watched her, declining, from a silent dell,
Not silent once, what time in rivalry
TASSO, GUARINI, waved their wizard-wands,
Peopling the groves from Arcady, and, lo!
Fair forms appeared, murmuring melodious verse,[212]
— Then, in their day, a sylvan theatre,
Mossy the seats, the stage a verdurous floor,
The scenery rock and shrub-wood, Nature's own;
Nature the architect.

MONTORIO.

GENEROUS, and ardent, and as romantic as he could be, MONTORIO was in his earliest youth, when, on a summer-evening not many years ago, he arrived at the Baths of * * *. With a heavy heart, and with many a blessing on his head, he had set out on his travels at day-break. It was his first flight from home; but he was now to enter the world; and the moon was up and in the zenith when he alighted at the Three Moors,[213] a venerable house of vast dimensions, and anciently a palace of the Albertini family, whose arms were emblazoned on the walls.

Every window was full of light, and great was the stir, above and below; but his thoughts were on those he had left so lately; and, retiring early to rest, and to a couch the very first for which he had ever exchanged his own, he was soon among them once more; undisturbed in his sleep by the music that came at intervals from a pavilion in the garden, where some of the company had assembled to dance.

But, secluded as he was, he was not secure from intrusion; and Fortune resolved on that night to play a frolic in his chamber, a frolic that was to determine the color of his life. Boccaccio himself has not recorded a wilder; nor would he, if he had known it, have left the story untold.

At the first glimmering of day he awaked; and, looking round, he beheld — it could not be an illusion; yet anything so lovely, so angelical, he had never seen before — no, not even in his dreams — a lady still younger than himself, and in the profoundest, the sweetest slumber by his side. But, while he gazed, she was gone, and through a door that had escaped his notice. Like a zephyr she trod the floor with her dazzling and beautiful feet, and, while he gazed, she was gone. Yet still he gazed; and, snatching up a bracelet which she had dropt in her flight, "Then she is earthly!" he cried. "But whence could she come? All innocence, all purity, she must have wandered in her sleep."[214]

When he arose, his anxious eyes sought her everywhere; but in vain. Many of the young and the gay were abroad, and moving as usual in the light of the morning; but, among them all, there was nothing like her. Within or without, she was nowhere to be seen; and, at length, in his despair he resolved to address himself to his hostess.

"Who were my nearest neighbors in that turret?"

"The Marchioness de * * * * and her two daughters, the ladies Clara and Violetta; the youngest beautiful as the day!"

"And where are they now?"

"They are gone; but we cannot say whither. They set out soon after sunrise."

At a late hour they had left the pavilion, and had retired to their toilet-chamber, a chamber of oak richly carved, that had once been an oratory, and, afterwards, what was no less essential to a house of that antiquity, a place of resort for two or three ghosts of the family. But, having long lost its sanctity, it had now lost its terrors; and, gloomy as its aspect was, Violetta was soon sitting there alone. "Go," said she to her sister, when her mother withdrew for the night, and her sister was preparing to follow, "go, Clara. I will not be long." And down she sat to a chapter of the *Promessi Sposi*.[215]

But she might well forget her promise, forgetting where she was. She was now under the wand of an enchanter;

and she read and read till the clock struck three, and the taper flickered in the socket. She started up as from a trance; she threw off her wreath of roses; she gathered her tresses into a net;[216] and, snatching a last look in the mirror, her eyelids heavy with sleep, and the light glimmering and dying, she opened a wrong door, a door that had been left unlocked; and, stealing along on tip-toe, (how often may Innocence wear the semblance of Guilt!) she lay down as by her sleeping sister; and instantly, almost before the pillow on which she reclined her head had done sinking, her sleep was as the sleep of childhood.

When morning came, a murmur strange to her ear alarmed her. — What could it be? — Where was she? — she looked not; she listened not; but, like a fawn from the covert, up she sprung and was gone.

It was she, then, that he sought; it was she who, so unconsciously, had taught him to love; and, night and day, he pursued her, till in the Cathedral of Perugia he discovered her at a solemn service, as she knelt between her mother and her sister among the rich and the poor.

From that hour did he endeavor to win her regard by every attention, every assiduity that love could dictate; nor did he cease till he had won it, and till she had consented to be his: but never did the secret escape from his lips; nor was it till some years afterwards that he said to her, on an anniversary of their nuptials, "Violetta, it was a joyful day to me, a day from which I date the happiness of my life; but, if marriages are written in heaven," and, as he spoke, he restored to her arm the bracelet which he had treasured up so long, "how strange are the circumstances by which they are sometimes brought about; for, if you had not lost yourself, Violetta, I might never have found you."

ROME.

I AM in ROME! Oft as the morning-ray
Visits these eyes, waking at once I cry,
Whence this excess of joy? What has befallen me
And from within a thrilling voice replies,
Thou art in ROME! A thousand busy thoughts
Rush on my mind, a thousand images;
And I spring up as girt to run a race!
Thou art in ROME! the city that so long
Reigned absolute, the mistress of the world;
The mighty vision that the prophets saw,
And trembled; that from nothing, from the least,
The lowliest village (what but here and there
A reed-roofed cabin by the river-side?)
Grew into everything; and, year by year,
Patiently, fearlessly, working her way
O'er brook and field, o'er continent and sea,
Not like the merchant with his merchandise,
Or traveller with staff and scrip exploring,
But ever hand to hand and foot to foot,
Through nations numberless in battle-array,
Each behind each, each, when the other fell,
Up and in arms, at length subdued them all.
Thou art in ROME! the city, where the Gauls,
Entering at sunrise through her open gates,
And, through her streets silent and desolate,
Marching to slay, thought they saw gods, not men;
The city, that, by temperance, fortitude,
And love of glory, towered above the clouds,
Then fell — but, falling, kept the highest seat,

And in her loneliness, her pomp of woe,
Where now she dwells, withdrawn into the wild,
Still o'er the mind maintains, from age to age,
Her empire undiminished.—— There, as though
Grandeur attracted grandeur, are beheld
All things that strike, ennoble[217] — from the depths
Of EGYPT, from the classic fields of GREECE,
Her groves, her temples — all things that inspire
Wonder, delight! Who would not say the forms
Most perfect, most divine, had by consent
Flocked thither to abide eternally,
Within those silent chambers where they dwell,
In happy intercourse?—— And I am there!
Ah! little thought I, when in school I sate,
A school-boy on his bench, at early dawn
Glowing with Roman story, I should live
To tread the APPIAN,[218] once an avenue
Of monuments most glorious, palaces,
Their doors sealed up and silent as the night,
The dwellings of the illustrious dead — to turn
Toward TIBER, and, beyond the city-gate,
Pour out my unpremeditated verse
Where on his mule I might have met so oft
HORACE himself[219] — or climb the PALATINE,
Dreaming of old EVANDER and his guest,
Dreaming and lost on that proud eminence,
Long while the seat of ROME, hereafter found
Less than enough (so monstrous was the brood
Engendered there, so Titan-like) to lodge
One in his madness;[220] and inscribe my name,
My name and date, on some broad aloe-leaf,
That shoots and spreads within those very walls

Where VIRGIL read aloud his tale divine,
Where his voice faltered and a mother wept
Tears of delight![221]

But what the narrow space
Just underneath? In many a heap the ground
Heaves, as if Ruin in a frantic mood
Had done his utmost. Here and there appears,
As left to show his handiwork not ours,
An idle column, a half-buried arch,
A wall of some great temple.—— It was once,
And long, the centre of their universe,[222]
The FORUM — whence a mandate, eagle-winged,
Went to the ends of the earth. Let us descend
Slowly. At every step much may be lost.
The very dust we tread stirs as with life;
And not a breath but from the ground sends up
Something of human grandeur.

We are come,
Are now where once the mightiest spirits met
In terrible conflict; this, while ROME was free,
The noblest theatre on this side heaven!
—— Here the first BRUTUS stood, when o'er the corse
Of her so chaste all mourned, and from his cloud
Burst like a god. Here, holding up the knife
That ran with blood, the blood of his own child,
VIRGINIUS called down vengeance. But whence spoke
They who harangued the people; turning now[223]
To the twelve tables,[224] now with lifted hands
To the Capitoline Jove, whose fulgent shape
In the unclouded azure shone far off,
And to the shepherd on the Alban mount
Seemed like a star new-risen?[225] Where were ranged
In rough array, as on their element,

The beaks of those old galleys, destined still[226]
To brave the brunt of war — at last to know
A calm far worse, a silence as in death?
All spiritless; from that disastrous hour
When he, the bravest, gentlest of them all,[227]
Scorning the chains he could not hope to break,[228]
Fell on his sword!
Along the Sacred Way[229]
Hither the triumph came, and, winding round
With acclamation, and the martial clang
Of instruments, and cars laden with spoil,
Stopped at the sacred stair that then appeared,
Then through the darkness broke, ample, star-bright,
As though it led to heaven. 'T was night; but now
A thousand torches, turning night to day,[230]
Blazed, and the victor, springing from his seat,
Went up, and, kneeling as in fervent prayer,
Entered the Capitol. But what are they
Who at the foot withdraw, a mournful train
In fetters? And who, yet incredulous,
Now gazing wildly round, now on his sons,
On those so young, well pleased with all they see,[231]
Staggers along, the last? — They are the fallen,
Those who were spared to grace the chariot-wheels;
And there they parted, where the road divides,
The victor and the vanquished — there withdrew;
He to the festal board, and they to die.
Well might the great, the mighty of the world,[232]
They who were wont to fare deliciously
And war but for a kingdom more or less,
Shrink back, nor from their thrones endure to look,
To think that way! Well might they in their pomp

Humble themselves, and kneel and supplicate
To be delivered from a dream like this!
  Here CINCINNATUS passed, his plough the while
Left in the furrow; and how many more,
Whose laurels fade not, who still walk the earth,
Consuls, Dictators, still in Curule state
Sit and decide; and, as of old in ROME,
Name but their names, set every heart on fire!
  Here, in his bonds, he whom the phalanx saved not,[233]
The last on PHILIP'S throne; and the Numidian,[234]
So soon to say, stript of his cumbrous robe,
Stript to the skin, and in his nakedness
Thrust under ground, "How cold this bath of yours!"
And thy proud queen, PALMYRA, through the sands[235]
Pursued, o'ertaken on her dromedary;
Whose temples, palaces, a wondrous dream
That passes not away, for many a league
Illumine yet the desert. Some invoked
Death and escaped;[236] the Egyptian, when her asp
Came from his covert under the green leaf;[237]
And HANNIBAL himself; and she who said,
Taking the fatal cup between her hands,[238]
"Tell him I would it had come yesterday;
For then it had not been his nuptial gift."
  Now all is changed; and here, as in the wild,
The day is silent, dreary as the night;
None stirring, save the herdsman and his herd,
Savage alike; or they that would explore,
Discuss and learnedly; or they that come
(And there are many who have crossed the earth)
That they may give the hours to meditation,
And wander, often saying to themselves,
"This was the ROMAN FORUM!"

A FUNERAL.

"Whence this delay?"—"Along the crowded street
A funeral comes, and with unusual pomp."
So I withdrew a little and stood still,
While it went by. "She died as she deserved,"
Said an Abatè, gathering up his cloak,
And with a shrug retreating as the tide
Flowed more and more.—"But she was beautiful!"
Replied a soldier of the Pontiff's guard.
"And innocent as beautiful!" exclaimed
A matron sitting in her stall, hung round
With garlands, holy pictures, and what not?
Her Alban grapes and Tusculan figs displayed
In rich profusion. From her heart she spoke;
And I accosted her to hear her story.
"The stab," she cried, "was given in jealousy;
But never fled a purer spirit to heaven,
As thou wilt say, or much my mind misleads,
When thou hast seen her face. Last night at dusk,
When on her way from vespers—none were near,
None save her serving-boy who knelt and wept,
But what could tears avail him, when she fell—
Last night at dusk, the clock then striking nine,
Just by the fountain—that before the church,
The church she always used, St. Isidore's—
Alas! I knew her from her earliest youth,
That excellent lady. Ever would she say,
Good-even, as she passed, and with a voice
Gentle as theirs in heaven!"—But now by fits
A dull and dismal noise assailed the ear,

A wail, a chant, louder and louder yet;
And now a strange fantastic troop appeared!
Thronging, they came — as from the shades below;
All of a ghostly white! "O, say!" I cried,
"Do not the living here bury the dead?
Do spirits come and fetch them? What are these,
That seem not of this world, and mock the day;
Each with a burning taper in his hand?" —
"It is an ancient Brotherhood thou seest.
Such their apparel. Through the long, long line,
Look where thou wilt, no likeness of a man;
The living masked, the dead alone uncovered.
But mark." — And, lying on her funeral couch,
Like one asleep, her eyelids closed, her hands
Folded together on her modest breast,
As 't were her nightly posture, through the crowd
She came at last — and richly, gayly clad,
As for a birth-day feast! But breathes she not?
A glow is on her cheek — and her lips move!
And now a smile is there — how heavenly sweet!
"O, no!" replied the dame, wiping her tears,
But with an accent less of grief than anger,
"No, she will never, never wake again!"
  Death, when we meet the spectre in our walks,
As we did yesterday and shall to-morrow,
Soon grows familiar — like most other things,
Seen, not observed; but in a foreign clime,
Changing his shape to something new and strange
(And through the world he changes as in sport,
Affect he greatness or humility),
Knocks at the heart. His form and fashion here
To me, I do confess, reflect a gloom,

A sadness round; yet one I would not lose;
Being in unison with all things else
In this, this land of shadows, where we live
More in past time than present, where the ground,
League beyond league, like one great cemetery,
Is covered o'er with mouldering monuments;
And, let the living wander where they will,
They cannot leave the footsteps of the dead.
  Oft, where the burial-rite follows so fast
The agony, oft coming, nor from far,
Must a fond father meet his darling child
(Him who at parting climbed his knees and clung)
Clay-cold and wan, and to the bearers cry,
"Stand, I conjure ye!"
                                    Seen thus destitute,
What are the greatest? They must speak beyond
A thousand homilies. When RAPHAEL went,
His heavenly face the mirror of his mind,
His mind a temple for all lovely things
To flock to and inhabit — when he went,
Wrapt in his sable cloak, the cloak he wore,
To sleep beneath the venerable Dome,[239]
By those attended, who in life had loved,
Had worshipped, following in his steps to Fame
('T was on an April day, when Nature smiles),
All Rome was there. But, ere the march began,
Ere to receive their charge the bearers came,
Who had not sought him? And when all beheld
Him, where he lay, how changed from yesterday,
Him in that hour cut off, and at his head
His last great work;[240] when, entering in, they looked
Now on the dead, then on that masterpiece,[241]

Now on his face, lifeless and colorless,
Then on those forms divine that lived and breathed,
And would live on for ages — all were moved;
And sighs burst forth, and loudest lamentations.

NATIONAL PREJUDICES.

"ANOTHER assassination! This venerable city," I exclaimed, "what is it, but as it began, a nest of robbers and murderers? We must away at sunrise, Luigi." — But before sunrise I had reflected a little, and in the soberest prose. My indignation was gone; and, when Luigi undrew my curtain, crying, "Up, signor, up! The horses are at the gate!" "Luigi," I replied, "if thou lovest me, draw the curtain." [242]

It would lessen very much the severity with which men judge of each other, if they would but trace effects to their causes, and observe the progress of things in the moral as accurately as in the physical world. When we condemn millions in the mass as vindictive and sanguinary, we should remember that wherever justice is ill-administered the injured will redress themselves. Robbery provokes to robbery; murder to assassination. Resentments become hereditary; and what began in disorder ends as if all hell had broke loose.

Laws create a habit of self-restraint, not only by the influence of fear, but by regulating in its exercise the passion of revenge. If they overawe the bad by the prospect of a punishment certain and well-defined, they console the injured by the infliction of that punishment; and, as the infliction is a public act, it excites and entails no enmity.

The laws are offended; and the community for its own sake pursues and overtakes the offender,—often without the concurrence of the sufferer, sometimes against his wishes.[243]

Now, those who were not born, like ourselves, to such advantages, we should, surely, rather pity than hate; and when, at length, they venture to turn against their rulers,[244] we should lament, not wonder at, their excesses; remembering that nations are naturally patient and long-suffering, and seldom rise in rebellion till they are so degraded by a bad government as to be almost incapable of a good one.

"Hate them, perhaps," you may say, "we should not; but despise them we must, if enslaved, like the people of ROME, in mind as well as body; if their religion be a gross and barbarous superstition."—I respect knowledge; but I do not despise ignorance. They think only as their fathers thought, worship as they worshipped. They do no more; and, if ours had not burst their bondage, braving imprisonment and death, might not we at this very moment have been exhibiting, in our streets and our churches, the same processions, ceremonials, and mortifications?

Nor should we require from those who are in an earlier stage of society what belongs to a later. They are only where we once were; and why hold them in derision? It is their business to cultivate the inferior arts before they think of the more refined; and in many of the last what are we as a nation, when compared to others that have passed away? Unfortunately it is too much the practice of governments to nurse and keep alive in the governed their national prejudices. It withdraws their attention from what is passing at home, and makes them better tools in the hands of ambition. Hence, next-door neighbors are held up to us from our childhood as *natural enemies*; and we are urged on like curs to worry each other.[245]

In like manner we should learn to be just to individuals. Who can say, "In such circumstances I should have done otherwise?" Who, did he but reflect by what slow gradations, often by how many strange concurrences, we are led astray; with how much reluctance, how much agony, how many efforts to escape, how many self-accusations, how many sighs, how many tears,— who, did he but reflect for a moment, would have the heart to cast a stone? Happily these things are known to Him from whom no secrets are hidden; and let us rest in the assurance that His judgments are not as ours are.[246]

THE CAMPAGNA OF ROME.

HAVE none appeared as tillers of the ground,[247]
None since they went — as though it still were theirs,
And they might come and claim their own again?
Was the last plough a Roman's?
From this seat,[248]
Sacred for ages, whence, as VIRGIL sings,
The Queen of Heaven, alighting from the sky,
Looked down and saw the armies in array,[240]
Let us contemplate; and, where dreams from Jove
Descended on the sleeper, where, perhaps,
Some inspirations may be lingering still,
Some glimmerings of the future or the past,
Let us await their influence; silently
Revolving, as we rest on the green turf,
The changes from that hour when he from TROY
Came up the TIBER; when refulgent shields,
No strangers to the iron-hail of war,

Streamed far and wide, and dashing oars were heard
Among those woods where Silvia's stag was lying,
His antlers gay with flowers; among those woods
Where by the moon, that saw and yet withdrew not,
Two were so soon to wander and be slain,[250]
Two lovely in their lives, nor in their death
Divided.

Then, and hence to be discerned,
How many realms, pastoral and warlike, lay
Along this plain, each with its schemes of power,
Its little rivalships! [251] What various turns
Of fortune there; what moving accidents
From ambuscade and open violence!
Mingling, the sounds came up; and hence how oft
We might have caught among the trees below,
Glittering with helm and shield, the men of TIBER;[252]
Or in Greek vesture, Greek their origin,
Some embassy, ascending to PRÆNESTE; [253]
How oft descried, without thy gates, ARICIA,[254]
Entering the solemn grove for sacrifice,
Senate and people! — each a busy hive,
Glowing with life!

But all ere long are lost
In one. We look, and where the river rolls
Southward its shining labyrinth, in her strength
A city, girt with battlements and towers,
On seven small hills is rising. Round about,
At rural work, the citizens are seen,
None unemployed; the noblest of them all
Binding their sheaves or on their threshing-floors,
As though they had not conquered. Everywhere
Some trace of valor or heroic toil!

Here is the sacred field of the Horatii.[255]
There are the Quintian meadows.[256] Here the hill[257]
How holy, where a generous people, twice,
Twice going forth, in terrible anger sate
Armed; and, their wrongs redressed, at once gave way,
Helmet and shield, and sword and spear thrown down,
And every hand uplifted, every heart
Poured out in thanks to Heaven.

Once again
We look; and, lo! the sea is white with sails
Innumerable, wafting to the shore
Treasures untold; the vale, the promontories,
A dream of glory; temples, palaces,
Called up as by enchantment; aqueducts
Among the groves and glades rolling along
Rivers, on many an arch high overhead;
And in the centre, like a burning sun,
The Imperial City! They have now subdued
All nations. But where they who led them forth;
Who, when at length released by victory
(Buckler and spear hung up — but not to rust),
Held poverty no evil, no reproach,
Living on little with a cheerful mind,
The Decii, the Fabricii? Where the spade,
And reaping-hook, among their household-things
Duly transmitted? In the hands of men
Made captive; while the master and his guests,
Reclining, quaff in gold, and roses swim,
Summer and winter, through the circling year,
On their Falernian — in the hands of men
Dragged into slavery with how many more
Spared but to die, a public spectacle,

In combat with each other, and required
To fall with grace, with dignity — to sink
While life is gushing, and the plaudits ring
Faint and yet fainter on their failing ear,
As models for the sculptor.
But their days,
Their hours are numbered. Hark! a yell, a shriek
A barbarous outcry, loud and louder yet,
That echoes from the mountains to the sea!
And mark, beneath us, like a bursting cloud,
The battle moving onward! Had they slain
All, that the earth should from her womb bring fort
New nations to destroy them? From the depth
Of forests, from what none had dared explore,
Regions of thrilling ice, as though in ice
Engendered, multiplied, they pour along,
Shaggy and huge! Host after host, they come;
The Goth, the Vandal; and again the Goth!
Once more we look, and all is still as night,
All desolate! Groves, temples, palaces,
Swept from the sight; and nothing visible,
Amid the sulphurous vapors that exhale
As from a land accurst, save here and there
An empty tomb, a fragment like the limb
Of some dismembered giant. In the midst
A city stands, her domes and turrets crowned
With many a cross; but they, that issue forth,
Wander like strangers[258] who had built among
The mighty ruins, silent, spiritless;
And on the road, where once we might have met
Cæsar and Cato and men more than kings,
We meet, none else, the pilgrim and the beggar.

THE ROMAN PONTIFFS.

Those ancient men, what were they, who achieved
A sway beyond the greatest conquerors;
Setting their feet upon the necks of kings,
And, through the world, subduing, chaining down
The free, immortal spirit? Were they not
Mighty magicians? Theirs a wondrous spell,
Where true and false were with infernal art
Close-interwoven; where together met
Blessings and curses, threats and promises;
And with the terrors of Futurity
Mingled whate'er enchants and fascinates,
Music and painting, sculpture, rhetoric,[259]
And dazzling light and darkness visible,[260]
And architectural pomp, such as none else!
What in his day the Syracusan sought,
Another world to plant his engines on,
They had; and, having it, like gods, not men,
Moved this world at their pleasure.[261] Ere they came,
Their shadows, stretching far and wide were known;
And two, that looked beyond the visible sphere,
Gave notice of their coming — he who saw
The Apocalypse; and he of elder time,
Who in an awful vision of the night
Saw the Four Kingdoms. Distant as they were,
Those holy men, well might they faint with fear! [262]

CAIUS CESTIUS.

WHEN I am inclined to be serious, I love to wander up and down before the tomb of CAIUS CESTIUS. The Protestant burial-ground is there; and most of the little monuments are erected to the young; young men of promise, cut off when on their travels, full of enthusiasm, full of enjoyment; brides, in the bloom of their beauty, on their first journey; or children borne from home in search of health. This stone was placed by his fellow-travellers, young as himself, who will return to the house of his parents without him; that, by a husband or a father, now in his native country. His heart is buried in that grave.

It is a quiet and sheltered nook, covered in the winter with violets; and the Pyramid, that overshadows it, gives it a classical and singularly solemn air. You feel an interest there, a sympathy you were not prepared for. You are yourself in a foreign land; and they are for the most part your countrymen. They call upon you in your mother-tongue — in English — in words unknown to a native, known only to yourself; and the tomb of CESTIUS, that old majestic pile, has this also in common with them. It is itself a stranger, among strangers. It has stood there till the language spoken round about it has changed; and the shepherd, born at the foot, can read its inscription no longer.

THE NUN.

'T IS over; and her lovely cheek is now
On her hard pillow — there, alas! to be
Nightly, through many and many a dreary hour,
Wan, often wet with tears, and (ere at length
Her place is empty, and another comes)
In anguish, in the ghastliness of death;
Hers never more to leave those mournful walls,
Even on her bier.
'T is over; and the rite,
With all its pomp and harmony, is now
Floating before her. She arose at home,
To be the show, the idol of the day;
Her vesture gorgeous, and her starry head —
No rocket, bursting in the midnight-sky,
So dazzling. When to-morrow she awakes,
She will awake as though she still was there,
Still in her father's house; and, lo! a cell
Narrow and dark, naught through the gloom discerned,
Naught save the crucifix, the rosary,
And the gray habit lying by to shroud
Her beauty and grace.
When on her knees she fell,
Entering the solemn place of consecration,
And from the latticed gallery came a chant
Of psalms, most saint-like, most angelical,
Verse after verse sung out how holily,
The strain returning, and still, still returning,
Methought it acted like a spell upon her,
And she was casting off her earthly dross;

Yet was it sad as sweet, and, ere it closed,
Came like a dirge. When her fair head was shorn,
And the long tresses in her hands were laid,
That she might fling them from her, saying, "Thus,
Thus I renounce the world and worldly things!"[263]
When, as she stood, her bridal ornaments
Were, one by one, removed, even to the last,
That she might say, flinging them from her, "Thus,
Thus I renounce the world!" when all was changed,
And, as a nun, in homeliest guise she knelt,
Distinguished only by the crown she wore,
Her crown of lilies as the spouse of Christ,
Well might her strength forsake her, and her knees
Fail in that hour! Well might the holy man,
He, at whose feet she knelt, give as by stealth
('T was in her utmost need; nor, while she lives,[264]
Will it go from her, fleeting as it was)
That faint but fatherly smile, that smile of love
And pity!

Like a dream the whole is fled;
And they, that came in idleness to gaze
Upon the victim dressed for sacrifice,
Are mingling in the world; thou in thy cell
Forgot, TERESA. Yet, among them all,
None were so formed to love and to be loved,
None to delight, adorn; and on thee now
A curtain, blacker than the night, is dropped
Forever! In thy gentle bosom sleep
Feelings, affections, destined now to die,
To wither like the blossom in the bud,—
Those of a wife, a mother; leaving there
A cheerless void, a chill as of the grave,

A languor and a lethargy of soul,
Death-like, and gathering more and more, till Death
Comes to release thee. Ah! what now to thee,
What now to thee the treasure of thy youth?
As nothing!
But thou canst not yet reflect
Calmly; so many things, strange and perverse,
That meet, recoil, and go but to return,
The monstrous birth of one eventful day,
Troubling thy spirit — from the first at dawn,
The rich arraying for the nuptial feast,
To the black pall, the requiem.[265] All in turn
Revisit thee, and round thy lowly bed
Hover, uncalled. Thy young and innocent heart,
How is it beating? Has it no regrets?
Discoverest thou no weakness lurking there?
But thine exhausted frame has sunk to rest.
Peace to thy slumbers!

THE FIRE-FLY.

There is an insect, that, when evening comes,
Small though he be and scarce distinguishable,
Like Evening clad in soberest livery,
Unsheathes his wings[266] and through the woods and glades
Scatters a marvellous splendor. On he wheels,
Blazing by fits as from excess of joy,[267]
Each gush of light a gush of ecstasy;
Nor unaccompanied; thousands that fling
A radiance all their own, not of the day,

Thousands as bright as he, from dusk till dawn,
Soaring, descending.
In the mother's lap
Well may the child put forth his little hands,
Singing the nursery-song he learnt so soon;[268]
And the young nymph, preparing for the dance[269]
By brook or fountain-side, in many a braid
Wreathing her golden hair, well may she cry,
"Come hither; and the shepherds, gathering round,
Shall say, Floretta emulates the Night,
Spangling her head with stars."
Oft have I met
This shining race, when in the TUSCULAN groves
My path no longer glimmered; oft among
Those trees, religious once and always green,[270]
That still dream out their stories of old ROME
Over the ALBAN lake; oft met and hailed,
Where the precipitate ANIO thunders down,
And through the surging mist a poet's house
(So some aver, and who would not believe?)[271]
Reveals itself.——Yet cannot I forget
Him, who rejoiced me in those walks at eve,[272]
My earliest, pleasantest; who dwells unseen,
And in our northern clime, when all is still,
Nightly keeps watch, nightly in bush or brake
His lonely lamp rekindling. Unlike theirs,
His, if less dazzling, through the darkness knows
No intermission; sending forth its ray
Through the green leaves, a ray serene and clear
As Virtue's own.

FOREIGN TRAVEL.

It was in a splenetic humor that I sat me down to my scanty fare at Terracina; and how long I should have contemplated the lean thrushes in array before me I cannot say, if a cloud of smoke, that drew the tears into my eyes, had not burst from the green and leafy boughs on the hearth-stone. "Why," I exclaimed, starting up from the table, "why did I leave my own chimney-corner?—But am I not on the road to Brundusium? And are not these the very calamities that befell Horace and Virgil, and Mæcenas, and Plotius, and Varius? Horace laughed at them.—Then why should not I? Horace resolved to turn them to account; and Virgil—cannot we hear him observing that to remember them will, by and by, be a pleasure?" My soliloquy reconciled me at once to my fate; and when for the twentieth time I had looked through the window on a sea sparkling with innumerable brilliants, a sea on which the heroes of the Odyssey and the Æneid had sailed, I sat down as to a splendid banquet. My thrushes had the flavor of ortolans; and I ate with an appetite I had not known before. "Who," I cried, as I poured out my last glass of Falernian[273] (for Falernian it was said to be, and in my eyes it ran bright and clear as a topaz-stone), "who would remain at home, could he do otherwise? Who would submit to tread that dull but daily round, his hours forgotten as soon as spent?" and, opening my journal-book and dipping my pen in my ink-horn, I determined, as far as I could, to justify myself and my countrymen in wandering over the face of the earth. "It may serve me," said I, "as a remedy in some future fit of the spleen."

Ours is a nation of travellers;[274] and no wonder, when the elements, air, water and fire, attend at our bidding, to transport us from shore to shore; when the ship rushes into the deep, her track the foam as of some mighty torrent; and, in three hours, or less, we stand gazing and gazed at among a foreign people. None want an excuse. If rich, they go to enjoy; if poor, to retrench; if sick, to recover; if studious, to learn; if learned, to relax from their studies. But, whatever they may say and whatever they may believe, they go for the most part on the same errand; nor will those who reflect think that errand an idle one.

Almost all men are over-anxious. No sooner do they enter the world than they lose that taste for natural and simple pleasures, so remarkable in early life. Every hour do they ask themselves what progress they have made in the pursuit of wealth or honor; and on they go as their fathers went before them, till, weary and sick at heart, they look back with a sigh of regret to the golden time of their childhood.

Now travel, and foreign travel more particularly, restores to us in a great degree what we have lost. When the anchor is heaved, we double down the leaf; and for a while at least all is over. The old cares are left clustering round the old objects; and, at every step, as we proceed, the slightest circumstance amuses and interests. All is new and strange.[275] We surrender ourselves, and feel once again as children. Like them, we enjoy eagerly; like them, when we fret we fret only for the moment; and here, indeed, the resemblance is very remarkable; for, if a journey has its pains as well as its pleasures (and there is nothing unmixed in this world) the pains are no sooner over than they are forgotten, while the pleasures live long in the memory.

Nor is it surely without another advantage. If life be short, not so to many of us are its days and its hours. When the blood slumbers in the veins, how often do we wish that the earth would turn faster on its axis, that the sun would rise and set before it does! and, to escape from the weight of time, how many follies, how many crimes, are committed! Men rush on danger, and even on death. Intrigue, play, foreign and domestic broil, such are their resources; and, when these things fail, they destroy themselves.

Now, in travelling we multiply events, and innocently. We set out, as it were, on our adventures; and many are those that occur to us, morning, noon and night. The day we come to a place which we have long heard and read of, and in ITALY we do so continually, it is an era in our lives; and from that moment the very name calls up a picture. How delightfully, too, does the knowledge flow in upon us, and how fast![276] Would he who sat in a corner of his library, poring over books and maps, learn more or so much in the time as he who, with his eyes and his heart open, is receiving impressions all day long from the things themselves?[277] How accurately do they arrange themselves in our memory, towns, rivers, mountains; and in what living colors do we recall the dresses, manners and customs, of the people! Our sight is the noblest of all our senses. "It fills the mind with the most ideas, converses with its objects at the greatest distance, and continues longest in action without being tired." Our sight is on the alert when we travel; and its exercise is then so delightful that we forget the profit in the pleasure.

Like a river, that gathers, that refines as it runs, like a spring that takes its course through some rich vein of mineral, we improve and imperceptibly — nor in the head only, but in the heart. Our prejudices leave us, one by one. Seas and mountains are no longer our boundaries. We learn to love, and esteem, and admire beyond them. Our benevolence extends itself with our knowledge. And must we not return better citizens than we went? For, the more we become acquainted with the institutions of other countries, the more highly must we value our own.

I threw down my pen in triumph. "The question," said I, "is set to rest forever. And yet —"

"And yet —" I must still say.[278] The WISEST OF MEN seldom went out of the walls of ATHENS; and for that worst of evils, that sickness of the soul, to which we are most liable when most at our ease, is there not, after all, a surer and yet pleasanter remedy, a remedy for which we have only to cross the threshold? A PIEDMONTESE nobleman, into whose company I fell at TURIN, had not long before experienced its efficacy; and his story he told me without reserve.

"I was weary of life," said he, "and, after a day such as few have known and none would wish to remember, was hurrying along the street to the river, when I felt a sudden check. I turned and beheld a little boy, who had caught the skirt of my cloak in his anxiety to solicit my notice. His look and manner were irresistible. Not less so was the lesson he had learnt. 'There are six of us, and we are dying for want of food.' — 'Why should I not,' said I to myself, 'relieve this wretched family? I have the means;

and it will not delay me many minutes. But what if it does?' The scene of misery he conducted me to I cannot describe. I threw them my purse; and their burst of gratitude overcame me. It filled my eyes . . it went as a cordial to my heart. 'I will call again to-morrow,' I cried. 'Fool that I was, to think of leaving a world, where such pleasure was to be had, and so cheaply!'"

THE FOUNTAIN.

It was a well
Of whitest marble, white as from the quarry;
And richly wrought with many a high relief,
Greek sculpture — in some earlier day perhaps
A tomb, and honored with a hero's ashes.
The water from the rock filled and o'erflowed;
Then dashed away, playing the prodigal,
And soon was lost — stealing unseen, unheard,
Through the long grass, and round the twisted roots
Of aged trees; discovering where it ran
By the fresh verdure. Overcome with heat,
I threw me down; admiring, as I lay,
That shady nook, a singing place for birds,
That grove so intricate, so full of flowers,
More than enough to please a child a-Maying.
The sun had set, a distant convent-bell
Ringing the *Angelus;* and now approached
The hour for stir and village-gossip there,
The hour REBEKAH came, when from the well
She drew with such alacrity to serve
The stranger and his camels. Soon I heard

Footsteps; and, lo! descending by a path
Trodden for ages, many a nymph appeared,
Appeared and vanished, bearing on her head
Her earthen pitcher. It called up the day
ULYSSES landed there; and long I gazed,
Like one awaking in a distant time.[279]
At length there came the loveliest of them all,
Her little brother dancing down before her;
And ever as he spoke, which he did ever,
Turning and looking up in warmth of heart
And brotherly affection. Stopping there,
She joined her rosy hands, and, filling them
With the pure element, gave him to drink;
And, while he quenched his thirst, standing on tiptoe,
Looked down upon him with a sister's smile,
Nor stirred till he had done, fixed as a statue.
Then hadst thou seen them as they stood, CANOVA,
Thou hadst endowed them with immortal youth;
And they had evermore lived undivided,
Winning all hearts — of all thy works the fairest.

BANDITTI.

'T IS a wild life, fearful and full of change,
The mountain-robber's. On the watch he lies,
Levelling his carbine at the passenger;
And, when his work is done, he dares not sleep.
Time was, the trade was nobler, if not honest;
When they that robbed were men of better faith[280]
Than kings or pontiffs; when, such reverence
The poet drew among the woods and wilds,

A voice was heard, that never bade to spare,[281]
Crying aloud, "Hence to the distant hills!
Tasso approaches; he, whose song beguiles
The day of half its hours; whose sorcery
Dazzles the sense, turning our forest-glades
To lists that blaze with gorgeous armory,
Our mountain-caves to regal palaces.
Hence, nor descend till he and his are gone.
Let him fear nothing." — When along the shore,
And by the path that, wandering on its way,
Leads through the fatal grove where Tully fell
(Gray and o'ergrown, an ancient tomb is there),
He came and they withdrew, they were a race
Careless of life in others and themselves,
For they had learnt their lesson in a camp;
But not ungenerous. 'T is no longer so.
Now crafty, cruel, torturing ere they slay
The unhappy captive, and with bitter jests
Mocking misfortune; vain, fantastical,
Wearing whatever glitters in the spoil;
And most devout, though, when they kneel and pray,
With every bead they could recount a murder;
As by a spell they start up in array,[282]
As by a spell they vanish — theirs a band,
Not as elsewhere of outlaws, but of such
As sow and reap, and at the cottage-door
Sit to receive, return the traveller's greeting;
Now in the garb of peace, now silently
Arming and issuing forth, led on by men
Whose names on innocent lips are words of fear,
Whose lives have long been forfeit. — Some there are
That, ere they rise to this bad eminence,
Lurk, night and day, the plague-spot visible,

The guilt that says, Beware; and mark we now
Him, where he lies, who couches for his prey
At the bridge-foot in some dark cavity
Scooped by the waters, or some gaping tomb,
Nameless and tenantless, whence the red fox
Slunk as he entered.
There he broods, in spleen
Gnawing his beard; his rough and sinewy frame
O'erwritten with the story of his life:
On his wan cheek a sabre-cut, well earned
In foreign warfare; on his breast the brand
Indelible, burnt in when to the port
He clanked his chain, among a hundred more
Dragged ignominiously; on every limb
Memorials of his glory and his shame,
Stripes of the lash and honorable scars,
And channels here and there worn to the bone
By galling fetters.
He comes slowly forth,
Unkennelling, and up that savage dell
Anxiously looks; his cruise, an ample gourd
(Duly replenished from the vintner's cask),
Slung from his shoulder; in his breadth of belt
Two pistols and a dagger yet uncleansed,
A parchment scrawled with uncouth characters,
And a small vial, his last remedy,
His cure, when all things fail.
No noise is heard,
Save when the rugged bear and the gaunt wolf
Howl in the upper region, or a fish
Leaps in the gulf beneath. But now he kneels;
And (like a scout, when listening to the tramp

Of horse or foot) lays his experienced ear
Close to the ground, then rises and explores,
Then kneels again, and, his short rifle-gun
Against his cheek, waits patiently.
Two monks,
Portly, gray-headed, on their gallant steeds,
Descend where yet a mouldering cross o'erhangs
The grave of one that from the precipice
Fell in an evil hour. Their bridle-bells
Ring merrily; and many a loud, long laugh
Reëchoes; but at once the sounds are lost.
Unconscious of the good in store below,
The holy fathers have turned off, and now
Cross the brown heath, ere long to wag their beards
Before my lady-abbess, and discuss
Things only known to the devout and pure
O'er her spiced bowl — then shrive the sisterhood,
Sitting by turns with an inclining ear
In the confessional.
He moves his lips
As with a curse — then paces up and down,
Now fast, now slow, brooding and muttering on;
Gloomy alike to him future and past.
But, hark! the nimble tread of numerous feet!
'T is but a dappled herd, come down to slake
Their thirst in the cool wave.
He turns and aims;
Then checks himself, unwilling to disturb
The sleeping echoes. — Once again he earths;
Slipping away to house with them beneath,
His old companions in that hiding-place,
The bat, the toad, the blind-worm, and the newt;

And, hark! a footstep, firm and confident,
As of a man in haste. Nearer it draws;
And now is at the entrance of the den.
Ha! 't is a comrade, sent to gather in
The band for some great enterprise.
Who wants
A sequel, may read on. The unvarnished tale,
That follows, will supply the place of one.
'T was told me by the Count St. Angelo,
When in a blustering night he sheltered me
In that brave castle of his ancestors
O'er Garigliano, and is such indeed
As every day brings with it — in a land
Where laws are trampled on and lawless men
Walk in the sun; but it should not be lost,
For it may serve to bind us to our country.

AN ADVENTURE.

Three days they lay in ambush at my gate,[283]
Then sprung and led me captive. Many a wild
We traversed; but Rusconi, 't was no less,
Marched by my side, and, when I thirsted, climbed
The cliffs for water; though, whene'er he spoke,
'T was briefly, sullenly; and on he led,
Distinguished only by an amulet,
That in a golden chain hung from his neck,
A crystal of rare virtue. Night fell fast,
When on a heath, black and immeasurable,
He turned and bade them halt. 'T was where the earth
Heaves o'er the dead — where erst some Alaric

Fought his last fight, and every warrior threw
A stone to tell for ages where he lay.
 Then all advanced, and, ranging in a square,
Stretched forth their arms as on the holy cross,
From each to each their sable cloaks extending,
That, like the solemn hangings of a tent,
Covered us round; and in the midst I stood,
Weary and faint, and face to face with one,
Whose voice, whose look dispenses life and death,
Whose heart knows no relentings. Instantly
A light was kindled and the bandit spoke.
"I know thee. Thou hast sought us, for the sport
Slipping thy blood-hounds with a hunter's cry;
And thou hast found at last. Were I as thou,
I in thy grasp as thou art now in ours,
Soon should I make a midnight spectacle,
Soon, limb by limb, be mangled on a wheel,
Then gibbeted to blacken for the vultures.
But I would teach thee better —— how to spare.
Write as I dictate. If thy ransom comes,
Thou liv'st. If not — but answer not, I pray,
Lest thou provoke me. I may strike thee dead;
And know, young man, it is an easier thing
To do it than to say it. Write, and thus."—
 I wrote. "'T is well," he cried. "A peasant-boy,
Trusty and swift of foot, shall bear it hence.
Meanwhile lie down and rest. This cloak of mine
Will serve thee; it has weathered many a storm."
 The watch was set; and twice it had been changed,
When morning broke, and a wild bird, a hawk,
Flew in a circle, screaming. I looked up,
And all were gone, save him who now kept guard

And on his arms lay musing. Young he seemed,
And sad, as though he could indulge at will
Some secret grief. "Thou shrinkest back," he said.
"Well may'st thou, lying, as thou dost, so near
A ruffian — one forever linked and bound
To guilt and infamy. There was a time
When he had not perhaps been deemed unworthy,
When he had watched yon planet to its setting,
And dwelt with pleasure on the meanest thing
Nature gives birth to. Now, alas! 't is past.
  Wouldst thou know more? My story is an old one.
I loved, was scorned; I trusted, was betrayed;
And in my anguish, my necessity,
Met with the fiend, the tempter — in RUSCONI.
'Why thus?' he cried. 'Thou wouldst be free and dar'st not.
Come and assert thy birthright while thou canst.
A robber's cave is better than a dungeon;
And death itself, what is it at the worst,
What but a harlequin's leap?' Him I had known,
Had served with, suffered with; and on the walls
Of PADUA, while the moon went down, I swore
Allegiance on his dagger.—— Dost thou ask
How I have kept my oath? Thou shalt be told,
Cost what it may. But grant me, I implore,
Grant me a passport to some distant land,
That I may never, never more be named.
Thou wilt, I know thou wilt.
                                        Two months ago,
When on a vineyard-hill we lay concealed
And scattered up and down as we were wont,
I heard a damsel singing to herself,

And soon espied her, coming all alone,
In her first beauty. Up a path she came,
Leafy and intricate, singing her song,
A song of love, by snatches; breaking off
If but a flower, an insect in the sun,
Pleased for an instant; then as carelessly
The strain resuming, and, where'er she stopt,
Rising on tiptoe underneath the boughs
To pluck a grape in very wantonness.
Her look, her mien and maiden ornaments,
Showed gentle birth; and, step by step, she came,
Nearer and nearer, to the dreadful snare.
None else were by; and, as I gazed unseen,
Her youth, her innocence and gayety,
Went to my heart! and, starting up, I breathed,
'Fly — for your life!' Alas! she shrieked, she fell;
And, as I caught her falling, all rushed forth.
'A wood-nymph!' cried RUSCONI. 'By the light,
Lovely as Hebe! Lay her in the shade.'
I heard him not. I stood as in a trance.
'What,' he exclaimed, with a malicious smile,
'Wouldst thou rebel?' I did as he required.
'Now bear her hence to the well-head below;
A few cold drops will animate this marble.
Go! 'T is an office all will envy thee;
But thou hast earned it.' As I staggered down,
Unwilling to surrender her sweet body;
Her golden hair dishevelled on a neck
Of snow, and her fair eyes closed as in sleep,
Frantic with love, with hate, 'Great God!' I cried
(I had almost forgotten how to pray; [284]
But there are moments when the courage comes),

'Why may I not, while yet — while yet I can,
Release her from a thraldom worse than death?'
'T was done as soon as said. I kissed her brow,
And smote her with my dagger. A short cry
She uttered, but she stirred not; and to heaven
Her gentle spirit fled. 'T was where the path
In its descent turned suddenly. No eye
Observed me, though their steps were following fast.
But soon a yell broke forth, and all at once
Levelled with deadly aim. Then I had ceased
To trouble or be troubled, and had now
(Would I were there!) been slumbering in my grave,
Had not Rusconi with a terrible shout
Thrown himself in between us, and exclaimed,
Grasping my arm, ''T is bravely, nobly done!
Is it for deeds like these thou wear'st a sword?
Was this the business that thou cam'st upon?
— But 't is his first offence, and let it pass.
Like the young tiger he has tasted blood,
And may do much hereafter. He can strike
Home to the hilt.' Then in an undertone,
'Thus wouldst thou justify the pledge I gave,
When in the eyes of all I read distrust?
For once,' and on his cheek, methought, I saw
The blush of virtue, 'I will save thee, Albert;
Again I cannot.'"

Ere his tale was told,
As on the heath we lay, my ransom came;
And in six days, with no ungrateful mind,
Albert was sailing on a quiet sea.
— But the night wears, and thou art much in need
Of rest. The young Antonio, with his torch,
Is waiting to conduct thee to thy chamber.

NAPLES.

THIS region, surely, is not of the earth.[285]
Was it not dropt from heaven ? Not a grove,
Citron or pine or cedar, not a grot
Sea-worn and mantled with the gadding vine,
But breathes enchantment. Not a cliff but flings
On the clear wave some image of delight,
Some cabin-roof glowing with crimson flowers,
Some ruined temple or fallen monument,
To muse on as the bark is gliding by.
And be it mine to muse there, mine to glide,[286]
From daybreak, when the mountain pales his fire
Yet more and more, and from the mountain top,
Till then invisible, a smoke ascends,
Solemn and slow, as erst from ARARAT,
When he, the Patriarch, who escaped the Flood,
Was with his household sacrificing there —
From daybreak to that hour, the last and best,
When, one by one, the fishing-boats come forth,
Each with its glimmering lantern at the prow,
And, when the nets are thrown, the evening-hymn
Steals o'er the trembling waters.

Everywhere
Fable and truth have shed, in rivalry,
Each her peculiar influence. Fable came
And laughed and sung, arraying Truth in flowers,
Like a young child her grandam. Fable came ;
Earth, sea and sky reflecting, as she flew,
A thousand, thousand colors not their own :
And at her bidding, lo ! a dark descent

To TARTARUS, and those thrice happy fields,
Those fields with ether pure and purple light
Ever invested, scenes by him portrayed[287]
Who here was wont to wander, here invoke
The sacred Muses,[288] here receive, record
What they revealed, and on the western shore
Sleeps in a silent grove, o'erlooking thee,
Beloved PARTHENOPE!
Yet here, methinks,
Truth wants no ornament, in her own shape
Filling the mind by turns with awe and love,
By turns inclining to wild ecstasy,
And soberest meditation. Here the vines
Wed each her elm, and o'er the golden grain
Hang their luxuriant clusters, checkering
The sunshine; where, when cooler shadows fall
And the mild moon her fairy net-work weaves,
The lute or mandoline, accompanied
By many a voice yet sweeter than their own,
Kindles, nor slowly; and the dance[289] displays
The gentle arts and witcheries of love,
Its hopes and fears and feignings, till the youth
Drops on his knee as vanquished, and the maid,
Her tambourine uplifting with a grace
Nature's, and Nature's only, bids him rise.

But here the mighty Monarch underneath,
He in his palace of fire, diffuses round
A dazzling splendor. Here, unseen, unheard,
Opening another Eden in the wild,
His gifts he scatters; save, when issuing forth
In thunder, he blots out the sun, the sky,

And, mingling all things earthly as in scorn,
Exalts the valley, lays the mountain low,
Pours many a torrent from his burning lake,
And in an hour of universal mirth,
What time the trump proclaims the festival,
Buries some capital city, there to sleep
The sleep of ages — till a plough, a spade,
Disclose the secret, and the eye of day
Glares coldly on the streets, the skeletons;
Each in his place, each in his gay attire,
And eager to enjoy.
Let us go round;
And let the sail be slack, the course be slow,
That at our leisure, as we coast along,
We may contemplate, and from every scene
Receive its influence. The CUMÆAN towers,
There did they rise, sun-gilt; and here thy groves,
Delicious BAIÆ. Here (what would they not?)
The masters of the earth, unsatisfied,
Built in the sea; and now the boatman steers
O'er many a crypt and vault yet glimmering,
O'er many a broad and indestructible arch,
The deep foundations of their palaces;
Nothing now heard ashore, so great the change,
Save when the sea-mew clamors, or the owl
Hoots in the temple.
What the mountainous isle[290]
Seen in the south? 'T is where a monster dwelt,[291]
Hurling his victims from the topmost cliff;
Then and then only merciful, so slow,
So subtle, were the tortures they endured.
Fearing and feared he lived, cursing and cursed;

And still the dungeons in the rock breathe out
Darkness, distemper. Strange, that one so vile[292]
Should from his den strike terror through the world;
Should, where withdrawn in his decrepitude,
Say to the noblest, be they where they might,
"Go from the earth!" and from the earth they went.
Yet such things were — and will be, when mankind,
Losing all virtue, lose all energy;
And for the loss incur the penalty,
Trodden down and trampled.

Let us turn the prow,
And in the track of him who went to die[293]
Traverse this valley of waters, landing where
A waking dream awaits us. At a step
Two thousand years roll backward, and we stand,
Like those so long within that awful place,[294]
Immovable, nor asking, Can it be?

Once did I linger there alone till day
Closed, and at length the calm of twilight came,
So grateful, yet so solemn! At the fount,
Just where the three ways meet, I stood and looked
('T was near a noble house, the house of Pansa),[295]
And all was still as in the long, long night
That followed, when the shower of ashes fell,
When they that sought POMPEII sought in vain;
It was not to be found. But now a ray,
Bright and yet brighter, on the pavement glanced,
And on the wheel-track worn for centuries,
And on the stepping-stones from side to side,
O'er which the maidens, with their water-urns,
Were wont to trip so lightly. Full and clear,
The moon was rising, and at once revealed

The name of every dweller, and his craft;
Shining throughout with an unusual lustre,
And lighting up this city of the dead.
Mark, where within, as though the embers lived,
The ample chimney-vault is dun with smoke.
There dwelt a miller; silent and at rest
His mill-stones now. In old companionship
Still do they stand as on the day he went,
Each ready for its office — but he comes not.
And there, hard by (where one in idleness
Has stopt to scrawl a ship, an armed man;
And in a tablet on the wall we read
Of shows ere long to be) a sculptor wrought,
Nor meanly; blocks, half-chiselled into life,
Waiting his call. — Here long, as yet attests
The trodden floor, an olive-merchant drew
From many an earthen jar, no more supplied;
And here from his a vintner served his guests
Largely, the stain of his o'erflowing cups
Fresh on the marble. On the bench, beneath,
They sate and quaffed and looked on them that passed,
Gravely discussing the last news from Rome.
But, lo! engraven on the threshold-stone,
That word of courtesy so sacred once,
Hail! At a master's greeting we may enter.
And, lo! a fairy-palace; everywhere,
As through the courts and chambers we advance,
Floors of mosaic, walls of arabesque,
And columns clustering in patrician splendor.
But hark, a footstep! May we not intrude?
And now, methinks, I hear a gentle laugh,
And gentle voices mingling as in converse!

— And now a harp-string as struck carelessly,
And now — along the corridor it comes —
I cannot err, a filling as of baths!
— Ah, no! 't is but a mockery of the sense,
Idle and vain! We are but where we were;
Still wandering in a city of the dead!

THE BAG OF GOLD.

I DINE very often with the good old Cardinal * *, and, I should add, with his cats; for they always sit at his table, and are much the gravest of the company. His beaming countenance makes us forget his age;[296] nor did I ever see it clouded till yesterday, when, as we were contemplating the sunset from his terrace, he happened, in the course of our conversation, to allude to an affecting circumstance in his early life.

He had just left the University of PALERMO, and was entering the army, when he became acquainted with a young lady of great beauty and merit, a Sicilian of a family as illustrious as his own. Living near each other, they were often together; and, at an age like theirs, friendship soon turns to love But his father, for what reason I forget, refused his consent to their union; till, alarmed at the declining health of his son, he promised to oppose it no longer, if, after a separation of three years, they continued as much in love as ever.

Relying on that promise, he said, I set out on a long journey; but in my absence the usual arts were resorted to. Our letters were intercepted; and false rumors were spread — first of my indifference, then of my inconstancy, then of my marriage with a rich heiress of SIENNA; and, when at length I returned to make her my own, I found her in a convent of Ursuline Nuns. She had taken the veil; and I, said he with a sigh — what else remained for me? — I went into the church.

Yet many, he continued, as if to turn the conversation, very many have been happy, though we were not; and, if I am not abusing an old man's privilege, let me tell you a story with a better catastrophe. It was told to me when a boy; and you may not be unwilling to hear it, for it bears some resemblance to that of the Merchant of Venice.

We were now arrived at a pavilion that commanded one of the noblest prospects imaginable; the mountains, the sea, and the islands illuminated by the last beams of day; and, sitting down there, he proceeded with his usual vivacity; for the sadness that had come across him was gone.

There lived in the fourteenth century, near BOLOGNA, a widow-lady of the Lambertini family, called MADONNA LUCREZIA, who in a revolution of the state had known the bitterness of poverty, and had even begged her bread; kneeling day after day like a statue at the gate of the cathedral; her rosary in her left hand and her right held out for charity, her long black veil concealing a face that had once adorned a court, and had received the homage of as many sonnets as PETRARCH has written on LAURA.

But Fortune had at last relented; a legacy from a distant relation had come to her relief; and she was now the mistress of a small inn at the foot of the Apennines, where she entertained as well as she could, and where those only stopped who were contented with a little. The house was still standing when in my youth I passed that way; though the sign of the White Cross,[207] the Cross of the Hospitallers, was no longer to be seen over the door; a sign which she had taken, if we may believe the tradition there, in honor of a maternal uncle, a grand-master of that order, whose achievements in PALESTINE she would sometimes relate. A mountain-stream ran through the garden; and, at no great distance, where the road turned on its way to BOLOGNA, stood a little chapel in which a lamp was always burning before a picture of the Virgin,—a picture of great antiquity, the work of some Greek artist.

Here she was dwelling, respected by all who knew her, when an event took place which threw her into the deepest affliction. It was at noon-day in September that three foot-travellers arrived, and, seating themselves on a bench under her vine-trellis, were supplied with a flagon of Aleatico by a lovely girl, her only child, the image of her former self. The eldest spoke like a Venetian, and his beard was short, and pointed after the fashion of Venice. In his demeanor he affected great courtesy, but his look inspired little confidence; for, when he smiled, which he did continually, it was with his lips only, not with his eyes; and they were always turned from yours. His companions were bluff and frank in their manner, and on their tongues had many a soldier's oath. In their hats they wore a medal, such as in that age was often distributed in war; and they were evidently subalterns in one of those free bands which were always ready to serve in any quarrel, if a service it could be called where a battle was little more than a mockery, and the slain, as on an opera-stage, were up and fighting to-morrow. Overcome with the heat, they threw aside their cloaks, and, with their gloves tucked under their belts, continued for some time in earnest conversation.

At length they rose to go; and the Venetian thus addressed their hostess: "Excellent lady, may we leave under your roof, for a day or two, this bag of gold?" "You may," she replied, gayly. "But remember, we fasten only with a latch. Bars and bolts we have none in our village; and, if we had, where would be your security?"—— "In your word, lady."

"But what if I died to-night? Where would it be then?" said she, laughing. "The money would go to the church; for none could claim it."

"Perhaps you will favor us with an acknowledgment." —— "If you will write it."

An acknowledgment was written accordingly, and she signed it before Master Bartolo, the village physician, who had just called on his mule to learn the news of the day; the gold to be delivered when applied for, but to be delivered (these were the words) not to one — nor to two — but to the three; words wisely introduced by those to whom it belonged, knowing what they knew of each other. The gold they had just released from a miser's chest in PERUGIA; and they were now on a scent that promised more.

They and their shadows were no sooner departed, than the Venetian returned, saying, "Give me leave to set my seal on the bag, as the others have done;" and she placed it on a table before him. But in that moment she was called away to receive a cavalier, who had just dismounted from his horse; and, when she came back, it was gone. The temptation had proved irresistible; and the man and the money had vanished together.

"Wretched woman that I am!" she cried, as in an agony of grief she threw herself on her daughter's neck, "what will become of us? Are we again to be cast out into the wide world? . . Unhappy child, would that thou hadst never been born!" and all day long she lamented; but her tears availed her little. The others were not slow in returning to claim their due; and there were no tidings of the thief; he had fled far away with his plunder. A process against her was instantly begun in BOLOGNA; and what defence could she make, — how release herself from the obligation of the bond? Wilfully cr in negligence she had parted with the gold,— she had parted with it to one, when she should have kept it for all; and inevitable ruin awaited her! "Go, GIANETTA," said she to her daughter, "take this veil which your mother has worn and wept under so often, and implore the counsellor Calderino to plead for us on the day of trial. He is generous, and will listen to the unfortunate. But, if he will not, go from door to door; Monaldi cannot refuse us. Make haste, my child; but remember the chapel as you pass by it. Nothing prospers without a prayer."

Alas! she went, but in vain. These were retained against them; those demanded more than they had to give; and all bade them despair. What was to be done? No advocate; and the cause to come on to-morrow!

Now GIANETTA had a lover; and he was a student of the law, a young man of great promise, LORENZO MARTELLI. He had studied long and diligently under that learned lawyer, GIOVANNI ANDREAS, who, though little of stature, was great in renown, and by his contemporaries was called the Arch-doctor, the Rabbi of Doctors, the Light of the World. Under him he had studied, sitting on the same bench with Petrarch; and also under his daughter NOVELLA, who would often lecture to the scholars when her father was otherwise engaged, placing herself behind a small curtain lest her beauty should divert their thoughts from the subject; a precaution in this instance at least unnecessary, LORENZO having lost his heart to another.[298]

To him she flies in her necessity; but of what assistance can he be? He has just taken his place at the bar, but he has never spoken; and how stand up alone, unpractised and unprepared as he is, against an array that would alarm the most experienced? — "Were I as mighty as I am weak," said he, "my fears for you would make me as nothing. But I will be there, GIANETTA; and may the Friend of the friendless give me strength in that hour! Even now my heart fails me; but, come what will, while I have a loaf to share you and your mother shall never want. I will beg through the world for you."

The day arrives, and the court assembles. The claim is stated, and the evidence given. And now the defence is called for — but none is made; not a syllable is uttered; and, after a pause and a consultation of some minutes, the judges are proceeding to give judgment, silence having been proclaimed in the court, when LORENZO rises and thus addresses them: "Reverend signors. Young as I am, may I venture to speak before you? I would speak in behalf of one who has none else to help her; and I will not keep you long. Much has been said; much on the sacred nature of the obligation — and we acknowledge it in its full force. Let it be fulfilled, and to the last letter. It is what we solicit, what we require. But to whom is the bag of gold to be delivered? What says the bond? Not to one — not to two — but to the three. Let the three stand forth and claim it."

From that day (for who can doubt the issue?) none were sought, none employed, but the subtle, the eloquent LORENZO. Wealth followed fame; nor need I say how soon he sat at his marriage-feast, or who sat beside him.

A CHARACTER.

One of two things Montrioli may have,
My envy or compassion. Both he cannot.
Yet on he goes, numbering as miseries
What least of all he would consent to lose,
What most indeed he prides himself upon,
And, for not having, most despises me.
"At morn the minister exacts an hour;
At noon, the king. Then comes the council-board;
And then the chase, the supper. When, ah! when,
The leisure and the liberty I sigh for?
Not when at home; at home a miscreant crew,
That now no longer serve me, mine the service.
And then that old hereditary bore,
The steward, his stories longer than his rent-roll,
Who enters, quill in ear, and, one by one,
As though I lived to write and wrote to live,
Unrolls his leases for my signature."
He clanks his fetters to disturb my peace.
Yet who would wear them[299] and become the slave
Of wealth and power, renouncing willingly
His freedom, and the hours that fly so fast,
A burden or a curse when misemployed,
But to the wise how precious — every day
A little life, a blank to be inscribed
With gentle deeds, such as in after-time
Console, rejoice, whene'er we turn the leaf
To read them? All, wherever in the scale,
Have, be they high or low, or rich or poor,
Inherit they a sheep-hook or a sceptre,

Much to be grateful for; but most has he,
Born in that middle sphere, that temperate zone,
Where Knowledge lights his lamp, there most secure,
And Wisdom comes, if ever, she who dwells
Above the clouds, above the firmament,
That seraph sitting in the heaven of heavens.
  What men most covet, wealth, distinction, power,
Are baubles nothing worth, that only serve
To rouse us up, as children in the schools
Are roused up to exertion. The reward
Is in the race we run, not in the prize;
And they, the few, that have it ere they earn it,
Having, by favor or inheritance,
These dangerous gifts placed in their idle hands,
And all that should await on worth well-tried,
All in the glorious days of old reserved
For manhood most mature or reverend age,
Know not, nor ever can, the generous pride
That glows in him who on himself relies,
Entering the lists of life.

PÆSTUM.

THEY stand between the mountains and the sea;[300]
Awful memorials, but of whom we know not!
The seaman, passing, gazes from the deck.
The buffalo-driver, in his shaggy cloak,
Points to the work of magic and moves on.
Time was they stood along the crowded street,
Temples of gods! and on their ample steps
What various habits, various tongues, beset

The brazen gates for prayer and sacrifice!
Time was perhaps the Third was sought for justice;
And here the accuser stood, and there the accused;
And here the judges sate, and heard, and judged.
All silent now! — as in the ages past,
Trodden under foot and mingled, dust with dust.
  How many centuries did the sun go round
From MOUNT ALBURNUS to the TYRRHENE sea,
While, by some spell rendered invisible,
Or, if approached, approached by him alone
Who saw as though he saw not, they remained
As in the darkness of a sepulchre,
Waiting the appointed time! All, all within
Proclaims that Nature had resumed her right,
And taken to herself what man renounced;
No cornice, triglyph, or worn abacus,
But with thick ivy hung or branching fern;
Their iron-brown o'erspread with brightest verdure!
  From my youth upward have I longed to tread
This classic ground. — And am I here at last?
Wandering at will through the long porticos,
And catching, as through some majestic grove,
Now the blue ocean, and now, chaos-like,
Mountains and mountain-gulfs, and, half-way up,
Towns like the living rock from which they grew?
A cloudy region, black and desolate,
Where once a slave withstood a world in arms.[301]
  The air is sweet with violets, running wild[302]
'Mid broken friezes and fallen capitals;
Sweet as when TULLY, writing down his thoughts,
Those thoughts so precious and so lately lost[303]
(Turning to thee, divine Philosophy,

Ever at hand to calm his troubled soul),
Sailed slowly by, two thousand years ago,
For ATHENS; when a ship, if north-east winds
Blew from the PÆSTAN gardens, slacked her course.
On as he moved along the level shore,
These temples, in their splendor eminent
'Mid arcs and obelisks, and domes and towers,
Reflecting back the radiance of the west,
Well might he dream of Glory! — Now, coiled up,
The serpent sleeps within them; the she-wolf
Suckles her young: and, as alone I stand
In this, the nobler pile, the elements
Of earth and air its only floor and roof,
How solemn is the stillness! Nothing stirs
Save the shrill-voiced cicala flitting round
On the rough pediment to sit and sing;
Or the green lizard rustling through the grass,
And up the fluted shaft with short quick spring,
To vanish in the chinks that Time has made.
In such an hour as this, the sun's broad disk
Seen at his setting, and a flood of light
Filling the courts of these old sanctuaries
(Gigantic shadows, broken and confused,
Athwart the innumerable columns flung) —
In such an hour he came, who saw and told,
Led by the mighty genius of the place.[304]
Walls of some capital city first appeared,
Half razed, half sunk, or scattered as in scorn;
— And what within them? what but in the midst
These Three in more than their original grandeur,
And, round about, no stone upon another?

As if the spoiler had fallen back in fear,
And, turning, left them to the elements.
'T is said a stranger in the days of old
(Some say a Dorian, some a Sybarite;
But distant things are ever lost in clouds) —
'T is said a stranger came, and, with his plough,
Traced out the site; and Posidonia rose,[305]
Severely great, Neptune the tutelar god;
A Homer's language murmuring in her streets,
And in her haven many a mast from Tyre.
Then came another, an unbidden guest.
He knocked and entered with a train in arms;
And all was changed, her very name and language!
The Tyrian merchant, shipping at his door
Ivory and gold, and silk, and frankincense,
Sailed as before, but, sailing, cried, "For Pæstum!"
And now a Virgil, now an Ovid sung
Pæstum's twice-blowing roses; while, within,
Parents and children mourned — and, every year
('T was on the day of some old festival),
Met to give way to tears, and once again
Talk in the ancient tongue of things gone by.[306]
At length an Arab climbed the battlements,
Slaying the sleepers in the dead of night;
And from all eyes the glorious vision fled!
Leaving a place lonely and dangerous,
Where whom the robber spares, a deadlier foe[307]
Strikes at unseen — and at a time when joy
Opens the heart, when summer-skies are blue,
And the clear air is soft and delicate;
For then the demon works — then with that air

The thoughtless wretch drinks in a subtle poison
Lulling to sleep; and, when he sleeps, he dies.
  But what are these still standing in the midst?
The earth has rocked beneath; the thunder-bolt
Passed through and through, and left its traces there;
Yet still they stand as by some unknown charter!
O, they are Nature's own! and, as allied
To the vast mountains and the eternal sea,
They want no written history; theirs a voice
Forever speaking to the heart of man!

AMALFI.

He who sets sail from Naples, when the wind
Blows fragrance from Posìlipo, may soon,
Crossing from side to side that beautiful lake,
Land underneath the cliff where, once among
The children gathering shells along the shore,
One laughed and played, unconscious of his fate;[308]
His to drink deep of sorrow, and, through life,
To be the scorn of them that knew him not,
Trampling alike the giver and his gift,
The gift a pearl precious, inestimable,
A lay divine, a lay of love and war,
To charm, ennoble, and, from age to age,
Sweeten the labor when the oar was plied
Or on the Adrian or the Tuscan sea.
  There would I linger — then go forth again,
And hover round that region unexplored,
Where to Salvator (when, as some relate,
By chance or choice he led a bandit's life,

Yet oft withdrew, alone and unobserved,
To wander through those awful solitudes)
Nature revealed herself. Unveiled she stood
In all her wildness, all her majesty,
As in that elder time ere man was made.
There would I linger — then go forth again;
And he who steers due east, doubling the cape,
Discovers, in a crevice of the rock,
The fishing-town, AMALFI. Haply there
A heaving bark, an anchor on the strand,
May tell him what it is; but what it was
Cannot be told so soon.[309]
The time has been,
When on the quays along the SYRIAN coast
'T was asked, and eagerly, at break of dawn,
"What ships are from AMALFI?" when her coins,
Silver and gold, circled from clime to clime;
From ALEXANDRIA southward to SENNAAR,
And eastward, through DAMASCUS and CABUL
And SAMARCAND, to thy great wall, CATHAY.[310]
Then were the nations by her wisdom swayed;
And every crime on every sea was judged
According to her judgments. In her port
Prows, strange, uncouth, from NILE and NIGER met,
People of various feature, various speech;
And in their countries many a house of prayer,
And many a shelter, where no shelter was,
And many a well, like JACOB'S in the wild,
Rose at her bidding. Then in PALESTINE,
By the way-side, in sober grandeur stood
A hospital, that, night and day, received
The pilgrims of the west; and, when 't was asked,

"Who are the noble founders?" every tongue
At once replied, "The merchants of AMALFI."
That hospital, when GODFREY scaled the walls,
Sent forth its holy men in complete steel;
And hence, the cowl relinquished for the helm,
That chosen band, valiant, invincible,
So long renownéd as champions of the cross,
In RHODES, in MALTA.
For three hundred years
There, unapproached but from the deep, they dwelt;
Assailed forever, yet from age to age
Acknowledging no master. From the deep
They gathered in their harvests; bringing home,
In the same ship, relics of ancient GREECE,
That land of glory where their fathers lay,
Grain from the golden vales of SICILY,[311]
And INDIAN spices. Through the civilized world
Their credit was ennobled into fame;
And, when at length they fell, they left mankind
A legacy, compared with which the wealth
Of Eastern kings — what is it in the scale? —
The mariner's compass.
They are now forgot,
And with them all they did, all they endured,
Struggling with fortune. When SICARDI stood
On his high deck, his falchion in his hand,
And, with a shout like thunder, cried, "Come forth,
And serve me in SALERNO!" forth they came,
Covering the sea, a mournful spectacle;
The women wailing, and the heavy oar
Falling unheard. Not thus did they return,[312]

The tyrant slain; though then the grass of years
Grew in their streets.
There now to him who sails
Under the shore, a few white villages
Scattered above, below, some in the clouds,
Some on the margin of the dark-blue sea
And glittering through their lemon-groves, announce
The region of AMALFI. Then, half-fallen,
A lonely watch-tower on the precipice,
Their ancient landmark, comes. Long may it last;
And to the seaman in a distant age,
Though now he little thinks how large his debt,
Serve for their monument! [313]

MONTE CASSINO.[314]

"WHAT hangs behind that curtain?"[315]—"Wouldst thou learn?
If thou art wise, thou wouldst not. 'T is by some
Believed to be his master-work who looked
Beyond the grave, and on the chapel-wall,
As though the day were come, were come and past,
Drew the Last Judgment.[316] But the wisest err.
He who in secret wrought, and gave it life,
For life is surely there and visible change,[317]
Life such as none could of himself impart
(They who behold it go not as they came,
But meditate for many and many a day),
Sleeps in the vault beneath. We know not much;
But what we know we will communicate.

'T is in an ancient record of the house;
And may it make thee tremble, lest thou fall!
  Once — on a Christmas-eve — ere yet the roof
Rung with the hymn of the Nativity,
There came a stranger to the convent-gate,
And asked admittance; ever and anon,
As if he sought what most he feared to find,
Looking behind him. When within the walls,
These walls so sacred and inviolate,
Still did he look behind him; oft and long,
With curling, quivering lip and haggard eye,
Catching at vacancy. Between the fits,
For here, 't is said, he lingered while he lived,
He would discourse, and with a mastery,
A charm by none resisted, none explained,
Unfelt before; but when his cheek grew pale
(Nor was the respite longer, if so long,
Than while a shepherd in the vale below
Counts, as he folds, five hundred of his flock),
All was forgotten. Then, howe'er employed,
He would break off and start as if he caught
A glimpse of something that would not be gone;
And turn and gaze and shrink into himself,
As though the fiend were there, and, face to face,
Scowled o'er his shoulder.
                                        Most devout he was;
Most unremitting in the services;
Then, only then, untroubled, unassailed;
And, to beguile a melancholy hour,
Would sometimes exercise that noble art
He learnt in FLORENCE; with a master's hand,
As to this day the sacristy attests,
Painting the wonders of the APOCALYPSE.

At length he sunk to rest, and in his cell
Left, when he went, a work in secret done,
The portrait, for a portrait it must be,
That hangs behind the curtain. Whence he drew,
None here can doubt; for they that come to catch
The faintest glimpse — to catch it and be gone —
Gaze as he gazed, then shrink into themselves,
Acting the self-same part. But why 't was drawn,
Whether, in penance, to atone for guilt,
Or to record the anguish guilt inflicts,
Or, haply, to familiarize his mind
With what he could not fly from, none can say,
For none could learn the burden of his soul."

THE HARPER.

It was a harper, wandering with his harp,
His only treasure; a majestic man,
By time and grief ennobled, not subdued;
Though from his height descending, day by day,
And, as his upward look at once betrayed,
Blind as old Homer. At a fount he sate,
Well known to many a weary traveller;
His little guide, a boy not seven years old,
But grave, considerate beyond his years,
Sitting beside him. Each had ate his crust
In silence, drinking of the virgin-spring;
And now in silence, as their custom was,
The sun's decline awaited.
                                        But the child
Was worn with travel. Heavy sleep weighed down

His eyelids; and the grandsire, when we came,
Emboldened by his love and by his fear,
His fear lest night o'ertake them on the road,
Humbly besought me to convey them both
A little onward. Such small services
Who can refuse? — Not I; and him who can,
Blest though he be with every earthly gift,
I cannot envy. He, if wealth be his,
Knows not its uses. So from noon till night,
Within a crazed and tattered vehicle,[318]
That yet displayed, in rich emblazonry,
A shield as splendid as the BARDI wear,[319]
We lumbered on together; the old man
Beguiling many a league of half its length,
When questioned the adventures of his life,
And all the dangers he had undergone;
His shipwrecks on inhospitable coasts,
And his long warfare.—They were bound, he said,
To a great fair at REGGIO; and the boy,
Believing all the world were to be there,
And I among the rest, let loose his tongue,
And promised me much pleasure. His short trance,
Short as it was, had, like a charmed cup,
Restored his spirit, and, as on we crawled,
Slow as the snail (my muleteer dismounting,
And now his mules addressing, now his pipe,
And now Luigi), he poured out his heart,
Largely repaying me. At length the sun
Departed, setting in a sea of gold;
And, as we gazed, he bade me rest assured
That like the setting would the rising be.
Their harp — it had a voice oracular,

And in the desert, in the crowded street,
Spoke when consulted. If the treble chord
Twanged shrill and clear, o'er hill and dale they went,
The grandsire, step by step, led by the child;
And not a rain-drop from a passing cloud
Fell on their garments. Thus it spoke to-day;
Inspiring joy, and, in the young one's mind,
Brightening a path already full of sunshine.

THE FELUCCA.[320]

Day glimmered; and beyond the precipice
(Which my mule followed as in love with fear,
Or as in scorn, yet more and more inclining
To tempt the danger where it menaced most)
A sea of vapor rolled. Methought we went
Along the utmost edge of this, our world,
And the next step had hurled us headlong down
Into the wild and infinite abyss;
But soon the surges fled, and we descried,
Nor dimly, though the lark was silent yet,
Thy gulf, La Spezzia. Ere the morning-gun,
Ere the first day-streak, we alighted there;
And not a breath, a murmur! Every sail
Slept in the offing. Yet along the shore
Great was the stir; as at the noontide hour,
None unemployed. Where from its native rock
A streamlet, clear and full, ran to the sea,
The maidens knelt and sung as they were wont,
Washing their garments. Where it met the tide,
Sparkling and lost, an ancient pinnace lay

Keel upward, and the fagot blazed, the tar
Fumed from the caldron; while, beyond the fort,
Whither I wandered, step by step led on,
The fishers dragged their net, the fish within
At every heave fluttering and full of life,
At every heave striking their silver fins
'Gainst the dark meshes.
Soon a boatman's shout
Reëchoed; and red bonnets on the beach,
Waving, recalled me. We embarked and left
That noble haven, where, when GENOA reigned,
A hundred galleys sheltered — in the day
When lofty spirits met, and, deck to deck,
DORIA, PISANI[321] fought: that narrow field
Ample enough for glory. On we went,
Ruffling with many an oar the crystalline sea,
On from the rising to the setting sun
In silence — underneath a mountain-ridge,
Untamed, untamable, reflecting round
The saddest purple; nothing to be seen
Of life or culture, save where, at the foot,
Some village and its church, a scanty line,
Athwart the wave gleamed faintly. Fear of ill
Narrowed our course, fear of the hurricane,
And that still greater scourge, the crafty Moor,
Who, like a tiger prowling for his prey,
Springs and is gone, and on the adverse coast
(Where TRIPOLI and TUNIS and ALGIERS
Forge fetters, and white turbans on the mole
Gather whene'er the crescent comes displayed
Over the cross) his human merchandise
To many a curious, many a cruel eye

Exposes. Ah! how oft, where now the sun
Slept on the shore, have ruthless scimitars
Flashed through the lattice, and a swarthy crew
Dragged forth, ere long to number them for sale,
Ere long to part them in their agony,
Parent and child! How oft, where now we rode[322]
Over the billow, has a wretched son,
Or yet more wretched sire, grown gray in chains,
Labored, his hands upon the oar, his eyes
Upon the land — the land that gave him birth;
And, as he gazed, his homestall through his tears
Fondly imagined; when a Christian ship
Of war appearing in her bravery,
A voice in anger cried, "Use all your strength!"
  But when, ah! when do they that can, forbear
To crush the unresisting? Strange, that men,
Creatures so frail, so soon, alas! to die,
Should have the power, the will to make this world
A dismal prison-house, and life itself,
Life in its prime, a burden and a curse
To him who never wronged them! Who that breathes
Would not, when first he heard it, turn away
As from a tale monstrous, incredible?
Surely a sense of our mortality,
A consciousness how soon we shall be gone,
Or, if we linger — but a few short years —
How sure to look upon our brother's grave,
Should of itself incline to pity and love,
And prompt us rather to assist, relieve,
Than aggravate the evils each is heir to.
  At length the day departed, and the moon
Rose like another sun, illumining

Waters and woods and cloud-capt promontories,
Glades for a hermit's cell, a lady's bower,
Scenes of Elysium, such as Night alone
Reveals below, nor often — scenes that fled
As at the waving of a wizard's wand,
And left behind them, as their parting gift,
A thousand nameless odors. All was still;
And now the nightingale her song poured forth
In such a torrent of heart-felt delight,
So fast it flowed, her tongue so voluble,
As if she thought her hearers would be gone
Ere half was told. 'T was where in the north-west,
Still unassailed and unassailable,
Thy pharos, GENOA, first displayed itself,
Burning in stillness on its craggy seat;
That guiding star so oft the only one,
When those now glowing in the azure vault
Are dark and silent. 'T was where o'er the sea
(For we were now within a cable's length)
Delicious gardens hung; green galleries,
And marble terraces in many a flight,
And fairy arches flung from cliff to cliff,
Wildering, enchanting; and, above them all,
A palace, such as somewhere in the East,
In Zenastan or Araby the blest,
Among its golden groves and fruits of gold,
And fountains scattering rainbows in the sky,
Rose, when ALADDIN rubbed the wondrous lamp;
Such, if not fairer; and, when we shot by,
A scene of revelry, in long array
As with the radiance of a setting sun,
The windows blazing. But we now approached
A city far-renowned; and wonder ceased.

GENOA.

THIS house was ANDREA DORIA'S.[323] Here he lived;[324]
And here at eve relaxing, when ashore,
Held many a pleasant, many a grave discourse
With them that sought him, walking to and fro
As on his deck. 'T is less in length and breadth
Than many a cabin in a ship of war;
But 't is of marble, and at once inspires
The reverence due to ancient dignity.
He left it for a better; and 't is now
A house of trade,[325] the meanest merchandise
Cumbering its floors. Yet, fallen as it is,
'T is still the noblest dwelling — even in GENOA!
And hadst thou, ANDREA, lived there to the last,
Thou hadst done well; for there is that without,
That in the wall, which monarchs could not give,
Nor thou take with thee,— that which says aloud,
It was thy country's gift to her deliverer.
'T is in the heart of GENOA (he who comes,
Must come on foot), and in a place of stir;
Men on their daily business, early and late,
Thronging thy very threshold. But, when there,
Thou wert among thy fellow-citizens,
Thy children, for they hailed thee as their sire;
And on a spot thou must have loved, for there,
Calling them round, thou gav'st them more than life,
Giving what, lost, makes life not worth the keeping.
There thou didst do indeed an act divine;
Nor couldst thou leave thy door or enter in,
Without a blessing on thee.

Thou art now
Again among them. Thy brave mariners,
They who had fought so often by thy side,
Staining the mountain-billows, bore thee back;
And thou art sleeping in thy funeral-chamber.
Thine was a glorious course; but couldst thou there,
Clad in thy cere-cloth — in that silent vault,
Where thou art gathered to thy ancestors —
Open thy secret heart and tell us all,
Then should we hear thee with a sigh confess,
A sigh how heavy, that thy happiest hours
Were passed before these sacred walls were left,
Before the ocean-wave thy wealth reflected,[326]
And pomp and power drew envy, stirring up
The ambitious man,[327] that in a perilous hour
Fell from the plank.

MARCO GRIFFONI.

War is a game at which all are sure to lose, sooner or later, play they how they will; yet every nation has delighted in war, and none more, in their day, than the little republic of Genoa, whose galleys, while she had any, were always burning and sinking those of the Pisans, the Venetians, the Greeks, or the Turks; Christian and Infidel alike to her.

But experience, when dearly bought, is seldom thrown away altogether. A moment of sober reflection came at last; and, after a victory the most splendid and ruinous of any in her annals, she resolved from that day and forever to live at peace with all mankind; having in her long career acquired nothing but glory and a tax on every article of life.

Peace came, but with none of its blessings. No stir in the harbor, no merchandise in the mart or on the quay; no song as the shuttle was thrown or the ploughshare broke the furrow. The frenzy had left a languor more alarming than itself. Yet the burden must be borne, the taxes be gathered; and, year after year, they lay like a curse on the land, the prospect on every side growing darker and darker, till an old man entered the senate-house on his crutches, and all was changed.

MARCO GRIFFONI was the last of an ancient family, a family of royal merchants; and the richest citizen in GENOA, perhaps in Europe. His parents dying while yet he lay in the cradle, his wealth had accumulated from the year of his birth; and so noble a use did he make of it when he arrived at manhood, that wherever he went he was followed by the blessings of the people. He would often say, "I hold it only in trust for others;" but GENOA was then at her old amusement, and the work grew on his hands. Strong as he was, the evil he had to struggle with was stronger than he. His cheerfulness, his alacrity, left him; and, having lifted up his voice for peace, he withdrew at once from the sphere of life he had moved in — to become, as it were, another man.

From that time, and for full fifty years, he was to be seen sitting, like one of the founders of his house, at his desk among his money-bags, in a narrow street near the Porto Franco; and he, who in a famine had filled the granaries of the state, sending to Sicily, and even to Egypt, now lived only as for his heirs, though there were none to inherit; giving no longer to any, but lending to all — to the rich on their bonds and the poor on their pledges; lending at the highest rate, and exacting with the utmost rigor. No longer relieving the miserable, he sought only to enrich himself by their misery; and there he sate in his gown of frieze, till every finger was pointed at him in passing, and every tongue exclaimed, "There sits the miser!"

But in that character, and amidst all that obloquy, he was still the same as ever, still acting to the best of his judgment for the good of his fellow-citizens; and when the measure of their calamities was full,—when peace had come, but had come to no purpose, and the lesson, as he flattered himself, was graven deep in their minds,—then, but not till then, though his hair had long grown gray, he threw off the mask and gave up all he had, to annihilate at a blow his great and cruel adversaries,[328] those taxes which, when excessive, break the hearts of the people; a glorious achievement for an individual, though a bloodless one, and such as only can be conceived possible in a small community like theirs.

Alas! how little did he know of human nature! How little had he reflected on the ruling passion of his countrymen, so injurious to others, and at length so fatal to themselves! Almost instantly they grew arrogant and quarrelsome; almost instantly they were in arms again; and, before the statue was up that had been voted to his memory, every tax, if we may believe the historian,[329] was laid on as before, to awaken vain regrets and wise resolutions.

A FAREWELL.[330]

AND now farewell to ITALY — perhaps
Forever! Yet, methinks, I could not go,
I could not leave it, were it mine to say,
"Farewell forever!" Many a courtesy,
That sought no recompense, and met with none
But in the swell of heart with which it came,
Have I experienced; not a cabin-door,
Go where I would, but opened with a smile;
From the first hour, when, in my long descent,
Strange perfumes rose, rose as to welcome me,
From flowers that ministered like unseen spirits;
From the first hour, when vintage-songs broke forth,
A grateful earnest, and the southern lakes,
Dazzlingly bright, unfolded at my feet;
They that receive the cataracts, and ere long
Dismiss them, but how changed — onward to roll
From age to age in silent majesty,
Blessing the nations, and reflecting round
The gladness they inspire.

Gentle or rude,
No scene of life but has contributed
Much to remember — from the POLESINE,
Where, when the south-wind blows and clouds on clouds
Gather and fall, the peasant freights his boat,
A sacred ark, slung in his orchard-grove;
Mindful to migrate when the king of floods[331]
Visits his humble dwelling, and the keel,
Slowly uplifted over field and fence,
Floats on a world of waters — from that low,

That level region, where no echo dwells,
Or, if she comes, comes in her saddest plight,
Hoarse, inarticulate — on to where the path
Is lost in rank luxuriance, and to breathe
Is to inhale distemper, if not death;[332]
Where the wild-boar retreats, when hunters chafe
And, when the day-star flames, the buffalo-herd,
Afflicted, plunge into the stagnant pool,
Nothing discerned amid the water-leaves,
Save here and there the likeness of a head,
Savage, uncouth; where none in human shape
Come, save the herdsman, levelling his length
Of lance with many a cry, or, Tartar-like,
Urging his steed along the distant hill
As from a danger. There, but not to rest,
I travelled many a dreary league, nor turned
(Ah! then least willing, as who had not been?)
When in the south, against the azure sky,
Three temples rose in soberest majesty,
The wondrous work of some heroic race.[333]
  But now a long farewell! Oft, while I live,
If once again in England, once again[334]
In my own chimney-nook, as Night steals on,
With half-shut eyes reclining, oft, methinks,
While the wind blusters and the drenching rain
Clatters without, shall I recall to mind
The scenes, occurrences, I met with here,
And wander in Elysium; many a note
Of wildest melody, magician-like
Awakening, such as the CALABRIAN horn
Along the mountain-side, when all is still,
Pours forth at folding-time; and many a chant,

Solemn, sublime, such as at midnight flows
From the full choir, when richest harmonies
Break the deep silence of thy glens, LA CAVA;
To him who lingers there with listening ear
Now lost and now descending as from Heaven!

AND now a parting word is due from him
Who, in the classic fields of ITALY
(If haply thou hast borne with him so long),
Through many a grove by many a fount has led thee,
By many a temple half as old as Time;
Where all was still awakening them that slept,
And conjuring up where all was desolate,
Where kings were mouldering in their funeral urns,
And oft and long the vulture flapped his wing —
Triumphs and masques.

Nature denied him much,
But gave him at his birth what most he values;
A passionate love for music, sculpture, painting,
For poetry, the language of the gods,
For all things here, or grand or beautiful,
A setting sun, a lake among the mountains.
The light of an ingenuous countenance,
And, what transcends them all, a noble action.[335]

Nature denied him much, but gave him more;
And ever, ever grateful should he be,
Though from his cheek, ere yet the down was there,
Health fled; for in his heaviest hours would come
Gleams such as come not now; nor failed he then
(Then and through life his happiest privilege)

Full oft to wander where the Muses haunt,
Smit with the love of song.
'T is now long since;
And now, while yet 't is day, would he withdraw,
Who, when in youth he strung his lyre, addressed
A former generation. Many an eye,
Bright as the brightest now, is closed in night,
And many a voice, how eloquent, is mute,
That, when he came, disdained not to receive
His lays with favor. * * * * *

1839.

NOTES.

(1) J. J. Rousseau. "J'arrive essoufflé, tout en nage; le cœur me bat; je vois de loin les soldats à leur poste; j'accours, je crie d'une voix étouffée. Il étoit trop tard." — *Les Confessions*, l. i.

(2) "Lines of eleven syllables occur almost in every page of Milton; but though they are not unpleasing, they ought not to be admitted into heroic poetry; since the narrow limits of our language allow us no other distinction of epic and tragic measures." — *Johnson.*

It is remarkable that he used them most at last. In the Paradise Regained they occur oftener than in the Paradise Lost in the proportion of ten to one; and let it be remembered that they supply us with another close, — another cadence, — that they add, as it were, a string to the instrument; and, by enabling the poet to relax at pleasure, to rise and fall with his subject, contribute what is most wanted, compass, variety.

Shakspeare seems to have delighted in them, and in some of his soliloquies has used them four and five times in succession; an example I have not followed in mine. As in the following instance, where the subject is solemn beyond all others:

"To be, or not to be," &c.

They come nearest to the flow of an unstudied eloquence, and should therefore be used in the drama; but why exclusively? Horace, as we learn from himself, admitted the Musa Pedestris in his happiest hours, in those when he was most at his ease; and we cannot regret her visits. To her we are indebted for more than half he has left us; nor was she ever at his elbow in greater dishabille than when he wrote the celebrated Journey to Brundusium.

(3) Bernard, Abbot of Clairvaux. "To admire or despise St. Bernard as he ought," says Gibbon, "the reader, like myself, should have before the windows of his library that incomparable landscape."

(4) The following lines were written on the spot, and may serve perhaps to recall to some of my readers what they have seen in this enchanting country.

I love to watch in silence till the sun
Sets; and Mont Blanc, arrayed in crimson and gold,
Flings his gigantic shadow o'er the lake;
That shadow, though it comes through pathless tracts,
Only less bright, less glorious than himself.
But, while we gaze, 't is gone! And now he shines
Like burnished silver; all, below, the Night's.
Such moments are most precious. Yet there are
Others that follow fast, more precious still;

When once again he changes, once again
Clothing himself in grandeur all his own;
When, like a ghost, shadowless, colorless,
He melts away into the heaven of heavens;
Himself alone revealed, all lesser things
As though they were not and had never been!

(5) The Castle of Joux, in Franche-Comté.

(6) See the *Odyssey*, lib. xix. v. 597, and lib. xxiii. v. 19

(7) The retreat of Amadeus, the first Duke of Savoy. Voltaire thus addresses it from his windows:

"Ripaille, je te vois. O bizarre Amédée," &c.

The seven towers are now no longer a landmark to the voyager.

(8) Ludlow.

(9) He has given us a very natural account of his feelings at the conclusion of his long labor there: "It was on the night of the 27th of June, 1787, between the hours of eleven and twelve, that I wrote the last lines of the last page in a summer-house in my garden. After laying down my pen, I took several turns in a *berceau* or covered walk of acacias, which commands the lake and the mountains. The sky was serene, the moon was shining on the waters, and I will not dissemble my joy. But, when I reflected that I had taken an everlasting leave of an old and agreeable companion," &c.

There must always be something melancholy in the moment of separation, as all have more or less experienced; none more, perhaps, than Cowper: "And now," says he, "I have only to regret that my pleasant work is ended. To the illustrious Greek I owe the smooth and easy flight of many thousand hours. He has been my companion at home and abroad, in the study, in the garden and in the field; and no measure of success, let my labors succeed as they may, will ever compensate to me the loss of the innocent luxury that I have enjoyed, as a translator of Homer."

(10) The burial-place of Necker.

(11) The Lake of the Four Cantons.

(12) In the course of the year they entertain from thirty to thirty-five thousand travellers. — *Le Père Biselx, Prieur.*

(13) Alluding to Barri, a dog of great renown in his day. He is here admirably represented by a pencil that has done honor to many of his kind, but to none who deserved it more. His skin is stuffed and preserved in the Museum of Berne.

(14) The Grande Chartreuse. It was indebted for its foundation to a miracle; as every guest may learn there from a little book that lies on the table in his cell, the cell allotted to him by the fathers.

"In this year the Canon died, and, as all believed, in the odor of sanctity; for who in his life had been so holy, in his death so happy? But how false are the judgments of men! For when the hour of his funeral had arrived, when the mourners had entered the church, the bearers set down the bier, and every voice was lifted up in the Miserere, suddenly, and as none knew how, the lights were extinguished, the anthem stopt! A darkness succeeded, a silence as of the grave; and these words came in sorrowful accents from the lips of the dead: 'I am summoned before a just God! . . . A just God judgeth me! . . . I am condemned by a just God!'"

"In the church," says the legend, "there stood a young man with his hands clasped in prayer, who, from that time, resolved to withdraw into the desert. It was he whom we now invoke as St. Bruno."

(15) Ils ont la même longueur que l'église de Saint-Pierre de Rome, et ils renferment quatre cents cellules.

(16) Vallombrosa, formerly called Acqua Bella.

(17) The words of Ariosto.

una badia
Ricca — e cortesa a chiunque vi venia.

(18) Ariosto and Milton. Milton was there at the fall of the leaf.

(19) Not that I felt the confidence of Erasmus, when, on his way from Paris to Turin, he encountered the dangers of Mont Cenis in 1507; when, regardless of torrent and precipice, he versified as he went; composing a poem on horseback,* and writing it down at intervals as he sat in the saddle,† — an example, I imagine, followed by few.

Much, indeed, of Childe Harold's Pilgrimage, as the author assured me, was conceived and executed in like manner on his journey through Greece; but the work was performed in less unfavorable circumstances; for, if his fits of inspiration were stronger, he travelled on surer ground.

(20) "Many able men have served under me; but none like him. He loved glory for itself."

(21) The Schreckhorn.

(22) The Jung-frau.

(23) The author of Lalla Rookh, a poet of such singular felicity as to give a lustre to all he touches, has written a song on this subject, called the Crystal-hunters.

(24) M. Ebel mentions an escape almost as miraculous. "L'an 1790, Christian Boren, propriétaire de l'auberge du Grindelwald, eut le malheur de se jeter dans une fente du glacier, en le traversant avec un troupeau de moutons qu'il ramenoit des pâturages de Bäniseck. Heureusement qu'il tomba dans le voisinage du grand torrent qui coule dans l'intérieur, il en suivit le lit par dessous les voûtes de glace, et arriva au pied du glacier. Cet homme est actuellement encore en vie." — *Manuel du Voyageur*.

(25) Lichen geographicus.

(26) Almost every mountain of any rank or condition has such a bridge. The most celebrated in this country is on the Swiss side of St. Gothard.

(27) When may not our minds be said to stream into each other? for how much by the light of the countenance comes from the child to the mother before he has the gift of speech; and how much afterwards in like manner comes to console us and to cheer us in our journey through life; for when even to the last cannot we give, cannot we receive what no words can convey?

And is not this the universal language, — the language of all nations from the beginning of time, — which comes with the breath of life, nor goes till life itself is departing?

(38) A tradition. Gesler said to him, when it was over, "You had a second arrow in

* "Carmen equestre, vel potius Alpestre." — *Erasmus.*
† "Notans in charta super sellam." — *Idem.*

your belt. What was it for?" — "To kill you," he replied, "if I had killed my son." There is a monument in the market-place of Altorf to consecrate the spot.

(29) The Eagle and Child is a favorite sign in many parts of Europe.

(30) "J'aime beaucoup ce tournoiement, pourvu que je sois en sûreté." — *J. J. Rousseau*, *Les Confessions*, l. iv.

(31) "Ou il y a environ dix ans, que l'Abbé de St. Maurice, Mons. Cocatrix, a été précipité avec sa voiture, ses chevaux, sa cuisinière, et son cocher." — *Descript du Valais.*

(32) Originally thus:

I love to sail along the LARIAN Lake
Under the shore — though not, where'er he dwelt,
To visit PLINY, — not, where'er he dwelt,
Whate'er his humor; for from cliff to cliff,
From glade to glade, adorning as he went,
He moved at pleasure, many a marble porch,
Dorian, Corinthian, rising at his call.

(33) "Hujus in littore plures villæ meæ." — *Epist.* ix. 7.

(34) *Epist.* i. 3, ix. 7.

(35) Il lago di Garda. His peninsula he calls "the eye of peninsulas;" and it is beautiful. But, whatever it was, who could pass it by? Napoleon, in the career of victory, turned aside to see it.

Of his villa there is now no more remaining than of his old pinnace, which had weathered so many storms, and which he consecrated at last as an *ex-voto.*

(36) Commonly called Paul Veronese.

(37) The lake of Catullus; and now called Il lago di Garda. Its waves, in the north, lash the mountains of the Tyrol; and it was there, at the little village of Limone, that Hofer embarked, when in the hands of the enemy and on his way to Mantua, where, in the court-yard of the citadel, he was shot as a traitor. Less fortunate than Tell, yet not less illustrious, he was watched by many a mournful eye as he came down the lake; and his name will live long in the heroic songs of his country.

He lies buried at Innspruck, in the church of the Holy Cross; and the statue on his tomb represents him in his habit as he lived and as he died.

(38) Petrarch, *Epist. Rer. Sen.* I. v. ep. 3.

(39) Mastino de la Scala, the Lord of Verona. Cortusio, the ambassador and historian, saw him so surrounded.

This house had been always open to the unfortunate. In the days of Can Grande all were welcome; poets, philosophers, artists, warriors. Each had his apartment, each a separate table; and at the hour of dinner musicians and jesters went from room to room. Dante, as we learn from himself, found an asylum there.

' Lo primo tuo rifugio, e'l primo ostello
Sarà la cortesia del gran Lombardo,
Che'n su la scala porta il santo uccello."

Their tombs in the public street carry us back into the times of barbarous virtue; nor less so do those of the Carrara Princes of Padua, though less singular and striking in themselves. Francis Carrara, the elder, used often to visit Petrarch in his small house at Arquà, and followed him on foot to his grave.

(40) See the *Heraclidæ* of Euripides, v. 203, &c.

(41) Originally thus:

My omelet, and a trout, that, as the sun
Shot his last ray through Zanga's leafy grove,
Leaped at a golden fly, had happily
Fled from all eyes;

Zanga is the name of a beautiful villa near Bergamo, in which Tasso finished his tragedy of Torrismondo. It still belongs to his family.

(42) *Hist. de Gil Blas*, l. i. c. 2.
After the concluding line in the MS.

That evening, tended on with verse and song,
I closed my eyes in heaven, but not to sleep;
A Columbine, my nearest neighbor there,
In her great bounty, at the midnight hour
Bestowing on the world two Harlequins.

Chapelle and Bachaumont fared no better at Salon, "à cause d'une comédienne, qui s'avisa d'accoucher de deux petits comédiens."

(43) Originally thus:

And shall I sup where JULIET at the masque
First saw and loved, and now, by him who came
That night a stranger, sleeps from age to age?

An old palace of the Cappelletti, with its uncouth balcony and irregular windows, is still standing in a lane near the market-place; and what Englishman can behold it with indifference?

When we enter Verona we forget ourselves, and are almost inclined to say, with Dante,

"Vieni a veder Montecchi, e Cappelletii."

(44) It has been observed that in Italy the memory sees more than the eye. Scarcely a stone is turned up that has not some historical association, ancient or modern; that may not be said to have gold under it.

(45) Fallen as she is, she is still, as in the days of Tassoni,

"La gran donna del Po."

(46) From the sonnet of Filicaja, "Italia! Italia!" &c.

(47) All our travellers, from Addison downward, have diligently explored the monuments of her former existence; while those of her latter have, comparatively speaking, escaped observation. If I cannot supply the deficiency, I will not follow their example; and happy shall I be if by an intermixture of verse and prose I have furnished my countrymen on their travels with a pocket companion.

Though the obscure has its worshippers, as well, indeed, it may, forever changing its aspect, and now and then, if we may believe it, wearing the likeness of the sublime; I have always endeavored, with what success I cannot say, to express my thoughts and my feelings as naturally and as clearly in verse as in prose, sparing no labor, and remembering the old adage, "Le Temps n'epargne pas ce qu'on fait sans lui."

It was the boast of Boileau — and how much are we indebted to him! — that he had taught Racine to write with difficulty, — to do as others have done who have left what will live forever.

"Weigh well every word, nor publish till many years are gone by," is an injunction which has descended from age to age, the injunction of one * who could publish only in manuscript, and in manuscript hope to survive; though now (such the energy of his genius, such the excellence of his precept and his practice) in every country, every language, and in numbers almost numberless, our constant companion wherever we go.†

What would he have said now, when many a volume, on its release from the closet, wings it way in an instant over the Old World and the New, flying from city to city during the changes of the moon; and when the words which are uttered in our senate at midnight are delivered to thousands at sunrise, and before sunset are travelling to the ends of the earth?

(48) There is a French proverb that must sometimes occur to an observer in the present age: Beaucoup de mal, peu de bruit; Beaucoup de bruit, peu de mal.

To Lord John Russell are we indebted for that admirable definition of a proverb, "The wisdom of many and the wit of one."

(49) A mirror in the sixteenth century is said to have revealed a secret that led to less tragical consequences.

John Galeazzo Visconte, Duke of Milan, becoming enamored in his youth of a daughter of the house of Correggio, his gayety, his cheerfulness left him, as all observed, though none knew why; till some ladies of the court, who had lived with him in great familiarity, and who had sought and sought, but never found, began to rally him on the subject, saying, "Forgive us our presumption, sir, but, as you are in love, — for in love you must be, — may we know who she is, that we may render honor to whom honor is due; for it will be our delight no less than our duty to serve her?"

The duke was in dismay, and endeavored to fly, if it were possible, from so unequal a combat. But in flight there is no security when such an enemy is in the field; and, being soon convinced that the more he resisted the more he would be assailed, he resolved at once to capitulate; and, commanding for the purpose a splendid entertainment, such as he was accustomed to give, he invited them, one and all; not forgetting the lovely Correggia, who was as urgent as the rest, though she flattered herself that she knew the secret as well as he did.

When the banquet was over and the table-cloth removed, and every guest, as she sate, served with water for her fair hands and with a tooth-pick from the odoriferous mastic-tree, a cabinet of rich workmanship was placed on the table. "And now," said he, with a gayety usual to lovers, "and now, my dear ladies, as I can deny you nothing, come, one by one, and behold her; for here she is!" As he spoke, he unfolded the doors of the cabinet; and each in her turn beheld the portrait of a beautiful girl.

The last to look and to see was Correggia, for so he had contrived it; but no contrivance was wanted; for, shrinking and agitated, she had hung back behind them all, till to her ear came the intelligence that the portrait was unknown, and with the intelligence came the conviction that her fond heart had deceived her.

But what were her feelings when she looked and saw; for at the touch of a spring the portrait had vanished, and in a mirror she saw herself! — *Ricordi di Sabba Castiglione*, 1559.

For this story, as indeed for many others, I am indebted to my friend, Sir Charles Lock Eastlake, President of the Royal Academy; and I am happy in this opportunity of acknowledging my obligations to him.

* Horace.

† Nineteen centuries have passed away, and what scholar has not now his pocket Horace?

(50) *Murato* was a technical word for this punishment.

(51) An old huntsman of the family met her in the haze of the morning, and never went out again.

She is still known by the name of Madonna Bianca.

(52) Several were painted by Giorgione and Titian; as, for instance, the Ca' Soranzo, the Ca' Grimani, and the Fondaco de' Tedeschi. Great was their emulation, great their rivalry, if we may judge from an anecdote related by Vasari; and with what interest must they have been observed in their progress, as they stood at work on their scaffolds, by those who were passing under them by land and by water! *

(53) Now an observatory. On the wall there is a long inscription: "Piis carcerem adspergite lacrymis," &c.

Ezzelino is seen by Dante in the river of blood.

(54) Bonatti was the great astrologer of that day; and all the little princes of Italy contended for him. It was from the top of the tower of Forli that he gave his signals to Guido Novello. At the first touch of a bell the count put on his armor; at the second he mounted his horse, and at the third marched out to battle. His victories were ascribed to Bonatti; and not perhaps without reason. How many triumphs were due to the soothsayers of old Rome!

(55) "Douze personnes, tant acteurs qu' actrices, un souffleur, un machiniste, un garde du magasin, des enfans de tout âge, des chiens, des chats, des singes, des perroquets; c' étoit l' arche de Noé. Ma prédilection pour les soubrettes m'arrêta sur Madame Baccherini." — *Goldoni.*

(56) The passage-boats are drawn up and down the Brenta.

(57) A pleasant instance of his wit and agility was exhibited some years ago on the stage at Venice.

"The stutterer was in an agony; the word was inexorable. It was to no purpose that Harlequin suggested another and another. At length, in a fit of despair, he pitched his head full in the dying man's stomach, and the word bolted out of his mouth to the most distant part of the house." — *See Moore's View of Society in Italy.*

He is well described by Marmontel in the *Encyclopédie.*

"Personnage de la comédie italienne. Le caractère distinctif de l'ancienne comédie italienne est de jouer des ridicules, non pas personnels, mais nationaux. C'est une imitation grotesque des mœurs des différentes villes d'Italie; et chacune d'elles est représentée par un personnage qui est toujours le même. Pantalon est vénitien, le Docteur est bolonois, Scapin est napolitain, et Arlequin est bergamasque. Celui-ci est d'une singularité qui mérite d'être observée; et il a fait long-temps les plaisirs de Paris, joué par trois acteurs célébres, Dominique, Thomassin, et Carlin. Il est vraisemblable qu'un esclave africain fut le premier modèle de ce personnage. Son caractère est un mélange d'ignorance, de naïveté, d'esprit, de bêtise et de grâce: c'est un espèce d'homme ébauché, un grand enfant, qui a des lueurs de raison et d'intelligence, et dont toutes les méprises ou les maladresses ont quelque chose de piquant. Le vrai modèle de son jeu est la souplesse, l'agilité, la gentillesse d'un jeune chat, avec une écorce de grossièreté qui rend son action plus plaisante; son rôle est celui d'un valet patient, fidèle, crédule, gourmand, toujours amoureux, toujours dans l'embarras, ou pour son maître, ou pour lui-même; qui s'afflige,

* Frederic Zucchero, in a drawing which I have seen, has introduced his brother Taddeo as so employed at Rome on the palace of Mattei, and Raphael and Michael Angelo as sitting on horseback among the spectators below.

qui se console avec la facilité d'un enfant, et dont la douleur est aussi amusante que la joie."

(58) Attila.

(59) "I love," says a traveller, "to contemplate, as I float along, that multitude of palaces and churches, which are congregated and pressed as on a vast raft." And who can forget his walk through the Merceria, where the nightingales give you their melody from shop to shop, so that, shutting your eyes, you would think yourself in some forest-glade, when, indeed, you are all the while in the middle of the sea? Who can forget his prospect from the great tower, which once, when gilt, and when the sun struck upon it, was to be descried by ships afar off; or his visit to St. Mark's church, where you see nothing, tread on nothing, but what is precious; the floor all agate, jasper; the roof mosaic; the aisle hung with the banners of the subject cities; the front and its five domes affecting you as the work of some unknown people? Yet all this may presently pass away; the waters may close over it; and they that come row about in vain to determine exactly where it stood.

(60) A poet of our own country, Mr. Wordsworth, has written a noble sonnet on the extinction of the Venetian republic.

"Once did she hold the gorgeous East in fee," &c.

(61) "Il fallut subsister; ils tirèrent leur subsistance de tout l'univers."—*Montesquieu.*

(62) A caravan.

(63) There was, in my time, another republic, a place of refuge for the unfortunate, and, not only at its birth, but to the last hour of its existence, which had established itself in like manner among the waters, and which shared the same fate; a republic, the citizens of which, if not more enterprising, were far more virtuous,* and could say also to the great nations of the world, "Your countries were acquired by conquest or by inheritance; but ours in the work of our own hands. We renew it day by day; and, but for us, it might cease to be to-morrow!"—a republic, in its progress, forever warred on by the elements, and how often by men more cruel than they; yet constantly cultivating the arts of peace, and, short as was the course allotted to it (only three times the life of man, according to the Psalmist), producing, amidst all its difficulties, not only the greatest seamen, but the greatest lawyers, the greatest physicians, the most accomplished scholars, the most skilful painters, and statesmen as wise as they were just.†

* It is related that Spinola and Richardot, when on their way to negotiate a treaty at the Hague in 1608, saw eight or ten persons land from a little boat, and, sitting down on the grass, make a meal of bread and cheese and beer. "Who are these travellers?" said the ambassadors to a peasant.—"They are the deputies from the states," he answered, "our sovereign lords and masters."—"We must make peace," they cried. "These are not men to be conquered."—*Voltaire.*

† What names, for instance, are more illustrious than those of Barneveldt and De Witt? But when there were such mothers, there might well be such sons.

When Reinier Barneveldt was condemned to die for an attempt to revenge his father's death by assassination, his mother threw herself at the feet of Prince Maurice. "You did not deign," said he, "to ask for your husband's life; and why ask for your son's?"—"My husband," she replied, "was innocent; but my son is guilty."

De Witt was at once a model for the greatest and the least. Careless as he was of his life when in the discharge of his duty, he was always careful of his health; and to the question how he was able to transact such a multiplicity of affairs, he would answer, "By doing only one thing at a time." A saying which should not soon be forgotten, and which may remind the reader of another, though of less value, by a great English lawyer of the last century, John Dunning. "I do a little; a little does itself; and the rest is undone."

(64) A national game of great antiquity, and most probably the "micare digitis" of the Romans. It is an old observation that few things are so lasting as the games of the young. They go down from one generation to another.

(65) Originally thus:

> With Punchinello, crying as in wrath
> "Tre! Quattro! Cinque!"—'T is a game to strike

(66) When we wish to know if a man may be accounted happy, we should perhaps inquire, not whether he is prosperous or unprosperous, but how much he is affected by little things,—by such as hourly assail us in the commerce of life, and are no more to be regarded than the buzzings and stingings of a summer fly.

(67) They were placed in the floor as memorials. The brass was engraven with the words addressed by the Pope to the emperor, "Super aspidem et basiliscum ambulabis," &c. Thou shalt tread upon the asp and the basilisk: the lion and the dragon shalt thou trample under foot.

(68) Alexander III. He fled in disguise to Venice, and is said to have passed the first night on the steps of San Salvatore. The entrance is from the Mercerìa, near the foot of the Rialto; and it is thus recorded, under his escutcheon, in a small tablet at the door: "Alexandro III. Pont. Max. pernoctanti."

(69) See Geoffrey de Villehardouin, in *Script. Byzant*, t. xx.

(70) See Petrarch's description of them and of the tournament, *Rer. Senil.* l. iv. ep. 2.

(71) Petrarch.

(72) Not less splendid were the tournaments of Florence in the place of Santa Croce. To those which were held there in February and June, 1468, we are indebted for two of the most celebrated poems of that age, the Giostra of Lorenzo de' Medici, by Luca Pulci, and the Giostra of Giuliano de' Medici, by Politian.

(73) "Recenti victoriâ exultantes," says Petrarch; alluding, no doubt, to the favorable issue of the war in France. This festival began on the 4th of August, 1364.

(74) Among those the most followed, there was always a mask in a magnificent habit, relating marvellous adventures, and calling himself Messer Marco Millioni. Millioni was the name given by his fellow-citizens in his lifetime to the great traveller, Marco Polo. "I have seen him so described," says Ramusio, "in the records of the republic; and his house has, from that time to this, been called La Corte del Millioni," the palace of the rich man, the millionnaire. It is on the canal of S. Giovanni Chrisostomo; and, as long as he lived, was much resorted to by the curious and the learned.

(75) "In atto di dar la benedittione," says Sansovino; and performing the same office as the Triton on the tower of the winds at Athens.

(76) Now called La Scala de' Giganti. The colossal statues were placed there in 1566.

(77) "Marin Faliero della bella moglie: altri la gode ed egli la mantiene."
"Locus Marini Faletri decapitati pro criminibus."

(78) Francis Carrara II.

(79) "Il Conte, entrando in prigione, disse: Vedo bene ch' io son morto, e trasse un grande sospiro."—*M. Sanuto.*

(80) Les prisons des plombs, c'est-à-dire ces fournaises ardentes qu'on avait distribuées en petites cellules sous les terrasses qui couvrent le palais ; les puits, c'est-à-dire ces fosses creusées sous les canaux, où le jour et la chaleur n'avaient jamais pénétré, étaient les silencieux dépositaires des mystérieuses vengeances de ce tribunal. — *Daru.*

(81) A deep channel behind the island of S. Giorgio Maggiore.

(82) "How fares it with your world ?" says his highness the Devil to Quevedo, on their first interview in the lower regions. "Do I prosper there ?"—"Much as usual, I believe." — "But tell me truly. How is my good city of Venice ? Flourishing ?" — "More than ever." — "Then I am under no apprehension. All must go well."

In a letter written by Francesco Priscianese, a Florentine, there is an interesting account of an entertainment given in that city by Titian.

"I was invited," says he, "to celebrate the first of August (ferrare Agosto) in a beautiful garden belonging to that great painter,* a man who by his courtesies could give a grace and a charm to anything festive ;† and there, when I arrived, I found him in company with some of the most accomplished persons then in Venice ; together with three of my countrymen, Pietro Aretino, Nardi the historian,‡ and Sansovino, so celebrated as a sculptor and an architect.

"Though the place was shady, the sun was still powerful ; and, before we sat down at table, we passed our time in contemplating the excellent pictures with which the house was filled, and in admiring the order and beauty of the garden, which, being on the sea and at the northern extremity of Venice, looked directly on the little island of Murano, and on others not less beautiful.

"Great, indeed, was our admiration, great our enjoyment, wherever we turned ; and no sooner did the sun go down than the water was covered with gondolettas adorned with ladies, and resounding with the richest harmonies, vocal and instrumental, which continued till midnight, and delighted us beyond measure, while we sat and supped, regaling ourselves with everything that was most exquisite."

(83) An allusion to the supper in *Candide* : c. xxvi.

(84) See Schiller's Ghost-seer, c. i.

(85) See the history of Bragadino, the Alchemist, as related by Daru. — *Hist. de Venise*, c. 28.

The person that follows him was yet more extraordinary, and is said to have appeared there in 1687. — *See Hermippus Redivivus.*

"Those who have experienced the advantages which all strangers enjoy in that city will not be surprised that one who went by the name of Signor Gualdi was admitted into the best company, though none knew who or what he was. He remained there some months ; and three things were remarked concerning him : that he had a small but inestimable collection of pictures, which he readily showed to anybody ; that he spoke on every subject with such a mastery as astonished all who heard him ; and that he never wrote or received any letter, never required any credit or used any bills of exchange, but paid for everything in ready money, and lived respectably, though not splendidly.

* Great as he was, we know little of his practice. Palma the elder, who studied under him, used to say that he finished more with the finger than the pencil. — *Boschini.*

† His scholar Tintoret, if so much could not be said of him, would now and then enliven the conversation at his table with a sally that was not soon forgotten. Sitting one day there with his friend Bassan, "I tell thee what, Giacomo," said he : "if I had thy coloring and thou hadst my design, the Titians and Correggios and Raphaels should not approach us." — *Verci.*

‡ Nardi lived long, if not so long as Titian. Writing to Varchi on the 13th of July, 1555, he says : "I am still sound, though feeble ; having on the twenty-first of the present month to begin to climb with my staff the steep ascent of the eightieth year of this my misspent life." — *Tiraboschi.*

"This gentleman being one day at the coffee-house, a Venetian nobleman, who was an excellent judge of pictures, and who had heard of Signor Gualdi's collection, expressed a desire to see them; and his request was instantly granted. After observing and admiring them for some time, he happened to cast his eyes over the chamber-door, where hung a portrait of the stranger. The Venetian looked upon it, and then upon him. 'This is your portrait, sir,' said he to Signor Gualdi. The other made no answer but by a low bow. 'Yet you look,' he continued, 'like a man of fifty; and I know this picture to be of the hand of Titian, who has been dead one hundred and thirty years. How is this possible?' 'It is not easy,' said Signor Gualdi, gravely, 'to know all things that are possible; but there is certainly no crime in my being like a picture of Titian's.' The Venetian perceived that he had given offence, and took his leave.

"In the evening he could not forbear mentioning what had passed to some of his friends, who resolved to satisfy themselves the next day by seeing the picture. For this purpose they went to the coffee-house about the time that Signor Gualdi was accustomed to come there; and, not meeting with him, inquired at his lodgings, where they learnt that he had set out an hour before for Vienna. This affair made a great stir at the time.

(86) A Frenchman of high rank, who had been robbed at Venice and had complained in conversation of the negligence of the police, saying that they were vigilant only as spies on the stranger, was on his way back to the Terra Firma, when his gondola stopped suddenly in the midst of the waves. He inquired the reason; and his gondoliers pointed to a boat with a red flag, that had just made them a signal. It arrived; and he was called on board. "You are the Prince de Craon? Were you not robbed on Friday evening?" — "I was." — "Of what?" — "Of five hundred ducats." — "And where were they?" — "In a green purse." — "Do you suspect anybody?" — "I do, a servant." — "Would you know him again?" — "Certainly." The interrogator with his foot turned aside an old cloak that lay there; and the prince beheld his purse in the hand of a dead man. "Take it; and remember that none set their feet again in a country where they have presumed to doubt the wisdom of the government."

(87) Une magistrature terrible, says Montesquieu, une magistrature établie pour venger les crimes qu'elle soupçonne. Of the terror which it inspired he could speak from experience, if we may believe one of his contemporaries.

In Italy, says Diderot, he became acquainted with Lord Chesterfield, and they travelled on together, disputing all the way; each asserting and maintaining as for his life the intellectual superiority of his countrymen; till at length they came to Venice, where Montesquieu was prosecuting his researches with an ardor all his own, when he received a visit from a stranger, — a Frenchman in a rusty garb, — who thus addressed him: "You must wonder at my intrusion, sir; but, when the life of a countryman is in danger, I cannot remain silent, cost me what it may. In this city many a man has gone to his grave for one inconsiderate word, and you have uttered a thousand. Nor is it unknown to the government that you write; and before the sun goes down — But I have said more than enough; and may it not be too late! Good-morning to you, sir. All I beg of you in return is, that, if you see me again under any circumstances, you will not discover that you have seen me before."

The president, in the greatest consternation, prepared for instant flight, and had already committed his papers to the flames, when Chesterfield appeared and began to reason with him on the subject.

"What could be his motive? Friendship?" — "He did not know me." — "Money?" — "He asked for none." — "And all, then, for nothing; when, if detected, he would be strangled on the spot! — No, no, my friend. He was sent, you may rest assured; and what would you say, — but let me reflect a little, — and what would you say, if you were indebted for this visit to an Englishman, a fellow-traveller of yours, to convince you by experience of what by argument he could never convince you; that one grain of our common sense, meanly as you may think of it, is worth a thousand of that *esprit* on which you all value yourselves so highly; for with one grain of common sense —"

"Ah, villain!" exclaimed Montesquieu, "what a trick you have played me! And my manuscript! my manuscript, which I have burnt!"

(88) La Biondina in Gondoletta.

(89) "C'était sous les portiques de Saint-Marc que les patriciens se réunissaient tous les jours. Le nom de cette promenade indiquait sa destination; on l'appellait *il Broglio.*" — *Daru.*

(90) When a despot lays his hand on a free city, how soon must he make the discovery of the rustic who bought Punch of the puppet-show man, and complained that he would not speak!

(91) For this thought I am indebted to some unpublished travels by the author of Vathek.

(92) Goldoni, describing his excursion with the Passalacqua, has left us a lively picture of this class of men.

"We were no sooner in the middle of that great lagoon which encircles the city, than our discreet gondolier drew the curtain behind us, and let us float at the will of the waves. At length night came on, and we could not tell where we were. 'What is the hour?' said I to the gondolier. — 'I cannot guess, sir; but, if I am not mistaken, it is the lover's hour.' — 'Let us go home,' I replied; and he turned the prow homeward, singing, as he rowed, the twenty-sixth strophe of the sixteenth canto of the Jerusalem Delivered."

(93) Premi o stali.

(94) At Venice, if you have *la riva in casa*, you step from your boat into the hall.

(95) Bianca Capello. It had been shut, if we may believe the novelist Malespini, by a baker's boy, as he passed by at daybreak; and in her despair she fled with her lover to Florence, where he fell by assassination. Her beauty, and her love-adventure as here related, her marriage afterwards with the grand duke, and that fatal banquet at which they were both poisoned by the cardinal, his brother, have rendered her history a romance.

(96) This circumstance took place at Venice on the first of February, the eve of the feast of the Purification of the Virgin, A. D. 994, Pietro Candiano, Doge.

(97) "E 'l costume era, che tutte le novizze con tutta la dote loro venissero alla detta chiesa, dov' era il vescovo con tutta la chieresia." — *A. Navagiero.*

(98) Among the *Habiti Antichi*, in that admirable book of wood-cuts ascribed to Titian (A. D. 1590), there is one entitled "Sposa Venetiana à Castello." It was taken from an old painting in the Scuola di S. Giovanni Evangelista, and by the writer is believed to represent one of the brides here described.

(99) San Pietro di Castello, the patriarchal church of Venice.

(100) "Una galera e una galeotta." — *M. Sanuto.*

(101) In the lagoons of Caorlo. The creek is still called *Il Porto delle Donzelle.*

(102) "Paululùm etiam spirans," &c. — *Sallust. Bell. Catal.* 59.

(103) They are described by Evelyn and La Lande, and were to be seen in the treasury of St. Mark very lately.

(104) "Le quali con trionfo si conducessero sopra una piatta pe' canali di Venezia con suoni e canti." — *M. Sanuto.*

(105) An English abbreviation. Rialto is the name, not of the bridge, but of the island from which it is called; and the Venetians say *Il ponte di Rialto*, as we say Westminster bridge.

In that island is the exchange; and I have often walked there as on classic ground. In the days of Antonio and Bassanio it was second to none. "I sottoportici," says Sansovino, writing in 1580, "sono ogni giorno frequentati da i mercatanti Fiorentini, Genovesi, Milanesi, Spagnuoli, Turchi, e d' altre nationi diverse del mondo, i quali vi concorrono in tanta copia, che questa piazza è annoverata fra le prime dell' universo." It was there that the Christian held discourse with the Jew; and Shylock refers to it, when he says,

"Signor Antonio, many a time and oft,
In the Rialto you have rated me —"

"Andiamo a Rialto," — "L'ora di Rialto," — were on every tongue; and continue so to the present day, as we learn from the comedies of Goldoni, and particularly from his *Mercanti.*

There is a place adjoining, called Rialto Nuovo; and so called, according to Sansovino, "perchè fù fabbricato dopo il vecchio."

(106) The Council of Ten and the Giunta, "nel quale," says Sanuto, "fu messer lo doge." The Giunta at the first examination consisted of ten patricians, at the last of twenty.

This story and the tragedy of the Two Foscari were published within a few days of each other, in November, 1821.

(107) She was a Contarini; a name coëval with the Republic, and illustrated by eight Doges. On the occasion of their marriage the Bùcentaur came out in its splendor; and a bridge of boats was thrown across the Cànal Grande for the bridegroom and his retinue of three hundred horse. Sanuto dwells with pleasure on the costliness of the dresses, and the magnificence of the processions by land and water. The tournaments in the place of St. Mark lasted three days, and were attended by thirty thousand people.

(108) Francesco Sforza. His father, when at work in the field, was accosted by some soldiers, and asked if he would enlist. "Let me throw my mattock on that oak," he replied, "and if it remains there, I will." It remained there; and the peasant, regarding it as a sign, enlisted. He became soldier, general, prince; and his grandson, in the palace at Milan, said to Paulus Jovius, "You behold these guards and this grandeur. I owe everything to the branch of an oak, — the branch that held my grandfather's mattock."

(109) It was a high crime to solicit the intercession of any foreign prince.

(110) "Va e ubbidisci a quello che vuole la terra, e non cercar più oltre."

(111) The state-inquisitors. For an account of their authority, see page 306.

(112) There is a beautiful precept which he who has received an injury, or who thinks that he has, would for his own sake do well to follow: "Excuse half and forgive the rest."

(113) "Veneno sublatus." The tomb is in the Church of St. Elena.

(114) A remarkable instance, among others in the annals of Venice, that her princes were merchants ; her merchants, princes.

(115) Count Ugolino. — *Inferno*, 32.

(116) Remember the poor Marcolini !

(117) " I visited once more," says Alfieri, " the tomb of our master in love, the divine Petrarch ; and there, as at Ravenna, consecrated a day to meditation and verse."

He visited also the house ; and in the album there wrote a sonnet worthy of Petrarch himself.

" O Cameretta, che già in te chiudesti
Quel Grande alla cui fama è angusto il mondo," &c.

Alfieri took great pleasure in what he called his poetical pilgrimages. At the birth-place and the grave of Tasso he was often to be found ; and in the library at Ferrara he has left this memorial of himself on a blank leaf of the *Orlando Furioso:* " Vittorio Alfieri vide e venerò. 18 giugno, 1783."

(118) The Côte Rotie, the Hermitage, &c.

(119) After which, in the MS.

A Crusoe, sorrowing in his loneliness —

(120) This village, says Boccaccio, hitherto almost unknown even at Padua, is soon to become famous through the world ; and the sailor on the Adriatic will prostrate himself when he discovers the Euganean hills. " Among them," will he say, " sleeps the poet who is our glory. Ah, unhappy Florence ! You neglected him, — you deserved him not."

(121) " I have built among the Euganean hills a small house, decent and proper ; in which I hope to pass the rest of my days, thinking always of my dead or absent friends." Among those still living was Boccaccio ; who is thus mentioned by him in his will : " To Don Giovanni of Certaldo, for a winter-gown at his evening studies, I leave fifty golden florins ; truly little enough for so great a man."

When the Venetians overran the country, Petrarch prepared for flight. " Write your name over your door," said one of his friends, " and you will be safe." — " I am not so sure of that," replied Petrarch, and fled with his books to Padua. His books he left to the republic of Venice, laying, as it were, a foundation for the library of St. Mark ; but they exist no longer. His legacy to his friend Francis Carrara the elder, a Madonna painted by Giotto, is still preserved in the cathedral of Padua.

(122) Thrice happy is he who acquires the habit of looking everywhere for excellences, and not for faults, — whether in art or in nature, — whether in a picture, a poem, or a character. Like the bee in its flight, he extracts the sweet, and not the bitter, wherever he goes ; till his mind becomes a dwelling-place for all that is beautiful, receiving, as it were by instinct, what is congenial to itself, and rejecting everything else almost as unconsciously as if it was not there.

(123) May I for a moment transport my reader into the depths of the Black Forest ? It is for the sake of a little story which has some relation to the subject, and which many, if I mistake not, will wish to be true.

" Farewell ! " said the old baron, as he conducted his guest to the gate. " If you must go, you must. But promise to write, for we shall be anxious to hear of your entire recovery ; though we cannot regret, as we ought to do, an illness by which we have been so much the gainers." The young man said nothing, but the tears were in his eyes ; and, as the carriage drove off, he looked back again and again on the venerable towers of the castle in which he had experienced such kindness. "Nor can I regret my illness," said he to himself, with a sigh.

Sick and a stranger, he had been received and welcomed from a miserable inn in the village below. By the baron he had been treated with the tenderness of a parent; and by his daughter — but the reader must fill up the sentence from what follows.

It was a younger son of the house of Modena, who was now travelling homeward along the banks of the Danube. What he thought at first to be gratitude, neither time nor distance could remove or diminish; and, having not long afterwards, by some unexpected circumstances, succeeded to the dukedom, he wrote instantly to invite her who had nursed him in his extremity to come and share his throne. "You have given me life," said he, "and you cannot refuse me that without which life would be of little value."

Her answer was soon received. She would not deny the pleasure, the emotion, with which she had read his letter. She would not conceal the friendship, — the more than friendship, — which she had conceived for him. "But I am no longer," says she, "what I was. A cruel distemper has so entirely changed me that you would not know me; and, grateful as I shall ever feel for the honor and the happiness you intended for me, I must, for your sake, for my own, decline them both, and remain hore to devote myself to my father in the obscurity in which you found me."

"No," he replied, "it was your mind, and not your person, beautiful as you then were, beautiful as in my eyes you must always continue to be, that won my regard. Come, — for come you must, — and bring him — my friend, my benefactor — along with you, that with you I may study to make him happy; nor can I fail of success, for it shall be the business of my life to make *you* so."

She came, and as lovely as ever. It was a *ruse* to try the strength of his affection; and from her is said to have descended the race that now occupies the throne of Modena.

(124) Affirming itself to be the very bucket which Tassoni in his mock heroics has celebrated as the cause of war between Bologna and Modena, five hundred years ago.

(125) *Inferno*, V.

(126) This story is, I believe, founded on fact; though the time and place are uncertain. Many old houses in England lay claim to it.

Except in this instance and another (p. 411) I have everywhere followed history or tradition; and I would here disburden my conscience in pointing out these exceptions, lest the reader should be misled by them.

(127) Commonly called Domenichino.

(128) How affecting are such demonstrations of grief!

We read of a father who lost an only child by a fall from a window, and who, as long as he lived, and however he might be employed, would suddenly break off and give the cry and the look and the gesture which he gave when it sprung from his arms and was gone.

It is said that Garrick was well acquainted with him, and that, when solicited by the actors in Paris to give some proof of his power, he gave what he had seen so often, and with a truth that overcame them all.

(129) See the Cries of Bologna, as drawn by Annibal Carracci. He was of very humble origin; and, to correct his brother's vanity, once sent him a portrait of their father, the tailor, threading his needle.

(130) The principal gondolier, il fante di poppa, was almost always in the confidence of his master, and employed on occasions that required judgment and address.

(131) "Adrianum mare." — *Cic.*

(132) See the *Prophecy of Dante.*

(133) See the tale as told by Boccaccio and Dryden.

(134) Such, perhaps, as suggested to Petrocchi the sonnet, "Io chiesi al Tempo," &c.

I said to Time, "This venerable pile,
Its floor the earth, its roof the firmament,
Whose was it once?" He answered not, but fled
Fast as before. I turned to Fame, and asked.
"Names such as his, to thee they must be known.
Speak!" But she answered only with a sigh,
And, musing mournfully, looked on the ground.
Then to Oblivion I addressed myself,
A dismal phantom, sitting at the gate;
And, with a voice as from the grave, he cried,
"Whose it was once I care not; now 't is mine." *

The same turn of thought is in an ancient inscription which Sir Walter Scott repeated to me many years ago, and which he had met with, I believe, in the cemetery of Melrose Abbey, when wandering, like Old Mortality, among the tomb-stones there.

The Earth walks on the Earth, glistering with gold;
The Earth goes to the Earth, sooner than it wold.
The Earth builds on the Earth temples and towers;
The Earth says to the Earth, "All will be ours."

(135) They wait for the traveller's carriage at the foot of every hill.

(136) Among other instances of her ascendency at the close of the thirteenth century, it is related that Florence saw twelve of her citizens assembled at the court of Boniface the Eighth, as ambassadors from different parts of Europe and Asia. Their names are mentioned in *Toscana Illustrata.*

(137) A chapel of the Holy Virgin in the church of the Carmelites. It is adorned with the paintings of Masaccio, and all the great artists of Florence studied there; Lionardo da Vinci, Fra Bartolomeo, Andrea del Sarto, Michael Angelo, Raphael, &c.

He had no stone, no inscription, says Vasari, for he was thought little of in his lifetime.

"Se alcun cercasse il marmo, o il nome mio,
La chiesa è il marmo, una cappella è il nome."

Nor less melancholy was the fate of Andrea del Sarto, though his merit was not undiscovered. "There is a little man in Florence," said Michael Angelo to Raphael, "who, if he were employed on such great works as you are, would bring the sweat to your brow." See Bocchi in his "Bellezza di Firenze."

(138) Il sasso di Dante. It exists, I believe, no longer, the wall having been taken down; but enough of him remains elsewhere. Boccaccio delivered his lectures on the Divina Commedia in the church of S. Stefano; and whoever happens to enter it, when the light is favorable, may still, methinks, catch a glimpse of him and his hearers.

(139) This quarter of the city was, at the close of the fourteenth century,† the scene of a romantic incident that befell a young lady of the Amieri family, who, being crossed in love

* For the last line I am indebted to a translation by the Rev. Charles Strong.
† October, 1396.

and sacrificed by her father to his avarice or his ambition, was, in the fourth year of an unhappy marriage, consigned to the grave.

With the usual solemnities she was conveyed to the cemetery of the cathedral, and deposited in a sepulchre of the family that was long pointed out; but she was not to remain there. For she had been buried in a trance; and, awaking at midnight "among them that slept," she disengaged in the darkness her hands and her feet, and, climbing up the narrow staircase to a gate that had been left unlocked, came abroad into the moonshine, wondering where she was, and what had befallen her. When she had in some degree recovered herself, she sought the house of her husband;* going forth in her grave-clothes and passing through the street, that was thenceforth to be called the Street of the Dead.† But, when she arrived there and he beheld her, he started back as from a spectre, and shut the door against her and fled.

To her father then she directed her steps, and afterwards to an uncle, but with no better success; and now, being everywhere rejected, and with horror, what, alas, had she to do but to die! — to return to the place from which in that garment she had wandered? For a while, in her agony, she is said to have sheltered herself under the porch of St. Bartholomew; till, the day beginning to break and the stir of life to gather round her, she resolved at once to fly for refuge to him who had loved her from their childhood, and who could never reject her.

Undistinguished in the crowd, he had followed the funeral-train; and, having taken a last look before she was removed from the bier, he was brooding at home on the past, when a voice came through the lattice, like a voice from heaven, and the interview let those imagine who can.

The sequel will surprise the reader, but we should remember when and where they lived. Her husband claiming her, she appealed to the ecclesiastical court; and, after due deliberation, it was decided that, having been buried with the rites of the church, and having passed through the grave, she was absolved from her vow, and at liberty to marry again. — *Firenza Illustrate. L'Osservatore Fiorentino.*

(140) *Inferno*, 33. A more dreadful vehicle for satire cannot well be conceived. Dante, according to Boccaccio, was passing by a door in Verona, at which some women were sitting, when one of them was overheard to say, in a low voice, to the rest, Do you see that man? He it is who visits hell whenever he pleases; and who returns to give an account of those he finds there. — I can believe it, replied another. Don't you observe his brown skin and his frizzled beard?

(141) "Movemur enim nescio quo pacto locis ipsis, in quibus eorum, quos diligimus, aut admiramur, adsunt vestigia. Me quidem ipsæ illæ nostræ Athenæ non tam operibus magnificis exquisitisque antiquorum artibus delectant, quàm recordatione summorum virorum, ubi quisque habitare, ubi sedere, ubi disputare sit solitus: studiosèque eorum etiam sepulchra contemplor." — *Cic. de Legibus*, ii. 2.

(142) A saying of Michael Angelo. They are the work of Lorenzo Ghiberti.

(143) "Mio bel san Giovanni." — *Inferno*, 19.

(144) Great, indeed, are the miseries that here await the children of genius; so exquisitely alive are they to every breath that stirs. But, if they suffer more than others, more than others is it theirs to enjoy. Every gleam of sunshine on their journey has a lustre not its own; and, to the last, — come what may, — how great is their delight when they pour forth their conceptions, when they deliver what they receive from the God that

* Nel Corso degli Adimari.

† La Via dell Morte, 'o, per dir meglio, della Morta.

is within them; how great the confidence with which they look forward to the day, however distant, when those who are yet unborn shall bless them!

(145) *Paradiso*, 17.

(146) The Chapel de' Depositi; in which are the tombs of the Medici, by Michael Angelo.

(147) He died early; living only to become the father of Catherine de Medicis. Had an evil spirit assumed the human shape to propagate mischief, he could not have done better.

The statue is larger than the life, but not so large as to shock belief. It is the most real and unreal thing that ever came from the chisel.

(148) The day of All Souls; Il dì de' Morti.

(149) "Exoriare aliquis nostris ex ossibus ultor!"

Perhaps there is nothing in language more affecting than his last testament. It is addressed "To God, the Deliverer," and was found steeped in his blood.

(150) Filippo Strozzi.

(151) The Tribune.

(152) Cosmo, the first Grand Duke.

(153) De Thou.

(154) Elenora di Toledo. Of the children that survived her, one fell by a brother, one by a husband, and a third murdered his wife. But that family was soon to become extinct. It is some consolation to reflect that their country did not go unrevenged for the calamities which they had brought upon her. How many of them died by the hands of each other! —*See* p. 448.

(155) De Thou.

(156) The Palazzo Vecchio. Cosmo had left it several years before.

(157) By Vasari, who attended him on this occasion. Thuanus, de Vitâ suâ, i.

(158) It was given out that they had died of a contagious fever: and funeral orations were publicly pronounced in their honor.

Alfieri has written a tragedy on the subject; if it may be said so, when he has altered so entirely the story and the characters.

(159) He was the father of modern painting, and the master of Giotto, whose talent he discovered in the way here alluded to.

"Cimabuè stood still, and, having considered the boy and his work, he asked him if he would go and live with him at Florence. To which the boy answered that, if his father was willing, he would go, with all his heart." — *Vasari.*

Of Cimabuè little now remains at Florence, except his celebrated Madonna, larger than the life, in Santa Maria Novella. It was painted, according to Vasari, in a garden near Porta S. Piero, and, when finished, was carried to the church in solemn procession, with trumpets before it. The garden lay without the walls; and such was the rejoicing there on the occasion, such the feasting, that the suburb received the name of Borgo Allegri, a name it still bears, though now a part of the city.

(160) His first instrument was presented by him to the Doge of Venice; and there is a tradition at Venice that he exhibited its wonders on the top of the tower of St. Mark.

His second, which discovered the satellites of Jupiter, and was endeared to him, as he says, by much fatigue and by many a midnight watch, remained entire, I believe, till very lately, in the Museum at Florence.

Kepler's letter to him on that discovery is very characteristic of the writer. "I was sitting idle at home, thinking of you and your letters, most excellent Galileo, when Wachenfels stopped his carriage at my door to tell me the news; and such was my wonder when I heard it, such my agitation (for at once it decided an old controversy of ours), that, what with his joy and my surprise, and the laughter of both, we were for some time unable, he to speak, and I to listen. At last I began to consider how they could be there, without overturning my Mysterium Cosmographicum, published thirteen years ago. Not that I doubt their existence. So far from it, I am longing for a glass, that I may, if possible, get the start of you, and find two for Mars, six or eight for Saturn," &c.

In Jupiter and his satellites, seen as they now are, "we behold, at a single glance of the eye, a beautiful miniature of the planetary system," and perhaps of every system of worlds through the regions of space.

(161) It is somewhere mentioned that Michael Angelo, when he set out from Florence to build the dome of St. Peter's, turned his horse round in the road to contemplate once more that of the cathedral, as it rose in the gray of the morning from among the pines and cypresses of the city, and that he said, after a pause, "Come te non voglio! Meglio di te non posso!"* He never, indeed, spoke of it but with admiration; and, if we may believe tradition, his tomb by his own desire was to be so placed in the Santa Croce as that from it might be seen, when the doors of the church stood open, that noble work of Brunelleschi.

(162) Santa Maria Novella. For its grace and beauty it was called by Michael Angelo "La Sposa."

(163) In the year of the Great Plague. See the Decameron.

(164) Once, on a bright November morning, I set out and traced them, as I conceived, step by step; beginning and ending in the Church of Santa Maria Novella. It was a walk delightful in itself and in its associations.

(165) I have here followed Baldelli. It has been said that Boccaccio drew from his imagination. But is it likely, when he and his readers were living within a mile or two of the spot? Truth or fiction, it furnishes a pleasant picture of the manners and amusements of the Florentines in that day.

(166) At three o'clock. Three hours after sunrise, according to the old manner of reckoning.

(167) Boccaccio.

(168) Decameron, vi. 10.

(169) Macchiavel.

(170) See a very interesting letter from Macchiavel to Francesco Vettori, dated the 10th of December, 1513.

(171) Since the invention of letters, when we began to write, how much, that will live forever, has come in solitude and in silence from the head and the heart! No voice delivers it when it comes; yet on by its own energy it goes through the world, come

* Like thee I will not build one. Better than thee I cannot.

whence it may, — from the distant, from the dead, — and on it will continue to go, enlightening millions yet unborn in regions yet undiscovered.

(172) La Verdea. It is celebrated by Rinuccini, Redi, and most of the Tuscan poets ; nor is it unnoticed by some of ours.

" Say, he had been at Rome and seen the relics,
Drunk your Verdea wine," &c.

Beaumont and Fletcher.

(173) It is difficult to conceive what Galileo must have felt, when, having constructed his telescope, he turned it to the heavens, and saw the mountains and valleys in the moon. Then the moon was another earth ; the earth another planet ; and all were subject to the same laws. What an evidence of the simplicity and the magnificence of nature !

But at length he turned it again, still directing it upward, and again he was lost ; for he was now among the fixed stars ; and, if not magnified as he expected them to be, they were multiplied beyond measure.

What a moment of exultation for such a mind as his ! But as yet it was only the dawn of a day that was coming ; nor was he destined to live till that day was in its splendor. The great law of gravitation was not yet to be made known ; and how little did he think, as he held the instrument in his hand, that we should travel by it so far as we have done ; that its revelations would ere long be so glorious !

Among the innumerable stars now discovered, and at every improvement of the telescope we discover more and more, there are many at such a distance from this little planet of ours, that " their light must have taken at least a thousand years to reach us." The intelligence which they may be said to convey to us, night after night, must therefore, when we receive it, be a thousand years old ; for every ray that comes must have set out as long ago ; and, " when we observe their places and note their changes," they may have ceased to exist for a thousand years.

Nor can their dimensions be less wonderful than their distances ; if Sirius, as it is more than conjectured, be nearly equal to fourteen suns, and there are others that surpass Sirius. Yet all of them must be as nothing in the immensity of space, and amidst the " numbers without number " that may never become visible here, though they were created *in the beginning*. — *Sir John Herschel.*

(174) Galileo came to Arcetri at the close of the year 1633 ; and remained there, while he lived, by an order of the Inquisition.* It is without the walls, near the Porta Romana.

He was buried with all honor in the church of the Santa Croce.

(175) *Il Giojello.*

(176) Ariosto himself employed much of his time in gardening ; and to his garden at Ferrara we owe many a verse.

(177) Milton went to Italy in 1638. "There it was," says he, "that I found and visited the famous Galileo, grown old, a prisoner to the Inquisition." "Old and blind," he might have said. Galileo, by his own account, became blind in December, 1637. Milton, as we learn from the date of Sir Henry Wotton's letter to him, had not left England on the 18th of April following. — *See Tiraboschi, and Wotton's Remains.*

(178) It has pleased God, said he, that I should be blind ; and must not I also be pleased ?

* For believing in the motion of the earth. " They may issue their decrees," says Pascal, " it is to no purpose. If the earth is really turning round, all mankind together cannot keep it from turning, or keep themselves from turning with it." — *Les Provinciales*, xviii.

(179) If we may judge from the progress which our language has made and is making, where, in what region, however distant, may it not prevail? And how inspiring, yet how awful is the reflection! for who among us can say where what he writes will not be read, — where the seed which he sows will not spring up to good or to evil?

"I care not," says Milton, "to be once named abroad, though perhaps I could attain to that; being content with these islands as my world." Yet where may he not be named, and with reverence? Where may not the verse which he delivered in trust to others, as he sate dictating in his darkness, be treasured up in the memories and in the hearts of men; his language being theirs?

(180) If such was their lot in life, if it was theirs to live under discountenance and in blindness, they were not without their reward; living, as so many have done, in the full assurance that their labor would not be lost, and that sooner or later the world would be the happier and the better for their having lived in it.

(181) They rise within thirteen miles of each other.

(182) Il Sagro Eremo.

(183) I cannot dismiss Pisa without a line or two; for much do I owe to her. If Time has levelled her ten thousand towers (for, like Lucca, she was "torreggiata a guisa d'un boschetto"), she has still her cathedral and her baptistery, her belfry and her cemetery; and from Time they have acquired more than they have lost.

If many a noble monument is gone,
That said how glorious in her day she was,
There is a sacred place within her walls,
Sacred and silent, save when they that die
Come there to rest, and they that live to pray,
For then are voices heard, crying to God,
Where yet remain, apart from all things else,
Four such as nowhere on the earth are seen
Assembled; and at even, when the sun
Sinks in the west, and in the east the moon
As slowly rises, her great round displaying
Over a city now so desolate —
Such is the grandeur, such the solitude,
Such their dominion in that solemn hour,
We stand and gaze and wonder where we are,
In this world or another.

(184) It was in this manner that the first Sforza went down when he perished in the Pescàra.

(185) Michael Angelo.

(186) A description of the Cartoon of Pisa.

(187) Petrarch, as we learn from himself, was on his way to Ancisa; whither his mother was retiring. He was seven months old at the time.

(188) "O ego quantus eram, gelidi cum stratus ad Arni
Murmura," &c. *Epitaphium Damonis.*

(189) There were the "Nobili di Torre" and the "Nobili di Loggia."

(190) Giovanni Buondelmonte was on the point of marrying an Amidei, when a widow of the Donati family made him break his engagement in the manner here described.

The Amidei washed away the affront with his blood, attacking him, says G. Villani, at the foot of the Ponte Vecchio, as he was coming leisurely along in his white mantle on his white palfrey; and hence many years of slaughter.

" O Buondelmonte, quanto mal fuggisti
Le nozze sue, per gli altrui conforti." — *Dante.*

(191) If war is a calamity, what a calamity must be civil war; for how cruel are the circumstances which it gives birth to!

"I had served long in foreign countries," says an old soldier, "and had borne my part in the sack of many a town; but there I had only to deal with strangers; and I shall never — no, never — forget what I felt to-day, when a voice in my own language cried out to me for quarter."

(192) The story is Bolognese, and is told by Cherubino Ghiradacci in his history of Bologna. Her lover was of the Guelphic party, her brothers of the Ghibelline; and no sooner was this act of violence made known, than an enmity, hitherto but half-suppressed, broke out into open war. The Great Place was a scene of battle and bloodshed for forty successive days; nor was a reconciliation accomplished till six years afterwards, when the families and their adherents met there once again, and exchanged the kiss of peace before the Cardinal Legate; as the rival families of Florence had already done in the place of S. Maria Novella. Every house on the occasion was hung with tapestry and garlands of flowers.

(193) The Saracens had introduced among them the practice of poisoning their daggers.

(194) It is remarkable that the noblest works of human genius have been produced in times of tumult, when every man was his own master, and all things were open to all. Homer, Dante and Milton, appeared in such times; and we may add Virgil.*

(195) As in those of Cosmo I. and his son Francis. — *Sismondi*, xvi. 205.

(196) A Sicilian, the inventress of many poisons; the most celebrated of which, from its transparency, was called Acquetta or Acqua Tophana.

(197) The Cardinal, Ferdinand de' Medici, is said to have been preserved in this manner by a ring which he wore on his finger; as also Andrea, the husband of Giovanna, Queen of Naples.

(198) Il Trabocchetto. — See *Vocab. degli Accadem. della Crusca.* See also *Dict. de l'Académie Françoise: art. Oubliettes.*

(199) Poggio-Caïano, the favorite villa of Lorenzo; where he often took the diversion of hawking. Pulci sometimes went out with him; though, it seems, with little ardor. See *La Caccia col Falcone*, where he is described as missing; and as gone into a wood, to rhyme there.

(200) The *Morgante Maggiore.* He used to recite it at the table of Lorenzo, in the manner of the ancient Rhapsodists.

* The Augustan age, as it is called, what was it but a dying blaze of the Commonwealth? When Augustus began to reign, Cicero and Lucretius were dead, Catullus had written his satires against Cæsar, and Horace and Virgil were no longer in their first youth. Horace had served under Brutus; and Virgil had been pronounced to be

" Magnæ spes altera Romæ."

(201) Bianca Capello.

(202) Caffaggiòlo, the favorite retreat of Cosmo, "the father of his country." Eleonora di Toledo was stabbed there on the 11th of July, 1576, by her husband, Pietro de' Medici; and only five days afterwards, on the 16th of the same month, Isabella de' Medici was strangled by hers, Paolo Giordano Orsini, at his villa of Cerreto. They were at Florence, when they were sent for, each in her turn, — Isabella under the pretext of a hunting-party, — and each in her turn went to die.

Isabella was one of the most beautiful and accomplished women of the age. In the Latin, French and Spanish languages, she spoke not only with fluency, but elegance; and in her own she excelled as an improvisatrice, accompanying herself on the lute. On her arrival at dusk, Paolo presented her with two beautiful greyhounds, that she might make a trial of their speed in the morning; and at supper he was gay beyond measure. When he retired, he sent for her into his apartment; and, pressing her tenderly to his bosom, slipped a cord round her neck. She was buried in Florence with great pomp: but at her burial, says Varchi, the crime divulged itself. Her face was black on the bier.

Eleonora appears to have had a presentiment of her fate. She went when required; but, before she set out, took leave of her son, then a child, weeping long and bitterly over him.

(203) I have here endeavored to describe an Italian sunset as I have often seen it. The conclusion is borrowed from that celebrated passage in Dante, "Era già l'ora," &c.

(204) Originally thus:

But let us hence. For now the sun withdraws,
Setting to rise elsewhere, — elsewhere to rise,
Gladdening the nations that expect him there;
And on to go, dispensing light and life,
On, while his absence here invites to sleep,
Far as the Indus and the numerous tribes
That on their faces fall to hail his coming.

(205) Before line 1, in the MS.

The sun ascended, and the eastern sky
Flamed like a furnace, while the western glowed
As if another day was dawning there.

(206) The Roman and the Carthaginian. Such was the animosity, says Livy, that an earthquake, which turned the course of rivers and overthrew cities and mountains, was felt by none of the combatants. — xxii. 5.

(207) A tradition. It has been called, from time immemorial, Il Sanguinetto.

(208) An allusion to the Cascata delle Marmore, a celebrated fall of the Velino, near Terni.

(209) A sign in our country as old as Shakspeare, and still used in Italy. "Une branche d'arbre, attachée à une maison rustique, nous annonce les moyens de nous rafraîchir. Nous y trouvons du lait et des œufs frais; nous voilà contens." — *Mém. de Goldini.*

There is, or was very lately, in Florence a small wine-house with this inscription over the door: "Al buon vino non bisogna frasca." Good wine needs no bush. It was much frequented by Salvator Rosa, who drew a portrait of his hostess.

(210) This upper region, a country of dews and dewy lights, as described by Virgil and

Pliny, and still, I believe, called *La Rosa*, is full of beautiful scenery. Who does not wish to follow the footsteps of Cicero there, to visit the Reatine Tempe and the Seven Waters?

(211) Perhaps the most beautiful villa of that day was the Villa Madama. It is now a ruin; but enough remains of the plan and the grotesque-work to justify Vasari's account of it.

The *Pastor Fido*, if not the *Aminta*, used to be often represented there; and a theatre, such as is here described, was to be seen in the gardens very lately.

(212) A fashion forever reviving in such a climate. In the year 1783, the *Nina* of Paesiello was performed in a small wood near Caserta.

(213) I Tre Mauri.

(214) What poet before Shakspeare has availed himself of the phenomenon here alluded to, a phenomenon so awful in his hands?

(215) A Milanese story of the 17th century, by Alessandro Manzoni.

(216) See the *Hecuba* of Euripides, v. 911, &c.

(217) Such was the enthusiasm there at the revival of art, that the discovery of a precious marble was an event for celebration; and, in the instance of the Laocoon, it was recorded on the tomb of the discoverer. "Felici de Fredis, qui ob proprias virtutes, et repertum Laocoöntis divinum quod in Vaticano cernes ferè respirans simulacrum, immortalitatem meruit, A. D. 1528."*

The Laocoon was found in the baths of Titus, and, as we may conclude, in the very same chamber in which it was seen by the elder Pliny. It stood alone there in a niche that is still pointed out to the traveller; † and well might it be hailed by the poets of that day! What a moment for the imagination, when, on the entrance of a torch, it emerged at once from the darkness of so long a night!

There is a letter on the subject, written by Francesco da S. Gallo, in 1567.

"Some statues being discovered in a vineyard near S. Maria Maggiore, the Pope said to a groom of the stables, 'Tell Giuliano da S. Gallo to go and see them;' and my father, when he received the message, went directly to Michael Angelo Buonarroti, who was always to be found at home (being at that time employed on the Mausoleum), and they set out together on horseback; I, who was yet a child, riding on the crupper behind my father.

"When they arrived there and went down, they exclaimed, 'This is the Laocoon of which Pliny makes mention!' and the opening was enlarged that the marble might be taken out and inspected; and they returned to dinner, discoursing of ancient things."

(218) The street of the tombs in Pompeii may serve to give us some idea of the Via Appia, that Regina Viarum, in its splendor. It is perhaps the most striking vestige of antiquity that remains to us.

(219) And Augustus in his litter, coming at a still slower rate. He was borne along by slaves; and the gentle motion allowed him to read, write and employ himself as in his cabinet. Though Tivoli is only sixteen miles from the city, he was always two nights on the road. — *Suetonius*.

(220) Nero.

* In the Church of Ara Cœli.

† The walls and the niche are of a bright vermilion. See Observations on the Colors of the Ancients, by Sir Humphrey Davy, with whom I visited this chamber in 1814.

(221) At the words "Tu Marcellus eris." The story is so beautiful that every reader must wish it to be true.

(222) From the golden pillar in the Forum the ways ran to the gates, and from the gates to the extremities of the empire.

(223) It was Caius Gracchus who introduced vehement action and the practice of walking to and fro when they spoke. — *Dio. fragm.* xxxiv. 90.

(224) The laws of the twelve tables were inscribed on pillars of brass, and placed in the most conspicuous part of the Forum. — *Dion. Hal.*

(225) "Amplitudo tanta est, ut conspiciatur a Latiario Jove." — *C. Plin.*

(226) The Rostra.

(227) Marcus Junius Brutus.

(228) We are told that Cæsar passed the Rubicon and overthrew the Commonwealth; but the seeds of destruction were already in the Senate-house, the Forum, and the Camp. When Cæsar fell, was liberty restored?

History, as well as poetry, delights in a hero, and is forever ascribing to one what was the work of many; for, as men, we are flattered by such representations of human greatness; forgetting how often leaders are led, and overlooking the thousand thousand springs of action by which the events of the world are brought to pass.

(229) It was in the Via Sacra that Horace, when musing along as usual, was so cruelly assailed; and how well has he described an animal that preys on its kind! It was there also that Cicero was assailed; but he bore his sufferings with less composure, as well indeed he might; taking refuge in the vestibule of the nearest house. — *Ad Att.* iv. 3.

(230) An allusion to Cæsar in his Gallic triumph. "Adscendit Capitolium ad lumina," &c. — *Suetonius.*

(231) In the triumph of Æmilus, nothing affected the Roman people like the children of Perseus. Many wept; nor could anything else attract notice till they were gone by. — *Plutarch.*

(232) "Rien ne servit mieux Rome, que le respect qu'elle imprima à la terre. Elle mit d'abord les rois dans le silence, et les rendit comme stupides. Il ne s'agissoit pas du degré de leur puissance; mais leur personne propre étoit attaquée. Risquer une guerre, c'étoit s'exposer à la captivité, à la mort, à l'infamie du triomphe." — *Montesquieu.*

(233) Perseus.

(234) Jugurtha.

(235) Zenobia.

(236) "Spare me, I pray, this indignity," said Perseus to Æmilius. "Make me not a public spectacle; drag me not through your streets." — "What you ask for," replied the Roman, "is in your own power." — *Plutarch.*

(237) Cleopatra.

(238) Sophonisba. The story of the marriage and the poison is well known to every reader.

(239) The Pantheon.

(240) The transfiguration; "la quale opera, nel vedere il corpó morto, e quella viva, faceva scoppiare l'anima di dolore à ogni uno che quivi guardava." — *Vasari.*

(241) "You admire that picture," said an old Dominican to me at Padua, as I stood contemplating a Last Supper in the Refectory of his convent, the figures as large as the life. "I have sat at my meals before it for seven and forty years; and such are the changes that have taken place among us, — so many have come and gone in the time, — that, when I look upon the company there, — upon those who are sitting at that table, silent as they are, — I am sometimes inclined to think that we, and not they, are the shadows."

The celebrated fresco of Lionardo da Vinci in the monastery of Santa Maria delle Grazie, at Milan, must again and again have suggested the same reflection. Opposite to it stood the prior's table, the monks sitting down the chamber on the right and left; and the artist, throughout his picture, has evidently endeavored to make it correspond with what he saw when they were assembled there. The table-cloth, with the corners tied up, and with its regular folds as from the press, must have been faithfully copied; and the dishes and drinking-cups are, no doubt, such as were used by the fathers in that day. — *See Goethe*, vol. xxxix. p. 94.

Indefatigable was Lionardo in the prosecution of this work. "I have seen him," says Bandello the novelist, "mount the scaffold at daybreak and continue there till night, forgetting to eat or drink. Not but that he would sometimes leave it for many days together, and then return only to meditate upon it, or to touch and retouch it here and there." The prior was forever complaining of the little progress that he made, and the duke at last consented to speak to him on the subject. His answer is given by Vasari. "Perhaps I am then most busy when I seem to be most idle, for I must think before I execute. But, think as I will, there are two persons at the supper to whom I shall never do justice, — our Lord and the disciple who betrayed him. Now, if the prior would but sit to me for the last —"

The prior gave him no more trouble.

(242) A dialogue which is said to have passed many years ago at Lyons (*Mem. de Grammont*, i. 3), and which may still be heard in almost every hôtellerie at daybreak.

(243) How noble is that burst of eloquence in Hooker! "Of law there can be no less acknowledged, than that her seat is the bosom of God, her voice the harmony of the world. All things in heaven and earth do her homage; the very least as feeling her care, and the greatest as not exempted from her power.

(244) As the descendants of an illustrious people have lately done.

> They know their strength, and know that, to be free,
> They have but to deserve it.

(245) Candor, generosity and justice, how rare are they in the world; and how much is to be deplored the want of them! When a minister in our parliament consents at last to a measure, which, for many reasons perhaps existing no longer, he had before refused to adopt, there should be no exultation as over the fallen, no taunt, no jeer. How often may the resistance be continued lest an enemy should triumph, and the result of conviction be received as a symptom of fear!

(246) Are we not also unjust to ourselves; and are not the best among us the most so? Many a good deed is done by us and forgotten. Our benevolent feelings are indulged, and we think no more of it. But is it so when we err? And when we wrong another and cannot redress the wrong, where are we then? Yet so it is, and so no doubt it should be, to urge us on without ceasing, in this place of trial and discipline,

> From good to better and to better still.

(247) The author of the Letters to Julia has written admirably on this subject.

> " All sad, all silent ! O'er the ear
> No sound of cheerful toil is swelling.
> Earth has no quickening spirit here,
> Nature no charm, and man no dwelling ! "

Not less admirably has he described a Roman beauty; such as "weaves her spells beyond the Tiber."

> " Methinks the Furies with their snakes,
> Or Venus with her zone, might gird her;
> Of fiend and goddess she partakes,
> And looks at once both Love and Murder."

(248) Mons Albanus, now called Monte Cavo. On the summit stood for many centuries the temple of Jupiter Latiaris. "Tuque ex tuo edito monte Latiaris, sancte Jupiter," &c. — *Cicero.*

(249) Æneid, xii. 134.

(250) Nisus and Euryalus. "La scène des six derniers livres de Virgile ne comprend qu'une lieue de terrain." — *Bonstetten.*

(251) Forty-seven, according to Dionys. Halicar. I. i.

(252) Tivoli.

(253) Palestrina.

(254) La Riccia.

(255) "Horatiorum quà viret sacer campus." — *Mart.*

(256) "Quæ prata Quintia vocantur." — *Livy.*

(257) Mons Sacer.

(258) It was not always so. There were once within her walls "more erected spirits."

"Let me recall to your mind," says Petrarch, in a letter to old Stephen Colonna, "the walk we took together at a late hour in the broad street that leads from your palace to the Capitol. To me it seems as yesterday, though it was ten years ago. When we arrived where the four ways meet, we stopped; and, none interrupting us, discoursed long on the fallen fortunes of your house. Fixing your eyes steadfastly upon me and then turning them away full of tears, 'I have nothing now,' you said, 'to leave my children. But a still greater calamity awaits me,— I shall inherit from them all.' You remember the words, no doubt; words so fully accomplished. I certainly do; and as distinctly as the old sepulchre in the corner, on which we were leaning with our elbows at the time." — *Epist. Famil.* viii. 1.

The sepulchre here alluded to must have been that of Bibulus; and what an interest it derives from this anecdote ! Stephen Colonna was a hero worthy of antiquity; and in his distress was an object, not of pity, but of reverence. When overtaken by his pursuers and questioned by those who knew him not, "I am Stephen Colonna," he replied, "a citizen of Rome !" and when, in the last extremity of battle, a voice cried out to him, "Where is now your fortress, Colonna ?" "Here !" he answered gayly, laying his hand on his heart.

(259) Music; and from the loftiest strain to the lowliest, from a Miserere in the Holy

Week to the shepherd's humble offering in advent; the last, if we may judge from its effects, not the least subduing, perhaps the most so.

Once, as I was approaching Frescati in the sunshine of a cloudless December morning, I observed a rustic group by the road-side, before an image of the Virgin, that claimed the devotions of the passenger from a niche in a vineyard wall. Two young men from the mountains of the Abruzzi, in their long brown cloaks, were playing a Christmas carol. Their instruments were a hautboy and a bagpipe; and the air, wild and simple as it was, was such as she might accept with pleasure. The ingenuous and smiling countenances of these rude minstrels, who seemed so sure that she heard them, and the unaffected delight of their little audience, all younger than themselves, all standing uncovered, and moving their lips in prayer, would have arrested the most careless traveller.

(260) Whoever has entered the Church of St. Peter's or the Pauline Chapel, during the exposition of the Holy Sacrament there, will not soon forget the blaze of the altar, or the dark circle of worshippers kneeling in silence before it.

(261) An allusion to the saying of Archimedes, "Give me a place to stand upon, and I will move the earth."

(262) An allusion to the prophecies concerning Antichrist. See the interpretations of Mede, Newton, Clarke, &c.; not to mention those of Dante and Petrarch.

(263) It was at such a moment, when contemplating the young and the beautiful, that Tasso conceived his sonnets, beginning "Vergine pia," and "Vergine bella." Those to whom he addressed them have long been forgotten; though they were as much perhaps to be loved, and as much also to be pitied.

(264) Her back was at that time turned to the people; but in his countenance might be read all that was passing. The cardinal, who officiated, was a venerable old man, evidently unused to the service, and much affected by it.

(265) Among other ceremonies, a pall was thrown over her, and a requiem sung.

(266) He is of the beetle-tribe.

(267) "For, in that upper clime, effulgence comes
Of gladness." — *Cary's Dante.*

(268) There is a song to the *lucciola* in every dialect of Italy; as, for instance, in the Genoese.

"Cabela, vegni a baso;
Ti dajo un cuge de lette."

The Roman is in a higher strain.

"Bella regina," &c.

(269) "Io piglio, quando il dì giunge al confine,
Le lucciole ne' prati ampj ridotte,
E, come gemme, le comparto al crine;
Poi fra l' ombre da' rai vivi interrotte
Mi presento ai Pastori, e ognun mi dice;
Clori ha la stelle al crin come ha la Notte."

Varano.

(270) Pliny mentions an extraordinary instance of longevity in the ilex. "There is one," says he, "in the Vatican, older than the city itself. An Etruscan inscription in letters of brass attests that even in those days the tree was held sacred."

(271) I did not tell you that just below the first fall, on the side of the rock, and hanging over that torrent, are little ruins which they show you for Horace's house, a curious situation to observe the

> " Præceps Anio, et Tiburni lucus, et uda
> Mobilibus pomaria rivis." *Gray's Letters.*

(272) The glow-worm.

(273) We were now within a few hours of the Campania Felix. On the color and flavor of Falernian consult Galen and Dioscorides.

(274) As, indeed, it always was, contributing those of every degree, from a *milord* with his suite, to him whose only attendant is his shadow. Coryate, in 1608, performed his journey on foot; and, returning, hung up his shoes in his village church as an ex-voto. Goldsmith, a century and a half afterwards, followed in nearly the same path; playing a tune on his flute to procure admittance, whenever he approached a cottage at night-fall.

(275) We cross a narrow sea; we land on a shore which we have contemplated from our own; and we awake, as it were, in another planet. The very child that lisps there lisps in words which we have yet to learn.

Nor is it less interesting, if less striking, to observe the gradations in language, and feature, and character, as we travel on from kingdom to kingdom. The French peasant becomes more and more an Italian as we approach Italy, and a Spaniard as we approach Spain.

(276) To judge at once of a nation, we have only to throw our eyes on the markets and the fields. If the markets are well supplied, the fields well cultivated, all is right. If otherwise, we may say, and say truly, these people are barbarous or oppressed.

(277) Assuredly not, if the last has laid a proper foundation. Knowledge makes knowledge as money makes money, nor ever perhaps so fast as on a journey.

(278) For that knowledge, indeed, which is the most precious, we have not far to go; and how often is it to be found where least it is looked for! "I have learned more," said a dying man on the scaffold, "in one little dark corner of yonder tower, than by any travel in so many places as I have seen." — *Holinshed.*

(279) The place here described is near Mola di Gaëta, in the kingdom of Naples.

(280) Alluding to Alfonso Piccolomini. "Stupiva ciascuno chè, mentre un bandito osservava rigorosamente la sua parola, il Papa non avesse ribrezzo di mancare alla propria." — *Galluzzi*, ii. 364. He was hanged at Florence, March 16, 1591.

(281) Tasso was returning from Naples to Rome, and had arrived at Mola Di Gaëta, when he received this tribute of respect. The captain of the troop was Marco di Sciarra. — See *Manso*, "*Vita del Tasso*." Ariosto had a similar adventure with Filippo Pacchione. — See *Garafalo.*

(282) " Cette race de bandits a ses racines dans la population même du pays. La police ne sait où les trouver." — *Lettres de Chateauvieux.*

(283) This story was written in the year 1820, and is founded on the many narratives which at that time were circulating in Rome and Naples.

(284) " Pray that you may pray," said a venerable pastor to one who came to lament that he had lost the privilege of prayer.

It is related of a great transgressor that he awaked at last to reflection as from a dream, and on his knees had recourse to the prayer of his childhood.

(285) Un pezzo di cielo caduto in terra. — *Sannazaro.*

(286) If the bay of Naples is still beautiful, — if it still deserves the epithet of *pulcherrimus*, — what must it not once have been; * and who, as he sails round it, can imagine it to himself as it was, when not only the villas of the Romans were in their splendor,† but the temples; when those of Herculaneum and Pompeii and Baiæ and Puteoli, and how many more, were standing, each on its eminence or on the margin of the sea; while, with choral music and with a magnificence that had exhausted the wealth of kingdoms, ‡ the galleys of the imperial court were anchoring in the shade, or moving up and down in the sunshine.

(287) Virgil.

(288) Quarum sacra fero, ingenti percussus amore.

(289) The Tarantella.

(290) Capreæ.

(291) Tiberius.

(292) "How often, to demonstrate his power, does he employ the meanest of his instruments; as in Egypt, when he called forth, not the serpents and the monsters of Africa, but vermin from the very dust!"

(293) The elder Pliny. See the letter in which his nephew relates to Tacitus the circumstances of his death. — In the morning of that day Vesuvius was covered with the most luxuriant vegetation; § every elm had its vine, every vine (for it was in the month of August) its clusters; nor in the cities below was there a thought of danger, though their interment was so soon to take place. In Pompeii, if we may believe Dion Cassius, the people were sitting in the theatre when the work of destruction began.

(294) Pompeii.

(295) Pansa, the Ædile, according to some of the interpreters; but the inscription at the entrance is very obscure.

It is remarkable that Cicero, when on his way to Cilicia, was the bearer of a letter to Atticus "ex Pansæ Pompeiano." ‖ (Ad. Att. v. 3.) That this was the house in question, and that in the street, as we passed along, we might have met him, coming or going, every pilgrim to Pompeii must wish to believe.

But, delighting in the coast and in his own Pompeianum (Ad. Att. ii. 1), he could be no stranger in that city; and often must he have received there such homage as ours.

(296) In a time of revolution he could not escape unhurt; but to the last he preserved his gayety of mind through every change of fortune; living right hospitably when he had the means to do so, and, when he could not entertain, dining as he is here represented, with his velvet friends — *en famille.*

(297) La Croce Bianca.

* "Antequam Vesuvius mons, ardescens, faciem loci verteret." — *Tacit.* "*Annal.*" iv. 67.

† With their groves and porticos they were everywhere along the shore, "erat enim frequens amœnitas oræ;" and what a neighborhood must have been there in the last days of the Commonwealth, when such men as Cæsar, and Pompey, and Lucullus, and Cicero, and Hortensius, and Brutus, were continually retiring thither from the cares of public life!

‡ "Gemmatis puppibus, versicoloribus velis," &c. — *Sueton.* "*Calig.*" 37.

§ Martial. IV. 44.

‖ According to Grævius. The manuscripts disagree.

(298) "Ce pourroit être," says Bayle, "la matière d'un joli problème : on pourroit examiner si cette fille avançoit, ou si elle retardoit le profit de ses auditeurs, en leur cachant son beau visage. Il y auroit cent choses à dire pour et contre là-dessus."

(299) I cannot here omit some lines by a friend of mine now no more.

For who would make his life a life of toil
For wealth, o'erbalanced with a thousand cares ;
Or power, which base compliance must uphold ;
Or honor, lavished most on courtly slaves ;
Or fame, vain breath of a misjudging world ;
Who for such perishable gauds would put
A yoke upon his free unbroken spirit,
And gall himself with trammels and the rubs
Of this world's business ? *Lewesdon Hill.*

(300) The temples of Pæstum are three in number ; and have survived, nearly nine centuries, the total destruction of the city. Tradition is silent concerning them ; but they must have existed now between two and three thousand years.

(301) Spartacus. See Plutarch in the Life of Crassus.

(302) The violets of Pæstum were as proverbial as the roses. Martial mentions them with the honey of Hybla.

(303) The introduction to his Treatise on Glory. — *Cic. ad Att.* xvi. 6. For an account of the loss of that treatise, see Petrarch, *Epist. Rer. Senilium*, xv. 1, and Bayle, *Dict.*, in Alcyonius.

(304) They are said to have been discovered by accident about the middle of the last century.

(305) Originally a Greek city under that name, and afterwards a Roman city under the name of Pæstum. It was surprised and destroyed by the Saracens at the beginning of the tenth century.

(306) Athanæus, xiv.

(307) The Mal'aria.

(308) Tasso. Sorrento, his birthplace, is on the south side of the Gulf of Naples.

(309) "Amalfi fell, after three hundred years of prosperity ; but the poverty of one thousand fishermen is yet dignified by the remains of an arsenal, a cathedral, and the palaces of royal merchants." — *Gibbon.*

(310) China. After this line, in the MS.

That wall, so massive, so interminable,
Forever, with its battlements and towers,
Climbing, descending, from assault to guard
A people numerous as the ocean sands,
And glorying as the mightiest of mankind ;
Yet where they are contented to remain ;
From age to age resolved to cultivate
Peace and the arts of peace, — turning to gold
The very ground they tread on, and the leaves
They gather from their trees, year after year.*

* An allusion to the porcelain and the tea of the Chinese.

(311) There is at this day in Syracuse a street called La Strada degli Amalfitani.

(312) In the year 839. See Muratori : Art. *Chronici Amalphitani Fragmenta.*

(313) By degrees, says Giannone, they made themselves famous through the world. The Tarini Amalfitani were a coin familiar to all nations ; and their maritime code regulated everywhere the commerce of the sea. Many churches in the East were by them built and endowed ; by them was founded in Palestine that most renowned military Order of St. John of Jerusalem ; and who does not know that the mariner's compass was invented by a citizen of Amalfi ?

Glorious was their course,
And long the track of light they left behind them.

(314) The Abbey of Monte Cassino is the most ancient and venerable house of the Benedictine order. It is situated within fifteen leagues of Naples, on the inland road to Rome ; and no house is more hospitable.

(315) This story — if a story it may be called — is fictitious ; and I have done little more than give it as I received it.

(316) Michael Angelo.

(317) There are many miraculous pictures in Italy, but none, I believe, were ever before described as malignant in their influence. At Arezzo, in the Church of St. Angelo, there is indeed over the great altar a fresco-painting of the fall of the angels, which has a singular story belonging to it. It was painted in the fourteenth century by Spinello Aretino, who has there represented Lucifer as changed into a shape so monstrous and terrible that he is said in that very shape to have haunted the artist in his dreams, and to have hastened his death ; crying, night after night, " Where hast thou seen me in a shape so monstrous ? " In the upper part St. Michael is seen in combat with the dragon : the fatal transformation is in the lower part of the picture. — *Vasari.*

(318) Then degraded, and belonging to a Vetturino.

(319) A Florentine family of great antiquity. In the sixty-third novel of Franco Sacchetti we read that a stranger, suddenly entering Giotto's study, threw down a shield and departed, saying, " Paint me my arms in that shield ; " and that Giotto, looking after him, exclaimed, " Who is he ? What is he ? He says, Paint me my arms, as if he were one of the Bardi ! What arms does he bear ? "

(320) A large boat for rowing and sailing, much used in the Mediterranean.

(321) Paganino Doria, Nicolo Pisani ; those great seamen, who balanced for so many years the fortunes of Genoa and Venice.

(322) Every reader of Spanish poetry is acquainted with that affecting romance of Gongora,

" Amarrado al duro banco," &c.

Lord Holland has translated it in his excellent Life of Lope de Vega.

(323) There is a custom on the continent well worthy of notice. In Boulogne we read, as we ramble through it, " Ici est mort l'Auteur de Gil Blas ; " in Rouen, " Ici est né Pierre Corneille ; " in Geneva, " Ici est né Jean-Jacques Rousseau ; " and in Dijon there is the Maison Bossuet ; in Paris, the Quai Voltaire. Very rare are such memorials among *us* : and yet, wherever we meet with them, — in whatever country they were, or of whatever

age, — we should surely say that they were evidences of refinement and sensibility in the people. The house of Pindar was spared

when temple and tower
Went to the ground ;

and its ruins were held sacred to the last. According to Pausanias, they were still to be seen in the second century.

(324) The Piazza Doria, or, as it is now called, the Piazza di San Matteo, insignificant as it may be thought, is to me the most interesting place in Genoa. It was there that Doria assembled the people, when he gave them their liberty (Sigonii *Vita Doriæ*) ; and on one side of it is the church he lies buried in, on the other a house, originally of very small dimensions, with this inscription : S. C. Andreæ de Auria Patriæ Liberatori Munus Publicum.

The streets of old Genoa, like those of Venice, were constructed only for foot-passengers.

(325) When I saw it in 1822, a basket-maker lived on the ground-floor, and over him a seller of chocolate.

(326) Alluding to the palace which he built afterwards, and in which he twice entertained the Emperor Charles the Fifth. It is the most magnificent edifice on the Bay of Genoa.

(327) Fiesco. For an account of his conspiracy, see Robertson's History of Charles the Fifth.

(328) Such as the Gabelles formerly in France ; "où le droit," says Montesquieu, "excédoit de dix-sept fois la valeur de la marchandise." Salt is an article of which none know the value who have not known the want of it.

(329) Who he is I have yet to learn. The story was told to me many years ago by a great reader of the old annalists ; but I have searched everywhere for it in vain.

(330) Written at Susa, May 1, 1822.

(331) The Po. "Chaque maison est pourvue de bateaux, et lorsque l'inondation s'annonce," &c. — *Lettres de Chateauvieux.*

(332) It was somewhere in the Maremma, a region so fatal to so many, that the unhappy Pia, a Siennese lady of the family of Tolommei, fell a sacrifice to the jealousy of her husband. Thither he conveyed her in the sultry time,

"tra'l Luglio e'l Settembre ;"

having resolved in his heart that she should perish there, even though he perished there with her. Not a word escaped from him on the way, not a syllable in answer to her remonstrances or her tears ; and in sullen silence he watched patiently by her till she died.

"Siena mi fe ; disfecemi Maremma.
Salsi colui, che'nnanellata pria,
Disposando, m'avea con la sua gemma."

The Maremma is continually in the mind of Dante ; now as swarming with serpents, and now as employed in its great work of destruction.

(333) The temples of Pæstum.

(334) Who has travelled and cannot say with Catullus,

"O quid solutis est beatius curis ?
Quum mens onus reponit, ac peregrino

Labore fessi venimus arem ad nostrum,
Desideratoque acquiescimus lecto."

(335) After this line, in the MS.

What though his ancestors, early or late,
Were not ennobled by the breath of kings;
Yet in his veins was running at his birth
The blood of those most eminent of old
For wisdom, virtue, — those who could renounce
The things of this world for their conscience' sake,
And die like blessed martyrs.

RECENTLY PUBLISHED

BY PHILLIPS, SAMPSON AND COMPANY,

THE COMPLETE

POETICAL WORKS OF THOMAS CAMPBELL;

WITH

AN ORIGINAL BIOGRAPHY, AND NOTES.

EDITED BY EPES SARGENT.

NOTICES OF THE PRESS.

A new edition of the Complete Poetical Works of Thomas Campbell, which possesses advantages over any hitherto published, both on account of its superior typographical appearance, and because it contains fifty more poems than any other edition extant, some of them unsurpassed by the poet's best pieces. All these are perfectly well authenticated, the sources from which they are taken being given in the notes.

A memoir of one hundred pages is prefixed, compiled from the ample materials furnished by Dr. Beattie, in his Life and Letters of Campbell, and by Mr. Cyrus Redding, in a Series of Reminiscences published in the New Monthly Magazine. The work has been edited by Mr. Epes Sargent, with great care and fidelity. — *Norton's (N. Y.) Literary Gazette.*

This is the finest library edition of Campbell that we have seen, being of goodly size, and of admirable type, paper and binding. The Memoir is the best brief sketch of the poet's life extant, and the notes sufficient and judicious. — *Puritan Recorder.*

Campbell is undoubtedly the finest of English lyric poets. The present edition contains a very full memoir. Fifty new poems, which have never before appeared in a permanent shape, are added; these are generally short, but many of them strikingly exhibit the poet's rare power of simple, concise, and yet magnificent expression. The volume is enriched with a portrait of Campbell when a young man, and also a pen-and-ink sketch, representing him in the ease and undress of his study. — *New York Courier and Enquirer.*

The merits of the present volume are marked; for it possesses several advantages over any previous edition that we have seen. — *Clark's Knickerbocker.*

An excellent edition, prepared by Epes Sargent, who has also prefixed an agreeable Memoir. It is most skilfully and entertainingly put together. — *Putnam's Magazine.*

This edition is first to be commended for its typographical beauty. The large, fine-cut letter sets off even Campbell to greater advantage, and in any garb he is *the* great lyrical poet of his age. And this is *the* edition of his work; indeed, the only edition of Campbell that can pretend to give anything like his *complete* poetical works. But we are not only indebted to Mr. Sargent for bringing together from isolated collections these well-authenticated productions of this eminent poet; we have also to thank him for the very full and entertaining Memoir prefixed to the work.

No library can be deemed a library without a copy of Campbell, and of the best edition. He is the first poet who ought to be placed in the hands of the young, for his English style is clear, simple and condensed, and his sentiments are always pure and elevated. No woman need ever blush for being caught with a poem of Campbell's in her hand. It is a gift-book that will prove a perennial. — *Boston Post.*

This is a fair book, as it should be, since it contains the finished productions of one of the purest and truest of English poets, who wrote nothing carelessly, and not a "line against religion or virtue." It has been carefully prepared by one well fitted, by taste and study, for his pleasant task. An original, gracefully-written, and full memoir, the materials of which were gathered from various sources, greatly increases its value. The publishers have done good service to literature in sending forth this completest collection of a bard whose "Gertrude of Wyoming" should give him a home in every American library and heart. We are glad to have such a volume bear Boston upon its title-page. — *Christian Register.*

By far the best edition which has been published. — *Dedham Gazette.*

This is a truly beautiful edition of Campbell, by far the most elegant and complete that has yet appeared in America. — *Yankee Blade.*

The only complete edition ever published. Every family, and, above all, every young person forming a literary taste, or cultivating a poetical talent, should own a copy of Campbell's complete works. — *True Flag.*

The chief feature in this beautiful edition of Campbell's Poems is the very full and excellent life of the poet, by Mr. Sargent. It is written in a clear and graceful style. — *Christian Examiner.*

Mr. Sargent appears to have spared no pains to render this acceptable volume worthy of the great poet, and creditable to his own reputation. — *Baltimore American.*

Phillips, Sampson & Co. have issued the most complete edition of the poems of Campbell that we have yet seen. It is well bound, and beautifully printed with large type. — *Sciota Gazette.*

What a delicious book is this new edition of Campbell, with its ample memoir, its full-length portraits of the poet, and the familiar poems, as finished, and as precious, and as everlasting as pearls! Mr. Sargent has executed his pious task with such *filial* care and completeness as to have linked his name imperishably with that of the poet. — *New York Home Journal.*

The present is indeed the *only* edition of Campbell that can pretend to give anything like his *complete* poetical works. We have also to thank Mr. Sargent for the very full and entertaining memoir prefixed to the work. — *Philadelphia Ledger.*

A most beautiful and acceptable edition of the great modern lyric poet of England, prefaced by a full and well-written biography from the pen of an American scholar. — *Southern (Richmond) Literary Messenger.*

A most attractive volume. It presents a more complete collection of Campbell's poetical writings than any edition before published. — *Troy (N. Y.) Budget.*

The most complete edition of the works of this beautiful poet. It contains about fifty additional poems. The full, well-written and highly entertaining biography adds much to the attractiveness of the volume. — *Presbyterian.*

A handsome and convenient volume of 460 pages, printed in the best style of the Boston press. — *New York Independent.*

The edition is one which, altogether, reflects great credit upon the American editor and publishers. — *Banner of the Cross.*

The most *complete* edition of Campbell's poetical works, and the most *desirable* by far. — *Norfolk (Va.) Democrat.*

www.ingramcontent.com/pod-product-compliance
Lightning Source LLC
LaVergne TN
LVHW020938110826
845150LV00004B/900